BIALL Handbook of Legal Information Management

BRITISH AND IRISH ASSOCIATION
OF LAW LIBRARIANS (BIALL)

The British and Irish Association of Law Librarians (BIALL) is the leading professional body in the UK and Ireland for information professionals working in the legal sector. BIALL is a self-supporting association which draws its income primarily from membership subscriptions. With over 700 personal and institutional members, the Association supports a number of different sectors including academic institutions, law firms, and barristers' chambers, as well as students entering the profession.

Continuing professional development is fundamental for legal information professionals, as it is vital they keep up to date with changes in the law. To this end, BIALL supports its members through the organization of regular training events, at both a national and regional level, and through the publication of its quarterly journal *Legal Information Management*. The Annual Conference is also an important event for BIALL members and non-members alike, providing an opportunity to learn about and discuss, formally and informally, the key issues affecting the legal information profession. BIALL has strong links with international legal information associations and offers bursaries to attend overseas conferences as well as its own conference.

Practical support and advice is also given for the day-to-day issues affecting legal information professionals through a number of schemes run by the BIALL committees and publications, including the BIALL *Newsletter*, the Handbook of Legal Information Management and the Annual Salary Survey.

BIALL Handbook of Legal Information Management

SECOND EDITION

Edited by

LOYITA WORLEY AND SARAH SPELLS

ASHGATE

Published by
Ashgate Publishing Limited
Wey Court East
Union Road
Farnham
Surrey, GU9 7PT
England

Ashgate Publishing Company
110 Cherry Street
Suite 3-1
Burlington
VT 05401-3818
USA

www.ashgatepublishing.com

British Library Cataloguing in Publication Data
A catalogue record for this book is available from the British Library

Library of Congress Cataloging-in-Publication Data
BIALL handbook of legal information management / By Loyita Worley and Sarah Spells.
-- Second edition.
      p. cm.
   Includes bibliographical references and index.
   ISBN 978-1-4094-2396-6 (hardback : alk. paper) -- ISBN 978-1-4094-2397-3 (ebook) -- ISBN 978-1-4724-0025-3 (epub)
   1. Law libraries--Great Britain--Handbooks, manuals, etc. 2. Law libraries--Ireland--Handbooks, manuals, etc. 3. Legal literature--Great Britain--Handbooks, manuals, etc. 4. Legal literature--Ireland--Handbooks, manuals, etc. I. Worley, Loyita, editor of compilation. II. Spells, Sarah, editor of compilation. III. Title: Handbook of legal information management.
   Z675.L2B52 2014
   026.34'00941--dc23

                                                                      2014003369

ISBN 9781409423966 (hbk)
ISBN 9781409423973 (ebk)
ISBN 9781472400253 (epub)

Printed in the United Kingdom by Henry Ling Limited, at the Dorset Press, Dorchester, DT1 1HD

SARAH SPELLS

3 August 1978–11 September 2012

Sarah was the Law Librarian and Deputy Head of Teaching and Research Support at SOAS Library, at the time of her sudden and tragic death.

She is much missed by all at BIALL and will be best remembered as the Chair of the Publications Committee, where under her leadership, the committee delivered an extra level of quality and depth to BIALL's portfolio of publications. Her key achievements included updating and republishing the Legal Research Packs in 2010 having been expanded to cover more legal topics; the redesign of the Newsletter to improve its look and feel and include a greater range of content for members; and updating the BIALL Careers Information leaflet to help promote law librarianship as a profession.

Sarah also took on the role as editor of this new edition of the BIALL Handbook and whilst she wasn't able to complete the project, the time she spent in organizing author submissions and working with Ashgate has been invaluable. To recognize her contribution BIALL is proud to dedicate this new edition of the BIALL Handbook of Legal Information Management to her memory.

CONTENTS

LIST OF FIGURES

LIST OF CONTRIBUTORS

EMILY ALLBON

Emily has been Law Librarian at City University London since 2000, having previously been a trainee at The Institute of Advanced Legal Studies. She is the creator of Lawbore [lawbore.net] and proud recipient of various awards including the BIALL/Wildy Law Librarian of the Year 2012 and Routledge/ALT Teaching with Technology Award 2013. Emily was named a National Teaching Fellow by the Higher Education Academy in June 2013. Emily tweets as lawbore.

JACKY BERRY

Jacky Berry has been an information professional for over 30 years and her experience ranges from being a school librarian in her early career days, working in the Inner London Education Authority, to being Head of Information Services at Linklaters, a global law firm. She also has experience of working in the property sector and with a firm of actuaries. She spent two years working at TFPL as their Training Manager before taking on a Project Manager role at the BMA. The role involved the relocation of the Library, analysing services for members and making changes accordingly, restructuring the department and installing a new Library management system. Since being made permanent in 2007, Jacky and her team are concentrating on making the BMA Library a 24/7 virtual environment for its members.

SARAH BRITTAN

Sarah is now entering her 21st year in legal information and has been the Library & Information Services Manager at Baker & McKenzie since 2008. Her main responsibilities include leading a team of information specialists, legal research training, information services, copyright compliance and financial planning. She has been a member of the BIALL Legal Information Group for the past three years.

PETER CLINCH

Peter retired in 2010 after more than 35 years in legal information work, latterly at Cardiff University. He has taught legal research skills to students at all levels of study, including for the Bar, as well as budding law librarians attending public courses run by Aslib and CILIP. The latest edition of his fourth book, *Legal Research: A Practitioner's Handbook*, was published by Wildy, Simmonds and Hill in 2013.

STEPHANIE CURRAN

Stephanie Curran has been the Librarian at the Royal Courts of Justice for three years, having worked elsewhere in other roles in jLIS and legal libraries in Australia.

ANGELA DONALDSON

Angela has been the Liaison Librarian for Law at Nottingham Trent University since 1999, looking after students on undergraduate, postgraduate and vocational law courses. She has been an active BIALL member for many years, serving as Secretary and as Chair of both the Membership Services Committee and the Awards & Bursaries Committee. Angela is a co-author of the *Unlocking Legal Learning* book.

FIONA FOGDEN

Fiona currently combines freelance law librarianship with a part-time role as Head of Customer Relations at Linex Systems – giving her experience from both the supplier and consumer perspectives. Prior to this, her roles included looking after the information, research and intranet needs of 28 offices for Baker Tilly and managing the Library & Information team at international law firm Baker & McKenzie.

ANN HEMMING

Ann now runs her own KM and L&D Consultancy, specializing in helping law firms and legal publishers develop their KM strategies and solutions. She has spent around 30 years working as a librarian and then KM director with a number of firms including Eversheds and Hugh James and is currently working with Thomas Eggar.

She has also worked with Tikit, a legal IT consultancy and Lexis Nexis on product development. Ann has an MBA in Law Firm Management and is a regular speaker and author on Legal IT and KM topics.

NICOLA HERBERT

Nicola has been a librarian since 2002. After working in the libraries of SJ Berwin, Ince & Co and the College of Law, she was employed as Information Officer in the legal department at Transport for London from 2006–11. She now works in the library at Cardiff Metropolitan University as Subject Librarian for Tourism, Hospitality and Events Management.

GUY HOLBORN

Guy has been Librarian of Lincoln's Inn Library since 1985, having previously held posts at the House of Lords Library and the Institute of Advanced Legal Studies. He is a past Secretary of BIALL, and was recipient of the first Wallace Breem Memorial Award, and of the Law Librarian of the Year Award 2007.

CHRIS HOLLAND

Chris Holland is Copyright and Permissions Officer at the University of Law. He has worked in law libraries for over 20 years, firstly in a large city firm and more recently as Librarian at the Law Society. Chris has also been the BIALL representative on the Library and Archives Copyright Alliance (LACA) for some years.

MICHAEL MAHER

Michael is Librarian of the Law Society of England and Wales and runs his own information management consultancy business, Info Service Solutions Ltd. Over the last 20 years he has spoken and written about many areas of legal library and information services, including financial management. He has been privileged to carry out a variety of BIALL responsibilities including being Chair and Treasurer.

DEAN MASON

Dean has worked in legal information for 12 years and is currently a Senior Librarian at Dentons. In the last couple of years he has researched, developed and rolled out a current awareness service at the legacy Salans firm now known as Dentons. His recent positions include Vice-Chair of the BIALL Publications Committee, which involved editing the association's newsletter published six times a year.

AMANDA McKENZIE

Amanda McKenzie has been at Olswang for 16 years and has been Head of Information Services since 1999. She was previously at Herbert Smith in the Know How team. In addition to managing the firm's team of information specialists, she is responsible for knowledge management projects, information architecture, legal research training and copyright compliance. She has written for various journals and presented at conferences on the subject of information and knowledge management.

CHRISTINE MISKIN

Christine was active in the worlds of legal information and legal publishing for many years. She worked as chief librarian in two major city law firms, ran her own legal publishing company and founded Legal Journals Index, a major bibliographical tool for law librarians. She was Editorial Director for Westlaw UK whilst employed by Sweet & Maxwell and has also been involved in developing the industry standard legal taxonomy. She is a Life Member of BIALL and was most recently Editor of Legal Information Management.

DIANA MORRIS

Diana was Librarian and then Research Services Manager for a major city law firm for nearly 23 years before retiring at the end of 2007 to work freelance for Sweet & Maxwell. Before that she worked in various public, special and academic libraries, including one at the Zimbabwe Institute of Development Studies in Harare, where she also taught cataloguing and classification on a City & Guilds course for library assistants. She was head of the Editorial Board for Moys Classification and Thesaurus for Legal Materials (5th edn, De Gruyter, 2012).

JAMES MULLAN

James is the Knowledge Management Systems Manager at Field Fisher Waterhouse where he is responsible for the firm's intranet, enterprise search tool, internal social media tools and other knowledge systems. During 2012–13 James was President of BIALL and has previously been a BIALL Council member and Chair of the Web Committee and Suppliers Liaison Group.

DIANE RAPER

Although originally acquiring both law and information/library qualifications, Diane Raper worked in both law and other subject areas during her career both as an information professional and as a manager. She ran large law firm libraries and the library of the Law Society before working in an academic law library as the law librarian between 2006 and 2010 when she was promoted to the position of Head of Academic Liaison, leaving her law library responsibilities. She retired in 2012.

RACHEL ROBBINS

Rachel Robbins was appointed as Senior Librarian at the Ministry of Justice in 2011 following circa 20 years' experience working in different libraries and information management teams in central government.

SALLY ROBERTS

Sally Roberts is Senior Knowledge Manager at Macfarlanes LLP, having previously worked at Clifford Chance LLP, Freshfields LLP and Thomson Reuters. Sally is responsible for the strategic development of knowledge solutions at Macfarlanes, including intranet, know how, enterprise search, e-learning technologies and social collaboration. Sally acts as the interface between the partners, fee earner and PSL communities and the IT department to ensure fluid and regular dialogue in the provision of the firm's knowledge and information resources.

KAREN SCOTT

Karen moved to freelance work in 1990 after a number of years' experience with a city law firm. Since then, she has set up and run information services in commercial and regulatory organizations, and in a wide variety of mid-range law firms with different specializations. She enjoys legal research, training people on effective use of resources, supporting business development and getting to grips with the needs of new clients.

PENNY SCOTT

Penny Scott has been the Chief Librarian and Head of Library and Information Services (jLIS) at the Ministry of Justice (MoJ) since 2006, having previously managed the Army Library and Information Service.

HEATHER SEMPLE

Heather Semple is a Chartered Librarian who joined the Law Society of Northern Ireland 24 years ago as a Library Assistant. For the past 17 years she has been Head of Library and Information Services at the Society and has been developing the range of services and facilities offered by the library to its membership. In recent years, for instance, she has introduced a Business Centre within the library. The library also occasionally publishes materials for the local legal community, both in hard copy and electronic format.

Heather is a member of the Society's Senior Management Team and has been responsible for achieving and maintaining ISO 9001:2008 accreditation throughout the Society.

KATE STANFIELD

Kate Stanfield has worked with law firms for over 23 years, with public library and business information experience prior to that. She ran the CMS Cameron McKenna Knowledge and Information Services as Head of KM for most of those 20 years, developing Information Services and KM within the firm. She has experience in implementing KM systems, document automation, project management and KM consulting within corporate clients.

In 2010 CMS Cameron McKenna announced a major BPO partnership with Integreon, which involved most of the business support services including the KIS team joining Integreon. Kate is now the VP Knowledge & Research for Integreon, with several law firm clients including CMS Cameron McKenna, as well as investment banks and other corporate organizations.

SOPHIE THOMPSON

Sophie has worked in the legal sector since 1999, starting with Osborne Clarke and then latterly with Integreon. She manages a large team of information professionals, providing a shared, outsourced library service to law firm clients, including delivery via a blended UK/India team.

KATHY TURNER

Kathy Turner has been the Ministry of Justice (MoJ) Librarian since 2011, having previously worked in the libraries at the Department of Constitutional Affairs and the Home Office.

MANDY WEBSTER

Mandy gained her law degree at the University of Nottingham and has worked as Library and Information Services Manager at Browne Jacobson since 1996, developing the online services, intranet resources and information skills training whilst carrying out increasing amounts of research and budgeting. Her previous experience includes working in the academic sector and for NHS information services.

JULES WINTERTON

Jules is Director and Librarian of the Institute of Advanced Legal Studies in the School of Advanced Study of the University of London. He is a member of the Board of the British and Irish Legal Information Institute, Convenor of the Libraries Committee of the Society of Legal Scholars and an Associate Professor at the Kwame Nkrumah University in Ghana. He was President of the International Association of Law Libraries 2004–10 and Chair of the British and Irish Association of Law Librarians in 1994–95.

LOYITA WORLEY

Loyita is Director of EMEA Library Operations at the global law firm Reed Smith. She has been working within the legal information sector for many years now and has been involved with BIALL for most of that time – most recently as editor of this handbook. She is interested in all aspects of information and knowledge management and also writes articles and speaks regularly at conferences.

LESLEY YOUNG

Lesley Young has worked in academic law librarianship for most of her career. After working in the History and British Government Publications sections of the University of London Library, she moved to the Institute of Advanced Legal Studies Library in 1983 to work with serials. She is currently Information Resources Manager, responsible for the selection, acquisition and management of the collections and is a member of the FLARE group and the Institute Library's senior management team.

FOREWORD

JAS BRESLIN
President, British and Irish Association of Law Librarians

The world in which we now work is very different to the workplace of 2006, the year in which the first edition of the *Handbook of Legal Information Management* was published. In the eight years since this book first appeared on the bookshelves of law firms and academic establishments, technology has transformed our profession, and indeed our lives, as we embrace social media tools, smartphones and 24/7 connectivity.

But the basic skills of our profession remain unchanged, and the need for a book such as this is no less now than it was back in 2006. In fact, as the global downturn continues to bite, and more is asked of information professionals, I would even argue that a publication such as the *Handbook* is now even more vital.

This new edition of the *Handbook* provides an up-to-date view of the many concerns and issues relevant for those who are involved in the management of legal information, in all of its many forms. Each chapter has been updated to reflect innovative techniques and forward thinking in its discrete areas.

There are new chapters on social networking, outsourcing and the Legal Services Act, and other such recent phenomena affecting legal information professionals. There are also updated chapters on the practical management of information and services in more traditional areas such as the organization of legal information and collection management; performance of legal research; the management of staff and teams; and pioneering technologies used in teaching information research and literacy skills.

Each chapter has been written by a leading authority in his or her field, and it is a credit to the collegial spirit of BIALL that we have so many talented and experienced individuals within our network who are able to share their expertise in the pages of this book.

This new edition will be as useful to our new generation of information workers as it will be to those who have been working in the field for many decades. I hope you will find it as useful and inspiring as I have done. And I just can't help but wonder what changes we will see in the third edition?

May 2014

PREFACE

A lot has happened since the first edition of this book was published, both in terms of legal information and the people connected with it.

When BIALL was approached about a second edition in 2010, having edited the first edition, I was happy to introduce the publishers to Sarah Spells, the then Chair of the BIALL Publications Committee. Having consulted her committee, it was decided that a second edition would be a good idea and Sarah enthusiastically volunteered herself as editor. She was the first to admit that it was a big task and so asked if I would help her having had previous experience. I was happy to do so and so began working alongside Sarah and the Publications Committee. I attended their meetings and helped Sarah identify possible contributors to the book. Sarah approached me to write one of the case studies which I gladly did and then when one of the contributors dropped out at the last moment, I volunteered to help out by rewriting a particular chapter for her. I had fully expected that simply giving a little more advice and encouragement along the way would be the end of my involvement. Sadly that was not to be and with Sarah's untimely and tragic death in September 2012, I was asked to take over the project. It has been a poignant experience and I have often thought of Sarah as I worked on the book. To me, one of Sarah's most endearing characteristics was her energy for every project that came her way and so I am both pleased and privileged that I was able to complete this one for her.

Within our profession, many legal information professionals will have faced some of the most challenging times of their careers over which they may have had little control with the financial recession which started in 2008. This had a direct impact on many libraries and information services from academic to law firm libraries and often resources were cut back – that is budgets and staff. We were required to make some difficult decisions and to think of new and different ways to supply our services to a still demanding client base. It has been more important than ever to align our strategy with that of the institution for whom we work and to assert ourselves to ensure that our efforts are recognized. We demonstrated our flexibility by continuing to provide high quality services with fewer resources, finding innovative ways to deliver new services and in some cases by taking on new responsibilities. Whilst at times difficult, this has also provided an opportunity for us to rise to the challenge to show what we are capable of. We have tried to reflect all of this in the *Handbook* and like its predecessor I would recommend it as a starting point to those who are new to the profession and as a reference tool to those with more experience.

The book concentrates on the law in England and Wales. However, Scotland, Northern Ireland and the Republic of Ireland are covered.

The text is up to date as of May 2014.

ACKNOWLEDGEMENTS

I would like to express my gratitude to the many contributors to this book – both from myself as well as BIALL – as without them the book would never have been possible. There were particular challenges but everybody remained patient and supportive throughout.

Lianne Sherlock, with whom I have worked at Ashgate, has been a great help and has gently nudged me along, keeping me focused and providing a second pair of hands when most needed.

Finally, I would like to thank my husband Martin for lending a good-natured ear and being so understanding of my working late to get the project completed.

GLOSSARY

AALL	American Association of Law Libraries – founded in the US in 1906 to promote and enhance the value of law libraries to the legal and public communities, to foster the profession of law librarianship, and to provide leadership in the field of legal information.
ALLA	Australian Law Librarians' Association – aims to provide a national focus for law librarianship and legal and business information in Australia.
ALT	Association for Learning Technology
Athens	AuTHENtication System – used by academic libraries to provide password authentication for their students.
AUSTLII	Australasian Legal Information Institute – provides free Internet access to Australasian legal materials.
BAILII	British and Irish Legal Information Institute – database providing access to British and Irish primary legal materials derived from a variety of sources. The database relies upon direct and indirect feeds by relevant courts, government departments and other organizations.
BILETA	British and Irish Law, Education and Technology Association – formed to promote the use of technology in legal education throughout the UK and Ireland.
BLDSC	British Library Document Supply Centre
BVC	Bar Vocational Course – this is the next part of training after the academic stage. Its purpose is to ensure that students intending to become barristers acquire the skills, knowledge of procedure and evidence, attitudes and competence to prepare them for the more specialized training in the 12 months of pupillage which follow.
CALL/ACBD	Canadian Association of Law Libraries/Association Canadienne des Bibliotheques de Droit – represents members from all types of

	Canadian law libraries (academic, corporate, court, government, law society and private law firms).
CDPA	Copyright, Designs and Patents Act
CELEX	CELEX is a complete and authoritative source of information on European Community law. It provides multilingual access to a broad range of legal instruments such as the founding treaties, secondary legislation, the opinions and resolutions of the institutions and bodies of the European Union and the case law of the Court of Justice and the Court of First Instance of the European Communities.
Citator	Volume or section of a volume containing tables of cases or legislation, with reference to their published sources and tables of cases and legislation that have been judicially noticed in subsequent cases.
CLA	Copyright Licensing Agency – a non-profit-making agency that licenses organizations for photocopying and scanning from magazines, books and journals.
Conflicts of interest	Situations where a firm may be acting in two or more separate capacities and the objectives in these capacities are not identical.
CPE	Common Professional Examination – this exam enables non-law graduates and, in some instances, non-graduates to complete the foundations of legal knowledge required by the academic stage of training.
DfES	Department for Education and Skills
DOI	Digital object identifier – a system for identifying content objects in the digital environment. DOIs are names assigned to any entity for use on digital networks. They are used to provide current information, including where they (or information about them) can be found on the Internet. Information about a digital object may change over time, including where to find it, but its DOI will not change.
ECR	European Court Reports – these contain all case law from the Court of Justice and Court of First Instance. They are available in all official EU languages.
HEFCE	Higher Education Funding Council for England
HEI	Higher Education Institutes
ICT	Information and communications technology
ISP	Internet service provider

JISC	Joint Information Systems Committee – supports further and higher education by providing strategic guidance, advice and opportunities to use information and communications technology (ICT) to support teaching, learning, research and administration. JISC is funded by all the UK post-16 and higher education funding councils.
JSI	Joint Study Institute – a study conference hosted in alternate years by AALL, ALLA, BIALL and CALL/ACBD.
Law Commission	This is the independent body set up by Parliament in 1965 (along with a similar Commission for Scotland) to keep the law of England and Wales under review and to recommend reform when it is needed.
LILI	Learning in Law Initiative
LNTV	Legal Network Television
LPC	Legal Practice Course – a key element of vocational training to become a solicitor: it must be completed by everyone who intends to qualify as a solicitor in England and Wales.
MLE	Managed learning environments – this refers to the whole range of information systems and processes that support learning and the management of learning within an institution. It includes virtual learning environments, administrative and other support systems.
MoJ	The Ministry of Justice is a ministerial department of the UK Government headed by the Secretary of State for Justice and Lord Chancellor (a combined position). The department is also responsible for areas of constitutional policy not transferred in 2010 to the Deputy Prime Minister, human rights law and information rights law across the UK.
NLP	Neuro-linguistic programming systems
NZLLA	New Zealand Law Librarians Association
PACE	Police and Criminal Evidence Act
PSL	Professional support lawyer – this is someone who is qualified as a lawyer, but who has decided to take a non-fee-earning role and works with lawyers within a law firm, providing them with information on latest legal developments as well as getting involved with producing precedents, marketing and training.
RELOAD	Reusable e-Learning Object Authoring and Delivery
RDN – VTS	Resource Discovery Network – Virtual Training Suite

SCONUL	Society of College, National and University Libraries
SCORM	Shareable Content Object Reference Model
SI	Statutory Instrument
SLS	Society of Legal Scholars (previously the Society of Public Teachers of Law or SPTL)
UCISA	Universities and Colleges Information Systems Association
UKCLE	UK Centre for Legal Education
UKLOM	UK Learning Object Metadata
URL	Uniform Resource Locator – a format for the address of an Internet document that is accessible using one of a variety of protocols.
VLE	Virtual learning environment – a set of teaching and learning tools designed to enhance a student's learning experience by including computers and the Internet in the learning process.
WIPO	World Intellectual Property Organization – an intergovernmental organization based in Geneva, Switzerland, and responsible for the promotion of the protection of intellectual rights throughout the world.
WORLDLII	World Legal Information Institute – a free, independent and non-profit-making global legal research database.

CHAPTER 1

LAW LIBRARIES AND THEIR USERS

JULES WINTERTON

INTRODUCTION[1]

Law libraries in Britain and Ireland form a distinct and dynamic group within the information world. They are defined by their focus on the discipline and practice of law and their close connection with, and mission to serve, the various parts of the legal system, notably the Bar, the courts and the judiciary, solicitors, government, those in professional legal education and those learning the law and researching it as an academic discipline.

Law libraries are a cross-sectoral group; they have parent institutions which range across the private and public spheres but they retain a common identity through their dealings with the legal profession in its various branches and their management of legal information in its various proliferations. Many libraries serve legal institutions directly; some are collections forming part of larger libraries, such as the national libraries and those of many of the universities. They are diverse in nature and size and in the ways in which they seek to provide for their users. Their scope and number have grown enormously in recent years. They include some of the most ancient libraries and the newest information units, repositories of centuries of learning and virtual systems distilling the knowledge bases of extraordinarily successful commercial firms.

Law librarians have responsibility for the selection, acquisition, maintenance, management and delivery of information of legal relevance in convenient and speedy ways suited to the nature of the legal research of their users. In doing this they play a vital part in the administration of justice, in the support of scholarship and legal education, and in the functioning of a social system which adheres to the rule of law.

Law librarians identify themselves as a distinct group within librarianship despite the wide diversity of their libraries and have formed an active and successful professional community. The British and Irish Association of Law Librarians

(BIALL) and many other local, regional and topical associations successfully sponsor professional development and the promotion of standards, professional collaboration and networking, on a cross-sectoral basis. Law librarianship in the latter part of the twentieth century became and remains a desirable career path, particularly in the commercial sector, despite the recent economic downturn. Law libraries have been at the forefront of many developments in information management and are currently at the leading edge of exploring new roles for libraries and librarians in serving their constituencies.

This chapter will describe and set law libraries in Britain and Ireland in context and relate their present state and their historical development to the various branches of the legal profession and the legal systems. There is a brief comparative outline of law libraries in other countries. The chapter will also describe professional collaboration, networking and professional associations of law librarians in Britain and Ireland and internationally. A survey of the underlying directions of change and strategic drivers as they affect law libraries concludes the chapter and seeks to give some sense of the future for law libraries. This can only be a brief survey and there is a need to define a research agenda in law librarianship[2] to investigate present practice and inform the redefinition of our profession.

THE ROLE OF LAW LIBRARIES

The law has always been information-based and information-intensive, particularly in common law systems. As organizations seek to harness and derive value from information ever more efficiently, the net for relevant information is thrown more widely, particularly in law firms. Relevant legal information is no longer contained solely in published form or in occasional 'unpublished' judgments. Information may take the form of in-house documentation, expertise, and information deriving from the practice of law and from discrete legal transactions. Many types of information are now drawn into more formal information systems and become intellectual capital within these vigorous competitive environments. This is a road along which other organizations in other sectors, such as universities, are also beginning to travel.

The know how database on the law firm's intranet and the management of intellectual assets and knowledge in other forms raise questions about the definition of law libraries and the roles of law librarians. This is a fundamental change from the situation described in the first chapters of the predecessors to this work, the two editions of the *Manual of Law Librarianship* (Daintree 1976, Logan 1987)[3] where the description of libraries could generally be satisfied by reference to libraries in the more traditional sense which dealt for the most part with published sources of information in print acquired from outwith the organization.

The complex series of processes conveniently swept up in the term globalization in all its manifestations and ramifications is noted at several points in this chapter and is having profound effects on legal practice and legal education and therefore on legal information management (Winterton 2011).

In contrast to these ongoing developments, the most dramatic single change from the corresponding chapter of the first edition of this book (Winterton 2006) is a more tangible development and derives from a defining moment in the constitutional history of the United Kingdom: the establishment of the new Supreme Court of the United Kingdom and its new library in a historic setting on Parliament Square in Westminster.[4]

TYPES OF LIBRARIES AND THEIR USERS[5]

Law libraries in Britain and Ireland date from medieval times and were established to serve legal institutions such as the Inns of Court and are closely tied to the development of those institutions.[6] There were still very few law libraries by the middle of the nineteenth century and they generally served professional organizations of barristers and solicitors and were located in the capital cities.

Since the middle of the nineteenth century there has been an enormous growth in all emanations of the legal system. Dramatic reforms of the legal system and the conduct of its business affected different branches of the profession at different times during the period. There is a detailed account of the development of the legal profession in England and Wales until 1988 by Richard Abel; he has also written a study of the legal profession in the 1990s, which was a period of particularly turbulent change (Abel 1988, 2003).[7]

The amount of legislation and litigation has increased the potential sources of law dramatically and there has been a growth in legal publishing to try to satisfy an inexorable desire to access more of that law. The impact of other national and international legal regimes and proliferating transnational legal relationships have increased both the quantity and the geographical extent of relevant law. The legal profession itself has grown and the legal educational systems which offer the routes to join that profession have grown in scope and number.

These increases fuelled an expansion in the numbers of law libraries and the number of law librarians. However, since 2006, particularly in the current economic climate, the value and sustainability of libraries have increasingly been questioned and there have been losses both of jobs and opportunities (Small 2009). Private and public institutions have sought to reduce overall costs or curtail the growth in costs and there has been a considerable process of institutional merger and consolidation, especially among law firms. Law libraries are no longer considered as a uniquely vital asset which they traditionally represented. Ironically library expenditure is seen by some institutions in terms of what libraries once were rather than the diverse and progressive services which they now supply.

LIBRARIES SERVING THE BAR IN ENGLAND AND WALES

The Bar is the branch of the practising legal profession which has enjoyed, until relatively recently, the exclusive right of audience in the higher courts.[8] This right has been conferred on their members since the sixteenth century by the four Inns of Court, independent and unincorporated bodies which developed a collegiate form: Gray's Inn, Inner Temple, Middle Temple and Lincoln's Inn.[9] They date from medieval times when there were a larger number of Inns in existence for those lawyers and others who needed to be in London when Parliament and the courts were in session. These four had reached a predominant position by 1400 and had developed into settled academic establishments. They became the source from which almost every judge was appointed and they remain the centre of the barristers' profession. They collectively bear responsibility for the regulation of the profession including matters of discipline, the admission of members and the required standards of legal education. In physical terms each Inn provides collegiate space in the centre of legal London near to the courts, renting out space as chambers for barristers to conduct their business, and each providing shared facilities and services including, from earliest times, a library.[10]

Practising barristers now number about 12,500 and a little over a third practise outside London.[11] In addition to advocacy, they are primarily concerned with drafting legal documents, writing opinions, advising clients and the preparation of pleadings. The Bar has traditionally been termed the senior or learned branch of the legal profession and has for generations provided the opportunity for specialization and been the source of expertise in particular areas of law.

Over the past 20 years the threat of competition to the Bar from law firms, especially those employing in-house specialists, and increased competition within a rapidly expanding Bar has led to fundamental changes within the profession and the modernization of the running of barristers' chambers and of the Inns. This has included the establishment of libraries, managed by trained staff, within some sets of chambers, building on the personal and shared collections of basic materials located there, and an increased recognition of the importance of the Inn libraries.

The libraries of the Inns maintain some of the few great collections of books on foreign and international law in Britain and Ireland, as well as magnificent collections on English law. Their early establishment ensured that their historical collections of legal materials and manuscripts are extremely rich and, where possible, they still supplement those collections with selected materials when they become available. The scope of the early collections was far wider than law. In common with most society and professional libraries of their age, they collected works of literature, history, topography, travel, biography and similar learned subjects. Much of this remains, though depleted through disposal in recent years.

The libraries of the Inns are private libraries not open to the general public; they serve members of their own Inn, including student members training for admission to the Bar, and barristers who have chambers in the Inn and their pupils. Barristers who are members of the other Inns and have chambers elsewhere are also admitted if their own Inn does not hold the material which they seek. Solicitors may be admitted by prior arrangement as a library of last resort for material unavailable in other London law libraries. Scholars are welcomed by appointment to use the rare books, manuscripts and archives of the Inns. The libraries of the Inns are principally reference collections rather than lending libraries, although lending was always extended to Benchers, those senior members who manage the affairs of their societies, and for the purposes of taking a particular item to court. The libraries of the Inns now offer automated catalogues[12] which can all be searched from each Inn, and union lists of current law reports, periodicals, looseleaf services and electronic resources.[13] They also provide a wide range of electronic services, distance services to members of the provincial Bar, collaborate over admission and opening hours, and have a co-operative collection development policy which concentrates provision for particular jurisdictions and subjects. Each Inn library maintains special collections and takes a primary responsibility for collecting the law of certain foreign and international jurisdictions and of other jurisdictions of Britain and Ireland in addition to its core collections of the law of England and Wales.[14] Overall co-operation is within the terms of reference of an Inns of Court Libraries Liaison Committee which reports to the Council of the Inns of Court and Bar. The issue of whether four such fine libraries, representing the heart of four societies with independent identities but carrying out similar functions, can be even more closely combined has yet to be resolved.[15]

LIBRARIES SERVING THE BAR IN SCOTLAND AND IRELAND

Scotland is a separate jurisdiction with a distinct legal system based on Roman civil law whereas the English common law forms the basis of the jurisdictions in Ireland. They do, however, share the practical implications of the relatively small size of their legal professions.

The Advocates Library[16] in Edinburgh is the private library of the Faculty of Advocates; it was founded in 1689 by a small professional society of lawyers and became a national cultural and intellectual institution; see Cadell and Matheson (1989), St Clair and Craik (1989), John (1992) and Longson (2009). In common with many libraries for lawyers it began to develop as a general scholarly library.

In 1710 it received copyright deposit status and by the nineteenth century it had begun to operate as a national library. This placed a huge burden on the private resources of the Faculty but it discharged them so successfully that, when the situation was resolved in 1925, it transferred by gift three quarters of a million volumes of non-legal holdings to form the National Library of Scotland.[17] From that date, retaining its copyright deposit privilege for legal materials, it has continued as a dedicated law library, it 'is widely regarded as the finest working law library in the British Isles'[18] and it possesses the best collection of continental European civil law works in Britain and Ireland and great collections of the papers of judges and advocates relating to court cases. Collections are also maintained in the High Court buildings in Edinburgh and Glasgow and at the Supreme Court in London. In common with the Law Library system in Dublin, the Faculty provides the working space and place of business for advocates and the administrative infrastructure to support them.

In Belfast the Bar Council of Northern Ireland operates the Bar Library, which is the base for all practising barristers in Northern Ireland, providing office and other support services as well as library and information services.[19] In a development similar to that in Dublin, new Bar Library accommodation was opened in April 2003 while retaining the Old Bar Library. The Main Library in the Royal Courts of Justice houses the printed collection of some 60,000 volumes and access to electronic services including OLIB, the in-house database of Northern Ireland law, is available to members in-house and remotely.

The King's Inns[20] in Dublin is a single society founded in 1541 which has a rather different history from the English Inns (Kenny 1992); it is the headquarters of the Benchers, who include all the judges of the Supreme and High Courts, and the home of the School of Law. It historically played a smaller role in the education of lawyers and is not a central physical focus of the Bar. Its library was formed in 1788 when it purchased the library of Mr Justice Robinson, but was not properly housed until 1832 when it was established in its present premises in Henrietta Street as part of a new complex of buildings giving the Inns its first dedicated home (Neylon 1973). The collections developed as a general learned and scholarly library, in common with the English Inns and the libraries serving the profession in Scotland, and 'about 40% of the library's 96,000 volumes are still today non-legal' (Holborn 2006: 457). Although it is an excellent law library, it is not the first resort for the practising Irish Bar since it does not form their place of business. For over 200 years the place of business for the Bar in Ireland has been at the Four Courts, housed in a magnificent building on the Quays, which provides accommodation both for the courts, ranged around a central Round Hall which has been imitated in other jurisdictions, and for barristers, first in the Hall and then in the Law Library.[21]

The Law Library Society was founded in 1816 when members of the Bar and subscribers to an existing library in the Four Courts bought that library from its impoverished owner (Aston 2011). The Benchers of the King's Inns provided a room in the Four Courts and the Library as it grew moved several times, occupying a purpose-built library in the east wing from 1897–1922. Today the Law Library provides the working desk space, consultation rooms, support services and meeting and hiring place for barristers as well as housing the law collection, now numbering over 130,000 volumes. The Library in the Four Courts was under tremendous pressure for space and in 1994 the Bar Council of Ireland bought its first property and built office space for barristers on Church Street. In 1998 it opened its second modern facility 100 yards away from the Four Courts, named the Distillery Building because it is built into the old walls of the Jameson's Distillery. This facility preserves and extends the Law Library way of working, providing desks as office space for barristers alongside a library which houses relatively small book collections but also makes extensive provision for electronic legal research. The building also houses the Dublin International Arbitration Centre.[22] Satellite libraries also operate at the Criminal Courts of Justice in Dublin and at Washington Street in Cork.

LIBRARIES SERVING THE COURTS AND THE JUDICIARY

Libraries serving the courts and the judiciary in London have experienced profound changes since 2006 because of constitutional changes and changes to government departments concerned with the legal system. The consequential changes to the libraries have been profound and the moves, mergers and transfer of materials have been a huge project and restructuring is continuing.

The new Supreme Court for the United Kingdom was established following the implementation of fundamental constitutional reform enacted in 2005 under government proposals to create a new 'free-standing Supreme Court, to separate the highest court of appeal for the United Kingdom from the second chamber of Parliament and the most senior judges from the legislature'(Constitutional Reform ... 2003).[23] The newly styled Justices of the Supreme Court of the United Kingdom, comprising professional judges who may be drawn from all jurisdictions of the United Kingdom, first sat in October 2009. The Court is now the final court of appeal for all United Kingdom civil cases, and criminal cases from England, Wales and Northern Ireland. Under the Constitutional Reform Act 2005, devolution cases from the jurisdictions of the United Kingdom are now heard by the Supreme Court.

The new Supreme Court is housed on Parliament Square in the refurbished and remodelled Middlesex Guildhall, in a location 'linked with justice and the law for over a millennium'[24] and in a building which housed courts since the nineteenth century and which itself replaced an earlier courthouse. The centrepiece of the new building is a magnificent triple-height library, newly created from legal materials transferred from the House of Lords Library, both the main library and the Law Lords' Collection, and from the Judicial Committee of the Privy Council, together with some additional material from the Royal Courts of Justice (Rowe 2009). This is a very large-scale investment in the Court's future accommodation and services, not least in the library services. The new building heralds an era of enhanced accessibility by accommodating visitors, offering exhibitions and tours, and also via the new website. The hearings are televised live both to monitors in the building and via the Sky broadcasting company.[25]

Until 2009 the Appellate Committee of the House of Lords formed the highest court of appeal in the United Kingdom. A volume with contributions by Law Lords and leading academics commemorated the achievements of the final court of appeal (Blom-Cooper, Dickson and Drewry 2009). The judicial role of the House of Lords had evolved over more than 600 years, originally from the work of the royal court. The professional judges were accommodated in the Palace of Westminster, were members of the House of Lords, styled Lords of Appeal in Ordinary, and drew on the Palace for the necessary support services including library services. The House of Lords Library was established in 1826 and was primarily devoted to the support of the appellate function of the House and continued to place considerable emphasis on that function. The library had considerable holdings of the law of England, Wales and Scotland, including early legislation, selected materials from other common law jurisdictions and collections on legislative drafting and statutory interpretation, European Union law and human rights (Jones 1998) and, in addition, a separate Law Lords' Collection was housed close to the offices of the judges. On the establishment of the new Supreme Court, relevant legal materials were transferred to form the core of the library serving the new Court. However, a considerable legacy of records relating to the judicial function of Parliament until 2009 remains in the Parliamentary Archives (Shenton 2011).

The Judicial Committee of the Privy Council[26] has also transferred to the new Supreme Court building from its Downing Street location. It continues to hear appeals from a reduced number of Commonwealth and former Commonwealth jurisdictions, from Overseas Territories, Crown Dependencies such as Guernsey, Jersey and the Isle of Man, and it has some other rarely used jurisdictions.[27] Selected library collections which were housed in the Downing Street building have been transferred. Some materials were donated to other major law libraries, a set of the judgments were made available to the British and Irish Legal Information Institute for digitization[28] and a set of the case papers was transferred to The National Archives.

The Ministry of Justice Library and Information Services[29] provides services to Her Majesty's Courts and Tribunals Service (HMCTS).[30] HMCTS was created on 1 April 2011, bringing together the separate Courts Service and the Tribunals Service, to provide support for the administration of justice in courts and tribunals in partnership with the judiciary. Library services are provided to the courts and the judiciary and tribunals in England and Wales and to the Law Commission. There are major libraries in London, including a library for the judiciary at the Royal Courts of Justice, and a regional library and information service with libraries based on the circuit system at Crown Courts and Combined Court Centres in England and Wales, and judges in chambers are provided with the necessary books, access to electronic information and a comprehensive reference service.[31] Services were formerly provided to the Judicial Committee of the Privy Council, whose library is now collocated with the library of the new Supreme Court.

An organized national library and information service in support of the courts and the judiciary is a fairly recent development (Holborn 2006: 459). Even within the Royal Courts of Justice, what was called the 'Supreme Court Library' was relatively recent, having been established in 1968, incorporating several earlier private ventures by the judiciary and the Bar, see Best (1983).[32] A separate library service based on the Bar Library, which had been originally established by the Inns when the Royal Courts of Justice were built in 1884, used to admit members of the legal profession and latterly litigants in person to consult material not readily available to them elsewhere; the Bar Library has now closed and this service no longer exists. The extensive collections of transcripts and indexes of transcripts from the Court of Appeal (Civil Division) (1951 onwards) and the Court of Appeal (Criminal Division) (1963 to 1989) as well as from the Employment Appeal Tribunal and the Immigration Appeal Tribunal appear to be no longer publicly available.[33] As noted above, the library collections remaining within the Royal Courts of Justice have been reorganized into a RCJ Library for the judiciary.

The short history and relative paucity of provision for the judiciary generally is in part explained by the availability of other library resources for judges, notably at their respective Inns or their own private libraries, but more importantly by the traditions of the English legal system in which judges do not rely on their own legal research but on research by counsel.

In Scotland the Supreme Courts Library serving the Court of Session and the High Court of Justiciary is located in Parliament House amid a concentration of other law libraries nearby, including of course the Advocates Library, described above. The Northern Ireland Courts and Tribunals Service, an agency of the Department of Justice for Northern Ireland,[34] maintains a library within the Royal Courts of Justice in Belfast and at its headquarters from which it serves the regional courts' offices and distributes most of its resources to the chambers of judges.

In Ireland, the Judges' Library housed in a building alongside the Four Courts, comprising over 20,000 volumes and a range of online subscription databases, provides services to the judiciary of the High Court and the Supreme Court and various branches of the administration of the court system, and also at a distance to judges of the District and Circuit Courts (Donnelly 1996, 2011). The King's Inns Library also serves as a resource for the judiciary.

LIBRARIES FOR SOLICITORS IN ENGLAND AND WALES

There are about 120,000 practising solicitors in England and Wales. The majority of solicitors' firms are distributed around the country and the high street business mainly comprises conveyancing, probate, family, employment and social welfare law. The city law firms however tend to deal primarily with civil law areas such as corporate finance, banking, financial services, media, pensions, litigation and so on. The profession in England and Wales first made provision for libraries not nationally but in the context of the formation of local law societies outside London in the late eighteenth and early nineteenth centuries, including Bristol,[35] Yorkshire, Manchester,[36] Plymouth and Birmingham.[37] These and many others[38] are independent non-profit organizations which do not form part of the Law Society of England and Wales; libraries often figured prominently in their original objectives[39] and still provide valuable services to their members (Martin 2001).

The Law Society of England and Wales[40] is the professional body for solicitors, first chartered in 1831 and established in Chancery Lane in London since 1832, some time later than some of the local law societies, and it was granted a Royal Charter in 1845 to regulate the profession.

The Law Society operated a library from the time of its establishment, and in common with the other professional libraries it amassed considerable collections of non-legal materials, but much of these have been disposed of over the past 30 years. The library maintains extensive working collections of the law of England and Wales, fine historical collections and an excellent collection of European Union legal material, housed in splendid rooms. Services to all solicitors, in larger firms in London and in practices around the country, include enquiry services and a speedy document delivery service. In common with many organizations, the Law Society has been seeking economies in recent years and reorganizations have affected the library and appear to have eliminated one of the most senior posts in law librarianship in the country.

The largest and most well-established law firm library services are found in firms in and around the City of London which are extremely large and successful global businesses and have generally weathered the economic downturn albeit with reductions in legal and business support teams. The largest law firm in 2010 had over 560 partners, 3,400 fee-earners worldwide in 33 offices in 23 countries and employed 6,300 staff; and fee income measured in hundreds of millions of pounds. Nationally some firms in metropolitan areas outside London have grown large enough to deal with large-scale commercial business or have formed groups and consortia to do so. The largest law firms are at the leading edge of law library development in the broadest sense; they invest heavily in information management both in terms of information itself, technology to store and manipulate it and in professional skills to devise and implement information and knowledge management strategy. Law firms have increasingly adopted legal process outsourcing, initially in support services, to deliver better value.

For many years there was little need for a significant library in a solicitor's office. In about 1900, 'the amount of legislation was not large, case reports tended to be short and pithy, and a legal library of 20 books was perceived as adequate' (Cruikshank 2003: 33). In 1976, in an earlier edition of this work, the existence of a small number of libraries in solicitors' firms was noted, 'in some cases a librarian has been appointed to exploit these materials ...' (Daintree 1976: 50–51). The large increase in professional law library jobs since the early 1970s, when the first professional law librarians were appointed in law firms, can be attributed to the growth of large law firms. The removal of the restriction in the number of partners to 20 by s.120 of the Companies Act 1967 was a major factor in the dramatic expansion in the size of law firms as they arose with the growth of financial and commercial activity in the City of London. The introduction of 'alternative business structures' regarding the ownership of law firms by non-lawyers in October 2011 may have an equally profound impact on the provision of legal services.[41]

LIBRARIES FOR SOLICITORS IN SCOTLAND

The Law Society of Scotland[42] was created by statute in 1949 and acts as the regulatory body for about 10,400 solicitors in around 1,200 firms but the formal organization of lawyers who were not advocates and came to be called solicitors began much earlier.

The Society of Writers to Her Majesty's Signet (WS)[43] dates from the Middle Ages and remains a private society of lawyers in general legal practice; the acronym WS appears after members' names. The Signet was the private seal of the early Scottish Kings, and the Writers to the Signet were those authorized to supervise its use and, later, to act as clerks to the Courts. The Society took definite shape in 1594, when the King's Secretary, as Keeper of the Signet, granted Commissions to a Deputy Keeper and 18 other writers.

The WS Society is particularly noted for its ownership of the Signet Library, whose history from 1722 has been fully chronicled by George Ballantyne in 1979, with a briefer account in 1971. The Signet Library is now housed in one of the finest Georgian buildings in Scotland which originally comprised a Lower Library for the Society, completed in 1815, and an Upper Library for the Faculty of Advocates, completed in 1822. The Faculty of Advocates moved to a newly constructed building soon after and the Society linked the Upper and Lower libraries. From the late eighteenth century and early nineteenth century the library expanded greatly and, in similar fashion to the Advocates Library, broadened its collections beyond law, and made its library available to general readers. The burden on a small society proved too much and, after increasing financial constraints, a period of contraction and sales began in 1958 and continued until 1979. In 1879 the library had contained about 65,000 volumes, at the turn of that century over 100,000 books, and today it again contains about 65,000, of which almost half are legal and, of the rest, about 15,000 are of historical and topographical interest devoted mainly to Scotland.[44] The collections and services are described by Bird (2009) and include the provision on a commercial basis of consultancy, research, document delivery and customized electronic information services. More recently restructuring has taken place, affecting the level of professional staffing of the library.

The other national society in Scotland is the Society of Solicitors in the Supreme Court (the SSC Society),[45] which was formed in 1784 and is incorporated by Royal Charter. It is located in Parliament House in Edinburgh and continues to play a central role in the life and work of the courts of Scotland and the legal profession generally. Membership is open to all solicitors who are members of the Law Society of Scotland but is mostly drawn from those involved in the conduct of litigation in the Court of Session, the High Court of Justiciary and Sheriff Courts throughout Scotland. The Library of the Society is a private library with particular collections of Scottish law as well as UK and European Union law.

Larger firms in the major cities operate their own libraries. Practitioners in the lower courts with local practices, called procurators, formed their own local organizations originally with rather more powers in regulating the profession than the local law societies in England. The Royal Faculty of Procurators in Glasgow[46] and the Society of Advocates in Aberdeen,[47] both founded in the second half of the seventeenth century, are the two remaining societies with libraries. Although both organizations sold collections in the second half of the twentieth century, they both maintain significant libraries and library services and that in Glasgow is 'the largest law library in the west of Scotland'.[48]

LIBRARIES FOR SOLICITORS IN IRELAND

A scholarly history of the Law Society of Ireland[49] provides considerable information about the profession (Hall and Hogan 2002) and Furlong (2011) provides a recent overview of the law firm sector with a statistical analysis of the profession. In 2010 there were about 8,200 practising solicitors in about 2,200 law firms; only 18 firms had ten or more partners.

The Society, originally granted a charter in 1852 as the Society of Attorneys and Solicitors in Ireland, existed in an earlier form from at least 1830. It is the professional body which educates, regulates and represents solicitors in Ireland. The Society and its library were provided with premises in the Solicitors' Buildings in the Four Courts by the Benchers of King's Inns, which governed the solicitors' profession until 1866. The library and its contents of approximately 3,000 volumes were destroyed in 1922 but the losses had been recouped by 1931 when the Society moved back into the rebuilt Four Courts complex. The Society moved from there to its present premises in Blackhall Place which opened in 1978. In 2000 the Society opened a new library in refurbished accommodation on the Blackhall Place campus serving members and students in conjunction with its new educational centre on the same site. The library with its history was described by Margaret Byrne (2002), Librarian from 1974 to 2010, and Mary Gaynor (2011) describes the past decade and the current services.

The Law Society of Northern Ireland[50] was set up under Royal Charter in 1922 and an authoritative account of its history has recently appeared (Hewitt 2010). The Society opened the new Law Society Hall in 2009[51] and its library, information services and business centre provides a range of services to over 2,300 solicitors currently practising in Northern Ireland.

LEGAL EDUCATION

The early history of legal education in England is described briefly by Baker (2002). The relatively modern origins of our current systems of legal education should be appreciated. Following a long decline, by 1850 professional legal education was completely moribund and academic legal education other than in the field of Roman law was virtually nonexistent. Even the House of Commons Select Committee on Legal Education could report in 1846, 'no legal education worthy of the name is at this moment to be had either in England or Ireland'.[52]

The recent history of legal education in England and Wales has not yet been fully documented although an extensive article by Boon and Webb (2008) gives a historical overview and a detailed account of recent years. Reference can also be made to the periodic official reviews touching legal education such as the Ormrod Report (Committee on Legal Education 1971), the Benson Report (Royal Commission on Legal Services 1979), the Marre Report (Committee on the Future of the Legal Profession 1988) and the reports of the Lord Chancellor's Advisory Committee on Legal Education and Conduct in the 1990s, together with the studies which they commissioned (Lord Chancellor's Advisory Committee ... 1996). A major new review of legal education and training, the Legal Education and Training Review, was published in mid-2013 by the Solicitors' Regulation Authority, the Bar Standards Board and the Institute of Legal Executives

Professional Standards.[53] These reviews generally concentrate on education for the legal profession rather than law as an academic discipline.

The education and training of solicitors has been under review by the Law Society of Scotland since 2006 and changes were implemented in 2011 (Campbell 2011).[54] In Northern Ireland there is a wide-ranging review by the Law Society of Northern Ireland of education and training to qualify as a solicitor, 'shaping the future of legal education'.[55] Paris and Donnelly (2010) provide a description of legal education in Ireland.

Useful summaries of legal education and the routes to professional qualification in England and Wales, Scotland and Northern Ireland, with links to relevant websites, used to be compiled by the UK Centre for Legal Education (UKCLE). UKCLE closed in July 2011 following the decision of the UK Higher Education Academy to discontinue funding to subject centres. Reference should be made to the regulatory bodies in each jurisdiction (see the section on professional legal education below).

In England and Wales, legal education is in three stages: academic, vocational and apprenticeship. One might now add continuing professional development. There has been scepticism among the practising profession in the past about the relevance of academic study of law as a preparation for practice. In 1883 Dicey gave an inaugural lecture at All Souls College entitled: 'Can English law be taught at the universities?' (Dicey 1883). He suggested that a body of eminent counsel would reply with unanimity 'that English law must be learned and cannot be taught, and the only places where it can be learned are the law courts or chambers'.

The existence of an 'academic' stage within the universities which is properly academic is now accepted. However, the tension between the vocational and the academic roles of university law schools, between the notion of the 'trade school' and the academic faculty has not been wholly left behind. The past dominance of the practising legal profession, particularly the Bar, in legal training and education limited the role of university law schools. The syllabus of a qualifying law degree is still the subject of considerable discussion between the academic branch of the profession and the professional bodies which monitor the syllabus on a subject by subject basis and allow exemptions from the professional examinations for 'core subjects' taught at the academic stage, conferring the status of 'qualifying law degree'.

Unlike the situation in other jurisdictions of Britain and Ireland, the vocational stage in England and Wales does not attract public funding and has for most of its history been conducted by privately financed and professional law schools outside the university system. The main interest groups have failed to agree an integrated and unified system of legal education which would operate within the scope of public funding. The recent franchising of the legal practice course and the Bar Professional Training Course, formerly the Bar Vocational Course, to be taught by individual universities has not changed that essential framework.

UNIVERSITY LAW SCHOOLS

The universities from earliest times taught civil and canon law but there was no formal and comprehensive system of education in the common law for much of its history. Blackstone's lectures at Oxford in the 1750s were primarily not for professional law students but for country gentlemen and clergymen. The publication of the lectures as the *Commentaries* in 1765–69 has a history of its own in terms of the understanding and the spread of the common law. However, the lectures and the subsequent endowment of the Vinerian chair in 1758 did not firmly establish the study of English law. During the next 50 years similar chairs were established at Trinity College Dublin and at Cambridge (the Downing Chair in English Law in 1800). The establishment of the law school at University College London (UCL) in 1826[56] was a radical departure in many ways as UCL was the first university in England founded to open up higher education to students of any race, class or religion and later the first university to welcome women on equal terms with men. Law departments were subsequently established at Queen's College Birmingham in 1850 (Pue 1989), at Owen College Manchester in 1880 and at University College Liverpool in 1892.[57]

The Society of Public Teachers of Law (SPTL), now the Society of Legal Scholars (SLS), held its first meeting in 1909 by which time the President, Henry Goudy, could speak in his introductory address of the reforms in legal education at Oxford and Cambridge and:

> ... the recent organization of legal studies in the metropolis both by the Inns of Court and the Law Society ... the prospects for the future development of a great Law Faculty in connection with the University of London ...the Schools of Law in the new universities in the provinces ... seven in number. (Goudy 1909)

A few years later the SPTL published a small booklet of legal curricula at 'various centres of public legal education in England and Wales'; it listed the Universities of Oxford, Cambridge, London, Manchester, Liverpool, Leeds, Sheffield and Wales and also the Council of Legal Education, the Law Society and eight Boards of Legal Studies which prepared students for the qualifying examinations of the Law Society (SPTL no date).[58] These Boards formed a focus for the collaboration of local law societies and universities in legal education. The Law Society had begun to provide grants to local law societies in the provinces in the late nineteenth century and, after the introduction of the compulsory one-year course in 1922 (the 'academic' or 'statutory' year), it gave grants directly to universities to teach the course until 1962. The provincial law faculties in universities were formally established or grew from this initiative and still continue a local co-operation with practitioners. A brief account of law teaching in many colleges, some of which were to become polytechnics and over time 'new universities', can be found in *A History of the Association of Law Teachers* (Marsh 1990).

University law schools were not the only, or even the preferred, route into the profession until relatively recently. Many distinguished lawyers of the period from 1850 to 1950 were not graduates or were graduates in other subjects, and there was a persistent view that members of the Bar, as members of a liberal profession, should be graduates in the humanities or other subjects and add law through vocational training at a professional law school at a later date.

Law is now a graduate profession and the law degree is generally the route for those intending to qualify as lawyers. The UK Centre for Legal Education lists 90 university law schools in England and Wales, 11 in Scotland and two in Northern Ireland and provides a directory of the law courses which they provide.[59] The Privy Council granted degree-awarding powers to the College of Law in 2006 and BPP College, a commercial provider, in 2007. BPP College of Professional Studies was awarded the university college title in 2010 in a move to involve the private sector further in higher education, a policy which may have a profound impact on the education landscape in future.

According to official statistics[60] there were 94,375 law students in higher education in the UK in 2009/10. Undergraduates numbered just over 72,000 compared to about 1,500 in 1938/39 (62 per cent at Oxbridge). In 2009/10 universities made 28,070 awards in law, of which 65.8 per cent were to women; 16,250 of the awards were first degrees. In common with most subjects, there has been an increase in part-time study and distance learning in recent years.[61] In common with most subjects there was a dramatic growth in the number of postgraduate students in law since the 1960s and an even faster growth since the 1980s in numbers of students reading for master's degree courses in specialized legal topics and the emergence of a global market for such LLM degrees. In 2009/10 there were 22,240 postgraduate law students in the UK including master's degree and doctoral students and those in vocational courses taught at universities, a slight drop from earlier in the decade probably occasioned by the recession, and 275 PhDs were awarded in law in the UK.[62]

The SLS and the Association of Law Teachers (ALT), whose existence as two organizations reflects their origins on the two sides of the binary divide, have both published surveys of legal education: Wilson (1966), Wilson and Marsh (1975), Wilson (1993), Harris and Bellerby (1993). The description and analysis in

Blackstone's Tower: The English law school by William Twining (1994) is essential reading and one might add *What Are Law Schools For?* (Birks 1996). The study of law has in recent years become broader and more diverse and has grown to value other disciplines in its study and begun to produce truly interdisciplinary study and research.[63] The increased mobility and diversity of students, before and after qualification, and of teaching staff have added new dimensions to the teaching of law; Crommelin and Hinchcliff (2011) discuss 'global legal education and its implications for legal information management'.

Much research in law includes a comparative element and this study grew at a fast pace in the second half of the twentieth century through the effects of the move to the UK of eminent legal scholars from continental Europe, the establishment of new international legal and economic orders and the effects of changes usually now signified by the term globalization. The effects of the inter-disciplinary patterns of study associated with socio-legal studies[64] have also had a profound impact on legal research. An 'inquiry on empirical research in law' reported in 2006 (Genn 2006) and a Centre for Empirical Legal Studies was established at University College London in 2007.[65] These developments will continue to have a direct impact on the range of library resources required.

ACADEMIC LAW LIBRARIES

The law library remains a crucial resource in legal education. University law libraries in Britain and Ireland have been well documented in recent years. In an admirable collaboration, the SLS and BIALL have carried out an annual survey of academic law libraries. This replaced a long-running annual survey of expenditure on legal materials in academic law libraries carried out by BIALL and published in the *Law Librarian*.[66] A report of the findings of each survey appears in *Legal Information Management*. The report of the 2008/09 survey of academic law libraries (Clinch 2010)[67] is based on 92 returns from a possible 111 law libraries. The detailed survey shows considerable diversity but gives a picture at the median of a typical law school with 694 students, in a separate location or shelved as a single identifiable unit, with one study seat for every 5.4 students and one computer workstation for every 3.44 students, open for 81 hours per week in term and 49.6 hours in vacation, spending £164,000 each year on legal materials (about £173 per student), including a little over £24,000 each year on provision of web-based legal databases, and 1.5 library staff with law service as their principal or sole function. A large number of law schools contribute directly towards the maintenance of the library resource and on average a typical law school provides £18,000 each year towards library funds. The analysis which appears in the report of these and other figures shows the considerable diversity concealed by these averages, particularly between types of institution such as 'old universities' and 'new universities'.

Academic law libraries generally provide for undergraduate students of law and also may support students of law as part of a non-law degree. Those universities which run vocational courses also make specific provision for their support. Academic law libraries often now support students on taught courses at master's degree level in certain specialized subjects which are an area of dynamic growth in law schools. Many law schools register students for research degrees in areas of particular expertise of their staff and the library has a responsibility to support their research along with the research needs of their academic staff, although this may well include recourse to other law libraries, regionally or nationally. The university law library may be the largest law library in the area and may well come to arrangements with readers other than those for whom it is funded, perhaps on payment of a fee, in order to support the needs of local practitioners and others.

Academic law librarians are likely to be more closely involved in the mission of the law school than ever before, to place greater emphasis on skills training, to be actively engaged in the teaching of information skills themselves and to be formally acquiring teaching skills, to be involved in the management, organization and delivery of electronic information locally and at a distance, perhaps be collaborating in constructing a portal or a virtual learning or research environment and be assisting in the selection and administration not only of information products but also their delivery mechanisms.

The law library as a physical place in universities is still important even though a great deal of legal information is now delivered remotely in electronic form. Recent data suggests that in 49 per cent of libraries' numbers of visits have remained constant and in 29 per cent visits have increased (Clinch 2009: 209). Law libraries have traditionally been used intensively and required the highest ratio of seats to students of any subject. There has also been some controversy in the past about the location of law libraries, whether in the law school or in an identifiable area within the main university library or interspersed among materials of other subjects. The precursor of this book devoted a section to 'centralization versus decentralization'. The scope of legal studies is increasingly inter-disciplinary and requires reference to materials relevant to other subjects although intensive use of core legal materials has not lessened. Current practice appears to show 37 per cent of academic law libraries are in a separate location, a third are not separated from the main university library but in a single identifiable unit, 8 per cent of academic law libraries' materials are dispersed wholly or partly among other subject collections and 23 per cent had several law libraries in separate locations.[68]

Although all academic law libraries may excel for the purpose for which they are designed, three libraries are outstanding in terms of their research collections, particularly of foreign, comparative and international law, and for their facilities:

the Bodleian Law Library at the University of Oxford,[69] the Squire Law Library at the University of Cambridge[70] and the Institute of Advanced Legal Studies at the University of London.[71] Representatives of the three libraries contributed to a symposium on law libraries (Symposium on Law Libraries 1964) to mark the opening in 1964 of the new Bodleian Law Library building designed by Sir Leslie Martin. In 1976 the Institute of Advanced Legal Studies was installed in a new building designed by Sir Denys Lasdun and most recently (1995) the Squire Law Library moved to the new Faculty of Law building by Sir Norman Foster. The librarians of the three libraries appeared together, with a representative of the British Library, at the Joint Study Institute in Cambridge in 1998. They each spoke about collaboration in a national context (National Legal Collections 1999) and soon after that the successful bid was launched for the Foreign Law Guide project, FLAG.[72]

The Bodleian Law Library holds the largest collections of law of any academic library in Britain and Ireland; it receives all law books deposited under the terms of the Copyright Act because it is administratively part of the Bodleian Library. All stock is on open access in a classified arrangement which renders the copyright deposit material much more accessible than material housed in the national libraries. 'The Codrington Library at All Souls College also has a fine law collection which often supplements the Bodleian in respect of older material' (Logan 1987: 25).

The Squire Law Library of the University of Cambridge has outstanding collections, particularly in international law, but its activities were constrained for a period until its move, by inadequate accommodation and less than generous staffing and funding. The Radzinowicz Library[73] of the Institute of Criminology at the University of Cambridge was founded in 1960 and has the most comprehensive collections in its subject in the UK and is now housed in modern accommodation alongside the Faculty of Law building.

The library of the Institute of Advanced Legal Studies (IALS) of the University of London performs many of the functions of a national legal research library and has a formal agreement for collaboration and co-ordinated collection development with the British Library.[74] The principle of co-operation on a national basis has always been at the heart of the IALS Library. Its primary constituency comprises the national academic legal research community and it admits postgraduate research students and academic staff from any university worldwide. It is also the postgraduate research law library of the University of London and forms the most prominent part of a network of law provision within the University, whose law-teaching colleges (Birkbeck College,[75] King's College London, the London School of Economics, Queen Mary University of London, the School of Oriental and African Studies and University College London) each have significant research collections in addition to their undergraduate provision.

Although established in 1947, the IALS Library is the second largest legal research library in the UK in terms of collections, with more than 300,000 volumes, and it has foreign law collections of international significance and the largest law library staff of any academic law library in Europe. It plays a significant role in the training of law librarians and legal research skills training. The library was well known for its printed bibliographical works including union lists and the *Index to Foreign Legal Periodicals*. Recently it is known better for its electronic publications such as the national internet portal for law, Eagle-i,[76] the Current Legal Research Topics database,[77] Current Awareness for Legal Information Managers,[78] hosting the British and Irish Legal Information Institute, BAILII and extensive collaborative digitization programmes.[79]

The IALS library is used, on a fee-paying basis, by members of the practising profession and by government and the judiciary. The library also operates a premium information and document delivery service and subscribers include many of the largest law firms and sets of chambers, both Houses of Parliament, the Courts and Tribunals Service, various government departments and overseas institutions. The service was introduced on the basis of full cost recovery after a review chaired by Sir Robert Megarry, recognizing the duty of the Institute to the profession, as a matter of public interest and as a contribution to the administration of justice (IALS 1986).

In Scotland, ten universities offer the Bachelor of Laws degree, either as an ordinary degree over three years or as an honours degree over four years.[80] These institutions and their libraries vary in size and age but include some of the oldest university institutions in Britain and their libraries also vary in size and scope and degree of separateness from the main university library system. The extensive law collections at Edinburgh University, comprising over 60,000 volumes, are in separate accommodation in the Law School alongside the Europa Library which includes the European Documentation Centre. There are recent descriptions of the libraries at the University of Glasgow (Munro 2009) and the University of Strathclyde (Ryan 2009), and there are plans to incorporate the law library at the University of Dundee into a separate area within the main library. As Scots law is a mixed legal system of civil law drawing on elements of common law, collections are likely to be stronger in civil law, Roman law, as well as the institutional writers of Scots law, than elsewhere in Britain and Ireland.

In Northern Ireland, Queen's University Belfast and the University of Ulster (on two sites) offer university legal education. Queen's University Belfast has its outstanding collection of law housed within the main library. The School of Law of the University has contributed to access to law in other ways through the Servicing the Legal System[81] programme which is the only regular publisher on Northern Ireland law.

In Ireland all seven universities offer law degrees, of which Trinity College Dublin has the most extensive collections of law and receives publications on copyright deposit both from Ireland and the United Kingdom. The Law Faculty at University College Cork hosts the Irish Legal Information Initiative[82] which complements the British and Irish Legal Information Institute.

PROFESSIONAL LEGAL EDUCATION AND LIBRARIES

The libraries supporting professional legal education have generally been those serving the legal profession in each jurisdiction and increasingly the academic law libraries of educational institutions now providing teaching for the professional examinations.

The Inns of Court and Chancery were once known as the third university of England and the early history of their role as teaching institutions is described by John Baker (Baker 1990, 2007):

> The Inns of Court were undoubtedly part of an educational system from the very beginning, a system which had been developing for at least eighty years before they came into existence and which, at its best, provided students with a rigorous introduction both to legal practice and to legal method. (Baker 2007: 9)

By the early fifteenth century an academic community had been established. An elaborate system of readings (lectures) and moots developed which provided for the instruction of aspiring barristers but the English Civil War effectively killed it off in the seventeenth century, '... so that the law student after the 1670s was left entirely to his own devices ...' (Baker 2007: 15). The primary means of education in the common law for lawyers became self-help and attendance at the courts and at lawyers' offices in London, and the discipline and regulation of the profession was lax. Many lawyers, until at least the middle of the nineteenth century, rather than study civil law at the universities, would read other subjects prior to their professional training, a tradition in England that lasted long beyond the establishment of modern law schools.

As university law schools began to teach the common law in the mid-nineteenth century, so the Inns revived their lectures and the Law Society began a course of lectures for articled clerks. The Council of Legal Education (CLE) was established by the Inns in 1856 and a compulsory Bar examination was introduced in 1872. In 1967 the CLE opened the Inns of Court School of Law (ICSL) near Gray's Inn as the principal place of education for the vocational stage of training for the Bar. In 1997 the Council ceased to operate[83] and transferred many of its responsibilities to the ICSL. The Law Society introduced examinations in 1836 and a three-tier system was instituted under the terms of the Solicitors Act 1860, although otherwise supervision of the profession was rudimentary. The Law Society established its own School of Law in 1903 which became the College of Law in the 1960s incorporating the tutorial firm Gibson and Weldon before becoming an independent provider in the late 1990s.

In recent years, following the end of the monopoly position of the Bar and the Law Society in the provision of professional legal education, there has been a rapid diversification of providers and access routes to professional qualification. In 2000 ICSL merged with the Department of Law of City University and in 2008 the ICSL name was discontinued and the City Law School created. The Bar Professional Training Course (BPTC), formerly the Bar Vocational Course, is now taught by several public and private institutions in England and Wales including the College of Law and universities. The College of Law, at several sites in England, was the body set up by the Law Society to teach and administer the vocational stage of education to qualify as a solicitor. A development similar to the arrangements for the BPTC has taken place and the Legal Practice Course (LPC) is taught by the College of Law and now by several universities. The College of Law was granted university title in November 2012 and in future will be known as the University of Law; at the same time it ceased to be an educational charity and became a for-profit provider.[84]

Study for these professional courses can now be extended to the award of a master's degree at several institutions, some by innovative means.[85] Other professional awards such as the Common Professional Examination, now known as the Graduate Diploma in Law,[86] the graduate entry LLB, or Institute of Legal Executives qualification are usually taught by the same institutions.

The Bar Standards Board and the Solicitors Regulation Authority are now the authorities in England and Wales which oversee standards for admission to the two branches of the profession but do not provide teaching.[87] Institutions offering the BPTC and the LPC have to meet a range of requirements in order to be validated, including the provision of particular library facilities which are monitored and assessed by means of a programme of visits by an expert panel. The Bar Standards Board, endorsing and building on the Standards for University Law Library Provision issued by the Society of Legal Scholars (SLS 2010),[88] and the Solicitors Regulation Authority promulgate guidance including requirements for library facilities (BSB 2011: A5.3, SRA 2011).[89] Several universities maintain collections and facilities separate from their university law library to support the courses. The former ICSL first opened a library in 1997, having formerly relied on the Inns of Court libraries, and opened a new Legal Training Resources Centre in 2002 with considerable emphasis on networked information services which has developed into the dedicated Gray's Inn campus library of the City Law School. The four Inns of Court libraries admit student members of their own Inn.

In Scotland and Northern Ireland vocational training remains within the university system, and within the public funding system, and library services are combined with the university systems. After completion of the LLB Degree or professional examinations, intending solicitors and advocates take the Diploma in Legal Practice, which is of 26 weeks' duration taught over one academic year, at the universities of Aberdeen, Dundee, Edinburgh, Glasgow, Strathclyde and Robert Gordon. The governing bodies for entry to the two branches of the profession are the Law Society of Scotland and the Faculty of Advocates.[90] In Northern Ireland the Institute of Professional Legal Practice was established at Queen's University Belfast to offer vocational training to trainee barristers and trainee solicitors and the University of Ulster now offers a postgraduate Diploma in Professional Legal Practice. The governing bodies are the Law Society of Northern Ireland and the General Council of the Bar.[91]

In Ireland, the governing bodies of the two branches of the profession not only play a regulatory role but are also still the sole providers of professional legal education for qualification to enter the profession. The Honorable Society of King's Inns,[92] whose library has already been described, administers the one-year vocational course at its Law School, somewhat confusingly called the 'degree course', enabling admission to the degree of barrister-at-law and to be called to the Bar of Ireland. The Education Department of the Law Society of Ireland[93] is responsible for the Law School which runs courses for those intending to become solicitors; their new combined education building and library has been described above. A report by the Competition Authority (2006) has urged reforms to achieve a diversification of providers of professional education and training.

NATIONAL LIBRARIES

The national libraries are generally more suitable as a supplementary resource for particular materials rather than a first choice for most legal research.

The British Library has very extensive collections of law books and official publications, including some of the founding collections of the British Museum Library, and it benefits from copyright deposit of publications from both Britain and Ireland (Cheffins 1999). It has particularly strong collections relating to legal history. However, the British Library has never been able to offer a legal research library service for foreign, comparative and international law and the UK has never had the equivalent of the Law Library of Congress in the US (Law Library of Congress 1982). In the British Library, no one person has overall responsibility for acquisition of legal publications; rather they are acquired by the language sections, other than those handled by the Legal Deposit Office or the Overseas English Section. The law books in the British Library are not arranged as a law library and have no unity as a collection. Access to the collection is in the Social Science Reading Room, as part of official publications and social sciences provision, which contains a reading area with a selection of legal textbooks and journals recently published in the UK along with key reference works and United Kingdom and European Union legislation. Until recently staffing did not include a legally qualified librarian or a trained law librarian even at junior level. A law and socio-legal studies librarian has recently been appointed in line with the strengths of the broader collections. A content strategy document is available,[94] drawn up after a review of collection development and provision which describes collecting policy, including for law, and a general description of the law and legal studies collection is also available.[95]

The British Library has for many years co-operated with the nearby Institute of Advanced Legal Studies rather than try to emulate the depth of expertise and collections there. Collaboration with existing centres of excellence was advocated, among other improvements, by the SPTL in their evidence to the National Libraries Committee in 1968 (SPTL 1968) and elaborated by the British Library Working Party on Provision for Law whose chair was the Director of the IALS and whose Secretary was the Librarian of IALS in the early 1980s (British Library Working Party [1985]). The recommendations of the latter were not implemented because central funding for the collaborative mechanisms was not forthcoming.

The British Library concluded a formal collaborative agreement with the IALS regarding services and collections some years ago. Some enquiries are referred to the IALS, staff training at the Institute is now attended by selected British Library staff, there is active investigation of gaps and overlaps in provision and joint events are held. Collaboration has further increased through the British Library's participation in the FLAG project and the more recent establishment of the FLARE partnership led by the IALS. This provides a means for the great academic law libraries in Oxford, Cambridge and London and the national library to collaborate (Bird, Wills and Winterton 2009).

The National Library of Scotland is in a unique position since it was created through the transfer of collections from the Advocates Library described above. There are arrangements to facilitate the consultation by members of the public in the National Library of the legal materials which are retained by the Advocates Library. The National Library of Wales receives UK copyright deposit material. The National Library of Ireland receives copyright deposit of Irish publications and naturally holds a good collection of Irish law. However, it should be noted that Trinity College Dublin receives both British and Irish publications by copyright deposit in addition to the extensive law collections held in support of its School of Law.

PUBLIC LIBRARIES

Generally law collections in public libraries in Britain and Ireland are limited to basic collections of the law of the local jurisdiction and European Union law, with an emphasis on official publications; they do not provide sufficient resources for in-depth legal research. It is thought that legal enquiries in public reference libraries do not form a significant percentage of all enquiries numerically but form a large proportion of complex enquiries, defined as those which take more than ten minutes of staff time to answer. Enquiries from the public pose difficult challenges in guidance and recommendation of materials while avoiding communicating legal advice. The number of such enquiries may well rise in the current climate when the public are likely to encounter more law-related problems at a time when funding difficulties are reducing the capacity of advice centres and other routes to free legal advice. Public libraries face considerable difficulties in maintaining collections of law in the face of declining budgets, price inflation on legal materials and difficulties in training staff adequately to perform legal reference work. Public libraries will usually be able to offer referral to local community legal advice services.

In London, English law reference collections can be found at the Westminster Reference Library,[96] at Hammersmith and Fulham by reason of an earlier allocation of law under the former LASER (London and South Eastern Library Region) subject specialization scheme among public libraries and at the Guildhall Library which realistically warns that it is not a law library and does not stock up-to-date legal textbooks although it holds a good collection of English law, including early material, and 'our files of English law reports are the most extensive likely to be found outside a specialist library'.[97] Holborn Library, which in the past had substantial holdings, now advertises only a small law collection. Central reference libraries of public library systems such as Birmingham, Manchester, Liverpool and Sheffield have a collection of law for the public and to support local government. Public library systems are now likely to subscribe to one of the major commercial online legal information databases although these too require training and practice to use effectively. They also make use of free-to-internet services such as the British and Irish Legal Information Institute,[98] and specialist services on citizen's rights such as the Citizen's Advice Network Information Service[99] and CANS Legal Information.[100]

In a paper from BIALL to the Library and Information Services Council in 1985, it was noted that:

> ... *perhaps because of the complexity of the literature and the absence of staff trained in its use, the standard of collections and level of legal reference service in public libraries is so abysmally low (with one or two honourable exceptions) as to be useless. (BIALL 1985)*

Very little research is available on actual provision of legal information by public libraries. A detailed study of access to legal information in East Kilbride, Glasgow and Paisley in 1997 did not go so far as the BIALL criticism (Mansfield 1997). The study nevertheless found that legal collections were out of date and basic in nature, collection development lacked a customer focus and training in legal reference work was woefully inadequate.

In part, but only in part, provision of legal information to the public has been overtaken by e-government initiatives. The UK government, somewhat later than in some other countries, has accepted that the statutes and other products of our democratic system should be made freely available on the internet and be available for republication by others. The range of government and non-profit initiatives to make legal material on the internet available without charge is detailed elsewhere. Government initiatives to publish legal materials on the internet in both the UK and Ireland form part of a larger agenda to make available national and local government services online.[101] However, although digital technology offers the possibility of making legal texts available to the general public, legal materials remain complex to retrieve and even more complex to read and interpret, and demand for meaningful legal information is likely to grow.

PARLIAMENTARY LIBRARIES

The parliamentary libraries in Britain and Ireland, which are complex and sophisticated information services, hold good collections of domestic and European Union law to serve legislators, among much broader collections in other subjects. The law collections are not generally of national significance. The libraries do not have large collections of foreign law, unlike their counterparts in some other countries, notably in the United States.

The House of Commons Library and the House of Lords Library are both within the Palace of Westminster. Until 2009 the House of Lords Library had much more extensive holdings of law since one of its main roles had been to serve the Appellate Committee of the House which was the highest court of appeal in the United Kingdom until the establishment of the new Supreme Court. The core of the new library of the Supreme Court was created with legal materials transferred from the House of Lords Library (see above under 'Libraries serving the Courts and the Judiciary'). The House of Commons Library[102] contains legal materials, with some emphasis on statutory law, for Members of Parliament and the considerable body of research officers serving them. The public are not admitted to the libraries and, in general, enquiries should be directed to the House of Commons Information Office or the House of Lords Information Office, although the House of Lords Library responds to research enquiries regarding unique historical materials held there. The House of Commons Information Office produces useful factsheets, a

Weekly Information Bulletin of activities of the House together with a *Sessional Information Digest* and various other materials including research briefings, which are all available in full text on the Parliament website.[103] The website itself now has extensive information about the workings of Parliament including the full text of Hansard, the record of proceedings of Parliament, back to November 1988, historic Hansard since 1803 and live television coverage of the debates via the internet. The sophisticated database of parliamentary business maintained by the Library, formerly POLIS, 'is no longer a free service' and enquirers are referred to the commercial Justis service for parliamentary data.[104]

The Scottish Parliament, the National Assembly for Wales and the Northern Ireland Assembly, which form the devolved parliaments and assemblies in the UK, have information services, whose coverage naturally includes law, for their members. They also place considerable emphasis on information to the public. The Scottish Parliament Information Centre (SPICe), for example, provides non-partisan research and information services to Members of the Scottish Parliament (Seaton 2000, Mansfield 2009) but it does not seek to emulate the accumulated collections of resources in the House of Commons Library and takes full advantage of an internet and intranet platform for the delivery of electronic services. The Scottish Parliament website was an innovation in providing a comprehensive account of all aspects of parliamentary business, both in the Chamber and committees. It includes information on forthcoming meetings, current motions, proposed Members' bills, as well as the progress of legislation, has a searchable database of the full text of all proceedings since May 1999 and a complete archive of all other parliamentary publications. In addition all SPICe research briefings are published including those relating to bills currently progressing through the Parliament.[105] The Library and Research Services of the national parliament of Ireland, the Houses of the Oireachtas, are described by Dennison (2011); physical access is restricted to Members of the Oireachtas, Deputies and Senators, but a comprehensive website is maintained.[106]

GOVERNMENT LIBRARIES

The Ministry of Justice was formed in May 2007 and is one of the largest government departments and this, together with the creation of the United Kingdom Supreme Court, precipitated a major reorganization of law collections in government libraries. The Ministry of Justice Library and Information Services (jLIS) operate a Headquarters Library, set up in December 2008 combining parts of the Home Office Library with the Department for Constitutional Affairs Headquarters Library, previously the headquarters library of the Lord Chancellor's Department, in the new headquarters building at 102 Petty France. The Headquarters Library provides services to the Lord Chancellor and Secretary of State, and the ministers and staff based in the Ministry's Headquarters as well as to Her Majesty's Courts and Tribunals Service and some of the agencies and bodies sponsored by the Ministry.

Although there was a substantial library at the Lord Chancellor's Department, latterly the Department for Constitutional Affairs, and significant provision of law library services to the courts, neither the UK nor Ireland have had a major government law library of the type facilitating comparative legal research maintained by continental European ministries of justice.[107] This was probably because of the dispersal of responsibility for aspects of the legal system among several government departments and perhaps through a historical disinclination to engage in comparative legal research.

Most government libraries hold official publications and basic legal materials within the area of the department's competence, particularly to assist in the preparation of legislation and allow the department's legal advisers to perform research. Government libraries are generally not open to the public; enquiries are sometimes directed to dedicated information hotlines or special public information units, and increasingly to websites.

In recent years government libraries with large accumulated collections have disposed of considerable amounts of stock which did not serve the current working needs of the department; this process often accompanied relocation. The FCO Library maintains collections of international law including treaties and collections of the law of British Overseas Territories. Its magnificent collection of legislation from Commonwealth countries since the earliest colonial times is held in trust by the IALS Library and complements the strong Commonwealth law collections there. Large collections of non-legal material were transferred to a range of other university libraries during the early 1990s. More recently the Inland Revenue has disposed of many overseas tax materials to other institutional libraries, retaining working collections of recent materials.

The library of the Law Commission, which is an independent body keeping the law of England and Wales under review and recommending reform, collects Commonwealth law reform publications in particular and is serviced through the Courts and Tribunals Service.

In Scotland lawyers working for the Government Legal Service for Scotland are served by the Solicitor's Legal Information Centre, which is based within the Scottish Government Legal Directorate in Edinburgh (Waldhelm 2009). The library's collections specialize in legislation, administrative and public law, human rights, European Union and Scots law and contain a number of historically rare and important works. The Scottish Law Commission in Edinburgh has an extensive collection of legal materials relating to Scotland, the UK and Commonwealth jurisdictions.

Lorrimer (2011) and Sleator (2011) describe a range of government legal libraries and information services in Northern Ireland. From the same issue of *Legal Information Management* in 2011, primarily devoted to Ireland, several articles focus on libraries serving the Irish government: the Office of the Attorney General, the Chief State Solicitor's Office, the Office of the Director of Public Prosecutions, the Legal Aid Board and the Law Reform Commission (O'Flaherty, Cassidy, McCabe, Melling, Kennedy – all 2011).

LAW LIBRARIES IN OTHER COUNTRIES

The types of law libraries and their users in many common law countries are similar to those in Britain and Ireland. Important law libraries are maintained by universities and by the legal profession. Court libraries may have a wider remit and readership than in Britain and Ireland. Very few countries provide law library services for the public and even in the USA there is considerable discussion of the role and funding of the 'county law libraries' or 'public law libraries' many of which have a mission to provide legal information and therefore access to the justice system to members of the local community (Adams and Smith 2006, Meadows 2006). The scale and level of sophistication of library services in private law firms in Britain are matched in very few other countries. In some countries, notably those with a civil law system, there is a major government legal research library with considerable amounts of comparative as well as domestic material, for example the library of the Italian Ministry of Justice. In many countries the parliamentary library holds one of the most significant legal collections; the parliamentary library may be combined with the national library. The Law Library of Congress[108] in the United States has the largest and most comprehensive collection of legal materials in the world, with over 2.6 million items.

There is no current international directory of law libraries.[109] Descriptive material about law libraries around the world can be traced in the professional literature, particularly in the publications of organizations noted under 'Professional Associations' below. For example, articles about law libraries in 22 countries or regions are listed in the cumulative index to the *International Journal of Law Libraries*. The *IALL International Handbook of Legal Information Management* has a chapter on law librarianship around the world (Danner and Winterton 2011, 135–179) which contains an account of the profession of law librarianship, its practice and regulation, the major law libraries and research resources, in several countries.[110]

Resources for law libraries and the availability of published legal materials are limited in many countries. The proceedings of the 22nd Annual Course in International Law Librarianship of the International Association of Law Libraries[111] describe examples of the varying circumstances of law libraries in several African countries. In many such countries a law library in one sector may service the research needs of large parts of the legal system. The rapidly developing library of the Constitutional Court of South Africa, in the Court's wonderful building on Constitution Hill in Johannesburg, is of particular significance and has the aim of becoming the heart of a national and international research centre.

There are outstanding legal research libraries in many countries, including great comparative legal research libraries such as those maintained by the Max Planck Society in Germany[112] or by the Institut suisse de droit comparé.[113] However, law libraries in their various forms are most fully represented in the United States, which has outstanding examples in all sectors. In addition to the Law Library of Congress, there are great law libraries at law schools including those at the universities of Harvard, Yale, Columbia, New York, Michigan, Minnesota, Texas and California (Berkeley), and also great public law libraries such as the Los Angeles Law Library. The annual *AALL Directory and Handbook*, published by the American Association of Law Libraries, lists approximately 2,000 law libraries. As described below under 'Professional Associations', there are more law librarians in the United States than in any other country and the branch of the profession was first formally recognized there. The profession has issued professional handbooks (for example Mueller and Kehoe 1983, Kehoe, Lyman and McCann 1995) as part of a continuing series of professional literature, and two contrasting histories of law libraries and law librarians in the US give a broad survey of their development (Brock 1974, Gasaway and Chiorazzi 1996).

COLLABORATION

One of the watchwords of librarianship is collaboration because no one collection can serve every need of its users. Collaboration is necessary to make the most efficient use of available funds and ensure that no project or initiative unnecessarily duplicates the efforts of another. Librarians need to combine to agree standards of performance and professional behaviour. In technical terms librarians adopt standards by utilizing international formats for data, for electronic manipulation of metadata and for metadata content. Professional librarians have always been convinced of the benefits of collaboration and have often worked hard to convince their institutional management. Networking and the formation of professional associations (see below) are themselves expressions of collaboration and many initiatives and collaborative projects rely on contacts, sometimes on contact between relatively few people.

BIALL in its second year of existence formed a Committee on Co-operation and the Committee issued a report in 1971 which remains an impressive document and an agenda for action to improve provision of legal information (BIALL 1971).[114] One can see the origin of most collaborative strategy in the report since it dealt with a national policy for acquisitions based on centres of excellence, standards for law collections and principles of access, recommendations on exchange of duplicates (the origin of the successful scheme operated by BIALL), standards for classification and cataloguing of legal materials, an early recognition of the need for co-ordination in the work of libraries in the harnessing of automation and training of law librarians.

Collaboration and Collections

The range of printed union lists of legal materials issued by the Institute of Advanced Legal Studies (IALS) between the late 1940s and 1987 were staple reference materials of their time. They helped law librarians to identify materials and locate holdings for their users and also encouraged co-ordination in acquisitions. The contacts made in the compilation of these lists also played a part in the growing awareness of the profession.

Today many law libraries have catalogues available on the web and the largest academic libraries contribute records to the joint catalogue of the Consortium of University Research Libraries, COPAC. However, there is no one place to easily ascertain law holdings of libraries across the country. Smaller libraries and private libraries do not necessarily make their catalogues freely available. The value of union lists in facilitating the sharing of legal resources among a group has been recognized by the City Legal Information Group, the Scottish Law Librarians Group and the BIALL Irish Group.

Collaboration in collection building has been promoted for many years. BIALL advocated on a number of occasions that a national service for rarer materials should be based on established centres of excellence, in particular the IALS Library and the Bodleian Law Library, and even that the British Library should help to fund inter-library loans posts at the two libraries. The British Library funded the purchase of foreign law reports at IALS for some years in the 1970s and early 1980s in recognition of the existing collections and expertise there. The informal collaboration between the British Library and its near neighbour, IALS, over the years was developed into the current formal agreement to enhance collaborative collection building, services and training.

The Foreign Law Guide (FLAG) was a major project on collaborative collection management undertaken from 1999 to 2002 by the IALS Library, the Bodleian Law Library, the Squire Law Library, the British Library and the library of the School of Oriental and African Studies. The project produced a major report on academic needs for foreign, comparative and international law materials (Clinch 2001), created a publicly accessible database of holdings based on a painstaking audit of UK law libraries which continues to be updated[115] and issued a final report on co-ordinated collection management (Clinch 2002). The FLAG project had drawn together the lead institutions to such an extent that they formed the Foreign Law Research group (FLARE)[116] at the conclusion of the project to take forward collaboration, co-ordination and the sustainable coverage of foreign law in the UK.

Collaboration and Standards

BIALL was from the outset concerned that law libraries should collect at least the basic materials of English law and it supported applications for financial provision by colleges of education to meet that standard. BIALL set up a Sub-Committee on Standards in 1973 and published the BIALL *Standards for Law Libraries* in 1981 (BIALL 1981). At that time the emphasis placed on services and staffing levels was in contrast to the other main work on standards by the Society of Public Teachers of Law (SPTL), now the Society of Legal Scholars (SLS).

The SPTL had provided guidance to law schools and law librarians since 1958 through statements of 'minimum holdings' of specified legal publications, which had a significant effect on the expansion of academic law libraries. In 1995, a new Statement of Standards for University Law Library Provision was prepared on behalf of the SPTL by a consultative group comprising all major stakeholders. This Statement was first published in 1995 with a major research report on law libraries and legal education in the UK which was funded by the Lord Chancellor's Advisory Committee on Legal Education and Conduct (SPTL 1995).

The new Statement takes account of major changes in university legal education as law schools have became more diverse in their resources, missions and styles of teaching and more thoroughly monitored and assessed for quality, including the quality of library provision. The standards recognize that a law library is more than collections of information but is a complex operation whose level and quality of services depend on a range of factors. The statement provides a comprehensive set of standards covering all aspects of law library provision from organizational relationship with the law school and staffing to space, equipment and collections of both print and electronic resources, but specifies no single prescription for adequate provision. The standards are accompanied by a detailed commentary incorporating data from an annual survey of academic law libraries financed in alternate years by BIALL and the SLS (Clinch 2010) to indicate current practice. The Statement was most recently revised in 2009 (SLS 2010). The SLS, representative of independent academic opinion, is unique in making this continuing commitment to the investigation, analysis and expression of what is needed for effective library provision for its discipline. The Standards, as noted above in the section of professional legal education, have been adopted by the Bar Standards Board and have drawn the interest of law schools in other countries (Crawford 2009a, 2009b).

Professional Ethics and Professional Liability

There has been limited engagement by BIALL with the ethical issues relating to the practice of law librarianship (Gordon-Till 2003, 2006) but there is a Statement of Ethical Principles and a more extended Code of Professional Practice promulgated by the Chartered Institute of Library and Information Professionals (CILIP).[117] CILIP also maintains an Ethics Panel to keep the Statement and Code up to date and also to be a source of confidential advice for professionals. The American Association of Law Libraries (AALL) adopted a statement of ethical principles in 1999.[118]

The work of many librarians inevitably involves them in responsibilities and sensitivities and calls for careful exercise of judgment and sometimes more than an intuitive ethical awareness. The information world is permeated with conflicting rights, some legal and some moral, whether it is privacy and the right to information, divulging patron information sometimes required by governments, taking a view of fair use or knowing the line between legal information and legal advice. Information ethics is now an established subject of academic study with journals dedicated to it.[119] Some of these ethical issues may be exacerbated in the legal field particularly within an adversarial system and the question of legal information rather than legal advice may be less than clear-cut particularly when assisting litigants in person. Many of these issues, with which librarians have been familiar for many years, are also now matters of legal compliance and the Information Commissioner's Office offers extensive guidance in the area of data privacy and freedom of information.[120]

The related matter of professional liability might have a direct impact on individuals and their employers. However, the legal liability of librarians for offering incorrect or incomplete information has been little more than a matter of academic speculation. It is rare for a law librarian to take out professional indemnity insurance and insurance cover extended by many employers to their employees may well not foresee this risk.[121] Cannan (2007) discusses the liability of law librarians in the US and the issue has been discussed in the context of medical and health-care librarians in the UK (Muir and Oppenheim 1995). Neither could cite a case of an information professional sued for liability in the provision of information. Healey reviews the literature on professional liability of law librarians and the unauthorized practice of law by giving legal advice but notes that 'an astonishing number of articles are written by non-lawyers who, in the course of telling people not to give legal advice or practice law, end up giving legal advice …' (Healey 2002: 134).

One of the ways to reduce liability is the adherence to good professional practice and that would include any guidelines produced by professional associations. The American Association of Law Libraries (2001) has produced an extremely useful and detailed framework of competencies for law librarianship which are useful in a wide variety of situations from drawing up job descriptions to matters of professional conduct.

PROFESSIONAL ASSOCIATIONS

The British and Irish Association of Law Librarians (BIALL)

BIALL[122] is well established as the professional group for law librarians in Britain and Ireland and provides support for all those working with legal materials across the four jurisdictions. The history of the Association has been documented by Mary Blake, its Honorary Secretary from 1976 to 1987 and its Honorary Archivist from that time until 2010 (Blake 2000), and a chronology of important events is available on its website.[123] Membership of BIALL has risen from 47 personal and institutional members in the year of its formation in 1969, to over 300 in 1986 to over 750 at present.[124]

The Association's membership is as diverse as the sector and draws its strength from the diversity of experience which is brought to its activities. At its formation, members were drawn primarily from academic law libraries, libraries of the Inns of Court and the law societies and from government departments. One obvious trend in membership, apart from the steady rise in numbers, has been the increase in the proportion of law firm librarians, after an initial wave of new academic librarians. There was one law firm librarian on the original 1969 list of members, six in 1970, 25 in 1980, 108 in 1988 and now over 350, about half of the total membership. In a recent BIALL salary survey, only 56 (possibly as many as 59)[125] people (38 per cent) claimed to be members or fellows of CILIP, although some respondents from Ireland might belong to the Library Association of Ireland (McTavish 2012: 40, Table 7.13).

BIALL was formed to fill a vacuum in support for those working with legal information. There was no doubt an awareness of the work of the American Association of Law Libraries (AALL) and the International Association of Law Libraries (IALL), itself a result of an initiative from AALL. The famous workshop in Harrogate in February 1968 which led to the foundation of BIALL was organized by Don Daintree of Leeds Library School and arose from the perceived need for training in legal bibliography:

> Following the final talk of the Workshop by Willi Steiner and Betty Moys on the International Association of Law Libraries (IALL) it was resolved to set up a British section, and an ad hoc Committee was appointed to look into the possibility and invite people's views. The members of this committee were Wallace Breem (who volunteered to send a circular to all law libraries), Don

Daintree, Betty Moys, Willi Steiner and Derek Way. Replies to the circular were so encouraging that at the second Workshop in April 1969 the Association of Law Librarians was formally established. (Blake 2000: 4)

The Association's current constitution, including governance and membership, is available on its website.[126] The organization is managed by a council comprising an annually elected president, four other elected officers and five elected council members. There is no permanent secretariat. There are standing committees on Awards and Bursaries, Conferences, Legal Information (the Legal Information Group to liaise with publishers), Membership Services, Nominations and Volunteers, PR and Promotions, Professional Development, Publications, Strategy and Finance, the Web and the Editorial Board of *Legal Information Management*.[127] This demonstrates the breadth of its activities.

BIALL has no powers to regulate law librarianship but undertakes a wide range of activities to support law librarians, provide opportunities for the discussion of law library work, promote the better administration of law libraries, promote the improvement of the position and qualifications of law librarians, promote and encourage bibliographical study and research, to publish and to collaborate with other organizations.

BIALL has provided continuing professional development for its members since its inception. There is a major annual study conference held since 1970, currently in June each year, which is now attended by over 400 people, supplemented by a regular pre-conference seminar. There have also been study weekends on key management skills. There are short courses such as a regular one-day course in 'legal reference materials' and various specialist one-day or half-day courses and visits. A regular Legal Foundations Course by distance learning through online lectures over a period usually from October to April is offered by the BIALL Professional Development Committee in conjunction with the University of Westminster, Department of Professional Legal Studies. The course originally began in 1984, with traditional lectures, as the 'Law for Law Librarians' course. The Association administers several bursaries to provide financial assistance for members to attend its own conference and to attend conferences overseas.

BIALL has published a journal, *Legal Information Management*, formerly the *Law Librarian*, since 1970, now published by Cambridge University Press, and issues a newsletter for members six times per year; both publications are available in electronic and print form. The BIALL Blog was launched in 2007.[128] The Association has published the leading work on law librarianship in Britain and Ireland, the *Manual of Law Librarianship* in two editions (Moys 1976, 1987), succeeded by the *BIALL Handbook of Legal Information Management* (Worley 2006) of which this volume is the second edition. The *Directory of British and Irish Law Libraries* was published in seven editions between 1876 and 2006. The

Association does not publish a membership list, although one did appear among the AGM papers until 1979 and subsequently appeared in the Law Librarian during the first half of the 1980s. The annual *BIALL Salary Survey* (McTavish 2012) has developed into a sophisticated statement of the profession in terms of age, experience and geographical and sectoral spread, as well as a tool for ascertaining best practice in rewards.

The Association has issued a range of other publications over the years including a timely bibliography of *Community Law* (Lutyens 1973), an *Index to Legal Essays 1975–79* (Tearle 1983), *Standards for Law Libraries* (BIALL 1981), the *Bibliography of Commonwealth Law Reports* (Breem and Phillips 1991), *Sources of Biographical Information on Past Lawyers* (Holborn 1999), the *History of the British and Irish Association of Law Librarians 1969–1999* (Blake 2000) and a series of legal research training packs now in their fourth edition (BIALL 2011). The Association, in addition to its own publishing, has sponsored or funded research including a survey of academic law libraries and a survey of trends in legal information provision. The Association also operates a duplicates exchange scheme to allow unwanted stock to be transferred to more appropriate libraries.

BIALL administer a range of awards for outstanding achievement in the profession. The Wildy-BIALL Law Librarian of the Year is a prestigious annual award, established in 2005 and sponsored by Wild & Sons Ltd. The Wallace Breem Memorial Award, sponsored by the Inner Temple and BIALL, is designed to recognize excellence through published contributions to law librarianship, or provide financial assistance for special research or other projects at doctorate level or above. The Award was inaugurated in 1990 in memory of Wallace Breem, former librarian of the Inner Temple Library and a founder member of BIALL (Noel-Tod 1990). In 2005 BIALL introduced awards for excellence which became, in conjunction with LexisNexis, the Halsbury's Awards in 2007 and which recognize dedicated performance and outstanding service by law libraries. BIALL also make an annual Legal Journals Award and a BIALL Supplier of the Year Award. The Willi Steiner Memorial Lecture was set up in 2004 by the Association in memory of Willi Steiner, an outstanding member of the law library profession, librarian of two outstanding law libraries, the Squire Law Library in Cambridge and the IALS in London and a founder member of BIALL (Winterton 2003).

BIALL, among many other activities, has a strong interest in the public policy arena although it has never been able to emulate the participation in advocacy, lobbying and policy-making at regional and national level achieved by the much larger AALL. BIALL has in the past submitted responses to various official enquiries including submissions to the British Library, the University Grants Committee, the Royal Commission on Legal Services, the Law Society and the Lord Chancellor's

Advisory Committee on Legal Education and Conduct. It responds to proposals for changes to copyright legislation although these issues are now increasingly decided on a global stage.

Other Professional Associations of Law Librarians in Britain and Ireland

There is a range of other groups within Britain and Ireland providing support and networking for law librarians in geographical areas, regions and cities, or concerned with particular subjects, or in similar law libraries, for example the BIALL One Man Band/Small Teams Group, the Freelancers and Solos Group and the BIALL Academic Law Librarian Special Interest Group. These groups are not necessarily explicitly affiliated to BIALL and are financially independent and self-sustaining but all maintain co-operation with BIALL, with which they share many of their members. There is a list of groups on the BIALL website[129] with contact details and a few are noted under member libraries in the *Directory of British and Irish Law Libraries* and in *A History of the British and Irish Association of Law Librarians* (Blake 2000: 86–88).

The City Legal Information Group (CLIG),[130] formerly the City Law Librarians Group, was established in 1976 and has over 300 members. It is one of the earliest specialist groups and one of the most prominent, with a fine website and a tradition of collaboration despite the intense competition of members' employers. An early project was a union list of law reports and serials held by its members. It provides both educational and social events convenient for legal information professionals in and around the City of London.

Groups based on geographical area offer a range of events which supplement those arranged by BIALL and form a focus for local issues. The groups include the Scottish Law Librarians Group (SLLG)[131] established in 1988 which has issued a Directory (Wilcox 1995) and a union list of serials (Wilcox 1997) and over a hundred members (Black 2009); the BIALL Irish Group formed in the late 1980s which issues a union list (Clavin 2000); ALLICE (Association of Law Librarians in Central England), established as the Birmingham Association of Law Librarians in 1987; BLINE, the Business and Legal Information Network based in the north-east of England, originally established in 1990 as the Newcastle Law Librarians Group; BRILL (Bristol Law Librarians Group) established in 1989; the Commercial, Legal and Scientific Group of CILIP with whom BIALL runs a graduate open day; the East Midlands Legal Information Professionals; the Liverpool Legal Information Group; the Manchester Legal Information Group established in 1990 with over 50 members; and the US Law Firms Librarians Network.[132] Many members of such groups are law firm librarians and others from the Court Service, barristers' chambers, local law societies and other sectors also belong.

Groups based on subject areas include government, insurance, business information and specialized subjects such as property legal information. The European Information Association,[133] formerly the Association of European Documentation Centre Librarians, though accommodating interests much wider than law, has produced many useful publications and runs courses relevant for law librarians.

Overseas and International Associations of Law Librarians

There are national or regional associations of law librarians in many countries, from the Nordic Countries to South Africa and from the United States to Russia, including recently formed associations in Turkey in 2007 and in China (the Beijing Law Libraries and Legal Information Research Society) in 2010. Many of these associations are listed on the BIALL website[134] and more comprehensively on IALL site.[135]

The American Association of Law Libraries (AALL)[136] is by far the largest and oldest law library association, founded in 1906, with a membership of over 5,000 and an annual meeting that attracts over 2,000, including a small contingent from Britain and Ireland each year. It publishes the quarterly *Law Library Journal* and a monthly magazine *AALL Spectrum*. Membership of AALL and attendance at its conference no doubt inspired some of those who founded BIALL. It has an extraordinarily broad range of activities, maintains a permanent secretariat in Chicago and an office in Washington DC responsible for government relations.

The International Association of Law Libraries, founded in 1959, is a worldwide organization dedicated to bringing together and facilitating the work of law librarians who use foreign and international legal resources. A brief description of its activities together with detailed lists chronicling its history appears in the *IALL International Handbook of Legal Information Management* (Danner and Winterton 2011, 358–375). It publishes the *International Journal of Legal Information* and holds a conference and annual course in international legal information and law in a different city around the world each year in association with prestigious legal institutions. The courses do not address transferable skills and other areas generally covered at the conferences of national associations; they address aspects of foreign and international legal systems both in substance and in their expression in legal information, seeking to give an understanding of the legal environment and the law underlying the information.

PROFESSIONAL NETWORKING IN BRITAIN AND IRELAND

Professionals form communities of practice to share knowledge and skills, both through personal contacts and through the formation of professional bodies such as those described above. Networking is an enjoyable and important part of professional life.

Networking can start at home and can be virtual. Many people participate through electronic lists and discussion groups, joining associations and reading their publications, and building up contacts by e-mail. Discussion lists provide much-needed expertise, support and the mobilization of opinion. Lis-law is the most commonly used electronic discussion list for law librarians in Britain and Ireland; it is hosted by JISCmail, an agency of the joint funding councils of UK universities, which offers web-based list management and maintains archives of messages posted.[137] The list has over 800 members mainly based in Britain and Ireland. There are many specialized lists and in fact there are so many lists that there is a searchable list of lists at the JISCmail site in order to identify the relevant one for your purpose. INT-LAW is a list for the discussion and sharing of information concerning foreign, comparative and international legal resources.[138] BIALL, in common with many associations, has a list open to its members only. Delia Venables maintains a list of blogs, news feeds, podcasts, video blogs and wikis.[139]

There is no substitute for meeting people in person. Conferences, such as the annual study conference of BIALL, often give you an insight into other approaches to law librarianship, perhaps the philosophical underpinnings of our profession or perhaps a good solution to a particular problem, a new way of expressing one's aspirations or a simple new procedure. Conferences of other organizations such as the SLS or the Society of Computers and Law can be equally rewarding.

INTERNATIONAL NETWORKING

Law librarians increasingly need to be aware of foreign and international legal systems, understand the sources of law and have recourse to expertise beyond local resources. Today there is not only a growth of transborder economic activity, but every aspect of law is affected by the interconnected nature of our world. International contacts not only broaden our horizons and make us aware of other legal systems and responsive to enquiries about them; contacts also give us back-up for materials, language and expertise (Winterton 2004, 2011).

Conferences overseas are opportunities to build those contacts. There is an international calendar of events on the IALL website and it also appears in the *International Journal of Legal Information*. Most of the national and regional associations hold a regular conference. Since 1998 the American, British and Irish and Canadian associations, now joined by the Australian Law Librarians Group, have held a biennial Joint Study Institute to cultivate interchange and give an opportunity to learn about the legal system, heritage and traditions of the host countries. The IALL conference is in a different country each year and over the past few years has taken place in association with the High Court in Mumbai, in Association with the University of Puerto Rico in San Juan, at the Bilgi University in Istanbul and at the Peace Palace, home of the International Court of Justice in The Hague.

The conference of the International Federation of Library Associations is a massive meeting and not one which concentrates on law librarianship. There are a couple of sessions each year to bring law library matters to the attention of a wider audience of librarians in different sectors, traditionally arranged by the IALL but now by a Section of Law Libraries[140] set up in 2005 and sessions organized by parliamentary and government librarians of interest to law librarians. However, the importance of IFLA is its role in international policy issues, such as intellectual property and international trade, which now impinges on all libraries so strongly. These issues were addressed for AALL by the late Robert Oakley (Oakley 2003).

BIALL has, with the financial assistance of law publishers, sent an official representative to the conferences of overseas law library organizations and has also offered bursaries to its members to attend overseas conferences since the early 1990s. IALL maintains a scholarship programme not limited to association members to provide financial assistance for law librarians to attend its conferences.

An extended visit to a library in another country can provide a more immersive experience than a conference and is potentially a much more valuable experience. The IALS has a Visiting Fellowship in Law Librarianship which brings eminent overseas law librarians to London and such visitors have given seminars and spoken at the BIALL Conference. There is no formal programme for job exchanges with overseas law librarians although AALL maintains a clearinghouse of information on job exchanges[141] and IALL now offers a grant to support international placements and internships.[142]

LAW LIBRARIANSHIP

Law librarianship has been an increasingly attractive career with the expansion of law libraries since the mid-1970s, especially in law firms. Advertisements for law librarians generally figured prominently and in large numbers over the past 20 years in the major recruitment publication for the wider profession.[143] Numbers in the law library profession have risen over the period, as the membership of BIALL demonstrates. There have been redundancies and a curtailment of recruitment following economic downturns and this was repeated rather more trenchantly after the ongoing financial crisis of 2008. A survey in 2002 (Young) appeared to provide reassurance that employment in the academic law library sector is at least stable and this conclusion is generally supported by the findings of the SLS/

BIALL annual survey of academic law libraries although there is a continuing fear that the roles of specialist law librarians may be diluted.

The annual *BIALL Salary Survey* gives a detailed statistical account of the employment of law librarians in Britain and Ireland (McTavish 2012). The survey for 2011/12 received 147 usable responses,[144] of which over half were from law librarians employed in the London area. The *Survey* reports salaries for full-time librarians ranging from £18,500 to £150,000 with a median of £35,954 (£30,885 in central and local government, £36,483 in the academic sector, £36,250 in law firms, £35,000 in professional bodies and £40,880 in the in-house sector). Salaries are analysed by a large number of factors including location; the highest salaries are paid in the City of London (a median salary of £41,995) and South East England (a median salary of £43,000) if one excludes responses by less than five people. The lowest full-time salaries are in North England (a median salary of £26,390) with Scotland not far behind (a median salary of £25,400). Eighty per cent of full-time and 85 per cent of part-time respondents were female. Generally those employed in law libraries are graduates with library and/ or information qualifications, predominantly postgraduate LIS qualifications. Of the 147 respondents, 129 had a LIS qualification and only 18[145] had a law degree.[146]

There are no specialist qualifications in law librarianship although several library schools offer options in legal information as part of their programmes. At the University of Aberystwyth it is possible to combine information management with law as a joint honours degree. There has been, since the establishment of BIALL, continuing professional education available for law librarians, but no formal system of the type introduced by the legal profession and proposed by CILIP. The specialist programmes of law librarianship in the United States and the difficulties of combining a postgraduate library/information course and the postgraduate JD law degree are described by Hazelton (2011).

There has been scope for lateral movement and increase in salary for successful law librarians, particularly in the law firm sector. There has generally been rather less mobility between sectors. Perhaps not surprisingly the larger law libraries (which have a staff structure which allows for a career progression) also participate in training, both by taking graduate trainees before they attend library school and by providing approved training schemes for career entrants after library school. The IALS Library, the Law Society Library and the Inns of Court libraries have acted as feeder libraries for those entering all sectors of the profession.

There is a small number of senior and prestigious posts in law libraries but, as noted some time ago by Logan (1987: 32), they are so few in number that they can scarcely be said to represent realistic career goals. In such posts, management skills become as important as specialist knowledge of legal information. Subject librarians engaged in day-to-day reference work in law may find it difficult to gain sufficient experience of management to achieve the most senior posts. If achieved, a blend of management and subject work may provide great satisfaction but it is often difficult to tackle the one while maintaining the other. Those who gain sufficient management expertise may move out of law libraries because opportunities in Britain and Ireland for further advancement in law libraries are limited.

THE FUTURE ROLE OF LAW LIBRARIANS

The impact of digital technology is mutating traditional models of information management. This goes far beyond difficult questions of collection development regarding format of material to be acquired and what particular nature of hybrid library to adopt at a particular time. It involves a redefinition of the role of law librarian (Danner 1998, 2011, Susskind 1999, 2011).

There has been a dramatic vertical integration of the processes of communication. Digital technology has allowed publishers to perform some functions of traditional libraries in the storage and delivery of information since it allows the publication of far more material than a system based on the traditional printed medium and allows delivery direct to the researcher. Long-term preservation of information which was once one of the roles of libraries now needs to be addressed at the birth of digital material and cannot be separated from its production, throwing the responsibility onto the producer, whether commercial or institutional.

During these changes, which might threaten the existence of libraries in the traditional sense, new opportunities have arisen for law librarians. Aspects of the work of law librarians can be identified in the capture and description of content, more sophisticated management of resources, in aspects of the publishing of information, in retrieving and packaging information for research and in education and training.

The paradigm shift in the role of law librarians has been exemplified in law firm libraries which are dynamic environments for the management of information rather than repositories of material (see Mansfield 1999, McTavish, Duggan 1999). The opportunities of emerging roles in information and knowledge management are accompanied by needs for re-skilling and by potential threats as the boundaries between roles of law librarians and practitioners become less well defined. Some aspects of the role of the professional support lawyer may suggest the emergence of a true hybrid post combining legal and information skills but this remains unproven and most firms do not presently require an information management qualification for those posts.

Although issues of disintermediation will continue to concern libraries as services are delivered and marketed directly to end-users, law librarians are taking responsibility for the management of increasingly broad definitions of information and services in a trend likely to reinforce the intermediary function. This may be seen as an extension of the traditional role of selecting and organizing content. Librarians are involving themselves further up the communication chain in the creation of information products; they capture content, organize it and make it available internally or externally on the internet, taking over some roles of publishers. Librarians are also involving themselves further down the communication chain by processing information for particular uses and by assisting and training end-users in using information. These roles may be an extension of the traditional role of advising the reader and may take the form of training in research skills, creating virtual learning or research environments or undertaking the research and pre-processing of information which amounts to part of the end-user's work. Roles including legal information officer, knowledge manager, publisher and teacher will require increasing subject expertise, increasing collaboration with others, a blurring of the boundaries of their roles and the roles of users and an evolving range of skills and attitudes.

THE FUTURE OF LAW LIBRARIES

The Future of Law, Transforming the Law and *The End of Lawyers* (Susskind 1998, 2000, 2008) are among the best known writings in the United Kingdom about the future development of the law and the legal profession. There are major pieces of research by law library organizations about the future of their profession. *Law and Order: Trends in legal information provision* is a study for BIALL of the key issues in the management and provision of legal information within the United Kingdom and Ireland (McTavish and Ray 1999). A series of articles appeared in *Legal Information Management* considering the future of law libraries and law librarianship in several sectors including a paper on the findings of the Sweet & Maxwell survey 'Information Managers in the 21st Century' (Allbon and Wakefield 2008, Holborn 2008, Steer 2008, Tearle 2008, Winter 2008).

Beyond the Boundaries is a report by the AALL Special Committee on the Future of Law Libraries in the Digital Age which contains the most comprehensive analysis of issues surrounding the evolution of virtual and physical law libraries in all sectors in the US (AALL 2002).[147] The findings and conclusions are summarized below. In 2006 a series of short articles by distinguished members of the US law library profession appeared in *AALL Spectrum* considering the future for law firm libraries (Todd 2006), academic law libraries (Axtmann 2006) and public law libraries (Meadows 2006). In 2009 a conversation between the librarians of Duke, Harvard and Yale law schools on the twenty-first century law library appeared in the *Law Library Journal* (Danner, Kauffman and Palfrey 2009) with comments from a US law firm perspective following two issues later (Heller 2009). In November 2011 AALL hosted a Futures Summit which focussed on maintaining the relevance of AALL to its members.[148]

In a period of rapid change, law librarians will continue to be flexible in serving lawyers and their parent organizations and innovative in defining the direction and boundaries of their mission. Law librarians will continue to balance a strong commitment to the legal system and the legal profession with a professional allegiance to the wider librarianship community. It is likely that many law librarians will work more closely with other information workers and become part of larger structures. The roles of law librarians will become blurred with other actors in the information chain and law librarians may adopt their skills more easily than others acquire the skills of the librarian. Although libraries serving the different sectors of the legal system will continue to develop differently and offer different levels and styles of services, common development themes can be discerned.

The strategic drivers for change operating on law libraries can be grouped into those centred on: legal publishing, the nature of access to legal information, preservation, authentication, intellectual property law and licensing, user expectations, information and communications technology, with globalization playing a part in each (AALL 2002: 3).

In commercial publishing the transition from print to electronic and the consolidation of publishing companies will continue. There will be considerable emphasis on customization and personalization of information products, embedding them within the workflow, aiming at the level of integration and market saturation of the type achieved by Microsoft. There will be competition between commercial publishers and a growing number of non-commercial and free-to-internet sources of information and increasing pressure on commercial companies to demonstrate real added value. Government delivery of information and services by electronic means will extend greatly. However, in terms of access to legal information, the digital divide both within Britain and Ireland and internationally will be an increasing concern. Law librarians will play an important role in making law available in a convenient and meaningful way to the citizen for whom access to legal support may become more limited.

Information and communications technology continues to evolve at a very rapid pace. While developments in electronic legal publishing tend to reduce the amount of clerical work in maintaining an up-to-date collection, other demands are being made which require higher skills. Law libraries not only need to be provided with support and development potential by their parent organization but also need in-house expertise among their staff as they build their intranets, extranets and portals.

The concern over the preservation of the print record and the born-digital record of the law will continue after the present period of transition with its inadequate measures for electronic record management. The need for limited numbers of print repositories should be considered. The issue of permanent URLs will need to be addressed or much of the work of cataloguing and evaluating materials on the web will become unsupportable, however far the generation of metadata is automated. Born-digital materials will require more rigorous authentication which was unnecessary for print materials. New models of publishing will require content creators to assign citations at the point of creation rather than publication, as the English courts have now started to do.

As libraries license content for access rather than owning content, their control over access becomes more stringently limited by private agreement rather than public law. The plethora of licence agreements under different terms for different materials and different users may be managed by sophisticated technology based on user identity and status but requires expertise in negotiation and contract management. It also strikes against some of the values of libraries in creating a shared resource and against practices of scholarship in the discovery of new relationships between unsought materials. The expansion of copyright protection and reduction of fair dealing (the doctrine of limitations and exceptions to copyright), database protection and the general absorption of scholarly material under the same terms as publishing of entertainment media will impact on many libraries and their users adversely.

User expectations have always driven libraries and in future there will be an expectation that all information should be accessible at any time and in any place. Remote 24-hour access has or will become a legitimate expectation of many users and, depending on licence restrictions and therefore on budget, this will be possible. However, greatly increased guidance and training both in individual systems and general information management will be required in order for users to fulfil their expectations of the efficiency of modern searching and to enhance critical awareness of the relative value of information retrieved. The issue of information literacy and the librarian's role in education will grow in importance (Bird 2011).

Law libraries will operate increasingly in a virtual environment and the library as a physical space will change. However, librarians and their users still generally believe that the hybrid library environment of both electronic and print, to different degrees in different sectors, will remain the dominant model for many years. The library is likely to remain, certainly in collegiate environments, a physical focus of the institution, and the librarian, even as manager of a virtual law library, will need to provide the human interface:[149]

> ... *law librarians have for long recognised that lawyering is a type of information processing and indeed much of their work has been built on this premise. Law librarians have also been some way ahead of most lawyers in*

> *embracing the power of IT and recognising the significance of the internet for legal practice ... With the explosive growth in various information technologies will come great vindication of the past claims and work of law librarians. Calls for better analysis of information needs, more rigorous management of content, greater vigilance in relation to security and privacy, deeper consideration of whether superior information control can offer competitive advantage – all of these and more will need to be answered by top managers in law firms, legal departments, and law faculties. (Susskind 2011)*

Law librarians will play an important role in strategic management within their institutions and in determining the information environment in which those institutions operate.

NOTES

1   This chapter was completed in November 2011 with minor corrections in November 2012 and May 2014. I am very grateful to Susan Mansfield, Jennefer Aston, George Woodman and other friends and colleagues who provided information to assist me.

2   The International Association of Law Libraries has recently produced a 'Research Agenda for International Law Librarianship' (Garavaglia 2011).

3   The chapters, then as now, were intended to include the historical background to the development of law libraries. There are other overviews of the contemporary state of law libraries by Daintree (1983) and also by Miskin (1981), the latter with more emphasis on electronic databases and the future of law libraries.

4   See below under 'Libraries Serving the Courts and the Judiciary'.

5   'Lawyers and their libraries' by Guy Holborn (2006), a chapter in the *Cambridge History of Libraries in Britain and Ireland*, provides a scholarly account, with detailed bibliography, of the practising legal profession and its libraries between 1850 and 2000 and is an invaluable source.

6   This chapter does not cover personal law libraries.

7   Abel (1988, 2003): both have very extensive bibliographies. See also Hogan (1986) for an earlier history in Ireland. Histories of particular institutions in the various jurisdictions such as the Faculty of Advocates or the Law Society of Ireland are cited below at the appropriate points.

8   The Courts and Legal Services Act 1990 and section 24 of the Law Reform (Miscellaneous Provisions) Scotland Act 1990 began the process throughout the 1990s of removing the exclusive rights of audience. The separate classification of libraries serving the Bar and those serving solicitors is a convenience here but is rooted in the history and the current provision of library facilities for the profession.

9   http://www.graysinn.org.uk/; http://www.innertemple.org.uk/; http://www. middletemple.org.uk/; http://www.lincolnsinn.org.uk/

10 There is a very considerable body of writing about the Inns. Inner Temple and Lincoln's Inn have recently published lavishly illustrated volumes (Rider and Horsler 2007;

Holdsworth 2007) and a history of Middle Temple appeared in 2011 (Havery 2011). Each has a useful section on the Inn's library.

11 The Bar Council provides extensive statistics about the composition of the Bar and entry to the Bar including analysis by gender and ethnicity at http://www.barcouncil. org.uk/about-the-bar/facts-and-figures/statistics/

12 http://www.innertemplelibrary.org/external.html. The catalogues are available independently. However, Inner Temple regularly uploads the records of the other three Inns into its system, providing a combined search facility. Lincoln's Inn and Gray's Inn produce their catalogue as a joint venture and their combined holdings can be searched.

13 http://www.innertemplelibrary.org.uk/collections/legal-collections/inns-of-court-libraries.htm

14 Commonwealth law and the law of Scotland in Inner Temple; Commonwealth law and the law of the Isle of Man and the Channel Islands at Lincoln's Inn; US law, European Union law and the law of Ireland in Middle Temple; and international law and the law of Northern Ireland in Gray's Inn, http://www.innertemplelibrary.org.uk/collections/legal-collections/special-collections.htm

15 There were discussions in 2009 between Inner Temple and Middle Temple about the possibility of joint library provision, beyond the current co-operative agreements, but no suitable arrangement was identified.

16 http://www.advocates.org.uk/library

17 Non-members of the Faculty can access the majority of the holdings of the Advocates Library via the National Library of Scotland.

18 From the 'Welcome to the Advocates Library' at http://www.advocates.org.uk/library/index.html

19 http://www.barlibrary.com/

20 http://www.kingsinns.ie/

21 http://www.lawlibrary.ie/

22 http://www.dublinarbitration.ie/

23 The Court was established by the relevant sections of the Constitutional Reform Act 2005.

24 http://www.supremecourt.gov.uk/about/middlesex-guildhall.html

25 http://news.sky.com/home/supreme-court. The ban on television broadcasting of other courts in England and Wales may be partially lifted following proposals in May 2012 http://www.justice.gov.uk/downloads/publications/policy/moj/broadcasting-filming-recording-courts.pdf. Powers to implement the proposals are in the Crime and Courts Bill, http://services.parliament.uk/bills/2012-13/crimeandcourts.html

26 http://www.jcpc.gov.uk/

27 http://www.jcpc.gov.uk/about/role-of-the-jcpc.html#UK gives details of the jurisdictions.

28 http://www.bailii.org/uk/cases/UKPC/

29 See also the section on Government Libraries below.

30 http://www.justice.gov.uk/about/hmcts/index.htm. Previously the Court Service was an executive agency of the Department for Constitutional Affairs.

31 The original law library rooms at Cardiff Crown Court and at Birmingham Magistrates'

Court are described on the HMCTS website as ideal spaces for drinks receptions or an intimate dinner party.

32   The Supreme Court Library at the time incorporated the Chancery Library, later the Probate Library, and the Bar Library.

33   It is to be hoped that they will be made freely available through a service such as the British and Irish Legal Information Institute rather than solely through an arrangement with a commercial supplier.

34   http://www.courtsni.gov.uk/

35   http://www.bristollawsociety.com/

36   The Manchester Incorporated Law Library serves and lends to both solicitors and barristers and is one of the oldest purpose-built law libraries in the UK. See http://www.manchester-law-library.co.uk/

37   http://www.birminghamlawsociety.co.uk/. Birmingham Law Society has come to a merger agreement with Aston University Library and Information Services and its collections are now housed at the University.

38   Links to the websites of 51 such local law societies can be found on the various regional pages of the Law Society of England and Wales website.

39   In the same way as 'law library associations' sprang up in the US during the same period; see Pound (1953: 215–219).

40   http://www.lawsociety.org.uk/

41   Legal Services Act 2007, Part 5.

42   http://www.lawscot.org.uk/. The Law Society of Scotland does not maintain a library for members, unsurprisingly given the alternatives available.

43   http://www.thewssociety.co.uk/

44   Special collections include the Scottish collection, comprising works published in or about Scotland and Scottish life, to which books are still added, and the Roughhead Collection on murders in Britain, donated by the late William Roughhead, editor of the Notable British Trials series, see http://www.thewssociety.co.uk/index.asp?lm=4

45   http://www.ssclibrary.co.uk/

46   http://www.rfpg.org/

47   http://www.socofadvocates.com/

48   http://www.rfpg.org/library.html. The library has been maintained since 1817 and is described with photographs by the Faculty Librarian, John McKenzie (2009).

49   http://www.lawsociety.ie/

50   http://www.lawsoc-ni.org/

51   See 'Official Opening of Law Society House', Writ: Journal of the LSNI, 200, Oct–Dec 2009, 4–10 available at http://www.lawsoc-ni.org/publications/

52   See the sections on university law schools and on professional legal education below for further description of the role of the Inns of Court and the establishment of law courses and law schools.

53   http://www.sra.org.uk/sra/news/letr-report-published.page and the Review's own website at http://letr.org.uk/

54   http://www.lawscot.org.uk/becomingasolicitor/

55   http://www.lawsoc-ni.org/joining-the-legal-profession/education-review/

56   Then London University 'but in 1836 the University was reconstituted as a federal body comprising the 1826 foundation (now given a new charter as University College) together with King's College (incorporated by charter in 1829, built on a site in the Strand, and opened in 1831). The new University of London was given the power to award degrees, and its Bachelor of Law degrees – the first university degrees in English law – were awarded three years later in 1839' (Baker 2007: 26–27).

57   The situation can be compared with legal education in the US of the period; see Stevens (1983).

58   The 'Boards of Legal Studies' were variously constituted but generally comprised representatives of the local university, the local law societies and individual solicitors and barristers practising in the district.

59   http://www.ukcle.ac.uk/students/directory/ but, as noted above, the website will not be updated from July 2011 onwards. Reference can be made to the regulatory bodies in each jurisdiction, for example the Bar Standards Board and the Solicitors Regulatory Authority in England and Wales which maintain lists of the qualifying law degrees and the institutions which offer them, https://www.barstandardsboard.org.uk/qualifying-as-a-barrister/academic-stage/

60   From the Higher Education Statistics Agency at http://www.hesa.ac.uk

61   Currently just over 23 per cent of university law students in the UK study part time.

62   In 2002/03 there were nearly 24,000 postgraduate law students and 255 doctorates were awarded.

63   Although 'We have not quite reached the point where the law is once again seen as one of the great humane subjects, along with history and literature, as it was in classical and medieval times …' (Twining 1994: 13).

64   The Socio-Legal Studies Association (SLSA) provides information about socio-legal studies on its website at http://www.slsa.ac.uk/

65   http://www.ucl.ac.uk/laws/socio-legal/index.shtml

66   The Survey contributes to the maintenance of the Standards for University Law Libraries maintained by the Society of Legal Scholars (SLS 2010); see the section on Standards below.

67   Clinch (2010) gives the references for previous survey reports which form a considerable body of data.

68   The responses citing 'several law libraries' may derive from the need to maintain a separate specialist library to serve the requirements of students on professional legal courses.

69   http://www.bodleian.ox.ac.uk/law

70   http://www.squire.law.cam.ac.uk/

71   http://ials.sas.ac.uk/library/library.asp

72   See below in the 'Collaboration' section

73   http://www.crim.cam.ac.uk/library/

74   http://ials.sas.ac.uk/flare/flare_origins.htm

75   Birkbeck College School of Law teaches law and carries out legal research but does not have extensive legal research collections in its college library.

76   http://ials.sas.ac.uk/eaglei/project/eiproject.htm. IALS contributed the law content to the national internet gateway, Intute. When Intute was discontinued by JISC, IALS added the data to its portal, Eagle-I, to maintain the national service.

77   http://ials.sas.ac.uk/library/clrt/clrt.htm

78   http://www.ials.sas.ac.uk/library/caware/caware.htm

79   http://www.bailii.org/

80   There are two-year accelerated programmes for graduates in another subject.

81   http://www.sls.qub.ac.uk/

82   http://www.ucc.ie/law/irlii/

83   Records of the Council of Legal Education were deposited at the Institute of Advanced Legal Studies Library, http://www.ials.sas.ac.uk/library/archives/cle.htm

84   http://www.college-of-law.co.uk/About-the-College/College-of-Law-change-of-ownership---FAQs/

85   For example, 'The Master of Laws degree (LLM) gives you the chance to build on your LPC or BVC qualification by topping this up to an LLM. This can be done by research into law in practice or a period of reflective legal practice', http://www.plymouth.ac.uk/courses/postgraduate/taught/3235/LLM+Legal+Practice although this programme is currently postponed.

86   'Conversion' courses which enable graduates in other subjects to obtain the same exemptions from the professional examinations as graduates with qualifying law degrees.

87   http://www.sra.org.uk/, http://www.barstandardsboard.org.uk/

88   See the section on Standards below.

89   The Bar Standards Board issues the *Bar Professional Training Course: Course Specification Requirements and Guidance.* London: BSB. 2011, available at https://www.barstandardsboard.org.uk/media/28049/bptc_final_pdf.pdf, see Part A 5.3, and the Solicitors Regulation Authority *Information for providers of Legal Practice Courses* 2012 London: SRA, available from http://www.sra.org.uk/lpc/

90   http://www.lawscot.org.uk/, http://www.advocates.org.uk/

91   http://www.lawsoc-ni.org/, http://www.barlibrary.com/about-us/the-general-council-of-the-bar-of-northern-ireland/

92   http://www.kingsinns.ie/

93   http://www.lawsociety.ie/

94   http://www.bl.uk/aboutus/stratpolprog/contstrat/contentstrategyappendices.pdf

95   http://www.bl.uk/reshelp/findhelpsubject/busmanlaw/legalstudies/intro/lawpage.html

96   http://www.westminster.gov.uk/libraries/special/law.cfm

97   http://www.cityoflondon.gov.uk/things-to-do/visiting-the-city/archives-and-city-history/guildhall-library/collections/Pages/English-law.aspx has guides to the law collections.

98   http://www.bailii.org/

99   http://www.citizensadvice.co.uk/en/about-us/CAS/Advicefinder/

100   http://www.cans.org.uk/

101   The UK programme is exemplified by http://www.gov.uk (although the website of the E-government Unit of the Cabinet Office has now been overtaken by

political developments and is archived, see http://webarchive.nationalarchives.gov.uk/20100807034701/http://archive.cabinetoffice.gov.uk/) or in Ireland by Citizens Information at http://www.citizensinformation.ie/en/

102 See the detailed factsheet dated September 2010 at http://www.parliament.uk/about/how/guides/factsheets/general/g18/

103 http://www.parliament.uk particularly the page offering the House of Commons Information Office publications at http://www.parliament.uk/mps-lords-and-offices/offices/commons/hcio/

104 http://www.polis.parliament.uk/. The factsheet dated 2010 noted that 'Members have access to the Parliamentary Information Management System (PIMS), a central database that provides access to the majority of information produced by parliament. A limited subscription based version of PIMS data is available to the public at www.polis.parliament.uk'.

105 http://www.scottish.parliament.uk/, http://www.wales.gov.uk/, http://www.niassembly.gov.uk/

106 http://www.oireachtas.ie/

107 Although in the scale of provision, the services to the courts, as opposed to government, were major law library services.

108 http://www.loc.gov/law/

109 The most recent such directory was published by the International Association of Law Libraries in 1988. Some law libraries are listed in more general directories and research guides and many have a presence on the Internet.

110 The countries are India, Moldova, Nigeria, the Philippines, Turkey and Vietnam. The International Association of Law Libraries intends to extend the coverage of these profiles to other countries and make them available on its website.

111 *International Journal of Legal Information*, 32: 2, Summer 2004.

112 There are libraries at eight legal research institutes of the Max Planck Society listed on its main website, http://www.mpg.de/english/portal/index.html, including the Institute for Comparative and International Private Law, http://www.mpipriv.de/ww/en/pub/news.cfm, and the Institute for Comparative Public Law and International Law, http://www.mpil.de/ww/en/pub/news.cfm

113 http://isdc.ch/

114 The Report is described in some detail by Blake (2000: 25–28).

115 The searchable database, final report and documentation are available at http://ials.sas.ac.uk/library/flag/flag.htm

116 http://ials.sas.ac.uk/flare/flare.htm

117 http://www.cilip.org.uk/professionalguidance/ethics/

118 http://www.aallnet.org/main-menu/Leadership-Governance/policies/PublicPolicies/policy-ethics.html

119 The International Centre for Information Ethics has useful pages at http://icie.zkm.de/

120 http://www.ico.gov.uk/

121 'When there is professional liability insurance for librarians we shall have really arrived' (Jeffries 1992: 92).

122 www.biall.org.uk

123   http://www.biall.org.uk/pages/history.html

124   'The Association has continued to increase its membership since its formation without recourse to any intensive recruitment drive' (Blake 2000: 69).

125   The *Survey* shows <5 where the number of respondents is less than five to preserve confidentiality.

126   Available from http://www.biall.org.uk/pages/about-biall.html

127   See http://www.biall.org.uk/pages/biall-committees.html for the remit and membership of the committees.

128   http://biall.blogspot.com/

129   http://www.biall.org.uk/pages/affiliate-groups-.html

130   http://www.clig.org/

131   http://www.sllg.org.uk/

132   The Cardiff Law Librarians Group was established in 1989 and the Leeds Law Librarians Group in 1990 but neither are currently listed on the BIALL website.

133   http://www.eia.org.uk/

134   List of national and international law library associations compiled by the British and Irish Association of Law Librarians, http://www.biall.org.uk/pages/useful-links.html

135   http://iall.org/linksOtherAssns.html

136   http://www.aallnet.org/

137   https://www.jiscmail.ac.uk/cgi-bin/webadmin?A0=lis-law, http://www.jiscmail.ac.uk

138   http://listserver.ciesin.columbia.edu/cgi-bin/wa?A0=Int-Law

139   http://www.venables.co.uk/blogs.htm

140   http://www.ifla.org/law-libraries

141   http://www.aallnet.org/sis/fcilsis/internships.html

142   http://iall.org/internships.html

143   Now named *CILIP Update*, available online as Lisjobnet at http://www.lisjobnet.com/

144   Compare this with 343 responses for the 2002/03 *Survey*; this introduces the risk that some results may be distorted by a small number of atypical responses.

145   Possibly as many as 24. Fewer than 5 responses, whether 1 or 4, are recorded as <5.

146   Fewer than 30 per cent of members of AALL hold a JD degree (Whisner 2008).

147   http://www.aallnet.org/Archived/Leadership-Governance/committees/final-report-including-appendices.pdf

148   http://www.aallnet.org/main-menu/Leadership-Governance/committee/cmte-final-reports/2011-2012/board-futuressummit.pdf

149   'The virtual law library offers many opportunities and challenges and we will each see our world changing to take advantage of these. Librarians can cement their roles in the virtual library by ensuring that the clients never forget that the human component is integral to any library, virtual or physical' (Whelan 2001: 16).

CHAPTER 2

SOURCES OF LEGAL INFORMATION AND THEIR ORGANIZATION

GUY HOLBORN

INTRODUCTION

Managing legal information requires a basic understanding of the different types of legal information that there are. This chapter aims to explain the sources of the law and the various legal materials. Although many law libraries hold foreign legal materials, this chapter is confined to materials typically used by UK lawyers or those studying UK law. As European law in its various guises is now integral to UK law that is also treated, and there is some discussion of international legal materials in so far as they impinge on UK law.

In using the expression 'UK law' it is important to appreciate that only in limited contexts is the law indeed the same throughout the UK. For most purposes it is necessary to distinguish the three separate jurisdictions that make up the 'United Kingdom of Great Britain and Northern Ireland' – England and Wales, Scotland and Northern Ireland. Each has a separate legal system, court structure and legal profession. And there is now also the further complication that though England and Wales share a legal system and 'English law' is the usual shorthand for the law applying in both England and Wales, Wales as explained below can now make its own legislation. It should be added that the Channel Islands and the Isle of Man while being dependencies of the UK are not part of it and are not dealt with here. Having, however, noted the distinct jurisdictions, the emphasis in this chapter is mostly on either UK-wide sources or English sources.

SOURCES OF UK LEGAL INFORMATION

There is a fundamental distinction between primary sources – what constitutes the law itself – and secondary sources, which describe, explain and comment on the law. For many practical purposes secondary sources are in fact more important than primary sources and will account for much of the content of the average law library. They are where the law student has to start, but they are also usually the starting point even for the experienced lawyer – someone else has already done the legal research and it is seldom that the raw data of the law has to be tackled from a completely cold start. Nevertheless, we need to start with primary sources, which comprise legislation on the one hand and the binding decisions of the courts on the other.

PRIMARY SOURCES

Legislation

Legislation is itself conventionally divided into 'primary' and 'secondary'. Primary legislation consists of statutes or – the terms are interchangeable – Acts of Parliament. The need for secondary legislation as well arises simply because it has long been accepted that it is not feasible for Parliament itself to provide in Acts all the detailed and frequently changing regulation needed in the governance of the modern state. Secondary legislation, which usually takes the form of Statutory Instruments (SIs), is more fully explained below.

Acts
The Parliament that passes Acts historically was that at Westminster. However, following the Scotland Act 1998 (substantially amended by the Scotland Act 2012) we also now have the Scottish Parliament, which passes Acts, abbreviated as 'asps', and following the Good Friday Agreement in 1998 the Northern Ireland Assembly, which (albeit after some vicissitudes) also passes its own Acts, as did the Northern Ireland Parliament from 1921 to 1972. On the other hand, the powers of the National Assembly for Wales to legislate and the terminology of the resulting forms of legislation have undergone some changes since devolution was first introduced. Originally under the Government of Wales Act 1998 the Assembly did not make its own primary legislation, only secondary legislation, which took the form of ordinary UK SIs. The Government of Wales Act 2006 introduced the power also to make 'Measures' which were a species of primary legislation, but the exercise of this power in specific areas had first to be sanctioned by Westminster. The 2006 Act also provided for the possibility in the future of full-blown 'Acts', still within devolved areas but without Westminster's say-so, subject to this extension of law-making powers being agreed by the citizens of Wales through a referendum. A referendum was duly held in 2011 resulting in a 'yes' vote, so thereafter 'Acts' replace 'Measures'.

Turning to describing Westminster Acts in more detail, there are two classes of Acts. First are Public General Acts which, as their name implies, apply generally to all places and persons. The second class, Local and Personal Acts, are encountered much less frequently. They apply only to a particular locality or to a particular person or body. Local Acts were very numerous in the nineteenth century when they were used in connection with, for example, local government, railways, canals and enclosure of common land. They continued to be used during the twentieth century, but on a much reduced scale, for other infrastructure projects, such as harbours and light transport systems, and also occasionally in connection with the constitutions of universities or other bodies (Lloyd's for instance). Since the Transport and Works Act 1992, they have become rarer still – only about half a dozen at most each year. In modern times there has been a sprinkling of Personal Acts (which are numbered as a separate series from the Local Acts), but none since 1987.

Before moving on to the more important Public General Acts it is worth explaining a small terminological point that can cause difficulty. You may hear Local and Personal Acts described as 'Private Acts' – and indeed *Current Law Statutes*, which has included them since 1991, so describes them. This is not wholly inaccurate since a fundamental distinction between Local and Personal Acts on the one hand and Public General Acts on the other is not so much their scope, but the Parliamentary procedure by which they are passed. Both Local and Personal Acts start as Private Bills, which go through an entirely different procedure from Public Bills. Until 1797 there were just two series of Acts, called Public and Private. In 1797 a separate series of Local Acts was started, but with the series of Private Acts also continuing. Gradually Private Acts were superseded for most purposes by Local Acts, and in 1948 Private Acts were renamed 'Personal Acts'. Thus 'Private Acts' may refer either loosely to all Acts other than Public General Acts, or more precisely to those Acts passed before 1948 under the Private Bill procedure that were not classified as Local.

Parliament in recent years has been legislating at the rate of anywhere between about 45 and 70 Acts each year. They may each amount to only a couple of pages, but can often run into hundreds of pages. There is considerable choice as to where best to lay your hands on the text of an Act, either in hard copy or online. The main permutations are text as originally enacted versus text as amended, and official text versus commercially published text, the latter generally carrying annotations or commentary.

To begin with official text: here in hard copy there is no choice as the only form in which it is published is as bare text as originally passed. These are the so-called 'Queen's Printer' copies of Acts published by The Stationery Office (TSO) as individual Acts as soon as each is passed, and then as bound (red) annual volumes with accompanying tables and indexes. New Acts are published simultaneously on the official and free government website www.legislation. gov.uk both as PDFs of the Queen's Printer copy and as web pages. All Acts from 1988 to date are available in those forms; many earlier ones are in the course of being added.

An alternative to the hard copy annual volumes of Queen's Printer copies is the statutes database on Justis. This service has the full text of all Public General Acts as passed from the earliest times, viz. 1235, to date. From 1870 the data is indeed taken from Queen's Printer bound volumes; before that date the data is taken from *Statutes at Large*, which is unofficial though widely relied upon. (Although Local Acts are beyond the scope of this chapter, it should also be mentioned that a very significant recent enhancement has been the addition of these to the Justis service, back to 1797.)

The main circumstance when the Queen's Printer copy is needed is for a very recent Act, simply because this is the first form in which it will be published. Otherwise their main use is for the text of repealed Acts, which are sometimes needed, and which may disappear from sources that only provide statutes in force. They also tend to be preferred for bundles of authorities for use in court on account of their official status though where the text has been heavily amended courts nowadays will readily see the convenience of using an unofficial version in amended form instead.

Much more usually it is the text of an Act, not as it was originally passed, but as it is now, in its amended form, that is wanted. There used also to be official texts of statutes in their amended state, the last edition of which was the looseleaf *Statutes in Force* which ceased in 1991. After a very long period of development it was replaced with the Statute Law Database. The latter is no longer a separate database and the data instead appears on www.legislation. gov.uk alongside Acts as originally enacted and other legislation. The data in question has a base date of 1991, so includes any Act wholly or partly in force at that time, and all since. A 'point in time' facility provides historic versions of the text back to 1991. There are ample warnings on the website, but note that the currency of the data leaves much to be desired – many Acts have numerous amendments awaiting incorporation into the text, though the amendments can be retrieved by laborious means. This limitation renders it next to useless for everyday purposes, though being free of charge it is useful in the limited circumstances where the end-user cannot get to the library and does not have access to the subscription databases.

Almost always it will be necessary to check the legislation part of either the Lexis or Westlaw databases. However, many lawyers prefer to start with hard copy (or having established the up-to-date position online, prefer to read from hard copy). In that case *Halsbury's Statutes* (published by LexisNexis) is generally the best place to go. *Halsbury's Statutes* provides in fifty-odd volumes, arranged by subject, the text of all Public General Acts relating to England and Wales in force as amended, with annotations. It also includes Local Acts relating to London, but does not include Acts applying only to Scotland. It is updated by the periodic reissue of particular volumes, an annual cumulative supplement and a looseleaf noter-up. There is also a 'pending tray' of looseleaf service volumes containing recent Acts awaiting incorporation in the appropriate bound volume at its next reissue. Although they are not distinguished typographically, the annotations are of two kinds. First are bare-bones 'textual' annotations, giving the source for amended or inserted text, commencements and so on. The second are 'value-added' annotations, for example referring to case law in which a provision has been judicially considered, or providing other explanatory matter. But it should be appreciated that even these annotations are not especially discursive, and do not offer much by way of detailed commentary, in contrast to those that appear in *Current Law Statutes*, discussed below.

When it comes to the main electronic rivals, Lexis and Westlaw, then if you subscribe to both it may boil down to personal preference as to which to use. But there are differences in the content. For Public General Acts Westlaw has as its base date 1991 (the same date as the Statute Law Database from which the data originally derived) – it includes all statutes at least partly in force at that date and all subsequent statutes. Where a statute is subsequently wholly repealed, the text remains. Lexis on the other hand includes all statutes that have featured in *Halsbury's Statutes* since it was first published in 1929 so may have more retrospective coverage. But once repealed the text goes, the title only remaining with a note of the repealing provision. Westlaw also has an excellent historic version facility (back to 1991); hence the presence of wholly repealed texts. Lexis, on the other hand, only currently provides historic versions as an e-mail request service and only back to 1998.

The other significant distinction between the two services is how annotations are provided. Lexis is able to provide the annotations as they appear in *Halsbury's Statutes*, though this is done in a slightly counter-intuitive way, as a result of how the database was originally compiled. The main database was originally compiled independently of the production of *Halsbury's Statutes* and carries only 'textual annotations'. The annotations as they appear in *Halsbury's Statutes* can indeed be accessed from a link on the results screen but the consequence is that the information in the 'textual annotations' is duplicated, though in a slightly different style, alongside the 'value-added annotations'. Furthermore, the annotations derived from *Halsbury's Statutes* are not necessarily provided at any greater currency than the hard copy version of *Halsbury's Statutes*, whereas the textual database is updated daily. Mindful that the annotations provided in *Halsbury's Statutes* are one of its selling points, Westlaw has now introduced an annotations service. It applies to all Acts from 2007, with annotations to earlier Acts gradually being added, such Acts generally being selected on their importance. These annotations are much more discursive than those that appear in *Halsbury's Statutes*, and include for example reference to significant Parliamentary debates on a particular section during its passage as a Bill. The service is currently, however, an add-on and is not part of the main subscription.

A further online source is Lawtel. The main selling point of this service is its case law coverage, but it also has a statutes section. It does now provide consolidated versions of selected statutes, but principally it provides the text as enacted (for Acts from 1987). There is a 'Statutory Status' table noting amendments and repeals (and commencement dates) with hypertext links to amending legislation, but in effect you are left to do the work of applying the amendments for yourself, so it is not a direct competitor to Lexis or Westlaw for legislation.

The core print product for legislation from Sweet & Maxwell has historically been *Current Law Statutes*, which performs a different function and fills a different niche in the market than *Halsbury's Statutes*. This provides the text of Public General Acts (and, as noted above, Local Acts from 1991) simply as passed – so are a commercially published equivalent of the TSO annual volumes – but with the addition of annotations and commentary. Since the first annotated volume was published in 1949 the annotations have steadily become fuller and the commentary more discursive, and are thus different in style and purpose from the annotations in *Halsbury's Statutes*. An expert in the field, who is identified as the author, provides the annotations. It is issued in loose booklets, which are replaced by bound volumes. For each Act, there is a general note at the start, which includes useful information on the legislative background, such as White Papers, Green Papers, Law Commission reports and so on. There may be further general notes relating to each part of an Act, and then specific annotations for each or most sections, including nowadays reference to significant mentions in Hansard during its passage as a Bill. Because the information is static – there is no updating mechanism as such – it is naturally of most use for recent Acts, particularly where standard textbooks on the topic have yet to take a new Act into account, but the information on the original legislative background remains useful whatever the date of the Act in question.

Looseleaf subject encyclopaedias generally are further sources of the text of an Act as amended. They are specifically designed to bring together all the legislation and related materials, such as government circulars, on a particular topic, with annotations and a greater or lesser amount of text by way of commentary. The extent to which such looseleaf works are simply collections of statutes and materials, as opposed to standing in lieu of an ordinary textbook, varies enormously. The looseleaf format is of course no particular guarantee of currency. It is imperative always to check the release notes carefully, and to distinguish the date of publication of a release from the date at which it states the law. Some looseleafs are also put out online as well, often as a part of subject modules or bundles on the publishers' main service.

Yet another source are the handy one-volume paperback collections of statutes and materials, such as the Butterworths Handbook series, mainly designed for the individual lawyer to have on his or her desk, or to pop in a briefcase. Students will also find there are paperback collections of statutes on particular topics aimed at them, either as separate books or in the 'cases and materials' style of book, and many practitioners' textbooks will reprint statutes as appendices (a cheap way for publishers to add to their bulk and price).

Statutory instruments and other secondary legislation
Although this form of legislation is often described as 'secondary' in distinction to 'primary' legislation, it is also known as 'subordinate', 'subsidiary' or 'delegated' legislation. The last term perhaps captures its nature best. Parliament delegates the power to make further legislation to another person or body, usually a minister. Thus the executive rather than Parliament makes this legislation. Parliament's role is usually confined only to very limited scrutiny after it has been made. The means of delegating is by including an enabling provision in an Act, and all secondary legislation must have such a parent Act. For example s. 41(1) of the Road Traffic Act 1988 provides that

> *... the Secretary of State may make regulations generally as to the use of motor vehicles ... on roads, their construction and equipment and the conditions under which they may be used.*

Sub-section (2) goes on: 'in particular, the regulations may make provisions with respect to ... width ... noise ... weight' and so on. Secondary legislation comes with a variety of labels: rules, regulations, orders, schemes and so on. But they are almost all published in the form of Statutory Instruments (SIs) – almost all, but unfortunately not quite all. The matter is governed by the Statutory Instruments Act 1946. To qualify as an SI the enabling Act must delegate the power either to a minister (the 'Secretary of State') or to the Crown generally. To get round this, the Act may deem another person to be a minister for the purposes of making regulations. But if it is not expedient to do so, the resulting legislation is not an SI. The two commonest examples encountered are practice rules and regulations made by the Law Society under the Solicitors Act 1974, and rules made by the Financial Services Authority under the Financial Services and Markets Act 2000. The Immigration Rules made under the Immigration Act 1971 are a further example – they are uniquely published as House of Commons Papers or Command Papers.

Since devolution in Scotland there has been a separate series of Scottish Statutory Instruments (SSIs) made under asps or under Westminster Acts applying only to Scotland, and there has always been, even before the latest form of devolution, a separate series of Northern Ireland Statutory Rules and Orders. On the other hand, in Wales the secondary legislation made by the National Assembly – and until 2006 the legislation the Assembly made was all secondary – is published in the same series as ordinary UK SIs. An additional Welsh number and parallel text in both Welsh and English (which are equally authentic), however, provide distinguishing features.

SIs are published by TSO individually as they are made, in analogous fashion to the Queen's Printer copies of Acts – at the rate of about 3,000 each year. Such SIs may be classified as general or local, though they share the same series numbering. There is a further class of local SIs that are not printed at all, though again they are allocated a number in the main SI series. From 2010 these are available on www.legislation.gov.uk: on where to obtain earlier ones, see the preface to the monthly or annual TSO *List of Statutory Publications* (where such SIs are now described as 'non-print' as opposed to 'unpublished'). There are also official annual bound volumes of SIs by published by TSO. Note that these annual volumes only include general SIs, not, with some minor exceptions, any local SIs, even if they were published in loose form. SIs of temporary duration or which have already been revoked are also excluded. The official bound volume series goes back to 1890. There was some secondary legislation before that date, but it was only published in ad hoc fashion. All those SIs that are published in loose form are available free on www.legislation. gov.uk from 1987, with some earlier ones back to 1947 being available very selectively. However www.legislation.gov.uk does not currently provide text as amended for SIs.

There were hard copy official revisions providing the text of all SIs (and Statutory Rules and Orders, as they were known before 1946) in force in amended form, but the last edition was in 1948 (the first was in 1896, and so these can be the source of pre-1890 secondary legislation if still in force in 1896 or later). As for Queen's Printer Acts, Justis provides an electronic alternative for SIs. But as with Acts on Justis, be aware of the scope of the data. The starting point of the data is the 1948 printed revision, that is, all those still in force at that date, the official bound annual volumes (so excluding even published local SIs) thereafter to 1986, and then all published SIs to date. There is a printed work for SIs under the Halsbury's brand, but *Halsbury's Statutory Instruments* differs significantly from *Halsbury's Statutes* in that it only prints in full text *selected* SIs, though that text is as amended.

The result of the foregoing is that for the text of SIs as amended you really need to use either Lexis or Westlaw. As with their respective coverage of Acts, their content is different. Lexis has greater retrospective coverage since it covers any SI that has been in force during the lifetime of *Halsbury's Statutory Instruments*, which first started publication in 1952. However, once an SI is wholly revoked the text is removed, though the title remains with details of the revoking instrument. Westlaw on the other hand is only comprehensive for SIs made from 1991, though some of the more important SIs back to 1948 have been added. As with Acts, Westlaw provides historic versions of the text back to 1991.

If you want to use hard copy, looseleaf encyclopaedias and subject handbooks are even more useful for SIs than they are for Acts, since they are the main source for amended text with annotations or commentary – there is no equivalent of *Current Law Statutes* for SIs, and the annotations in *Halsbury's Statutory Instruments* are not generally discursive. Two areas that are particularly well covered in this respect are tax, with *Tolley's Yellow* and *Orange Handbooks* (and similar rivals from other publishers), and social security, where Sweet & Maxwell's annual *Social Security Legislation* volumes are indispensable.

Case Law

Case law forms the other primary source of law. It is the 'common law' in one of that expression's several senses. (For an excellent explanation of its different meanings in different contexts, see Glanville Williams (2010).[1] It also goes on to provide a similarly useful explanation of another term that can be opaque to the non-lawyer – 'equity'). Certain areas of law are governed by the decisions of the courts as developed over the centuries, and do not derive from legislation. For example, large parts of the law of contract and of torts (civil wrongs, such as negligence, nuisance, libel and so on) rest merely on case law. There are even criminal offences that have never been put into a statute, and so are said to be common law offences – not many now, but murder is one. Legislation, however, continually and cumulatively intervenes, so the areas of law that can be described as pure common law gradually become smaller. Nonetheless, legislation itself frequently needs to be interpreted by the courts, so what the courts have to say on the meaning of a statute in turn becomes part of the law.

Case law acts as a source of law through the doctrine of precedent. Like cases have to be decided alike and the decisions of the higher courts have to be followed by the lower courts. It should be appreciated, however, that most cases that come before the courts, particularly the lower courts, involve no dispute as to the law. The court has only to resolve disputes of fact. Case law is nowadays promulgated in two distinct forms, traditional law reports on the one hand and transcripts of unreported judgments on the other.

Law Reports

Law reports have historically been and continue to be the means of selecting cases that decide new points of law or clarify existing law. The structure of most full series of law reports is similar. The full text of the judgment or judgments is provided, preceded by various pieces of editorial apparatus, the most important of which is the headnote. Here the law reporter distils the essence of the case and what was *held*, that is, the kernel of the case, or in technical terms the 'ratio'. However, a central feature of legal reasoning and argument in common law systems is deciding precisely what the ratio of a case is, and how widely or narrowly it should be interpreted in later cases. The extent to which the case represents a novel point of potential precedent value is not necessarily transparent. Opinion may thus genuinely differ as to what is 'reportable'. However, as explained below strong commercial forces are also at play. These two factors are the reason that there is such proliferation of different series of law reports, with much duplication of coverage.

Law reporting has never been in official hands. With the exception discussed below of the Incorporated Council of Law Reporting, law reporting has always been a matter of commercial free enterprise. The main law reports until 1865 were prepared by individual law reporters and editors who covered particular courts, and then lent their name to a particular series. Hence they are known as the nominate reports. The nominate reports as originally published form something of a higgledy-piggledy collection of material – long series, short series, obscure series, well-used series, different editions, some large folios, others small octavos. Furthermore few law libraries, let alone individual lawyers, have complete sets of every series as they were published from about 1571 to 1865. Early in the twentieth century nearly all were reprinted, with the original text but rearranged by court rather than reporter, as the *English Reports* in a manageable 178 volumes. As it is in the form of the *English Reports* that they are found in most law libraries, the nominate reports in general are sometimes loosely referred to as the *English Reports*. The full text of the *English Reports* is now widely available online: free of charge on CommonLII (the amalgamated site of BAILII and the other 'legal information institutes' from the common law jurisdictions), and on Westlaw and HeinOnline.

Growing dissatisfaction with the varying editorial standards and duplication of coverage of the nominate reports led to the formation in 1865 of the Incorporated Council of Law Reporting, a non-profit making body under the control of the profession itself. Its aim was the creation of a single, authoritative set of law reports. It was successful in the second part of its aim but not in the first. Its reports, known just as *The Law Reports*, indeed became the most authoritative reports, based on the highest editorial standards, with the added advantage that the judgments are checked by the judge. For this reason they are the series that must be cited in court in preference to any other. However, commercial competition did not simply wither away. *The Law Reports* were slow to appear and there remained a willing market for cases they did not deign to report. The multiplication of series of law reports in the latter decades of the twentieth century took the form of topic-based series in particular, often with competing series on the same subject area from rival publishers – for example *British Company Cases* and *Butterworths Company Law Cases*, and the *Building Law Reports* and the *Construction Law Reports*. Due to saturation of the market, and the availability of transcripts online (discussed below), this proliferation has slowed down, but new series do continue to pop up from time to time.

The Incorporated Council finally faced up to the challenge of timeliness by publishing the *Weekly Law Reports*, which started in 1953. These are published in three volumes each year. The cases in Volumes 2 and 3 are those that are destined for publication in *The Law Reports* proper, once they have been checked by the judge and a report of counsel's argument (a unique feature of *The Law Reports*) has been added. Cases in Volume 1 are those deemed to be of lesser importance. Each weekly part thus comprises two halves, Volume 1 cases and, depending on the time of year, either Volume 2 or Volume 3 cases.

The *All England Law Reports*, which started in 1936, is the main commercially published general series of law reports (and rank equally with the *Weekly Law Reports* for use in court – see Chapter 3, p. 93). As well as separate series, there are law reports that appear in conjunction with journals, either as brief reports for current awareness (such as the *New Law Journal*), or as full reports (such as the *Estates Gazette*) or with expert commentary (for example, the *Criminal Law Review*). The law reports in the newspapers, particularly of course *The Times*, obviously fulfill the function of speediness in reporting. Many will be reported more fully elsewhere in due course, but some are not, and so, particularly for older cases not available as a transcript on a database, this will remain all that there is to go on.

Most modern published series of law reports are now available in full text online. *The Law Reports* themselves offer the greatest retrospective coverage in electronic form, since the whole series from 1865 is available – from the Incorporated Council's own online service, and on both Lexis and Westlaw. Lexis and Westlaw each carry those series where Butterworths and Sweet & Maxwell respectively are the publisher, since they own the content. Both services, but Lexis in particular, have in the past carried in addition content licensed from third party publishers. However, there has been a worrying trend for third party publishers to withdraw from such arrangements in order to set up their own online services, which means that it is no longer the case that if you carried out a search on both those services you could be satisfied that your results were as near comprehensive as possible.

Transcripts of unreported judgments
Notwithstanding the proliferation of printed law reports, they do remain selective and there are commercial limitations as to what it is economic to put into print. The advent of the online database, allowing the wholesale uploading of virtually limitless amounts of text at little cost, has removed that limitation. But why should anyone want or need a transcript? The first reason is simply timeliness. Many of the services are able to put up cases within 24 hours of them being decided, long before they might appear in a printed law report. Being found to be out of date is the perpetual worry of any lawyer. Secondly, the uninitiated may be surprised to learn that the binding nature of a decision does not depend on whether it is reported in a series of law reports or not. As has been seen, a degree of editorial judgment goes into selecting cases for publication in a law

report, so a case may have got overlooked, or a point seeming trivial at the time may subsequently assume importance because of other developments in the law. Thirdly, lawyers sometimes find it helpful to look at previous cases, not with an eye to their precedent value, but simply as being illustrative. They may want to see whether a particular set of facts that they are dealing with has cropped up before. Or, if they have to advise in an area where the courts can exercise a lot of discretion, such as in family cases, they may wish to get a feel for current judicial thinking.

Before describing the various online services, a word needs to be said about transcripts in hard copy – a case may be needed which is either too old to be on the online services or is recent but has escaped the services for some reason. In the first eventuality, it should be appreciated that for only very limited categories of cases is there any form of archive of transcripts. The main exception is the judgments of the Court of Appeal (Civil Division), which have been preserved since 1951, though there are one two other examples. The main reason, which is also relevant to what is available on the online services, is that transcripts have never been in the public domain per se. The preparation of transcripts of cases is contracted out by the Court Service to private firms of shorthand writers, and they in effect own the transcripts, which they sell to those that need them. Furthermore the shorthand writers do not generally retain transcripts or tapes more than six years old, so in the first eventuality they will be no help. If it is the second eventuality that you are faced with then you would need to identify the relevant shorthand writer and pay the fairly high fee they exact. Fortunately in this whole area help is at hand in the form of Inner Temple Library's guide to transcripts (2011)[2] last issued in 2011. It covers not only the courts but a very wide range of tribunals, giving details of holdings and access, where to obtain hard copies and the cost and availability on websites.

Although the shorthand writers retain a commercial interest in a *transcript*, technically the text of the judgment itself is Crown copyright. Where a judgment is handed down (as opposed to actually being transcribed) it can be freely disseminated. In the past judges in particular cases have directed that their judgments be put up on the Courts Service website. This brings us to BAILII – the British and Irish Legal Information Institute, the free not-for-profit service that has been running since 2001. Their aim is to bring together all judgments that have been put in the public domain. In pursuing this aim they work closely with the courts, but it should be appreciated that it has yet to achieve by any means complete comprehensiveness.

This is one reason why there remains such a strong market for the commercial services. The other reason is that the commercial providers can provide value-added content, particularly in the form of indexing and abstracting, which would be beyond the resources of BAILII. Given the limitations of pure free-text searching, particularly on what is now such a vast body of material, the provision of summaries, subject headings and so on is a real benefit. This also makes the material amenable for use as a current awareness tool, as opposed to a research tool – all the commercial services provide alerter services of various kinds, which can be tailored to a particular user's areas of practice or interest.

The four main services currently available are Lexis, Lawtel, Westlaw and Casetrack. (There are also one or two specialist services, such as the Electronic Immigration Network, and recently launched is a service from Justis, which includes the archive of Court of Appeal judgments back to 1951 and High Court cases from 1996). Lexis was the first in the market as long ago as 1980. This historical depth of coverage is among its strongest points. It is important, however, to appreciate that the scope of its original coverage was not as wide as it now is, it then being much more selective for High Court first instance decisions. Also in its original form it merely loaded the text of the transcript, so you were entirely reliant on free-text searching. Since 1995, however, it has provided its All England Reporter service (cited as All E R (D)), which provides summaries having the appearance of the opening part of a printed law report, with catchwords and a headnote, and which generally appear in advance of the full transcript.

Lawtel also started life in 1980, though the full text of the transcripts only goes back to the 1990s. The main record is a relatively full summary. Usefully the transcripts themselves are PDFs. Westlaw came on the scene in 2000. 'Case analysis' documents, giving a summary of the case, citator-type information and so on, are given in the same style as they are for reported cases, making for a seamless approach.

Casetrack is a slightly different product from the other three. It is produced by Merrill Legal Solutions (previously Smith Bernal) who have been the official shorthand writers for the Court of Appeal and Administrative Court since April 1996. For those courts it is thus comprehensive. It is also likely to be the first service to put up a case from those courts. It also aims to provide wide coverage from the other divisions of the High Court, which started from July 1998.

As with law reports series, there is very heavy duplication of coverage between the services, though there may be small differences in timeliness. The main class of case where different results may be obtained is first instance High Court cases where judgment is given *ex tempore* (that is, orally by the judge at the close of the case). These have to be transcribed in the true sense, and so are subject to delay. Also greater editorial judgment as to whether they are worth obtaining has to be exercised.

SECONDARY SOURCES

Textbooks

Textbooks come in all shapes and sizes: nutshell guides for cramming students, substantial academic texts intended for undergraduates, but which have wider reputations (for example *Treitel on Contract* or *Smith & Hogan on Criminal Law*), handy introductions aimed at busy practitioners, major practitioner works that continue to be published in new editions long after their original authors are dead (for example *Chitty on Contracts* or *Archbold*), guides to new Acts produced very quickly after they appear, academic monographs, perhaps based on a doctoral thesis (such as those published by Hart), and the major looseleaf encyclopaedias (which have already been touched upon in connection with their coverage of legislation).

As well as deciding which current textbooks to stock, which will depend on the library's clientele, there is also the thorny question of retention of superseded editions. Only the Inns of Court, the Law Society and the major research libraries routinely retain old editions on a large scale. There are good reasons for lawyers needing old law. In many libraries, there is simply no choice for reasons of space – ruthlessness must rule the day. In the law firm setting, you may need to be aware of any major long-term litigation or other matter in hand, before throwing out material that has just been superseded. Short back runs of annual tax handbooks, for example, may be needed where clients' tax liabilities for previous accounting periods are in dispute.

Most self-respecting academic law libraries and the major professional society libraries will also hold copies of the classic legal treatises (which are also widely available in various forms of reprint), such as *Coke's Institutes of the Laws of England* (1628), *Hale's Pleas of the Crown* (1736) or *Blackstone's Commentaries on the Laws of England* (1765–69). These are by no means only of interest to the academic legal historian. They are regarded as authoritative statements of the common law at the time, and thus are frequently cited in court for that reason. It should also be appreciated that, though textbooks are not a source of law as such, modern works by eminent authors, whether academics or practitioners, are frequently cited in court as persuasive sources.

Journals

Again there is a huge range: the general weeklies such as the *Solicitors Journal* or the Law Society's *Gazette*, specialist newsletters often prepared by law firms partly as marketing tools, heavyweight learned journals (either general such as the *Law Quarterly Review*, or specialist such as *Lloyd's Maritime and Commercial Law Quarterly*), the gossipy 'legal business' publications such as *The Lawyer* aimed mostly at law firms and law reviews put out by university law departments.

They perform a variety of functions. Current awareness is high on the list, but where in-depth articles are provided they are a source of information on new topics or new developments before they have been incorporated into the textbooks. They are also a vehicle for specialist in-depth treatment of topics that are not covered by the textbooks at all. Equally, the handy two-page article in the *New Law Journal*, or the highly practical coverage in *Property Law Journal* may be exactly what is being looked for by the practitioner in a hurry or by the trainee solicitor in a panic.

Forms and Precedents

Forms and precedents represent an important secondary source of legal information. They provide samples of common legal documents as aids to drafting. They are used by practitioners to avoid reinventing the wheel and help them understand what information it will be necessary to provide in the documentation for any particular transaction. ('Precedent' in this context thus has a different sense from 'precedent' in the context of case law.)

They are used in two distinct fields. One is drafting documents such as contracts, leases, loans, trusts, wills and so on, that is, where the lawyer is doing transactional or non-contentious work. The other is drafting the documents required to conduct litigation. The latter, 'court forms', may be statutory where the court rules lay down prescribed content and format, as is the case with a variety of notices or orders that are served on the parties or issued by the court, or they may simply be suggested examples where no particular requirement is laid down, for example statements of claim. Forms and precedents will set out a typical example of the document with blanks left to fill in particular details, such as relevant names and dates, but where they are non-statutory the lawyer is of course free to tailor them as necessary, and indeed has to take care not to follow them blindly. Usually they are accompanied by commentary or annotations on the relevant substantive or procedural law – this commentary can in fact often be a very useful substitute for a conventional textbook.

Most law firms maintain databases of precedents that they have previously used, and these may be particularly useful as they will be geared to their areas of practice. But there are a variety of published sources. Even where these are printed sources they are often also offered in electronic form, for ease of word processing. The two main general encyclopaedic collections covering each of the main types described above are the *Encyclopaedia of Forms and Precedents* and *Atkin's Encyclopaedia of Court Forms in Civil Proceedings* (both published by LexisNexis and available on LexisLibrary). In hard copy these are very large multi-volume works with the updating mechanisms of replacement volumes and looseleaf supplements on similar lines to *Halsbury's Laws* and *Statutes*. There are also individual works covering particular areas of law, for example *Practical Commercial Precedents* or *Precedents for the Conveyancer* (both Sweet & Maxwell looseleafs). Statutory court forms will be found in volumes accompanying *Civil Procedure* (the White Book) and its competitors, but there are also collections of forms and precedents for particular courts such as *Admiralty and Merchant Shipping Court Forms and Precedents 3rd ed.* (Chambers and Parsons 2013). Many standard textbooks have appendices of forms and precedents, for example *Rayden & Jackson on Divorce and Family Matters* (available on LexisLibrary).

Finally, another excellent source of precedents is *PLC*. *PLC* is an online database that delivers practical guidance, analysis and materials. The database covers 20 practice areas including sets of standard documents for each. For example it contains eight different share purchase agreements and a complete subset of standard clauses relating to them. *PLC* is a resource that is used extensively by law firms to complement primary resources and textbooks.

Official Publications

Apart from legislation, there is a wide range of official publications to which lawyers need access. Perhaps the most important are those relating to law reform proposals and pre-legislative materials. They are needed by both academics and practitioners for current reasons (to explain or advise on forthcoming changes in the law) and for retrospective research (to explain, particularly in the context of statutory interpretation, how the law came about). New legislation may arise from recommendations in a one-off report of a Royal Commission or a committee of inquiry, or from a Law Commission report. More frequently, new legislation is heralded first by a government Green Paper (that is, a consultation paper), and then by a White Paper setting out the government's intentions in light of the consultation. Green Papers are typically departmental publications, though they may also be published by the TSO or even occasionally be Command Papers. Nowadays they are invariably published on the internet (sometimes only on the internet). White Papers are typically Command Papers, which, together with House of Commons Papers and Bills, are one category of House of Commons parliamentary papers. Though Command Papers are all published in print form, again White Papers will invariably be available on the internet.

Once prospective legislation is set to go through Parliament most major Bills now go through 'pre-legislative scrutiny' – a procedure first introduced experimentally in 1998. A draft Bill is considered by a Select Committee of one or other House or by a joint committee. Written and oral evidence is taken from outside interested parties. The committee reports and evidence are published as House of Commons or House of Lords papers.

After the Bill proper has started its passage, there are three further classes of materials that need be consulted. First, there are the Bills themselves. They are reprinted, incorporating the changes to date, as they go through – usually there are five prints, two for the Commons and three for the Lords. These prints and the amendment papers have been retained on the Parliament website[3] since session 2006/2007. Secondly, there are the Explanatory Notes to Bills, which were introduced in 1999. These are prepared by the government department sponsoring the Bill and are published at the same time as the Bill is first printed for the Commons and again when it is first printed for the Lords. A final version, to the Act, appears soon after it is passed. Lastly, there are the parliamentary debates. Hansard is published in two series, for the Commons and for the Lords. It comes out in daily and weekly unrevised parts, then in official bound volumes incorporating editorial amendments (and shifts in column numbering). As well as containing a near-verbatim record of all proceedings on the floor of each House, they include written parliamentary questions and their answers, and ministerial statements – these are a mine of information on any official activity. Apart from the two main series of Hansard, there is a separate series of House of Commons Public Bill Committee debates (before session 2006/2007 'Standing Committee' debates) since in the Commons the committee stage on a Bill is not usually taken on the floor of the House. These three series are available on the Parliament website, but with varying start dates.

Traditionally reference to what was said in Parliament during the passage of a Bill was not permitted in court as an aid to statutory interpretation. That rule was relaxed by the House of Lords in *Pepper v Hart* [1993] AC 593. Thus researching Hansard tends to be called by practitioners '*Pepper v Hart* research'. Since there is no particular age limit on a statute that might require to be interpreted with the aid of Hansard, old materials, not available on the internet, may be needed, and in any event *Pepper v Hart* research remains one of the few categories of legal research where hard copy research is unquestionably preferable.

Official publications not related to law reform and the legislative process are infinitely various, as are the uses to which lawyers may put them. These can include annual reports, statistics, decisions of regulatory bodies and ombudsmen, non-legislative parliamentary materials such as Select Committee reports, or one-off inquiries. There is really no way to predict in what form they will be published – as a parliamentary paper, as a TSO publication or put out by the body itself. If the item is relatively recent, there is absolutely no shame and a lot of sense in simply doing a Google search.

EUROPEAN SOURCES

When the expression 'European law' arises, it is important to distinguish the senses in which it might be meant. First there is the law of the European Union – with its headquarters in Brussels and its court in Luxembourg. Then there is the law arising from treaties that originate with the Council of Europe, notably, but by no means exclusively, the European Convention on Human Rights. The Council of Europe currently has 47 member states, in contrast to the European Union's 27, and has its headquarters in Strasbourg, which is also the seat of the European Court of Human Rights. Lastly it might refer to the comparative law of European countries, either EU member states or generally.

EU Sources

The EU has its origins in three separate 'communities', the European Coal and Steel Community (ECSC) founded in 1952, followed by the European Economic Community and the European Atomic Energy Community (Euratom) in 1957. The ECSC Treaty expired in 2002, but until the Treaty of Lisbon which came into force at the end of 2009 there were two communities in the plural. The Maastricht Treaty in 1992 created the European Union, which was defined as three 'pillars'. The first pillar was the European Communities, and at that time it remained the source of the distinctive European law as we know it – Directives, Regulations, European Court of Justice (ECJ) decisions and so on. This was technically 'EC law', rather than 'EU law', and the names of the principal institutions matched this, for instance the 'Commission of the European Communities'. The other two pillars were foreign and security policy on the one hand and justice and home affairs on the other; there were no powers to make law under these two pillars in the same way as under the first. The Lisbon Treaty did away with this structure and the 'EC', making the European Union a single legal entity in its own right, incorporating the second and third pillars, and with matching change of terminology – so now the 'Commission of the European Union'.

The sources of EU law are the original EC treaty (renamed post-Lisbon, the 'Treaty on the Functioning of the European Union'), the subsequent amending treaties and treaties of accession of new member states. This constitutes the EU's primary legislation. Secondary legislation takes the form of Directives, Regulations and Decisions. Directives provide a framework, which member states have to transpose into their own domestic law within a certain time. In the UK transposition is almost always by means of an SI, the enabling power for making the SI being the European Communities Act 1972. Occasionally, however, for major Directives implementation may require a new Act. Regulations, in contrast, have direct effect – they form part of UK law without further ado. Nonetheless in practice many regulations require adjustment of existing UK legislation to accommodate them. Directives and Regulations apply throughout all member states. Decisions, on the other hand, are directed to particular member states, or to particular undertakings or bodies. If directed to the UK, an SI may have to ensue. The official vehicle for publishing all EU legislation is the *Official Journal*, L series. The vast bulk of the legislation is freely available on EUR-Lex, the official EU website.

Court decisions are the other source of EU law. The Court of Justice of the European Union, which is now the overarching name, comprises the European Court of Justice – the main court, still abbreviated as the 'ECJ' – the General Court (formerly the Court of First Instance or CFI founded in 1989) and the Civil Service Tribunal (which deals with staff cases which the CFI used to handle). All of the decisions of the ECJ and the General Court are published in the official series the *European Court Reports* and on the court's website,[4] but are widely available elsewhere in print and online. Note that an important part of ECJ case law is not just the judgment of the court but the Advocate-General's opinion, which precedes it. Both appear in the reports.

European Human Rights Sources

The Human Rights Act 1998 incorporated into UK law the European Convention on Human Rights, which was signed in 1950. The text of the Convention forms a schedule to the Act, which came into force in October 2000. (Scotland felt the effect a year earlier, by virtue of the Scotland Act 1998.) The courts in this country can now recognize Convention rights and provide remedies for their breach, without the need to visit the European Court of Human Rights in Strasbourg. In doing so, under s. 2 of the Act, the court *must* take into account all previous Strasbourg case law. It is thus important to be aware of the different categories of Strasbourg case law. A major restructuring of the system of human rights adjudication at Strasbourg came into effect on 1 November 1998. This impinges on where case law is to be found before and after 1998. Before 1998 two separate bodies were involved, the European Commission of Human Rights and the European Court of Human Rights. The former performed a filtering role. Initial application was made to the Commission, who decided whether it was admissible. Once admitted, the Commission proceeded to investigate the merits of the case, and produced a report. Thus there were two categories of Commission case law: *decisions* (on admissibility) and *reports* (on the merits). Both categories were officially published in the Commission's *Decisions and Reports* (DR, or previously *Collection of Decisions*, CD) – though in the case of admissibility decisions, only the most important. Depending on the outcome at the Commission stage, the case would then be referred to the Court, so the third category of case law is *judgments of the Court*. The 1998 reforms abolished the Commission. The Court itself now decides admissibility, and the intermediate stage represented by the Commission's report on the merits has gone. But there remain two types of case law emanating from the Court, decisions on admissibility and judgments. There is an official series *Reports of Judgments and Decisions* (before 1995 called *Publications of the European Court of Human Rights Series A*), but the commercially published *European Human Rights Reports* (EHRR, which also used to include, selectively, Commission materials) is the much more widely used series (and acceptable in court). However, the Strasbourg database of case law, HUDOC,[5] has almost all that is needed free of charge – the main exception is most pre-1986 Commission materials. Furthermore the text of case law taken off HUDOC is also acceptable for use in court (see the Practice Direction accompanying part 39 of the Civil Procedure Rules).

INTERNATIONAL LAW SOURCES

It is important to distinguish the two types of international law. One is private international law. This is law in a domestic setting where there is a foreign element. Its alternative name, conflict of laws, perhaps describes it better. It comes to the fore in the international commercial context. If a British ship owner carries cargo purchased from Argentina by an Australian buyer and has a collision in Hong Kong, is the relevant law that of England, Argentina, Australia or Hong Kong? But it can arise in any number of everyday contexts. Public international law, on the other hand, is the law as it applies between states (or between states and certain international organizations). Here we are dealing with such matters as international boundaries, the law of the sea, the law of war, diplomatic immunity and so on.

The main sources of public international law are, firstly, treaties – binding agreements between states, whether just two states (bilateral treaties) or between many states (multilateral treaties). Treaties come with a variety of labels; 'Convention' is the most common for a multilateral treaty. A 'Protocol' is usually a treaty amending a principal treaty. Treaties to which the UK is a party are published as Command Papers. Secondly, there is the case law of international courts and tribunals, such as the International Court of Justice at The Hague. Under the constitutional arrangements which apply in the UK (it may differ elsewhere), public international law does not form part of domestic law applied directly by our courts, unless it is expressly incorporated by separate legislation, which may be an Act or an SI. The status of the European Convention on Human Rights in the UK before and after the 1998 Act now makes this a familiar concept.

The sources for private international law are in the first place simply ordinary domestic sources of law – each jurisdiction has its own rules for the conflict of laws, but clearly it would be chaotic if there were not some uniformity of the rules between different jurisdictions, and in most important areas, such as commercial law, shipping law, arbitration, family law and children, there are international regimes in place, with a greater or lesser number of participant countries, so that courts in different countries arrive at the same answer in a conflict situation. Those regimes are usually established by means of treaties (which if applicable in the UK will be incorporated by an Act), so there is some overlap between private international law and public international law.

It is also worth noting that since the Treaty of Amsterdam in 1997 the EU has been competent to legislate directly in the field of private international law. So much European cross-border law is now made by directly effective Regulations, rather than as previously by conventional international treaties (which required the individual consent of each member state).

NOTES

1   Williams, G. (2010), *Learning the law*, 14th edn. Sweet & Maxwell, pp. 21–22.
2   Inner Temple Library (2011), *Transcripts of judicial Proceedings in England and Wales: a Guide to Sources*.
3   www.parliament.uk
4   http://curia.europe.eu
5   www.echr.coe.int/echr/en/hudoc

CHAPTER 3

LEGAL RESEARCH – TECHNIQUES AND TIPS

PETER CLINCH

THE CONTEXT OF LEGAL RESEARCH

What is Legal Research?

An effective law librarian is like high-grade oil in the engine of a top-performance legal organization. The law librarian is the intermediary between the enquirer and the sources of law. Even though more and more sources are available electronically and networked throughout organizations, the role of the librarian remains to assist in identifying resources, arrange for acquisition or licensing, provide easy access to and, where appropriate, train enquirers in effective use of those sources.

An organization having all the sources described by Guy Holborn in Chapter 2 of this handbook, yet without a law librarian experienced in legal research techniques, will not be as effective or efficient as one where resources have been selected appropriate to needs, with the assistance of an information professional who knows how to exploit those resources to best advantage.

The information professional as intermediary is an established concept and applies particularly in the conduct of legal research. A legal information professional usually undertakes research on behalf and for the benefit of someone else and is in fact assisting in the fulfillment of the middle stage in the process of legal research. Generically, the three stages of legal research are:

- identifying and analysing a problem
- finding appropriate information to solve the problem
- presenting the results of the analysis and research in an appropriate and effective manner (Clinch 2006: 20[1]).

Ideally, before approaching an information professional, the enquirer has carried out the first stage and identified the relevant areas of law and perhaps developed some relevant keywords. Members of the public cannot be expected to have analysed the relevant areas of law. Even in law firms and universities, many enquirers, including professional lawyers and students, will not have undertaken the first stage and information professionals will need to undertake some steps (such as selecting keywords) in this first stage in collaboration with the enquirer.

The second stage is where the skills of an information professional come into play. It is a matter of matching the sources to the problem to provide solutions. It demands an understanding of the structure of legal literature and the media through which it is made available, understanding how to use indexes and search tools effectively, using and interpreting legal citations and abbreviations, checking the currency of information and ensuring the information provided to the enquirer is up to date.

The third stage is usually in the hands of the enquirer who will use the product of the search of legal sources to create a written or verbal report containing an argument, opinion or advice on the law in relation to the legal problem defined initially. It is about applying the law to the original problem and presenting the result effectively. At this stage legal advice is given. An information professional must be on guard to avoid straying into this third stage. We are not qualified to provide advice on the law, merely to find what we believe are the statements of law relevant to the problem posed by the enquirer. Leave legal interpretation to those qualified to do so or, in the case of a member of the public posing the problem, to them. Of course, the information professional may make a written report to the enquirer about the second stage and use similar principles of good presentation in that report, but keep the content to information on where the relevant sources can be found and avoid interpreting or applying it.

Who Are Our Enquirers?

In Chapter 1 Jules Winterton defined our 'audience'. In terms of legal research needs, it can be split crudely into those requiring academic sources and those requiring practitioner sources, with many overlaps. Universities are responsible for the delivery of the 'academic' stage of legal education where, normally, students will be working towards a degree qualification in law or exempting qualification (the Common Professional Examination or CPE). The Ormrod Report (1971, para. 102) stated that the law degree means teaching

> ... legal principles and the basic subjects ... without which no one can begin to be a lawyer, and developing the intellectual processes which are usually referred to as 'thinking like a lawyer'.

Teaching staff will be engaged in research into the law from a critical or creative perspective. The academic stage therefore considers the law as a topic for study, analysis and discussion.

Following the 'academic' stage of legal education is the 'vocational' stage of legal training (note the change in emphasis from education to training). At this stage, the focus is on developing professional skills – 'acting like a lawyer', that is, developing the skills of a barrister or solicitor. Such training can take place either through vocational courses (such as, in England and Wales, the Legal Practice Course (LPC) or the Bar Professional Training Course (BPTC)) or in-house, within a law firm. The focus of training is to meet the specific legal needs of a particular client, through the provision of focused advice, creating legal documents or representing the client in court. The sources a practitioner uses will include those on the practice and procedure of the courts as well as non-litigious materials. In addition, those lawyers with corporate business clients will need access to business and financial information that will keep them informed of changes in their client's business sector and identify relevant legal issues. Business information is also valued in law firms to enable them to prepare effective presentations, the so-called 'beauty parades', where law firms compete to gain contracts to act as legal advisors to national and international businesses.

So, lawyers in practice, including those training to be practising lawyers, are going to pose quite different research questions from those engaged in the academic study of law.

Those working for professional bodies or central government may be dealing with both types of legal enquiry, the academic as well as the practice-oriented. For example, in central government, departments formulating policy on an aspect of law may be required to investigate the law from an academic standpoint as a prelude to devising and proposing practical measures. In local authorities, public libraries and citizens' advice bureaux, which deal directly with the public, generally legal research will be focused on searching sources to provide information aimed at the solution of the needs of a particular client. Public libraries, in addition, may deal with some academic enquiries from students.

Academic and vocational lawyers require access to a wide range of legal sources, but a central core, comprising the primary sources of law (legislation and case law), will be common to both.

THE FIVE FUNDAMENTALS OF LEGAL RESEARCH

There are five key points to bear in mind before attempting legal research.

Jurisdiction

Parliaments or legislatures – the bodies responsible for making or amending laws – have their own 'sphere of influence' or, more correctly, 'jurisdiction', limited to a particular geographical area. For example, the law of the United Kingdom of Great Britain and Northern Ireland comprises four distinct jurisdictions: England, Wales, Scotland and Northern Ireland. Note that the Isle of Man and the Channel Islands are not included in these jurisdictions. The concept of jurisdiction has implications for the way in which legal information is organized and the conduct of legal research.

Each jurisdiction has its own court structures, hierarchies, procedures and traditions. The courts administer justice and interpret the law made by the legislature.

Overlaying what might be termed the domestic UK jurisdiction are the Treaties, Regulations, Directives and other legislation of the European Union (EU), supplemented by the decisions of the European Court of Justice. The EU aims to harmonize laws between member states. The main instruments are EU Regulations and Directives.

Jurisdiction is also significant when finding legal information about countries with state and federal legal systems, as in the US. Time can be wasted if you are unsure whether the information required involves federal law or a particular state or a number of states.

Key pointers

When dealing with an enquiry, make sure you know for which jurisdiction the information is required. Ensure the information sources used (both paper and electronic) cover that jurisdiction. Remember that law libraries usually collect the greatest amount of information about the jurisdiction in which they are situated or with which their users normally deal. Do not expect the collection to contain much about other jurisdictions. Electronic sources have gone some way to removing this barrier to information flow. Finally, never assume that the law of another jurisdiction is going to be available in English unless the official language/s of that jurisdiction includes English. An English translation of a law originally enacted in another language must be treated with caution, unless there is clear evidence that the translation has been authorized and is approved by the original law-making body. English translations that are not authoritative at best should be used as a general guide to the law, not as a basis for interpretation or challenge in the courts.

Variations in Legal Systems

Whilst the United Kingdom comprises several jurisdictions, there are many similarities between the way the four are structured and operate. Consequently there are similarities in the legal information they produce. However the legal systems of countries such as England, France, Poland and Japan, for example, are quite different from each other. Be aware that there are families of legal systems so that knowledge of the structure of legal literature in one member of a particular family may assist information-seeking in relation to the law of a member of the same family. The UK is part of the 'common law' legal system, as are those countries colonized by the UK and which on independence have decided to keep the same system of law. So, in general there are similarities between the UK, Ireland, many Commonwealth countries and the US.

It is interesting to note that Scotland is in fact a mixed legal system, sharing common law features with a tradition linked to the continental approach.

Key pointers

Do not expect to find the same types of law publication or terminology used in your own country in a country with a different legal tradition. Within the same legal family (such as the common law family) there will be similarities. But, although the roots of legal systems may be the same, over the centuries the law has developed in different ways, with different publications, terminology and techniques to research the law.

Change

There is one constant in the law – change. New laws are enacted, courts interpret them and settle legal disputes, new codes and standards of practice are authorized. Some publications and electronic databases print the text of a piece of legislation but have no means of informing the user that the legislation may have been amended or even repealed or revoked by later legislation. Similarly, publications containing the text of the decisions of the courts usually do not indicate whether a particular decision has been overtaken by a later decision and is therefore no longer 'good law'. Many years ago, the looseleaf publishing format was devised to overcome these difficulties. More recently, electronic databases have speeded up reporting the law, but even so some do not make clear whether the information about legislation or court decisions contains updates or not.

Even electronic databases cannot keep users entirely up to date. There are often delays of days and sometimes weeks between legislation being approved by Parliament and the text appearing on a database. Similarly, court decisions can take days or weeks to appear in full text form. Whilst the internet has reduced delay times, as will be seen later in this chapter, particular databases are better at timeliness than others.

Key pointers

When researching legal information in paper format, use a publication with a looseleaf format wherever possible. Note that not all subjects are published in looseleaf format, only those where there is a considerable practitioner market. So, academic topics like jurisprudence and legal history or 'general' topics not applied to a particular practice area such as tort or negligence are not represented by looseleaf encyclopaedias. Check that the looseleaf has been kept up to date: look at the date of the last release given in the Filing Record or Filing Instructions pages. Check the Filing Record to make sure the subscription has been constant and that no releases of replacement pages have been missed. A hardback can be years out of date. Always check the title page or preface for a statement about the date up to which the law stated is correct. Check if there is or should be a separately published supplement volume which brings the book up to date. Carry out searches in a number of sources to bring the statement of law as close to the present as possible. If this is not possible, make clear to the enquirer that what you are providing is information 'correct to' a particular date, which may not be the current situation.

Unpublished Material

Not every legal document is published. The natural assumption is that all the law made by the legislature and the courts of a country will be published and readily accessible to the public. In some common law jurisdictions, such as the UK, this is not so. For example, in England and Wales the courts hear and decide over 200,000 cases each year but only about 2,500 (or 1.25per cent) are published, or, as lawyers say, reported. Only those cases that develop the law, setting new precedents, are reported. The rest remain either as unpublished (unreported) transcripts or go totally unrecorded.

Although electronic databases such as LexisLibrary and Westlaw UK carry the full text of a selection of unreported decisions of the English higher courts, transcripts of the vast majority of English cases are not made publicly available. An invaluable, comprehensive guide to what is available and how to obtain it (*Transcripts of Judicial Proceedings in England and Wales: a Guide to Sources* (2011)) has been compiled by Sally Mclaren of the Inner Temple Library and is only available on the internet for a charge on the web at www.innertemplelibrary. org.uk/Transcripts/TranscriptsGuide.htm.

Key pointers

Regardless of jurisdiction, do not assume all court decisions are readily available in either printed or electronic form. Information about cases decided in the lower courts of common law jurisdictions may be difficult or even impossible to obtain.

Abbreviations

Lawyers often use abbreviations and special forms of citation to refer to a particular legal source or type of document – indexes to these are available and will enable you to correctly identify the information required.

Key pointers

The most comprehensive paper index to legal abbreviations is the third (2008) edition of Donald Raistrick's *Index to Legal Citations and Abbreviations*, published by Sweet & Maxwell. It covers not just the United Kingdom and Ireland, but also the Commonwealth, the US, member countries of the European Union, other European countries, Africa, Asia and South America. The contents include not only abbreviations for publications but abbreviations relating to personalities and procedures in the law. A more up-to-date source of abbreviations, for publications only, is the Cardiff Index to Legal Abbreviations at http:// www. legalabbrevs.cardiff.ac.uk. It covers even more jurisdictions than Raistrick's *Index*, is updated frequently, permits searching without punctuation and allows searches to be conducted in either direction: from abbreviation to title and from title to abbreviation.

ANSWERING LEGAL ENQUIRIES

Asking the Right Questions

The major key to a successful piece of legal research is to understand exactly and correctly what information the enquirer wants.

An enquiry is usually presented either as a focused or an unfocused question. Focused questions are easier to deal with as they frequently name the document that the enquirer is seeking: 'I am looking for SI 1995/1027' or 'Do you have a copy of the latest version of the PACE codes?' So long as you can recognize the legal shorthand (SI means Statutory Instrument and PACE refers to the Police and Criminal Evidence Act) it should not be too difficult to find the material required. 'Do you have a model mortgage deed for the purchase of an aircraft?' is still a focused query but made difficult by being based in a relatively specialist area of law.

To answer an unfocused question needs more skill and thought: 'Who is responsible for maintaining an unadopted road?'; 'What interests do MPs need to declare?'; 'Is a coroner allowed to hold an inquest on a Sunday?'; or 'How is a company registered in Italy – is the procedure available in an English translation?'

Not all enquiries are presented so clearly. Some enquirers have not fully worked out what they need, so the enquiry as posed can be in general terms: 'I need information on the law relating to the carriage of goods by sea', or superficially focused but unclear: 'Where do you keep cases on discrimination heard in Europe?'

There are a number of questioning techniques which can be employed to help you (and the enquirer) gain a clearer idea of what is really wanted. Funnelling questions help the enquirer to focus in from the general to the particular: 'What aspects of the law of carriage of goods by sea interest you?'; 'Why do you need the information?'; 'Do you need it to answer a specific query or to commence study of the area of law in general?'; 'Do you need the current law or a historical description?'; 'Are you concerned with the law effective in the UK or internationally?'

Probing questions seek further details when you are not sure what the enquirer wants: 'When you say Europe, do you mean cases heard in the courts of individual countries or do you mean cases heard in the European Court of Human Rights or the European Court of Justice?'; 'What forms of discrimination do you have in mind: racial, gender, age, religious?'; 'Have you the name of a particular case in mind?'

The form of the individual question used falls into one of several categories:

- an open question, which invites the enquirer to supply further details without you specifying what additional information would be helpful ('What aspects of the law of carriage of goods by sea interest you?') – but such a question can leave too many options open;
- a closed question, which forces the enquirer to give a yes or no answer ('Have you the name of a particular case in mind?') – but it should be used only when you are certain what the options are;
- a forced choice question, which forces the enquirer to choose between alternatives ('What forms of discrimination do you have in mind: racial, gender, age, religious?') – but you have to know what the alternatives are before you pose the question.

There are other types of question that may be used in a reference interview such as:

- a leading question (which leads the enquirer in the direction of the answer you want – but this imposes your assumption on the enquirer's request);
- a hypothetical question (where you create a question about a hypothetical situation to glean insights into the information required).

These are little used in legal research work and difficult to construct. With the latter in particular, there may be difficulty interpreting the response. Questions should revolve around the five Ws:

- *who* – the kinds of people or organizations involved in the legal information sought; apart from the enquirer, identifying who needs the information sought;

- *what* – the activities those people or organizations are undertaking; establishing what the enquirer wants to do with the information;
- *when* – the time-span of information required: current, consolidated (in-force), recent, historical, original and unamended;
- *where* – the jurisdiction/s for which the information is required;
- *why* – the purpose for which the information is required.

Once you have clarified in your mind exactly the information the enquirer is seeking, it can help to rephrase the question as you now understand it and ask for confirmation before searching for the final answer. This technique may be useful where the original enquiry is garbled or has arrived as a brief e-mail or other written request, and you do not have any verbal and non-verbal clues to assist in identifying the actual information sought.

During the interview it is also important to identify four other variables:

- By when does the enquirer need the information – within the hour, tomorrow, next week?
- Is the full text of the information or only a summary or digest required?
- In what form does the enquirer want the information – an original document, photocopy, fax, e-mail?
- If external, fee-charging information services need to be used, is the enquirer prepared to pay for the information?

What to Do if You Do Not Understand the Legal Terminology

Ask the enquirer to explain what the terms mean. Consult the Oxford English Dictionary and its supplements (published by Clarendon Press). Use a law dictionary. The list is in approximate order of increasing size of publication!

For the law of England and Wales:

- *Mozley and Whiteley's Law Dictionary* (2001), 12th edn, London: Butterworths
- *A Dictionary of Law* (2013), 7th edn, Oxford: Oxford University Press
- *Osborn's Concise Law Dictionary* (2013), 12th edn, London: Sweet & Maxwell
- *Jowitt's Dictionary of English Law* (2010) and supplements, 3rd revised edn, London: Sweet & Maxwell
- *Stroud's Judicial Dictionary of Words and Phrases* (2012) and supplements, 8th edn, London: Sweet & Maxwell
- *Words and Phrases Legally Defined* (2009) and supplements, 4th edn, London: LexisNexis
- Use the index volumes to *Halsbury's Laws* (2008–), 5th edn, London: LexisNexis Butterworths.

For Scots law:

- *Bells' Dictionary and Digest of the Law of Scotland* (1890), 7th edn, Edinburgh: Bell & Bradfute
- *Glossary of Scottish and European Union Legal Terms and Latin Phrases* (2003), 2nd edn, Edinburgh: LexisNexis UK
- *Glossary of Scottish Legal Terms* (2009), 5th edn, Edinburgh: W Green & Son
- *Trayner's Latin Maxims* (1894), 4th edn, Edinburgh: W Green & Son.

For Irish law:

- Murdoch, H. (2008), *Dictionary of Irish Law*, 5th edn, Dublin: Tottel.

To gain insight into the interrelationship of legal terms use:

- Miskin, C. (1999), *A Legal Thesaurus*, 3rd edn, Hebden Bridge: Legal Information Resources.

Identifying the Right Materials

Once the query posed has been analysed and you are clear exactly what the enquirer wants, it is necessary to correctly 'classify' the type of information so that the most appropriate sources can be selected. A query on UK law may be classified into any one or a number of the following categories:

- words and phrases – where the meaning of a legal term is required, defined either by statute or through interpretation by the judges in case law;
- substantive law – the actual law embodied in legislation and the decisions of the courts as opposed to procedural law;
- procedural law – law dealing with the procedure of the courts (litigation) or with the preparation of legal documents for use in transactions outside the courts (non-litigious procedure) such as wills, mortgages, leases and so on;
- updating known law – checking that a known Act or SI is still good law and whether there have been any amendments or repeals which affect the validity of the legislation; similarly, for a case, establishing whether the judgment is still good law or has been adversely commented on in court or overruled by a later decision;
- commentary on the law – opinions and explanations of the law, whether on a particular piece of legislation or case or a subject in general;
- pre-legislative proposals – consultation papers, working papers, official reports, Bills, parliamentary debates;
- governmental administrative documents – materials such as circulars, memoranda, policy papers issued by government departments to assist

public bodies (local authorities, health services and so on) in applying the law;

- non-governmental documents – administrative or procedural materials published by such organizations as the Stock Exchange, the Bank of England, the British Standards Institution and professional bodies such as the British Medical Association;
- business information – company accounts, annual reports, directories and business news;
- information about people or personalities connected with the law, law firms or chambers.

A similar classification may be applied to EU legal queries:

- finding specific legislation or a case
- updating known law
- tracing law on a topic
- finding commentary, news and forthcoming developments in EU law.

Choosing the Right Medium

Legal and business information is available in three different formats: printed, compact disc (CD-ROM) and online (now almost entirely over the internet). Each has particular characteristics that will influence which one or combination is chosen in the search for information.

1. Printed sources: easy to handle; user-friendly; many important sources only in this format; usually possess indexes which have been compiled by experts which not only highlight all references to a topic but frequently indicate with the use of bold type where the fullest treatment of a matter is to be found in the text; no search charges; usually a clear statement of how up to date the information is; BUT out of date, slow to use and inflexible.

2. CD-ROM databases: fast; flexible; usually no running costs; sometimes offer more advanced and complex search facilities than internet equivalents; BUT not always user-friendly; often no index but keyword search can produce a large volume of results not sorted according to relevance; limited capacity; out of date and sometimes no clear indication of the date of the information. This format has been almost completely overtaken by online services.

3. Online services: may be up to date but rarely indicate clearly how up to date the information is; may be fast and flexible; BUT sometimes do not make clear what information is held; can have high search costs; sometimes not user-friendly; often no index but keyword search can produce a large volume of results not sorted according to relevance.

Some Points to Bear in Mind

Authority of information
Lawyers need to be assured that the information provided in response to a query is authoritative. Always check the authority of information – has it been compiled by an official organization? Is there an alternative and more authoritative source?

This is especially true of information gleaned from the internet. Watch out for the tilde sign (~) in the URL of a site. This sign represents the personal directory of an individual, and indicates that the information and opinions are personal and are not official. It does not necessarily mean the information is of poor quality but merely that it is not official. The tilde sign can be found occasionally within some official sites.

Similarity of paper and electronic versions
The printed and electronic versions of the same publication may not have precisely the same characteristics or content. You may need to check this.

Choosing the most appropriate electronic source
There are many different legal online databases. Each offers different content. Legal information professionals need to become masters of the skill of identifying the appropriate database to meet the particular information need. This not only applies when dealing with an enquiry but also when evaluating the purchase of a database. In those organizations where end-users are given desktop access to databases, information professionals need to ensure through training, promotional publicity and personal contact that end-users are fully aware of what each database offers and that they use expensive resources wisely.

The limitations of search engines
Search engines are one of the least useful ways of finding large quantities of relevant legal information. They are valuable only if all other internet avenues have failed. Why?

First, the internet is growing faster than search engines can index it. Most commentators estimate that no search engine covers more than about 17 per cent of the entire internet.

Second, the parts of the internet containing the most useful 'added-value' information are hidden from search engines. For example, they may be behind passwords or registration forms or search forms; on pages comprising separate frames of information from which search engines cannot collect information; or on results pages created 'on the fly' from a search query put to a database. The 'hidden web' is of special value to lawyers.

Third, some search engines take months to capture a new site, index it and add it to their database. Some search engines are programmed to collect the most popular sites only. So, search engines are better at collecting news, current affairs and leisure sites rather than technical or academic sites.

If you are going to use a search engine, in general, Google performs best.

CHOOSING THE RIGHT SOURCES

The most appropriate sources for the information required are identified below. For further description of the sources listed, see Chapter 2. To avoid unnecessary repetition, the full bibliographical reference for a publication is given only when the title is first mentioned. Remember that when searching for internet-based resources several major law portal sites provide valuable links.

For legal sites and resources in the UK and Ireland, look at:

- www.venables.co.uk/ – thousands of links of most use to the law practitioner created by computer consultant, Delia Venables.

For legal information on the internet, look at:

- Lawlinks – http://kent.ac.uk/lawlinks/ – links of most use to the academic lawyer
- Access to Law – http://www.accesstplaw.com/ – over 1,300 annotated links to free UK and commonwealth law websites, focusing especially on the needs of the practitioner.

Of course, there will be times when most law librarians will need to answer enquiries about overseas law. The three portals mentioned above have sections of links relevant to overseas law. Here is a select list of other websites:

- EISIL – http://www.eisil.org/ – Electronic Information System for International Law, a selective listing of authoritative websites for primary and secondary international law materials, arranged under broad subject headings.
- Eagle-i – ials.sas.ac.uk/eagle-i.htm – links to law websites in over 200 jurisdictions and major governmental and international organizations. Now incorporates the highly regarded Intute: Law service, which is a searchable database of over 3,500 quality law websites selected from across the world, each site described in detail. Unfortunately, updating this part of the Eagle-i service ceased in July 2011.

- Worldlii – www.worldlii.org/ – free, independent global collection of over 270 databases of primary law materials for more than 40 jurisdictions in over 20 countries.
- Foreign Law Guide (FLAG) – http://193.62.18.232/dbtw-wpd/textbase/collsearch.htm – a web inventory of the collections of foreign, comparative and international law held in UK universities, the British Library, the Inns of Court and the Public Record Office, Kew. Collections of printed versions of law for over 200 countries and over 60 international organizations are described.

It is important to remember that there are still some countries of the world which have very few law resources freely available on the internet. This is especially true for law made in the pre-internet era or made in developing countries.

Words and Phrases in Statutes

Search for the particular statute and section in which the words or phrases occur, using any of the following printed or online sources.

Printed sources
For England and Wales:

- *Current Law Legislation Citator*, annual, London, Sweet & Maxwell; and latest updates in *Current Law Statutes Binder*, looseleaf, London: Sweet & Maxwell
- *Halsbury's Laws* and *Cumulative Supplement and Noter-Up* (2008), 5th edn, London: LexisNexis Butterworths
- *Words & Phrases Legally Defined* (2009) and supplements, 4th edn, London: LexisNexis
- *Stroud's Judicial Dictionary* (2012), 8th edn, London: Sweet & Maxwell
- *Halsbury's Laws*, near back of final index volume
- The Law Reports, irregular, London: Incorporated Council of Law Reporting for England and Wales, consolidated and current indexes.

Update these using *Current Law Monthly Digest* (London: Sweet & Maxwell), index of words and phrases.

For Ireland:

- Murdoch's *Dictionary of Irish Law* (2008), 5th edn, Dublin: Tottel.

Online sources
- Westlaw UK
- LexisLibrary
- *Westlaw.ie*

Words and Phrases in Cases

Search under the particular word or phrase using any of the following sources.

Printed sources
For England and Wales:

- *Words and Phrases Legally Defined* and supplements
- *Stroud's Judicial Dictionary* and supplements
- *Halsbury's Laws*, near back of final index volume
- *The Law Reports*, consolidated and current indexes.

Update all of these using *Current Law Monthly Digest* index of words and phrases.

For Scotland:

- *Scottish Contemporary Judicial Dictionary of Words and Phrases* (1995), Edinburgh: W. Green & Son
- *A Dictionary of Words and Phrases Judicially Defined and Commented on by the Scottish Supreme Courts* (1946), Edinburgh: W. Green & Son
- *Faculty Digest* and supplements (1868 onwards), Edinburgh: W. Green & Son
- *Scots Digest* (up to 1947)
- *Scottish Judicial Dictionary* (1946).

For Northern Ireland:

- Entries relating to Northern Ireland will be found in Stroud, *Words and Phrases*, *Current Law Monthly Digest* and *Current Law Yearbook*.

For Ireland:

- *The Irish Digests* 1894 to 1999
- Murdoch's *Dictionary of Irish Law* (2008), 5th edn, Dublin: Tottel.

Online sources
For England and Wales:

Westlaw UK offers a facility to search for definitions of words appearing in legislation, but, to research definitions determined by the courts in case law, the use of an electronic database is not recommended. It will be very difficult to limit the results to places where a specific word or phrase is defined rather than merely mentioned in passing.

Substantive Law

Where the subject matter is recognizable
Use practitioner textbooks, including their supplements, and student textbooks to glean references to legislation and case law. Update textbook references found using online sources (see below).

Where the subject matter is not recognizable
For England and Wales:

Use *Halsbury's Laws* and update through its *Cumulative Supplement and Noter-Up*. Follow through by updating this information using electronic sources (see below). Note that it can be easier to use the printed version of *Halsbury's Laws* for this type of query. Whilst the electronic version does reproduce the index, the inexperienced user may find the ability to browse more easily in the print version an advantage.

For Scotland:

- *Laws of Scotland* (also referred to as the *Stair Memorial Encyclopedia*). An electronic version is available through LexisLibrary.

For Ireland, there is no true encyclopaedia of Irish law but the following may help:

- Byrne, Raymond, et al. (2009), *The Irish Legal System* 5th edn, Haywards Heath: Bloomsbury Professional
- Ussher, P. and B.J. O'Connor (eds) (1992), *Doing Business in Ireland*, looseleaf, New York: Matthew Bender.

Legislation

Printed sources – official and semi-official
For England and Wales:

All these titles reproduce the legislation in the form originally passed and do not include subsequent amendments or notes on repeals or revocations:

- Queen's Printer's copies (QPC) – loose issues of legislation
- Public General Acts and General Synod Measures, annual, The Stationery Office – bound volumes of QPC
- Law Reports Statutes, irregular, The Incorporated Council of Law Reporting for England and Wales
- Statutory Instruments, The Stationery Office.

For Scotland:

- Acts of the Scottish Parliament, The Stationery Office
- Scottish Statutory Instruments, The Stationery Office.

For Northern Ireland:

- Northern Ireland Statutes, Belfast: HMSO
- Statutes Revised, Northern Ireland, Belfast: HMSO
- Northern Ireland Statutory Rules and Orders, Belfast: HMSO.

For Ireland:

- Acts of Oireachtas 1922–, Dublin: Stationery Office
- Statutory Rules and Orders 1922 to 1947, Dublin: Stationery Office
- Statutory Instruments 1948–2011, Dublin: Stationery Office.

Printed sources – unofficial
For England and Wales:

All of the following titles provide text in its consolidated version (that is, in force as at the present time) but only if information in the main volume is updated using appropriate supplements:

- *Halsbury's Statutes of England* (1985), 4th edn, London: LexisNexis
- *Halsbury's Statutory Instruments* (1986), 2nd edn, London: LexisNexis
- *Current Law Statutes Annotated*, London: Sweet & Maxwell.

For Scotland:

- *Current Law Statutes Annotated*, London: Sweet & Maxwell
- *Parliament House Book*, looseleaf, Edinburgh: W. Green & Son.

For Ireland:

- *Irish Current Law Statutes Annotated*, looseleaf (1984), Dublin: Round Hall Sweet & Maxwell.

Online sources – subscriber databases
- LexisLibrary – consolidated version (that is, in force at the present time) – can take several weeks for complex, amending legislation to be incorporated. It covers legislation made at Westminster applying to the United Kingdom as a whole, England and Wales together and Wales only; also covers Measures of the National Assembly for Wales (NAW), but not Statutory Instruments

made by the NAW. Also includes Public and General Acts and Scottish Statutory Instruments (SSI) made by the Scottish Parliament at Holyrood. Does not include legislation made by the Northern Ireland Assembly.

- Westlaw UK – consolidated version (that is, in force at the present time) – coverage similar to LexisLibrary but does include SIs made by the NAW.
- Lawtel – original version only. Contains digests of UK statutes from 1984 onwards with links to the full text of legislation from 1987 onwards on the free, Legislation.gov.uk website, see below. Also includes Measures of the NAW, SIs made by the NAW and Acts of the Scottish Parliament and Scottish Statutory Instruments.
- *Justis UK Statutes* – original version only, from 1267 onwards but with cross-references between amended and amending legislation. Does not include legislation made by the NAW or the Northern Ireland Assembly, but includes Acts of the Scottish Parliament and SSIs.
- *Westlaw.ie* – original Acts from 1984 to date with annotations and commentary. Commentary up to date to the date of the publication of the Act only.

Online sources – free
- Legislation.gov.uk – www.legislation.gov.uk – searchable, authoritative database of revised legislation dating from 1987 onwards, with most pre-1987 material in original form only. Links on the home page to substantial responses to FAQs set out the content and limitations in revision of legislation held on the site.
- National Assembly for Wales – http://new.wales.gov.uk/legislation/?lang=eng – original version only, Assembly Measures, Legislative Competence Orders and SIs. Note that under additional powers approved in the referendum of 2011 the NAW will be able to make Assembly Bills and Acts, and this website is the most authoritative source for NAW legislation. A Welsh language version of all the NAW web pages is available.
- Scottish Acts and Scottish Statutory Instruments made at Holyrood by the Scottish Parliament – held on Legislation.gov.uk, above.
- Northern Ireland Statutes (made at Westminster) and Acts of the Northern Ireland Assembly – held on Legislation.gov.uk, above.
- BAILII – www.bailii.org – reproduces material obtained from the same source as Legislation.gov.uk, above, but in unconsolidated, original form only.
- Ireland:
    - http://www.irishstatutebook.ie/ – Statutes 1922–2011, Statutory Instruments 1922–2011, Legislation Directory (tracking amendments to Statutes, 1922–November 2010)
    - www.oireachtas.ie – Bills, Oireachtas Debates
    - www.bailii.org – Acts 1922–2011, Statutory Instruments, 1922–2011
    - www.irlii.org – Acts 1999–2011, Statutory Instruments, 2002–08.

Case Law

Which report of a case do I cite? The courts have determined an order of priority for the citation of reports of cases reported in different law reports. Practice Statement (Supreme Court: Judgments) [1998] 1 W.L.R. 825, at paragraph 8 states that:

> *If a case is reported in the official Law Reports published by the Incorporated Council of Law Reporting for England and Wales, that report should be cited. These are the most authoritative reports; they contain a summary of argument; and they are the most readily available. If a case is not (or not yet) reported in the official Law Reports, but is reported in the Weekly Law Reports or the All England Law Reports, that report should be cited. If a case is not reported in any of these series of law reports, a report in any of the authoritative specialist series of reports may be cited.*

So, when providing a report of a case to an enquirer it would be wise to follow this order of priority when selecting a particular report of the judgment. The Statement later notes that occasions arise where one report is fuller than another or when there are discrepancies between reports. On such occasions the practice outlined need not be followed. 'It is always helpful if alternative references are given'. This is sound advice when providing an enquirer with references: give as full a list of alternatives as possible. Ideally the list of alternative reports of a case should be given in the order of priority set out in the Practice Statement.

The Court of Appeal has made two similar Practice Directions – Practice Direction (Court of Appeal: Citation of Authority) [1995] 1 W.L.R. 1096 – www.hmcourts-service.gov.uk/cms/797.htm and Practice Direction (Judgments: Form and Citation) [2001] 1 W.L.R. 194.

In Scotland the Court of Session has issued Practice Note (No. 5 of 2004): Form of Opinions and Neutral Citation, 16 November 2004, which says that where a case has been reported in the series Session Cases it must be cited from that source. Other series of reports may only be used when a case is not reported in Session Cases. The High Court of Justiciary has issued Practice Note (No. 2 of 2004) which is on similar lines and requires cases reported in Justiciary Cases to be cited from that source.

No Directions on this point appear to have been issued by the courts in Northern Ireland.

How do I cite reports of cases published on the internet and also in printed reports? In 2001, following the increased publication of cases on the internet prior to publication in printed law reports, the courts gave directions on how such cases should be cited: the rules on neutral citation of judgments. As far as answering law enquiries is concerned, it is important to note that in Practice Direction (Judgments: Form and Citation) [2001] 1 W.L.R. 194 – www.hmcourts-service. gov.uk/cms/485.htm – at paragraph 2.3 it states that:

> *When the judgment is reported, the neutral citation will appear in front of the familiar citation from the law reports service. Thus:* Smith v Jones *[2001] EWCA Civ 10, [2001] Q.B. 124, [2001] 2 All E.R. 364 etc.*

So, when citing a list of alternative reports of a case that has been given a neutral citation, ensure the list commences with the neutral citation.

In Scotland both the Court of Session and the High Court of Justiciary have made Practice Notes (P.N. (No. 5 of 2004) and P.N.(No. 2 of 2004) respectively) relating to neutral citation in the Scottish courts.

No Directions on this point appear to have been issued by the courts in Northern Ireland.

Printed sources
See Chapter 2 by Guy Holborn.

Online sources
Take care that you distinguish between reported and unreported judgments. Reported cases are taken from published law reports. Transcripts and unreported cases do not have any of the value-added features provided by law report publishers. An unreported case lacks (amongst other features): catchwords, a headnote, lists of cases referred to and cross-references to encyclopaedias. Where possible, lawyers generally prefer to have a reported version of a case, since it will possess a headnote which summarizes the issues for them.

Is there one electronic database that contains all the cases I shall need? Each online source contains electronic versions of reported cases drawn from either the particular publications the database company owns or for which it has been able to obtain licences to include in the database. No single database will therefore satisfy all users' needs. Further, the content of each electronic database is subject to frequent and sometimes unannounced change, when the database provider fails to successfully retain the licence to include a particular title in its contents.

Subscriber databases – full text
These usually include sophisticated search features. A selection of the major providers includes:

- LexisLibrary – the full text of cases published by Butterworths and a few other publishers with whom Butterworths has a licence agreement. This database probably contains the most extensive collection of reported and unreported cases, but it does not include the text of cases appearing in the *Weekly Law Reports* or law reports published under the Lloyd's or Jordan's imprints. There are links from each case to a citator providing information on whether the case is still good law and to other materials such as the text of statutes cited. But a disadvantage is that there is no direct link from the text of the case to a list of journal articles on the decision.
- LexisLibrary includes the Irish Reports from 1950 and unreported decisions from 1985. Whether access to Irish law is available will depend on the terms of your organization's contract with LexisLibrary.
- Westlaw UK – the full text of cases published by Sweet & Maxwell and a few other publishers with whom Sweet & Maxwell has a licence agreement. The collection of reported and unreported cases is substantial but does not include the full text of cases appearing in the *All England Law Reports*, nor cases published under the Lloyd's or Jordan's imprints. There are links from each case to a citator providing information on whether the case is still good law and to other materials such as the text of statutes cited and, advantageously, lists of journal articles on the decision. Limited access to Irish law is available from *Westlaw.ie*.
- Justis – contains databases of the major law report series reproduced on screen exactly as in the paper versions. The Irish Reports and the Irish Digests from 1919 to date are also available.

For Ireland:

- *Firstlaw.ie* – provides the full text of all cases circulated by the courts since 1999 together with a headnote and abstract.
- *Westlaw.ie* – provides the full text of the Irish law reports monthly, from 1976 to date, and the Employment Law Reports, from 1990 to date, together with unreported judgments from 2002.

Regardless of jurisdiction, various internet and CD products each cover the contents of a single series of law reports only.

Subscriber databases – digests and indexes
- Lawtel – digest with access to a full text version of transcript. For Scotland, it covers only those cases reported in the 'English' series of law reports.
- *JustCite* – index of citations to law report series from all publishing houses.
- *Justis.com – Irish Digests* from 1919 to 1999.
- *Westlaw.ie* – case digests taken from both *Irish Current Law Monthly Digest*, 1995 onwards, and all cases from the Superior Courts. It also contains tables of cases giving cumulative listings of all cases digested,

plus details of all authorities cited, both reported and unreported, and *Irish Law Times Digests*, 1983 onwards.

Subscriber databases for current legal information:

- David Swarbrick's *Lawindexpro* – www.swarb.co.uk/index.php?option=com_wrapper&view=wrapper&Itemid=13 – index to over 200,000 cases dating from January 1992 onwards, with well over 55,000 as case summaries. Links to the full text of over 170,000 decisions.

For Ireland:

- Justis (formerly *Firstlaw.ie*) – provides full text of all judgments circulated by the Courts service with a headnote to all acts and statutory instruments from 1999, in addition to items from the daily newspapers. Provides subscribers with updates twice a week containing all material processed in the previous three days.
- *Westlaw.ie – Irish Current Law Monthly Digest* provides digests of all cases from the Superior Courts. It also contains tables of cases giving cumulative listings of all cases digested, plus details of all authorities cited, both reported and unreported, together with abstracts of all statutory material, journal articles and recent books. The service also provides a current awareness service.

Free databases – official and full text.
Search features can be limited. Here is a selection:

- Supreme Court – www.supremecourt.gov.uk/decided-cases/index.shtml
- Transcripts of all judgments delivered from 1 October 2009 onwards. There is a link on this page to the archive of House of Lords judgments from 14 November 1996 to 30 July 2009.
- Scottish Courts – http://www.scotcourts.gov.uk/opinionsApp/index.asp?txt=False.

Free databases – unofficial and full text

- BAILII – www.bailii.org/ – free law portal to transcripts of cases from 1996 onwards, and a selection of earlier landmark decisions selected by university law lecturers – includes England, Wales, Scotland, Northern Ireland and Ireland decisions.
- www.irlii.org – complementary site to BAILII containing the most recent
- information prior to its loading on the BAILII site. The site covers all judgments, statutory instruments and acts.

Free databases – digests and indexes

- ICLR Case Search – http://cases.iclr.co.uk/Subscr/Search.aspx – searchable database of over 75,000 decisions in summary form reported by the Incorporated Council of Law Reporting since 1865.

Procedural Law

Criminal procedure
For England and Wales:

- Anthony and Berryman, *Magistrates' Court Guide*, annual, London: Butterworths
- Archbold, *Criminal Pleading, Evidence and Practice*, biennial, London: Sweet & Maxwell – also available online via Westlaw UK
- *Blackstone's Criminal Practice*, annual, Oxford: Oxford University Press – also available electronically on the OUP website and LexisLibrary.

For Scotland:

- Renton and Brown, *Criminal Procedure according to the Law of Scotland* (1996), 6th edn, looseleaf, Edinburgh: W. Green & Son.

For Northern Ireland:

- *Magistrates' Courts Rules (Northern Ireland) 1984*, Belfast: The Stationery Office, a single volume updated by amendments available only via the web at www.courtsni.gov.uk/en-GB/Publications/Legislation/.

For Ireland:

- O'Malley, Thomas (2009), *The Criminal Process*, Dublin: Round Hall
- Walsh, *Criminal Procedure* (2002), Dublin: Round Hall
- Woods, James V., *District Court Practice and Procedure in Criminal Proceedings*, 3rd ed., Limerick: Woods.

Civil procedure
For England and Wales:

- *Atkin's Encyclopedia of Court Forms in Civil Procedure* (1961), 2nd edn, London: Butterworths, including looseleaf noter-up – also available online via LexisLibrary
- *Bullen & Leake & Jacob's Precedents of Pleadings* (2007), 16th edn, London: Sweet & Maxwell – also available online via Westlaw UK
- *Butterworths Civil Court Precedents* (1991–) looseleaf, London: LexisNexis
- *Butterworths Costs Service* (1996–) looseleaf, London: LexisNexis
- *Civil Court Practice* ('The Green Book'), annual, London: LexisNexis, including supplements – also available online via LexisLibrary
- *Civil Procedure* ('The White Book'), annual, London: Sweet & Maxwell, including supplements – also available online via Westlaw UK

- *The Court Service* (forms and guides) free online service at http://hmctscourtfinder.justice.gov.uk/HMCTS/FormFinder.do%3bjsessionid=BE05E9EDE97BA78A999E555991A3C783
- Fordham, *Judicial Review Handbook* (2012), 6th edn, Oxford: Hart Publishing
- Lawtel *Civil Procedure* – online service
- *Practical Civil Court Precedents* (1999-) looseleaf, London: Sweet & Maxwell
- *Stone's Justices' Manual*, annual, London: LexisNexis – also available as CD
- Westlaw UK *Civil Procedure* – online subscription service.

For Scotland:

- *Green's Litigation Styles* (1994–) looseleaf, Edinburgh: W. Green & Son – also available as CD.

For Northern Ireland:

- *Rules of the Supreme Court (Northern Ireland) 1980*, Belfast: The Stationery Office, single volume updated by amendments available only via the web at www.courtsni.gov.uk/en-GB/Publications/Legislation
- Valentine, B.J.A.C. and Barry J.A.C. have compiled a series of useful texts all published by SLS Legal Publications (NI): *Civil Proceedings: the County Court* (1999), *Civil Proceedings: the Supreme Court* (1997) and *Supplement to Civil Proceedings: the Supreme Court* (2000).

For Ireland:

- Delany and McGrath, *Civil Procedure in the Superior Courts* (2012), 3rd edn, Dublin: Round Hall
- Dowling, Karl, *Civil Procedure in the Circuit Court* (2008), Dublin: Round Hall
- Dowling, Karl, *Civil Procedure in the District Court* (2009), Dublin: Round Hall
- O'Floinn, B., *Practice and Procedure in the Superior Courts* (2008), 2nd edn, Dublin: Tottel
- Deale, J., *Circuit Court Practice and Procedure* (1994), 2nd edn, Dublin: Fitzbaggot Publications
- Woods, James V., *District Court Practice and Procedure in Civil, Licensing and Family Law Proceedings* (1997), Limerick: Woods.

Non-litigious situations
For England and Wales:

- *Encyclopedia of Forms and Precedents* (1985), 5th edn, London: Butterworths. Includes looseleaf noter-up – also available online via LexisLibrary

- *EveryForm*, available on CD from LexisNexis Butterworths as a subscription service.

For Scotland:

- *Greens Practice Styles* (1995–) looseleaf, Edinburgh: W. Green & Son, also available as CD.

Updating Known Legislation: Acts

Printed sources
All the under mentioned cover England and Wales, and some include Scots legislation. Use:

Either

Current Law Legislation Citator updating through *Current Law Statutes Service File Citator* and *Current Law* monthly parts, covering more recent changes via one of: LexisLibrary, Westlaw UK and finally sweeping up the most recent developments using Lawtel

Or

Halsbury's Statutes, with its Cumulative Supplement and Noter-Up, covering more recent changes via one of: LexisLibrary, Westlaw UK and finally sweeping up the most recent developments using Lawtel.

For Ireland:

- Irish Current Law Statutes Annotated 1994.

Online sources
- Westlaw UK
- Lawtel
- *Westlaw.ie.*

Updating Known Legislation: SIs

Printed sources
For England and Wales:

- *Halsbury's Statutory Instruments*, updating through the monthly update in Service Binder 1, then sweep up latest developments using LexisLibrary and finally Lawtel

- *Current Law Legislation Citator*, London: Sweet & Maxwell.

For Scotland:

- Current Law Legislation Citator, London: Sweet & Maxwell.

For Ireland:

- Irish Current Law Statutes Annotated.

Online sources
- Westlaw UK
- Lawtel
- *Westlaw.ie*

Case Law

Printed sources
For England and Wales, and Scotland:

- *Current Law Case Citator*, following through using *Current Law* monthly parts and sweeping up latest developments using Lawtel.

For Ireland:

- *Irish Current Law* – monthly, yearbook and parts and sweeping up latest developments using *Westlaw*.ie.

Online sources
- LexisLibrary
- Westlaw UK

Commentary on the Law

Journals and textbooks
Use your organization's library catalogue to trace textbooks. For current awareness of new commentary on the law in England and Wales use *Current Law Monthly Digest* or *Halsbury's Laws Monthly Review*. For Scotland use *Current Law Monthly Digest*. For Ireland use *Irish Current Law Monthly Digest*.

Online sources
- Westlaw UK – includes probably the most comprehensive journal indexing service (*Legal Journals Index*) of all online products, commencing in 1986 and now offering summaries from over 600 English language law journals.

If commentary on a particular statute or case is required, search for that item: when found, use the link at the left side of the screen to journal articles. If a more general search is required use the Journals library. Westlaw UK also has a large number of UK law journals in electronic format which can be searched.

- *Legal Journals Index* (which is embedded within the Journals library of Westlaw UK) is available through *Current Legal Information* (CLI), another Sweet & Maxwell product. The service also indexes Irish journals.
- The *Bulletin of Northern Ireland Law* (1981–), Belfast: SLS Legal Publications (NI) fulfills the role of *Current Law* in Northern Ireland.
- LexisLibrary – includes a substantial newspaper database and a wide range of UK law journals in electronic format.
- *JustCite* – a subscriber-only service indexing over 130 law and law-related journals published within and outside the UK, carrying English language articles. The majority of indexing commences from 2000 onwards.
- Lawtel's Articles Index contains summaries of articles from more than 60 journals and starts in the late 1990s.

Pre-Legislative Proposals

Printed sources
See Chapter 2 by Guy Holborn.

Online sources
- Parliament – www.parliament.uk/ – full text of materials for Westminster Parliament including Bills, Weekly Information Bulletin and Hansard Debates from 1989 onwards.
- Directgov – www.directgov.uk/ – links to central and local government departments, agencies and services and some non-governmental organizations.
- Scottish Parliament – www.scottish.parliament.uk/
- Welsh Assembly – www.new.wales.gov.uk/
- Northern Ireland Assembly – www.niassembly.gov.uk/.

Governmental Administrative Documents

Printed sources
See Chapter 2 by Guy Holborn.

Online sources
- Directgov – www.direct.gov.uk/. Links to central and local government departments, agencies and services and some non-governmental organizations.

- UK official publications on the internet – www.official-documents.co.uk/. Links to the full text of UK official documents from May 2005 onwards which are on the internet and a selection back to 1951.
- Welsh Assembly Government – //wales.gov.uk/?skip=1&lang=en (English language) or http://wales.gov.uk/?skip=1&lang=cy (Welsh language)
- Scottish Government – //home.scotland.gov.uk/home
- Ireland – www. gov.ie/.

Non-Governmental Documents

Trace the website of the relevant organization using either the UK law portals mentioned earlier, or by running a search in Google – www.google.co.uk/.

Business Information

Company accounts – subscriber-only databases
- *FAME* – financial information for public and private British companies;
- *Thomson Research* – critical company information and analysts' research reports for international and US companies;
- *Hoover's Online* – financial data on approximately 4,000 international public and private companies;
- *Datastream* – financial statistical database of company accounts and share price information for UK quoted and overseas companies;
- *Bankscope* – financial and ownership information on 9,500 banks worldwide;
- *Companies House Direct* – //direct.companies.gov.uk/;
- *Perfect Filings* – database of over 5 million company filings;
- *Dun & Bradstreet* – well-known company analysts providing business and credit information on UK and international companies;
- *Companies Registration Office* www.cro.ie.

Company annual reports
- Try the company's own website as many have their reports online;
- Companies House – www.companies-house.gov.uk/ – free basic information;
- For subscribers only, *Companies House Direct* provides greater detail from filed reports;
- CAROL – www.carol.co.uk/ (*Company Annual Reports On-Line*) Free access to thousands of annual reports;
- Hemscott – www.hemscott.co.uk/ – key company financial information and details of shareholders – some services free, others for a fee;
- Thomson Research (see above).

Company directories
- *Kompass Register* – www.kompass.com/ – details of 1.5 million UK companies. Basic information free. Registration required to access detailed

data. Also available in printed form (East Grinstead: Kompass, Reed Business Information).

- *Waterlow Stock Exchange Yearbook* (incorporating Crawford's Directory of City Connections) – subscriber-only details of companies and securities listed on the London and Dublin stock exchanges. Also available in printed form, annual, London: Waterlow Professional Publishing.
- The Biz – www.thebiz.co.uk/ – free directory of websites of UK companies.

Business news – selected online sources
- Nexis UK – subscriber only database covering UK (full text of national and local newspapers), US, European and Asian news including Global News Wire;
- FT.com – www.ft.com/home/uk/ – free access to search for current news and to access some articles after which payment is required to read further articles and access archives;
- Factiva.com – www.factiva.com/ – subscriber only service incorporating materials from 25,000+ leading news and business publications;
- Research Index – www.researchindex.co.uk/.

Information about People or Personalities Connected with the Law, Law Firms and Chambers

Printed sources
For England and Wales:

- *Law Society's Directory of Solicitors and Barristers*, annual, London: Law Society
- *Bar Directory*, annual, London: Sweet & Maxwell
- *Butterworth's Law Directory*, annual, London: LexisNexis
- *Chambers UK. Client's Guide to the Legal Profession*, annual, Chambers & Partners
- *Who's Who*, annual, London: A & C Black
- *Havers' Companion to the Bar*, annual, London: Havers' Directories Ltd
- *Legal 500 UK: The Client's Guide to UK Law Firms*, annual, London: Legalease
- *Biographical Dictionary of the Common Law* (1984), London: Butterworths – for historical biography
- *Dictionary of National Biography*, Oxford: Oxford University Press.

For Scotland:

- *Scottish Law Directory* – usually referred to as 'The White Book', annual, Edinburgh: LexisNexis UK.

For Ireland:

- *The Law Directory*, annual, Dublin: Law Society of Ireland.

Online sources
Use the law portal www.venables.co.uk/ to trace individual websites of law firms and chambers. Directory websites include:

For England and Wales:

- Bar Directory – www.legalhub.co.uk/legalhub/app/appinit
- Find a Solicitor – www.lawsociety.org.uk/choosingandusing/findasolicitor. law
- Lexis Nexis Lawyer Locator – www.lawyerlocator.co.uk.

For Scotland:

- Law Society of Scotland – www.lawscot.org.uk/.

For Ireland:

- Law Society of Ireland – www.lawsociety.ie
- Bar Council – www.lawlibrary.ie – searchable database of all practicing barristers.

EU Law: Finding Specific Legislation or a Case in Full Text

Printed official sources
- *Official Journal of the European Communities*, Luxembourg: Office for Official Publications of the EC
- *Official Reports of Cases before the Court* – better known as European Court Reports (ECR), Luxembourg: Court of Justice of the European Communities.

Printed unofficial sources
- All England Law Reports: European Cases, London: Butterworths
- Common Market Law Reports, London: Common Market Law Reports Ltd
- European Community Cases, London: Sweet & Maxwell
- European Union Law Reporter, London: Sweet & Maxwell.

Online official sources
- Official Journal of the European Union – http://eur-lex.europa.eu/JOIndex. do?ihmlang=en
- Court of Justice of the European Communities – http://curia.europa.eu/ jurisp/cgi-bin/form.pl?lang=en.

Online unofficial sources
These sources usually provide added value information in the form of details of national legislation implementing EU obligations and for case law, details of journal articles and commentary on the decision.

- *Eurolaw*
- Justis-CELEX
- Lawtel EU
- LexisLibrary
- Westlaw UK

EU: Updating Known Law

Printed unofficial sources
- *European Current Law*, monthly, London: Sweet & Maxwell
- *Current Law Monthly Digest*, London: Sweet & Maxwell.

Online official sources
- *Eur-Lex*

Online unofficial sources
These sources usually provide added value information in the form of details of national legislation implementing EU obligations and for case law, details of journal articles and commentary on the decision.

- *Eurolaw*
- Justis-CELEX
- Lawtel *EU*
- LexisLibrary
- Westlaw UK

EU: Tracing Law on a Topic

Printed sources
- *Halsbury's Laws*
- *Encyclopedia of European Community Law*, looseleaf, London: Sweet & Maxwell.

Online official sources
- *Eur-lex*

Online unofficial sources
These sources usually provide added value information in the form of details of national legislation implementing EU obligations and for case law, details of journal articles and commentary on the decision.

- *Eurolaw*
- Justis-CELEX
- LexisLibrary
- Westlaw UK

Finding Commentary, News and Forthcoming Developments in EU Law

Printed official sources
- *Bulletin of the European Union*, monthly, Luxembourg: Office for Official Publications of the EC.

Printed unofficial sources
- *European Current Law*
- *Current Law*
- *European Law Review*, London: Sweet & Maxwell.

Online sources
- *European Sources Online*, formerly *Know Europe and European Access*
- Lawtel *EU*
- Lawtel *UK*, LexisLibrary and Westlaw UK include article or journal libraries with summaries and, in some cases, the full text of articles on EU law.

Still stumped?
Look for outside help. Use electronic discussion lists such as:

- Lis-law – www.jiscmail.ac.uk/lists/lis-law.html
- BIALL Mailing List (open to BIALL members only) – mailtalk.ac.uk/biall. htm.

Use other 'external sources':

- If your firm is a member of the Law Society contact The Law Society Library in Chancery Lane, London, or your local Law Society library (the 'BIALL Directory' – *Directory of British and Irish Law Libraries* (2006), 8th edn, BIALL – has details).
- Barristers' chambers may be able to obtain help from the Inns of Court Libraries (Gray's Inn, Inner Temple, Lincoln's Inn, Middle Temple) in London (details in the BIALL Directory).
- In Scotland, the Signet Library – www.thewssociety.co.uk/index. asp?cat=Library/ – offers a range of document supply and research services to members of the WS Society, as does the Royal Faculty of Procurators in Glasgow Library – www.rfpg.org/library.html – to its members, and more

limited services are available from the Society of Advocates in Aberdeen Library – www.socofadvocates.com/resources.php. For advocates, the Advocates Library in Edinburgh – www.advocates.org.uk/library/index. html – provides services to members of the Scottish Bar.

- In Northern Ireland, the Law Society of Northern Ireland Information Service – www.lawsoc-ni.org/lib.htm – provides services to its members and the Bar Library, Belfast – www.barlibrary.com – services to members of the Northern Ireland Bar.
- In Ireland, the Law Society of Ireland Library – www.lawsociety.ie provides services to its members (solicitors) and trainee solicitors. The Bar Council of Ireland Law Library – www.lawlibrary.ie – provides services to the Irish Bar.
- Your local university library may be able to offer assistance but check the BIALL Directory for any conditions and fees payable.
- Use the BIALL Directory and Members Information Pack to trace other libraries or organizations that may be able to help – for example, regional groups such as the City Legal Information Group (CLIG) covering London.

REPORTING BACK

- Always keep the enquirer informed of difficulties so that you can both be thinking of alternative strategies.
- Offer a compromise answer, perhaps less relevant or less up to date.
- Finally, check that the information found does match the request made.
- Do not supply all the information traced but select the best and most relevant.
- Make sure you provide a citation for every piece of information and indicate where it might differ from the original.
- Remain within copyright and licensing restrictions – this applies particularly when photocopying material for commercial purposes which is controlled by the terms of licences and a voucher payment scheme run by the Copyright Licensing Agency.

ACKNOWLEDGEMENTS

Parts of this chapter have been inspired by or adapted from the following:

Clinch, Peter (2000), *Legal Information: What it is and where to find it*, 2nd edn, London: ASLIB.

Clinch, Peter (2013), *Legal Research: A Practitioner's Handbook*, 2nd edn, London: Wildy, Simmonds & Hill.

The City Law School (2012), *Opinion Writing and Case Preparation*, 2nd edn, Oxford: Oxford University Press.

Ormrod Report (1971), *Report of the Committee on Legal Education*, Cmnd 4595, London: HMSO.

Owen, Tim (2000), *Success at the Enquiry Desk*, 3rd rev. edn, London: LA Publishing.

My thanks also to Mary Gaynor of the Law Society of Ireland for kindly checking and updating the Irish references.

NOTE

1   http://www.ukcle.ac.uk/resources/teaching-and-learning-strategies/tlr/

CHAPTER 4

LEGAL TECHNOLOGIES

CONTRIBUTORS:
DEAN MASON
SALLY ROBERTS
MANDY WEBSTER

CURRENT AWARENESS SYSTEMS

DEAN MASON

INTRODUCTION

A key challenge of any law library and information service is enabling users to keep up to date with the shifting landscape of rules and regulations and, at the same time, to be commercially aware. 'Current awareness' is the term that is used to describe services that meet this information need and it is often the law library that is responsible for its provision. The service can take many forms, but the three models commonly employed by information professionals, and often in combination, are:

- manually filtering, selecting and publishing relevant information in a specific format for their users;
- using their searching skills to automate alerts through various services, which are accessible by users in a specific format; or
- adopting a 'self-service' approach by providing users with the relevant links and instructions for setting up the services.

The current awareness service (CAS) is far from being a new concept and was defined by Kemp in 1979 as 'a system or publication for reviewing newly available documents, selecting items relevant to the needs of an individual or group, and recording them so that notifications may be sent to those individuals or groups to whose needs they are related'. This definition touches on some of the fundamental elements of a CAS: currency, relevance and the information needs of the user or group receiving the service. The other elements to add to this definition are the sources, format and method of delivery, as well as the cost (versus benefit) of providing the CAS (Fourie 1999).

Law libraries have a range of online tools at their disposal, based on the above principles, which they can use to provide a CAS. The aim of this chapter is to provide an overview of these key tools and their characteristics. This information is intended to inform the decisions of those who are considering creating, rationalising or maintaining a CAS to meet the information needs of their users. While it is not possible to provide solutions to those who fall into these categories, as every institution has its own specific needs, guidance will be provided on areas to consider when looking for a solution. This chapter is written from experience of operating a CAS in a commercial law firm context, but will equally apply to other legal sectors.

FINDING A SOLUTION

The motivation for information professionals to consider the effectiveness of the CAS that is operating in their organizations can be fuelled by many different concerns. Examples include information overload or the underperformance of the CAS, which can become apparent through user feedback or analysis of usage statistics, or the need to rationalize the service due to budget and staffing changes. There could just be the need to create a new service from scratch. A more reliable framework for deciding whether a CAS needs attention, or as a guide to creating a service, is to consider the following reasoning by Fourie (1999) on what a CAS should deliver:

- [The] right information, to the
- Right user, at the
- Right time, in the
- Right format, covering the
- Right sources, at the
- Right cost, and with the right amount of effort to keep users up to date.

The information professional should have a good idea of whether to carry out a more formal information needs assessment by using the above framework, which if successful should confirm whether the needs of users are being met and the CAS that is required to meet these needs. It is outside the scope of this chapter to discuss the assessment of information needs in detail, but a good work to assist is *Assessing Information Needs in the Age of the Digital Consumer* by David Nicholas (2009). As an overview, however, the above framework is a good place to start to help decide what information is required in order to assess the service and therefore the questions to ask. In terms of collecting the information, it is a good idea to use a variety of methods – such as surveys, interviews and focus groups – as each could yield different but useful information (Nicholas 2000), the result of which can be combined to get a more rounded understanding of users' requirements. An assessment will also be a useful benchmark to allow you to carry out a later study to see how effective a solution has been and if any further changes are required.

The culture and structure of your organization will also have an impact on your CAS. On the topic of current awareness, Fahy (2008) notes that 'the cultural awareness of the librarian is integral to success'. A successful needs assessment should give you details of the information habits of users and groups, but not necessarily an understanding of the broader structure of your organization. It will be useful to know the practices or services your organization covers and – more relevant to law firms – the sector, client and project teams (McKenzie 2008). McKenzie notes that these teams can be difficult to define as there can be cross-over, but it is well worth charting the various groups, so that the flow of information from the CAS can be tailored to fit this structure. A collaboration with Business Development could be useful when reviewing a CAS to increase participation (Platt 2007), but also to assist with an understanding of the various groupings. The other impacts on a CAS to consider are your organization's commercial strategy or development plan, if they have one, and any other project work that is taking place, as these will most likely have implications for a CAS review. You may also need to consider the trends that are taking place in your organization such as part-time working, remote access from multiple locations, application of tools to assist blind users and other similar employment related concerns.

When it comes to looking at technologies there are various criteria to consider in addition to the needs identified above. The sections that follow will look at each type of technology in turn. In general terms, however, it is worth speaking to information professionals in other organizations to get their opinion on the vendor, the service they provide and how it is being utilized. It is also worth determining the level of support from the vendor you are likely to receive and the input you have into the future development of the service. If you have a pre-existing subscription service that you are looking to cancel, check the cancellation clauses in your contact as you may be required to give notice. If so, notify the vendor of your intention to cancel, even if you may not do so (Fogden 2010).

LEGAL INFORMATION PROVIDERS

For the benefit of this chapter, information providers are essentially publishers who provide an online database of content. Users can search for materials on these databases and use the built-in current awareness tools to be notified of new additions or changes to the data. While it is not possible to consider all the legal resources available, the popular subscription services are: Westlaw UK, Lawtel,

Practical Law Company (PLC), LexisLibrary and Justis. A few free sites are: Legislation.gov.uk and the British and Irish Legal Information Institute (BAILII).

As with any database, the current awareness tools available are often dictated by the type of information that is provided. Legal information is no exception, with indexing that covers an array of subjects and legal concepts, which is extremely useful when setting up alerts. Westlaw UK, LexisLibrary and Lawtel, make good use of their indexing, by allowing users to create alerts based on a number of 'tick-box' criteria, which includes various types of materials and topics. These type of alerts are particularly useful for daily updates featuring primary legal materials (for example employment legislation and cases), combined with value-added commentary such as journal articles. These three services and Justis also allow users to create alerts based on keyword searches, which could be useful to follow a specific area of interest, for example tracking legislation or a case. Westlaw UK also allows users to create a case alert to monitor specific changes, for example if there has been an appeal, or citation of the case in other cases or articles. The flexibility of these current awareness tools means they are adaptable to the general daily needs of users, as well as the ad hoc requirements dictated by workflow. It is worth noting that not all facilities are automatically switched on. At the time of going to press Westlaw UK has an RSS function that is included in the core subscription, but is only turned on upon request. It is therefore essential to liaise with the vendor about your goals in advance.

The alerts provided by PLC are highly regarded by users, as much of the content has added value by providing practical guidance and analysis (PLC 2012). However, unlike the services mentioned above, PLC adopts a much more standardized approach to their current awareness by offering a range of predefined practice-based alerts that users can subscribe to. The advantage of these is that they support the self-service model effectively, as it is easy for users to tick a box to receive an alert. The downside is the inability to save searches to follow a particular area of interest. The predefined alert model is similar to the one used by Legislation.gov.uk and BAILII, and many providers of freely available content.

All of the above legal databases provide RSS feeds, so users can aggregate content from the various services and view this information through a specific platform (see section below on aggregators for further details). Westlaw UK and Lawtel go one step further and allow you create your own RSS feeds based on a saved search, which is particularly useful when a standard feed does not provide what you need. The others provide predefined feeds, which are still useful if they are relevant. It is evident that some sites, like Legislation.gov.uk and BAILII, have chosen to offer RSS feeds over e-mail. However, e-mail still remains to be a commonplace way to deliver and receive content and therefore, because of this, it can be more effective. The text used in RSS feeds can be limited and therefore uninformative. E-mail might be a better option unless you can convince the publisher to make the feeds they provide more descriptive.

The current awareness tools on the legal databases discussed are on the whole designed to be self-serving, that is, users can set up and subscribe to alerts themselves. They do not allow information professionals to adopt a centralized approach to providing a CAS, that is, library-administered set-up and delivery of alerts to users and groups. The only concession to this model is a useful e-mail circulation list option, featured on Westlaw UK, LexisLibrary and Justis, to allow you to create an e-mail alert and deliver this to a group of users. It should be noted that vendor support can often overcome the lack of features, as they are often happy to set up alerts for users based on your specification.

NEWS AND BUSINESS INFORMATION PROVIDERS

There is often a need for lawyers to be commercially aware, particularly in law firms. This awareness usually involves keeping abreast of what is happening in the legal market, as well the activities of current and potential clients. To enable lawyers to tap into the intelligence they need there are a huge amount of services online, free or subscription-based, that offer news and business information content and current awareness tools to deliver this information. The popular services used in the legal industry are: LexisNexis Publisher, Reuters with Newsroom used in conjunction with Westlaw UK Watch (the former is the news database and the latter is the tool for administering and delivering alerts) and Google News. In terms of business information, sources used are: Mergermarket, Bureau Van Dijk (BvD) and FT.com.

Like the legal information databases above, the indexing on the LexisNexis and Thomson Reuters news products is incredibly useful, allowing users to set up alerts with various filters applied to focus the results, for example to a particular jurisdiction, industry or company. As the providers are responsible for the content the indexing should, in theory, be applied consistently and therefore the searches should be more in-depth and relevant. Similarly, Google News processes and indexes a range website news content, much of which is freely available, to provide users with an aggregated list of results. However, unlike the other services, the index on the 'Alert Hub' of FT.com and Google News is 'hidden' from users. It is only available to search via key words, as opposed to more conscious filtering by selecting the categories you need from a list. As with any service that provides indexing, it is a good idea to familiarize yourself with how the indices are structured and applied, as this will enable you to use it more effectively. A good tip from Nina Platt (2007) is to also ensure that the indices are complete, as it is possible that the metadata has not been assigned correctly or is incomplete.

The services provided by LexisNexis, Thomson Reuters and FT.com provide seamless access to the underlying materials, as you are not just paying for the functionality, but also the content. In comparison, access to materials via Google News is not necessarily seamless and users can be faced with pay walls or registration screens for particular websites. In terms of searching, however, all the services allow you to focus on particular parts of the text and to determine the sources used, allowing you to control the relevancy and access to the full text of materials.

The alerts on all the news services, except FT.com, can be created from saved searches using keywords and the aforementioned indexing. Alerts have to be set up separately on FT.com in their 'Alerts Hub'. They all offer delivery via e-mail or by an RSS feed, but the LexisNexis and Thomson Reuters services allow more control of how information appears in emails and the delivery criteria. It is interesting to note that Google have introduced a new feature to allow users to 'set the volume' of results in e-mail alerts. Users can either choose to receive 'only the best results', or 'all results'. Google notes that the former option: 'tries to filter the results so that they are relevant to your query and high quality' (Google 2012).

The delivery of alerts on the whole for all of the databases is automated, but LexisNexis, Thomson Reuters and FT.com allow for some human intervention, which is useful when a search string cannot produce the level of relevancy that is required. This generally works by allowing information professionals to carry out a search and to select the relevant results from a list that can be automatically formatted and delivered to users.

The Thomson Reuters and LexisNexis products appear to be designed as library administered services, as they offer advanced search capabilities and the ability to deliver information to various users and groups. It is possible for these products to be self-service, but the design of the platforms and licensing of the products can be prohibitive. FT.com is also mainly user-centric, but also allows the distribution of news using their 'clippings' service and allows individuals to subscribe to other users' 'clippings'. Google is the opposite and provides an effective self-service model, as users can carry out a search and turn this into an e-mail alert or RSS feed in seconds, but it does not provide any features for users to administer and distribute this information. The availability and ease of use of Google News means it is a very useful and popular product for users, but it also means that users may not be receiving the information that is appropriate to their needs, as set out in Fourie's framework (1999) in the 'Finding a solution' section above. Therefore, it is worth including consideration of any personal e-mail updates users are receiving in your needs assessment.

There is also useful information available in business information databases that users can extract to aid their commercial awareness. Three key services are

Mergermarket, Bureau Van Dijk (BvD) and FT.com. Mergermarket is a mergers and acquisitions intelligence service comprising a deals database and rumours about future deals. BvD provides company reports and profile information. FT.com provides news (as covered above) and data-related information, such as share prices and exchange rates. The three databases all provide e-mail alerts based on either new materials added or changes to their current information. Mergermarket and FT.com also provide RSS feeds, which in the case of the former may need to be activated and in the latter are predefined. This functionality will allow you to deliver alerts to various users through an aggregator (as discussed below). In the case of BvD you can distribute e-mail alerts to multiple users. However, to make the best use of the information on these services for current awareness purposes would require the appropriate amount of licensing. This would enable users to have seamless access between alerts and the underlying information. It should be noted that this is less of a problem for FT.com, as some of the data-related content is free to access.

RSS AGGREGATORS

RSS (often known as Really Simple Syndication) has become a commonplace way for publishers to 'push' content in the form of feeds to users, which can be combined and accessed in web-based services or software known as aggregators or feed readers. Users can also access these feeds via specific versions of Outlook that support RSS, or via an intranet platform. RSS feeds and aggregators have transformed how publishers deliver information and how users receive it; and with smartphone technology users can now access feeds remotely. The obvious advantage of using RSS feeds and aggregators is that users can check updates from various publishers in one place, which can be a useful way to save time and increase productivity, as opposed to visiting a series of websites individually. The key subscription-based aggregating services used in the legal market are Linex Smart Alerts and LexisNexis Ozmosys. For comparison purposes, and to provide a free alternative, The Old Reader will also be discussed.

The Linex and LexisNexis products are very flexible and have a whole range of tools that can be adapted to the information needs of a legal organization. The basic premise of the services is that you can add all the RSS feeds you need to monitor and allocate the content to particular users or groups. The services will then automatically consolidate the content and deliver in a newsletter-type e-mail (with items ordered by publisher or industry). The content can also be published as an RSS feed for users who would prefer to use their own readers, or pushed to an intranet. It is true that not all websites have RSS feeds, but Linex also allows you to also pull in website content, for example from the news section of a company website. Furthermore, if there is an e-mail you receive from a third party that you find useful you can also have this delivered into Linex and the content will be aggregated along with your other feeds. These products have essentially provided the solution to the issue that an effective CAS often needs to use different sources, publishers, formats and delivery criteria in order to meet users' needs.

One of the key benefits of the Linex, Ozmosys and The Old Reader services is that you do not necessarily have to procure additional content, like with the subscription news products considered above, in order to make use of the products. These products enable you to use the content you already have more effectively and increase the return on investment on your subscription services, as well as using freely available materials. The LexisNexis service can integrate with its Publisher product to provide an additional source collection if needed. Where The Old Reader does not match up to the other two is by not allowing you to automatically apply a level of filtering and indexing to the feeds aggregated. This is possible, however, with the Linex and Ozmosys services and particularly useful when a service does not allow you to create your own feed, or you if need general filters covering many feeds.

The Linex and Ozmosys products are primarily designed to be library administered. The Linex platform, however, is also self-service by allowing users to have direct access to the feeds they subscribe to, so they can make their own decisions about what appears in their daily update. The Old Reader is very much designed with the user in mind and not as a distribution system. Where The Old Reader stands out from the other two services is by providing an additional range of organizational and social tools that allow users to share and interact with the information. At a basic level, you can opt to follow other users and others can follow you to receive updates on your activity, which consists of items you opt to 'like' and any notes you choose to add to articles. Users can even share items via their own RSS feed generated by the service. Users who subscribe to your feed will be alerted when anything is shared, which could be useful to flag items of interest on a particular company or topic. While The Old Reader is not designed to dispense information to various groups and users, the sharing functionality could certainly assist with this.

SOCIAL MEDIA

The emergence of social media has made a huge impact on how people generally interact with information and the services law libraries provide. In a basic sense, social media sites are designed for users to engage in a conversation and share information, as opposed to just being flat consumers of published materials. On the whole, using social media to deliver a CAS is considered to provide a service that is: more timely, cost-effective, value-added, flexible, innovative and engaging. However, one of the major barriers to using social media to deliver a CAS is an organization's culture (Mullan 2009) and a major shift could be required for users to embrace and make the best use of such technologies. We have already discussed the social tools available on The Old Reader and there are various other services available to facilitate a CAS in your organization. These generally fall under the categories of: wikis, social networking, social bookmarking, blogs and microblogging. The sites this section will specifically look at are: Twitter, Facebook and LinkedIn.

The social media site that has had the biggest impact is Twitter, with many legal organizations now providing tweets on their activities. The basic premise of the service is that users of Twitter can post short messages (tweets), which can be read by anyone who decides to 'follow' them and you can read the tweets of others that you have chosen to 'follow'. The result is an aggregated list of content that users can access via Twitter, or choose to receive via another platform. In the same way as building a useful collection of sources, users can build up a useful stream of information by following particular users and organizations to suit their needs and 'deliver' their own current awareness by tweeting. Users can also opt to keep an eye on 'trending' information, by following particular Hashtags. These Hashtags are generated by users adding terms to their tweets. This informal use of indexing is useful to monitor real-time events and, as noted by Fiona Fogden in her talk at 2011 BIALL Conference, allow users to tap into the rumour mill for particular companies or events often before the details are published. Mullan (2009) notes that Hashtags can easily be abused, due to fact that anyone can create or use one. Similarly, regular audits may be required to weed out any people or organizations that you 'follow' that do not meet your current awareness needs.

The social networking sites, LinkedIn and Facebook, can also be useful tools for delivering a CAS. Like Twitter you can post status updates and connect to other users and organizations and see their posts and activity. Facebook and LinkedIn, however, also allow you create and join topics or organizational-based groups. The idea is the members can post and share information relevant to these groups. Where LinkedIn perhaps has the edge over Facebook in the professional arena, is because of a service they provide called 'LinkedIn Today'. This service centralizes the articles people share on LinkedIn and Twitter. Users can see the news that is 'trending' and follow a particular industry, as well as searching across this trending information for a more specific topic.

The current awareness aspects of these services are not designed to be library administered, like some of the publishing solutions previously mentioned, as they are social by nature therefore need to be user-driven to reach their potential. However, law libraries can create pages and groups on LinkedIn and Facebook with relevant information that users can subscribe to. The information professional's role, to benefit from such services, is to raise their profile and provide guidance on their ability to contribute to a CAS. If should be noted that social media sites can often be blocked in law firms due to concerns regarding confidentiality. There are, however, similar enterprise versions of such social media that can be implemented behind an organization's firewall.

Facebook and LinkedIn provide RSS feeds for some of their content, to allow you to aggregate relevant information in a reader (as discussed above). Unfortunately, Twitter has removed its RSS functionality, so it is not possible to incorporate this content and it would have to be utilized separately (Scott 2011). However, users of Linex are able to include Twitter content in their alerts, which can be republished as RSS feeds. If there is a clear need for a library administered social media based CAS, then using a blog to deliver this information could be the answer. An excellent example is the Inner Temple Library's Current Awareness blog (see http://www.innertemplelibrary.com/). This blog draws information from a variety of sources and allows users to subscribe to an e-mail update or various RSS feeds.

THE FUTURE

Social media has paved the way for technologies to work together to provide a seamless information-rich environment. Third party and official technologies exist to allow users to pull content from one service into another, for example LinkedIn content can be added to Twitter. However, these advancements are often fuelled by commercial reasons and therefore can also work in reverse, for example Google announcing their intention to shut Google Reader (Thomas 2013) and Twitter removing RSS feeds from its service (Scott 2011). Legal organizations are similarly looking for better integration of their key technologies behind their firewalls to increase efficiencies and a CAS has the potential to play a part in this, for example users could subscribe to a feed to let them know when a book is automatically added to the library catalogue, or when know how is generated or when there is any activity regarding a key client or prospect on a client relationship management (CRM) system.

The aim of this chapter was to provide an overview of the landscape of the key current awareness technologies that are available to law libraries and information professionals and how to go about finding a solution. The technologies discussed will inevitably evolve over time to meet the changing needs of users and to make existing services more efficient, seamless and intelligent. With all these changes the underlying principles of what a CAS should deliver are still important, as is the involvement of the information professional in the process. The various technologies have been shown to rely on different models to deliver a CAS, that is, a library-administered service, or one in which the user is responsible themselves for the set-up and delivery of information. With the former, library administration of RSS aggregation can result in a better knowledge management policy. Profile information regarding individuals' preferences for alerts, sources and searches can be retained by the library when they leave, or shared with other users. It could be argued that with the latter, and with the increasing intelligence of CAS solutions, that the information professional's role is decreasing in the delivery of such services. However, this role is one that is still fundamental but also has the potential to be more advisory, for example by assessing needs, researching and implementing a solution and carrying out reviews, rather than just the physical act of delivering information.

LAW FIRM INTRANETS

SALLY ROBERTS

INTRODUCTION

So, you've been asked to get involved in your firm's intranet project. Until recently, intranets suffered from a lack of ownership in all organizations, but in more recent times organizations have begun to see the value of an intranet as an essential communication and business tool.

Intranets have tended to suffer as they are not client facing systems, so often have fewer resources devoted to them than a public facing website. Again, more and more organizations are beginning to see the value in investing in systems that are going to be used by employees day in, day out.

Whether you are embarking on a brand new implementation or refreshing your existing site, this chapter aims to provide some ideas on how you can improve your intranet, and increase its usage and profile within your organization.

LET'S TALK STRATEGY

Ask most intranet managers (me included) what their intranet strategy is and they may struggle to show you any formal documentation. However it is important and shows the organization that 'you mean business'. Your strategy does not need to be a 20-page long document, but instead a concise A4 sheet that captures where the intranet is at, overall goals and direction, short-term deliverables and long-term direction. A lack of strategy can contribute to a lack of support and resourcing.

Establishing Ownership and Getting Stakeholder Support

Who is going to run this project? Large-scale intranet projects will demand input from all departments in the firm, and if it is a global project, all offices need to be consulted. Buy-in is important for future success, but it does need to have a team at the helm in order to project manage and take the project forward.

It will be imperative to have senior stakeholder sponsorship. In a law firm, this would ideally come from a partner or a group of partners – the highest level of seniority in the firm. Intranets only succeed if they have support from the highest level.

Content Ownership

As well as having an overall intranet manager/owner, you need a content owner and content editor for each section of the site. The owner and editor may be the same person in a smaller organization, but in essence you need someone who is able to make decisions about the content on the site, and someone who is actually able to create, update and amend the content.

It's important that anyone responsible for updating content on the intranet is aware of the necessary standards you have for creating content on the site and you might want to look at providing some materials specifically on writing for the web. See http://www.useit.com/papers/webwriting/ for many useful resources.

Being an intranet content editor needs to become part of the job description for those who are responsible for it to avoid intranet work being pushed to the bottom of a busy person's 'to do' list. Speak to HR about incorporating this where relevant.

CHOOSING YOUR INTRANET PLATFORM

The most popular platform for intranets at the moment is SharePoint. It provides a flexible solution that can work for all types of organization. It also provides for social elements such as wikis and blogs.

Increasingly other products are building web parts to integrate with SharePoint: PLC and enterprise search providers Recommind are just two examples. SharePoint may also already be in use within the firm for document management or know how portal solutions so the intranet will be an obvious next step.

In choosing a platform you should be aware, however, that SharePoint is not an out-of-the box solution. Configuration can be time-consuming and costly. Some firms are set up to be able to manage and deliver on this kind of project, however other organizations may not have this kind of expertise in-house and would therefore have to outsource a SharePoint project.

There are, however, lots of alternatives to SharePoint which might be more suitable if you wanted to implement an 'off the shelf' intranet package which will only require a minimal amount of development and customization.

- Ask your peers;
- Go and see intranets in action;
- Look outside the law. Corporate intranets often have big budgets and well-resourced intranet teams rolling out sophisticated solutions – we can learn a lot from them;
- Think about what systems you already have and whether your intranet will need to be able to integrate with them, for example your document management system, practice management, know how and CRM systems.

Look Forward

Your firm may not be ready for Facebook-style feeds on your intranet right now, but your site needs to be able to expand and move with the times as your users do. Even the most basic of intranets, if done well, will continue to develop.

Relaunch or Redesign

When asked to relaunch an out-of-date and ineffective intranet, a common response is to start a redesign project. This can be a lengthy (and costly) process, especially if external designers and agencies are used. There may be nothing to show to the business for several months and sometimes this kind of project is out of the question – you just need some quick fixes which demonstrate improvement to your stakeholders. Whilst there is appetite to improve the site, you should act on it.

Task-based improvements
Staff come to the intranet with a particular task in mind – fee earners are busy people who rarely visit to see what's new or just to look around. The value of a site can often be found in how well it supports common tasks.

What are the top five things your users go to the intranet for:

- To find an appraisal form?
- To find a colleague's phone number?
- To book some holiday?
- To book a room?
- To claim expenses?
- To find a HR form?

Ask your users how they go about finding this information. Do they search? Or browse? Do they have links to items stored as favourites in the browser?

Once you have decided which task to focus on (taking one task at a time), you need to talk to your users to find out how they perform the task. You should choose a good cross-section of employees across the organization for example, a secretary, a trainee, a solicitor, a partner and some business services team representatives. It is important to engage at all levels as the intranet should be a tool for everyone at the firm.

- Ask for 10–15 minutes with a few staff who regularly perform the task;
- Sit with them and watch/record how they perform the task at the moment;
- Ask them to think aloud so you can capture any problems.

Use the results of these activities to make changes to the site and, where possible, find ways to measure the improvements or receive feedback from users.

Never skip user testing in any of this process, ensure you have any changes tested with your users prior to launch.

Everyone Wants a Piece of Me!

In any organization the home page is a hotly contested piece of real estate. Invariably your users are coming to the site to carry out a task or to look for a piece of information. The key to a great site is to get them to stay a while once they're there. If it's unattractive and unintuitive, your users will switch off on arrival.

However, in law firms you are faced with the additional burden of trying to find a home page that meets the needs of everyone in the firm. The information needs of fee earners are very different from those of people working in the Finance department. It is important to engage with all users and make them feel that the intranet is theirs too. Make the home page for all users, not just for the partners/ management, and use it to feature active, dynamic and changing content.

Can one size fit all?
When faced with the dilemma of trying to get a home page that will meet everyone's needs, often organizations go down the customization route: 'I know, let's allow them to decide what they want on their home pages!' Unfortunately, research shows that only five to ten per cent of users will actually make use of this functionality.

A more realistic option might be to tailor or target content or pages to a particular user's needs. For example, if they are banking lawyers – give them the banking practice area home page. If you go down this route, you will need to make sure they still get all the information they need to know what's going on around the firm – but with some added-value information which is just relevant to them.

Key components of the home page

- News – this should include items such as new client wins, recently completed deals, appointments and new joiners;

- Navigation – this does not have to mean just the top-level menu bar. Navigation can include quick links and lists of departments or services;

- Collaboration and community – an area for all users to contribute. This could be as basic as an online notice board, right through to collaborative document drafting through wiki pages;

- Internal marketing – a space for teams to promote new initiatives or events that are going on around the firm;

- Key tools – make sure that your search and people finder are available on every page.

This list of content should provide a balanced mix of functionality on the home page.

Make them pay for it

There may not be room to keep all the content you need on the home page at the same time. You can have spaces on the home page that teams can 'rent out' for a set period of time. Keep a running schedule of ideas for this advert space or spotlight area. Get this policy approved at a high level from the outset to avoid any issues.

Keep it all above the fold?

The phrase 'keep it above the fold' refers to the requirement that all intranet pages (especially the home page) should fit within the parameters of one screen, so that users do not have to scroll to get to the content.

This is a slightly outdated rule as users are used to scrolling through content now – look at the BBC, Guardian or Sky News websites as examples. These sites all contain a lot of content on their home pages and users know to scroll down to see more.

The key is to apply some 'information scent' so that users know there is more to find 'below the fold'. This can be done by showing that there is content further down the screen.

PEOPLE SEARCH

A firm's most important asset is, of course, its people and therefore a powerful people search is an essential on any intranet. A good people search should include photos and skills. Your people finder should be easy to update so that users can add to their profiles.

Some organizations also like to include small biographies listing previous roles or experience. This may not seem necessary in small organizations but if faced with the situation where you are pitching to be on the legal panel of ABC bank, it would be useful to know that the latest lateral hire in the corporate department used to work at ABC bank and may have some useful insights for you.

'I CAN NEVER FIND ANYTHING ON OUR INTRANET'

A common complaint of intranets is that the users can't find what they are looking for. This can be down to poor information architecture, confusing navigation or an ineffective search engine.

What is navigation?
Navigation allows users to browse an intranet to find the information they need. Getting the navigation right is essential to the success of your intranet. Even if you're not attempting to redesign the navigation at this moment in time, checking that your navigation still works is a valuable exercise.

Card sorting
Card sorting is a technique used to gain input into the design of a structure of an intranet. It is a quick, simple and cost-effective way to involve users in the design process.

Card sorting involves:

- Getting a group of employees together;
- Providing them with a set of cards, each labelled with a piece of content or functionality that currently appears on your site;
- Asking your users to group the cards into sets that make sense to them;
- Once the sets of cards have been determined, asking your users to create a label for each set.

The groups and labels are then used as input into the site structure. The labels and groups can be used to form suggestions for menus and headings.

Card sorting does not produce a final structure but can be provide useful input and can be used to validate proposed and existing structures. For further information see Spencer (2011).

Once you have come up with your draft site structure, select some users to test it out on. Mock up some screenshots that can be used throughout your testing.

Krug (2005) provides invaluable advice on this kind of user-centred design process. He states:

- If you want a great site, you've got to test;
- Testing one user is 100 per cent better than testing none;
- Testing one user early in the project is better than testing 50 near the end;
- The point of testing is not to prove or disprove, but to inform;
- Testing is iterative (test > fix > test again).

Search

No matter how much time is spent on card sorting and other similar exercises, tirelessly trying to get the navigation right, it won't work for 100 per cent of the people 100 per cent of the time. That's why a good intranet search is important.

- Put search on every page in the same place with a white query box;
- Deliver comprehensive search results with relevant results and a well-presented search results page;
- Use good page titles, tags and summaries to help the search engine and also help users pick out results from a list;
- Review your search statistics regularly to make sure you're delivering the best results.

Identify popular search terms
Look at search statistics for common search terms and ensure that frequently searched information is easily accessible from the home page or from a menu.

'Best bets'
Some search engines will enable you to make use of 'best bets' such as Recommind Decisiv Search. This is where you can identify frequently searched terms and ensure the right results always appear at the top of the results list – this is achieved by hard-coding results into the search engine. 'Best bets' can, however, be an administrative burden as they need to be kept up to date and reviewed regularly so they should not be used extensively if resource is likely to be an issue.

Remove redundant content
You can substantially increase the chances of your users finding relevant information by removing all unnecessary content – and this does not just mean out-of-date content. You may need to conduct a content audit and look at usage statistics to see what content is not being looked at.

IT'S ALL IN THE NAME

Giving your intranet a name is another device you can use to promote your site. A name will give the site its own identity which can be useful if you're trying to raise awareness and increase engagement.

Think about your audience and consider what type of name will suit your organization. One approach is to run an intranet naming competition to run alongside the relaunch (with prizes, of course!). Beware of renaming, then relaunching the intranet without making significant improvements to the site though – your users won't fall for it!

The key to adoption of an intranet name is consistent usage. Reinforce the name throughout the launch campaign and afterwards in marketing materials and by word of mouth. See http://intranet-matters.de/intranet-names/ for some inspiration on what to call your site.

Working Out the Brand

It's important to note that your intranet does not need to match the external brand. What works on a website that greets external visitors on an occasional basis may not suit intranet users that need to visit the site daily.

Your intranet should have:

- A consistent set of colours, page designs and style sheets that are used throughout the site; and
- Consistent labelling and terminology – for example if you call your news section 'Local News' in one area, don't call it something else like 'London News' in another. It will confuse users (and cause havoc with search results).

You can align the intranet brand with the external look and feel (perhaps by fonts and colours), but you do not need to copy it directly. Once the brand is established, the brand does not need to be over-managed (so that it results in lengthy brand manuals and a non-scalable model), it just needs to flow naturally through the site and onto any collateral that the site produces, for example brochures, quick guides and e-learning materials.

If you are struggling to define your intranet 'brand', a useful activity can be to use the Microsoft Product Reaction cards. The cards contain words that can be used to describe your intranet in its current state and help you define where you want to get to. You should aim to choose around eight cards to describe the intranet both as is, and words that describe the site you would like to launch.

The cards can be found at: www.microsoft.com/usability/UEPostings/Product ReactionCards.doc.

Spreading the Word

Once your site or feature is ready to go live, you need to start talking about it. Promotion of the intranet is never-ending – you'll find that you need to constantly advertise the intranet to your users.

Use a variety of communication methods to market the new site or the new feature. If the site has a new name, be sure to use this as much as possible in your advertising. Posters, emails, e-learning, presentations, floor-walking, handouts and brochures are all good ways of communicating the message to your users.

You can also add weight by using your senior stakeholders to communicate the changes for you. You can do the hard work by putting the promotional materials together, but if the message is delivered from the top, it's more likely to be taken on board.

Other ways to promote your site or applications once live include:

- Birthdays – celebrating the launch a year on;
- E-mail links to the intranet – replace attachments in emails with links to relevant intranet pages to pull people in;
- Brochures – support your intranet with a brochure detailing features and benefits, along with screenshots;
- What's new emails – staff may not be aware of new content or features being added and it also spreads the message to those who don't visit the site regularly;
- Autoload on start-up – if it doesn't already, make sure the intranet page loads when your users log on in the morning;
- Catch them on day one – get a demonstration of the intranet on the induction programme.

DON'T STOP MOVING

A good intranet is always a work in progress – constantly in development and must keep pace with the ever-changing digital world. Without going very far though you have a wealth of information which can help keep the site moving:

- Site analytics – this will tell you what your users are using and what they are not using. It will not tell you why they are using it, but will point you in the right direction.
- User surveys – regular surveys that combine rating-style and open-ended questions will give you a good steer.
- Onsite feedback – 'was this helpful' tabs, thumbs-up buttons and instant feedback forms provide ways to get real-time feedback from users.

- Focus groups – simply getting users around tables always generates great ways to improve usability.
- Expert reviews – do your research and ask a web/intranet guru to take a look at your site. Buy them lunch afterwards!

If you don't build it, they won't use it.

LIBRARY MANAGEMENT SYSTEMS (LMS)

MANDY WEBSTER

INTRODUCTION

Since the first edition of this book, written in 2005, several developments have increased, if possible, the importance of having an LMS fit for present purposes and adaptable for future needs. The consolidation of LMS vendors has continued to gather momentum making some older systems obsolete or unsupported and leaving migration as a bigger issue than choosing a first system. Few organizations requiring an LMS will not have one by now and some may have already migrated to a different system at least once. Advances in technologies have transformed the environment LMSs operate in and the way they operate. The ever-tightening stranglehold on budgets has created impetus for extracting increasing value from all purchases and subscriptions, including the LMS itself. Thinking about the costs of maintaining current systems helps to focus on any areas where the system has not provided satisfactory performance.

The process of selecting an initial system or migrating to a new one happens so infrequently in a professional's career that the unfamiliarity raises its own stresses and difficulties. It is worth visiting exhibitions and trade shows every few years even if a migration is not currently contemplated, to see the latest developments in LMS capabilities as they change frequently. New colleagues joining from other organizations may have used a system which has added benefits not considered before. Seeing the latest possibilities can help to focus arguments about where the current system fails to deliver or does not save as much time as it possibly could when all services are being required to do more with less. Trade stands should be able to offer a broad estimate of costs including site licences, data conversion and whether training and support is included initially along with annual costs for subsequent years. The LMS is still at the heart of well-run Library and Information Services (LIS) and an efficient, effective choice is fundamental to maintaining the service's reputation. Using an outdated system can reflect badly on the reputation of the LIS. Whichever system is selected, it is worthwhile considering how easily it can be customized to fit in with the LIS branding to remind users which resources and databases are supplied by the LIS.

MIGRATION

Any purchase requires a soundly reasoned business case but in the current economic climate additional spending will undergo extremely close scrutiny. If there are no clear reasons why the current LMS is no longer fit for purpose, fund-holders will rightly reject the idea of spending what will probably be a substantial sum in the initial cost, data conversion and ongoing support/maintenance costs. Compelling reasons for change are likely to include outdated software incompatible with the organization's own IT systems, duplicated inputting to different systems wasting staff time, poor OPAC searching and inadequate reporting, amongst others. End-users familiar with sites such as Amazon expect OPACs to be as simple to search and offer useful extra information. Some LMSs have not kept up with changing operating systems, such as Windows 2000 to XP to Vista, and although it may be comforting to have a system which has survived for many years, it may no longer be the most efficient means of performing the necessary tasks. It always needs to be demonstrable that the new system will help to achieve the organization's objectives.

A major problem could be from a risk management perspective in that the current LMS does not adequately identify missing issues of journals and looseleaf updates or that a module of the LMS was not purchased and a manual system is in use, making tracing missing items inefficiently time-consuming. Particularly for law it is vital for fee earners to be confident of working from the most up-to-date versions of texts and in using journals for current awareness to be certain they are not missing out on current issues.

The LMS should avoid any unnecessary duplicates being purchased because nobody knows what is currently held and save valuable time tracking down what is held by clearly identifying where items are or who currently has them on loan. This can be particularly effective if staff catalogue items ready to order them through an acquisitions module which flags up potential duplicate records of items already held before any unnecessary order is placed. How important each issue is depends on the individual LIS and what may be crucial to one service may only be a nice to have elsewhere. The choice to migrate a system, like the initial purchase, has to be founded on the individual needs of the organization and not be a blind following of what other similar sized organizations have chosen.

The best LMS can help the Library & Information Service (LIS) to save money by providing information to help make informed decisions about whether to buy new editions based on past loan records. Exceptional systems will allow staff to record items being used for reference without being borrowed, avoiding a false report of no loans against items often consulted only briefly but frequently. Commonly law firms may have several offices and may want to divide payments – perhaps in instalments – across different cost codes for each office. Any system should make this a simple process. Financial management is a key issue and any LMS needs to be capable of revealing the financial health of the budget quickly: details of what has been spent, how much is unspent and, of that, how much is already committed to subscriptions and ideally which month of the financial year each subscription or part of a subscription is due. If any monthly or quarterly financial reports need to be submitted to managers outside the LIS without access to the LMS, can relevant data be extracted in a suitable format such as a Word document or spreadsheet thereby regularly saving staff time? A perfect solution would be for the LMS to fully integrate with the accounts system so data need only be entered once and making it easy to track payments should questions about whether a subscription has lapsed arise.

For the benefit of new starters a simple means of obtaining lists of journals on a topic or all holdings in a location or subject area is needed. This should be capable of being emailed as a Word document for example to save time. On the topic of new starters, circulation lists should be easily amendable to permit the addition of new recipients at any position on the list without having to delete the entire list and re-enter it as some systems require.

Some systems include enquiry tracking software as a module. It is worth considering this as an extra module at some stage, as once staff are familiar with using the LMS a similar enquiry module should be simple to use and will provide statistical evidence of workloads and resources which could be used to justify the information service existence if required. It can also be used to demonstrate time spent on business development and save staff time if a similar enquiry has recently been asked and only needs the response updating. It can help to monitor deadlines and staff workloads. Whether research time is charged back to clients or not a stopwatch function on enquiry software offers LIS staff the option to let fee earners know how long the research took and then decide whether it is to be charged back to clients or to illustrate how LIS staff have saved fee earner time.

Automatic cataloguing based on entering an ISBN or ISSN helps to save valuable staff time. Where this is also linked to an acquisitions module sending orders to suppliers in an acceptable standard format, this offers an additional time-saving for staff rather than duplicating work by emailing orders to suppliers. Serials modules can be one of the most problematic parts of any LMS. If issues arrive out of sequence or several sites have their own copies of the same journal title, some systems handle these common situations inadequately with only the first site being able to log the arrival of an issue and other sites then being unable to identify whether they have received their copy or need to claim for a missing issue. The report for identifying missing issues to claim should be simple to run and include all the relevant information needed to make the claim without having to search the system to identify the number of the last issue received and all the necessary contact details of the supplier and account information by a couple of clicks at most. Time-saving automation is a valuable bonus permitting tasks such as temporary changes, including exclusion from circulation lists whilst users are on maternity leave, long-term sick leave or even long holiday, without having to remove them completely and then being able to reinstate them on their return. If the system permits end dates for these temporary changes this frees up even more staff time.

Any migration requires the assurance of the best quality data and many LMS suppliers will be happy to illustrate how a few sample records from the current system will look on migration to the new system. A great time-saver would be if the circulation lists and orders could be migrated without having to be input manually and there may be value in having the borrowing history of users transferred. Some systems can integrate with staff intranets to avoid having to enter borrower details twice, which saves users time if they log loans or requests from their own PCs by not having to repeatedly enter their user details if they wish to borrow more than one item. The expense of buying in barcodes can be saved if the system includes barcoding software and an ability to print any other labels required such as classmarks in a suitable format for spine labels. These have the added bonus of saving staff time if they can be tagged for printing in batches at the end of a cataloguing session. If the LIS has its own esoteric classification system it is worth checking how the system will deal with this as well as the spine labelling. If existing items have already had barcodes inserted, compatibility with the new system is essential to minimize disruption and wasted time in re-barcoding existing stock.

Where the LMS is to be used to access seminar notes and counsels' opinions, copyright permitting, the ability to include fields such as 'key cases cited' and 'legislation' will improve the quality of search results for users. If the formats are also compatible with any citation checking software to link to cases and legislation, the risk management and time-savings are potentially invaluable. Newer systems should be able to capture data about webinars and podcasts and link directly to these. Some systems already provide for author videos and this could be adapted for webinars.

Compatibility with any internally used thesaurus will improve relevance of retrieval and encourage user satisfaction. It might be appropriate to consider the size of the abstract field to allow the full text of a seminar note to be included to help with keyword searching, or a form of federated searching included for searching the full text of linked pdf or Word documents. It is worth checking how effective full text searching of scanned documents is. If there is some form of federated searching, does that extend to full text articles and chapters in e-journals and e-books and how well does it work in practice? Some systems have very restricted abstract fields which may be inadequate.

Users may appreciate being able to register to be alerted to new acquisitions in their specified areas of interest to help them get value from the system. This should be simple to set up and amend, for example for trainees moving to new seats with new areas of interest. If the LIS operates across multiple sites, an ability to reserve items and request they be sent to a different site could be an advantage. For users on the move, access on smartphones or tablets in an easily readable format is an obvious benefit.

The simplest form of self issue helps to avoid items being removed out of hours without being logged out and then subsequently missing. At any demonstration or trial of potential systems only the users can honestly assess how simple the process is. Only if end-users can easily check out loans will they bother to do so. This maintains an up-to-date trail of borrowers and saves valuable fee earner time looking for items.

Searching must be intuitive as users may not use the system often enough to become familiar with any quirks and will not want to read help pages. It may be helpful for users to be able to check their own loan history, if they have recently borrowed an item and cannot remember all the details but need to consult it again, especially outside normal working hours. A history of recently viewed items can be helpful as some users dismiss items as irrelevant but later in the searches decide a previous hit looked more relevant after all. Ease of returning to search results needs to be clear and options for both advanced searching by fields and basic Google-type searching options would be advantageous for users familiar with field-searching on legal databases and ubiquitous Googling.

An important consideration could be how easily data can be extracted and the format it is available in, not only for any future migration to another system but, for example, to answer user requests for holdings at a particular location or journals circulated on a particular subject, and would ideally be available in a format easily attached to an e-mail. The ability to include images of book covers initially may not seem a very appealing extra for law libraries with sets of similarly bound books, but it can help users to find items more quickly if they know the book is a particular colour and can help to make the OPAC seem more attractive and like familiar websites. On a similar theme, users already familiar with Amazon and LibraryThing[1] will probably appreciate a review, extract, author information, recommend and rating option with tagging. This may not spring to mind for legal textbooks but should add value if, for example, seminar notes or know how are included on the LMS with options for users to add comments; and LibraryThing for libraries can already integrate book reviews into some LMSs. The ability to link to groups with similar research interests, blogs and subscriptions as envisaged by Library 2.0 would help to attract more users to the LMS and make it more central to the business. Options to link to any floor plans of the organization to save time tracing where items are offer distinct advantages, as would a link to a plan of the library shelf linked to a particular classmark. Some systems offer the option of browsing books on nearby shelves to a selected item, adding a layer of serendipity to online browsing and helping to exploit expensive items which might be overlooked, particularly items available online rather than in printed formats. A few systems offer a link to show other local institutions holding an item if a search of the OPAC reveals it is not held. This would be appropriate if a large public library is close by or a university library where the organization has arranged borrowing rights, or among small consortiums with inter-lending arrangements to save time contacting them to check on holdings; avoiding users being disappointed, wanting to buy an item they only need to use once or having to log in to other online catalogues.

Where the LMS is used as a portal to annotate websites or to link to online versions of resources, broken link checking software offers a worthwhile time-saver and maintains the image of LIS efficiency when run regularly. Copyright Licensing Agency audits can take up a lot of staff time which can be avoided if a formatted report can be quickly generated.

THE UNITED KINGDOM CORE SPECIFICATION

UKCS: http://www.cilip.org.uk/professionalguidance/lms/corespecification. htm) is intended for large academic and public libraries but could be trimmed and adapted to form an initial list of requirements for smaller institutions. Grading each area as either essential or desirable helps to measure systems against each other and is an opportunity for the organization to personalize the selection process by weighting different factors according to how important they are for that particular LIS. Any invitation to tender must include a deadline for responses and eventually two or three systems are selected for more detailed scrutiny. This clear itemizing of what is required from the LMS also helps to gain support from internal management for a well-thought-out and financially sound proposal.

Reputable suppliers should not object to supplying the names and contact details of referees willing to be approached and asked about the system and supplier. This can give a valuable insight into how customers are treated, how quickly their requests are dealt with and reactions to any suggested improvements to the system. It should clarify who decides how urgent requests for help are dealt with, the supplier grading them or the customer, which may be important under the service level agreement. An active user group is a good sign of a supplier responsive to users' needs and keen to provide upgrades users appreciate. It can give a useful overview of recent upgrades and how effective training is. A successful customer retention record demonstrates a commitment to customer service and that the system itself has probably evolved and been updated to satisfy changing customer needs. Similarly vendors expanding their product development teams would seem to indicate a commitment to maintaining and developing the product to increase its longevity.

Most suppliers will provide a sample system on request for staff to examine in more detail. For both traditional systems and remotely hosted ones it is important for all LIS staff to test the product. All suppliers tend to claim their systems are intuitive and user-friendly but only by carrying out each process can staff fully evaluate how many clicks each task requires and how difficult it is to move between different screens for different processes such as cataloguing, issue and return of items and receipt of issues. End-users will not appreciate having to keep returning to the main menu to move to another process. It may be important for the organization to be able to customize menus, particularly if the system is to be used to hold less usual items like webinars or seminar notes. It should be a simple process to change these and to change, say, locations listings. It saves staff time to be able to click from a receipts screen directly into suppliers' details to claim missing issues. This also offers an opportunity to test how easily predefined fields can be customized. Locations may need to be changed frequently if offices relocate, collections are centralized or dispersed and to cover new locations after mergers and take-overs. The simpler the process the more staff time it will save.

CLOUDS

A recent growing trend has seen data stored on remotely hosted servers rather than pc hard drives and local servers of organizations. In terms of LMS this means dedicated software no longer has to be downloaded and maintained, saving memory space and making the data accessible from anywhere, sometimes without licences for administration rights or following the traditional model of separating licence costs into administrative and end-user licences. Linking to such systems from the intranet probably means end-users do not notice any difference to traditional LMSs.

There may be important security issues to consider if counsels' opinions, internal seminar notes and precedents are linked to from the LMS and concerns about users' personal data and financial information regarding LIS budgets. It would be particularly catastrophic if the supplier went out of business and data was lost before being extracted by users where the data is held by the supplier remotely giving due diligence an added significance.

On a more positive note, remotely hosted servers may offer a cheaper alternative, at least initially. Costs are likely to include an element for hosting the data and for licensing the software on a monthly, quarterly or annual basis rather than the more traditional upfront purchase of software in a single payment with annual maintenance and upgrades in subsequent years. The option of dividing payments into smaller but more regular instalments may be advantageous from a cash flow perspective. It is always worth asking for details of price increases over the last few years as an indication of likely future increases to avoid unpleasant shocks. Users could be more vulnerable to future increases if the supplier charges for upgrades and insists on their acceptance. It would not be a wise move with any system to abandon upgrades and allow it to become obsolete, but in dire financial necessity it would be simpler to take that route with a traditional LMS. The more traditional LMS suppliers have of necessity become more flexible regarding the payment terms under which they are prepared to supply systems, with some allowing instalments, making these decisions less clear-cut and always worth bringing into negotiations.

Remotely hosted systems can avoid the cost of having suppliers visit to install software or the organization's own IT team spends time installing software, but training costs could remain an issue where many remotely hosted systems suppliers are based in other countries. It may be possible to have training for staff remotely by webinars but if the suppliers need to visit to carry out training on-site it needs to be clearly stated in the contract who pays for that training, and even if the training is included as part of the total cost, and who will pay for the trainer's travel and any accommodation costs. Similarly if training is held at the supplier's premises, any staff travel and accommodation could be an expensive factor. Ongoing software upgrades are less disruptive as they are carried out remotely by the host, saving IT staff time which can often be a hidden cost to the organization. It also avoids any conflict about allocating IT staff time to install upgrades, which, although essential to be carried out relatively quickly, sometimes proves problematic for traditional LMSs.

CONTRACTS

It is imperative to investigate the financial stability of any LMS supplier but the issue may be of greater concern for a relatively new company. New products may be heavily discounted initially to attract users. Generally suppliers should have a greater incentive to keep customers satisfied in order to retain their interest in renewing at annual intervals on hosted systems. There is also a risk of provider downtime frustrating users. Speaking to other users about their experiences with the supplier should help to allay such concerns. Performance relies on the subscribing organization's internet connection so having a sample database to use and test is insightful.

As with any contract the terms need to be studied carefully in relation to how data will be extracted if there is a further migration to another system. Having to pay an additional cost to extract data the organization has created should be avoided even if the organization has to write its own clause into the purchase agreement to that effect. Any extracted data should be available in a common standard format for it to be easily used in other applications if needed. Similarly data back-up may be provided as part of the cost but it should be checked to see if it is of a satisfactory standard. Where a remotely hosted system is used, cancellation clauses are particularly significant should the organization wish to change supplier at a later date. The notice period or any penalty clauses should not be prohibitively expensive or lengthy.

For traditional and remotely hosted systems the details of licences are vital. For remotely hosted systems it can be more common to find restrictions on the number of records because of the storage space provided by the suppliers or price banding based on numbers of records, numbers of users and numbers of sites and possibly where those sites are based. A site licence could cover all users working for that organization on its premises or extend to users working remotely from home or on secondment. If the licences are for a number of concurrent simultaneous users it is a careful exercise to decide how many licences are required to avoid blocked users becoming frustrated. It is worth considering how close the organization is to the top of the current band for however many records it has and the financial implications of wanting to move into the next band. Less easy to quantify in advance but something to consider in negotiations is the possibility of the organization merging, taking over or being taken over by another organization. Whether the LMS is remotely hosted or in-house, how will software licences be affected for the new entity?

Contracts will usually be on a standard form but in a keenly competitive market suppliers are more open to making amendments for a specific situation which a purchaser feels is important. Generally it is worthwhile taking advantage of the legal expertise within the purchasing entity to check all vital elements of the contract are clear and levels of service specified and satisfactory.

OPEN SOURCE

North American libraries have been quicker to adopt open source LMS software as a solution to the rising costs of proprietary systems and a perceived lack of support and development devoted to some systems. Open Source Software (OSS) allows users to improve and modify software and has witnessed some communities of users grow into support networks. For internal IT teams seeking greater integration to lighten workloads, a difficulty for commercial organizations is their reliance on Microsoft where some OSS use Unix-based systems.

One of the most successful open source systems is Evergreen,[2] currently only used in the UK by a consortium led by Sterling libraries in Scotland. Initially developed five years ago it is used in over 870 libraries including 18 consortia. Evergreen seems to evoke positive feedback from its users and a community spirit to make changes happen. Whilst it does not offer everything proprietary systems offer it is constantly developing. One of the first OSS packages for LMS, Koha,[3] is now maintained by a group of users around the world with an active e-mail list, blog and wiki. It has been used for federated searching of other libraries' holdings as well as host organizations. Koha seems to be one of the more sophisticated OSS in being able to communicate with suppliers' databases, allow user tagging, reviews, setting up alerts, social bookmarking, RSS feeds and support multiple budgets.

The major issue with any OSS is the level of skill required to install the initial software and to maintain upgrades. In the UK, Koha and Evergreen are supported by PTFS Europe Ltd, offering Koha on a cloud computing platform hosted on a designated server. Annual savings of between £4,000 and £8,000 in maintenance costs have been claimed for some OSSs (Raven 2011a). Support is not tied to a provider so if it is not suitable the provider can be changed and the system retained. OSS is less susceptible to mergers as the software is not owned by a provider but there has been consolidation among support providers such as Libline merging with PTFS.

Some organizations have used Microsoft Access to create their own LMS and there have been courses specifically to cover this. It does not offer sophisticated searching and is not successful where several staff need to catalogue items simultaneously or where an organization has a large number of records but it can offer a cheap alternative and can link to associated online resources such as e-journals.

FUTURE

The pace of change grows ever faster making it very difficult to foresee what systems in five or ten years' time may be capable of – or longer term whether they will still exist. Due to the pressures of having fewer LIS staff but needing more time for areas such as research there is likely to be a demand for greater automation, possibly with systems automatically contacting publishers or suppliers to claim missing issues of serial publications based on identified regular patterns of receipt. Some systems already run reports for reviewing circulation lists but this may be another task which could be run at predetermined intervals to automatically contact users and check they are still seeing only those items of interest, saving them time and maintaining the LIS proactive stance. The time-saving element of integration with other systems will be increasingly important. Some systems already integrate with SharePoint and can download information direct from suppliers. If webinars and so on are accessed via the system, integration with HR and e-learning monitoring would be advantageous. Hybrid LISs are likely to exist for many years yet and systems originally developed to handle printed resources need to be versatile enough to deal with electronic media and add value through areas such as creating more reliable usage statistics for databases accessed through OPACs where supplier generated statistics are often not comparable.

Developments will continue to be driven by end-user expectations. Users take for granted the same type of additional content, such as 'see inside', available on frequently used websites such as Amazon. SOPAC (Social OnLine Public Access Catalog)[4] is a free, open source social discovery platform for library bibliographic data and already claims to be the first social library OPAC for special libraries with a view to transforming libraries from being cost centres to knowledge networks. It enables a two-way exchange of vetted content from top down and bottom up with users tagging, reviewing and rating holdings. To survive, OPACs will need to be versatile and relevant to end-users' work and to look beyond internally held resources to federated searching and offer options about other similar items on the topic or other locally held and accessible resources.

To continue in existence any LMS must be capable of handling e-journals and e-books. Although legal publishers have been slow to develop e-books they are gradually becoming available. Different publishers with different licensing arrangements can make these particularly difficult for the traditional LMS to deal with. It unnecessarily complicates and duplicates effort to have 'loans' on the publisher's system and financial information and so on on the LMS. If the traditional LMS is being used to capture loan information as part of making purchasing decisions on new editions, this loses credibility and value if separated from a publisher's system controlling loans of e-books. If the legal sector publishers follow some education sector ideas where publishers lease contents of book chapters or journal articles for a fixed period which are then subsequently deleted from the system or device, the LMS will need to deal with access, licensing dedicated or concurrent user(s) and financial records for such transitory items whilst generating meaningful management information about how they were used. This will help to aid future decisions on similar resources or advise where the tipping point for permanent access to an item becomes viable.

Discovery platforms are opening up alternatives to federated searching and are still improving. Options like Primo[5] offer OPACs with a personal e-shelf and provide access by mobile devices. Searches across OPACs, e-journals and other digital resources can be carried out from one search, saving time and maximizing use of expensive resources. Discovery platforms rely on relevancy rankings, increasing the need for good information literacy training on focusing searches and using faceted searching. One of the major impediments to further uptake of discovery platforms is currently publishers' resistance (Buckley Owen, 2011).

NOTES

1 http://www.librarything.com/
2 http://evergreen-ils.org/
3 http://koha-community.org/
4 http://thesocialopac.net/
5 http://www.exlibrisgroup.com/category/PrimoOverview

CHAPTER 5

FINANCIAL MANAGEMENT

CONTRIBUTORS:
SARAH BRITTAN
MICHAEL MAHER
FIONA FOGDEN

PLANNING AND BUDGETING

SARAH BRITTAN AND MICHAEL MAHER

INTRODUCTION

This chapter is aimed at library managers and anybody responsible for financial management within a library and information service (LIS). It is examined from a practical perspective with the aim being to show you how to do it. This is particularly crucial within a modern information world facing threats of outsourcing and cutbacks and disappearing under the catch-all label of knowledge management. Financial management, whether it be on the expenditure or the income side of the balance sheet, is a skill that the LIS manager has to develop and be seen to display.

FINANCIAL PLANNING

LIS financial planning is divided into three major practical components: namely, *awareness*; *budgets*; and *control*. They interact and influence one another but, for convenience, this chapter treats each one of them as a separate unit. Different libraries exist to cater for different user groups operating within different sectors. Within the legal sector, libraries are categorized under one of four types: academic, court service, law firm and professional society. Each type of library exists as part of a larger, parent organization which acts as their main funding body, providing annual budgets to cover staffing, stock and maintenance costs. These library budgets are normally managed by the library manager who will follow an agreed financial planning process based on whatever the organization's firm-wide finance processes are.

This library financial planning process will cover everything from basic administrative tasks, such as procedures for paying invoices, to management tasks such as budget preparation and financial controls. All the tasks that make up the process should be documented and readily available to anybody who carries out LIS financial responsibilities. Although these individual financial tasks may vary from one library to another, they should all fit under the three umbrella components highlighted above that make up the financial planning process. Each of these components is analysed below.

AWARENESS

Awareness may not be the first point that springs to mind when considering LIS financial planning but it acts as a key part of the process, not least because libraries need to continually prove their value to the organization they work for. With information now readily available on the desktop, questions will be asked about the need for the traditional library set-up and LISs have to react to these questions by working harder at justifying their existence. An essential tool to help them is awareness. At the very least they need to be aware of what is expected of their service and how it fits the bigger organizational set-up. They should know the different information needs of the user groups they cater for and make sure these are being fully met. Although different law libraries have different awareness needs, three groupings common to all are looked at below.

Organizational Awareness

Organizational structure
Within the legal sector, libraries tend to operate as a smaller part of a larger organizational body such as a law firm or university. Therefore, it is essential that the law library manager is fully aware of how the larger organization is structured, and where the LIS department fits within that structure. They need to be familiar with organizational development plans and strategies, not just those covering the LIS, but ones covering all aspects of the business. This knowledge allows the manager to evaluate how well or poorly the LIS supports the organization's needs. It gives them the opportunity to identify new areas of the business into which the LIS can expand its services. Without such awareness LIS services may become stale and be increasingly seen as old style or, worse still, obsolete.

Mission statement
A second area the LIS manager will need to be aware of is the organization's mission statement. This is normally some broad message summing up the organization's purpose and vision and will be linked to their major strategies and objectives. The LIS manager should also be using it as the foundation block for the LIS's strategic plans and objectives, including any dealing with finance and

financial processes. As Jim Basker states: 'The vision of the organisation is very important to the information service because it confers legitimacy.'[1] LIS planning needs to fit in with wherever the organization sees itself or aims to be. Existing information services and library resources need to regularly reviewed in light of the organization's mission statement so that finances can be shown to be justified.

Financial set-up
The overall organizational financial set-up is a third awareness area. Is there a central finance team? Where is it located and how is it organized? If there isn't one, then who has financial responsibility? Who does the LIS department financially report to? What precisely is it expected to report on? Does it set its own budget? When is it set and what does it cover – just stock acquisitions or other items such as staffing, building maintenance, IT? All basic questions, but ones that the library manager must be able to answer.

On the financial procedural side, there must be familiarity with the internal procedures used by the organization; for example, what to do to raise a cheque or to pay an invoice in euros; how and when payment runs are made; and who has authority to sign off invoices. The library manager should know and have access to all the internal financial documentation that is used, such as purchase vouchers, expense claim forms, payment requisition forms and the like. These may be available in an operations manual or be a printable document off the intranet.

On the financial management side, what processes are in place to find out LIS current budgetary spend? Does the LIS receive updated internal monthly expenditure reports? If not, then get them set up.

User information demands
A second grouping to be aware of is library users, and in particular their information needs as these will clearly impact on the LIS financial planning processes in terms of what library stock is bought in and what information services are provided. Over time needs may well change and evolve. For example, UK law firms in the late 1980s had libraries catering solely for the firm's fee earners whose information needs centred around access to law and practice management material. Thirty years on and UK law firm libraries cater not only for fee earners but for other groups within the firm, such as business development, human resources and practice lawyers. They may also cater for clients' information needs.

User information delivery
Delivery of information has also undergone radical changes over recent years with today's user expecting the law library to be able to provide information in a variety of formats. The traditional hard copy collections remain and there is little evidence to suggest UK law libraries moving away from them, but there is now also demand for desktop access as more and more services and sources become web-delivered.

This has impacted on financial planning in that the library manager now has to budget for *access to* rather than *ownership of* a service. Purchasing a book is a relatively straightforward product to budget for in that it has a fixed price irrespective of how many times you use it. Budgeting access costs to an online product is much more difficult because the price is much more variable. It may be charged on a pay-as-you-go basis and, thus, difficult to predict in advance. Alternatively, it may be based on the number of fee earners within the firm, or on what parts of the product the library wants access to. In the main, the more you use a commercial online product, the more you face additional financial penalties. One thing that is clear is that library managers are having to become experts at financial negotiating when it comes to renewing online subscriptions.

User location

This follows on from user demand in that LIS financial planning also needs to reflect user demand to be able to access information from anywhere, not just from the physical library itself. Providing information is comparatively easier and cheaper if all the users are based in the one location. The more locations the library has to cater for, the greater the pressure to duplicate stock. Multiple locations also mean a need to recruit additional library staff to manage the additional site collections. Recent shifts in lifestyle trends have added to the number of possible locations the LIS will need to cover in that some users may now demand access to information from their homes. This impacts on LIS financial planning in that it will need to deal with demands for 'personal' home copies of key works, and increased remote PC access to commercial online sources.

Marketplace Awareness

Suppliers

Looking outside the organization, the third grouping the library manager needs to be aware of is the library publishers and suppliers. On the development stock side, what new titles are planned? Are there going to be new editions of current key titles? Are there any titles going to be cancelled or merged? What is the anticipated inflation rate for renewing existing subscriptions? The answers to these questions impact on the size of budget and how best to allocate it.

But it is not just stock development: delivery of information can also impact on financial plans. A look at services such as LexisLibrary and Westlaw shows how far publishers have moved towards offering electronic versions of more and more of their popular titles. Electronic delivery introduces a different range of cost considerations for the LIS financial planner, not least of which is the accompanying licence required to access and deliver the information.

One final supplier area to be aware of is payment method. Typically, payment processes are dictated by the financial management and invoice systems used by the parent organization and the supplier. A large proportion of law library purchases are simply renewals of existing stock and so it may be possible to negotiate a single annual figure to cover everything rather than paying for each and every release and title. An alternative is to make a single payment of the monthly statement. It makes sense to have a single contact point at both the supplier and library ends when dealing with payments as this helps to improve communication and to build relationships and understanding of each other's businesses.

Competitor market
There are several areas to examine here. Firstly, just because two libraries purchase the same book it does not follow that they have paid the same price for it. Nowadays, the price you pay can be negotiated rather than fixed. Negotiation skills are covered in the accompanying chapter.

BUDGETS

The second component of the financial planning process is the budgetary process, which is divided into *budget planning*, *budget preparation* and *budget presentation*. Normally, a budget is approved in advance. The type of budget an LIS is expected to prepare will depend upon the requirements of the parent organization, which might want a very detailed financial breakdown of expected expenditure covering all operational costs, or just a single bottom-line figure. Alternatively, they may not require any direct budget at all because LIS expenditure has already been accounted for within another department's budget. Whatever budget is required will fall under one of the following types:

- *Operating budget* – most familiar to LIS departments and represents routine day-to-day budgets covering expenditure on material, staffing and utilities.
- *Capital expenditure* – for one-off items of expenditure such as library management systems and may well be accounted for over the life of the purchase as a depreciation figure spread over several years.
- *Internal recovery* – covers expected internal revenue to be raised during the life of the budget, revenue derived from cross-charging other departments and internal users for library services.
- *Income budget* – covers predicted income to be generated during the life of the budget. This may be revenue raised by photocopying charges, fines, sales of material and the like. LIS income and charging will be looked at in-depth in the second part of this chapter.

Budget Preparation

Methods
The LIS's strategic plan is the base on which to build the LIS budget. The budget itself can be prepared following several defined methods, all of which are

examined in Duncan McKay's guide, *Effective Financial Planning for Library and Information Services*.[2] Listed in increasing level of complexity they are:

- line item budgeting
- formula budgeting
- programme budgeting
- performance budgeting
- planning programming budgeting system
- zero based budgeting.

What category the LIS uses may depend upon the preferred method of the parent organization. It is also possible to combine two or more categories. However, many libraries tend to prepare their budget by using the simple line item system, an example of which, Figure 5.1, is shown opposite. This shows how a law firm library might choose to lay out its budget proposal. Starting from the left-hand side, the first column lists proposed expenditure under a couple of broad headings and revenue under a single heading for the forthcoming year. Each in turn is broken down into the individual cost groups that make up the broad heading. Thus, the Departmental Costs heading comprises of all of the firm's practice group's book budgets plus the renewal budgets for other library subscriptions such as journals and newspapers. The second column indicates the nominal budget codes for each of these cost groups. Putting each one under its own code makes it is easier to identify any overspend and underspend.

The remaining columns concentrate on the actual budget figures and spend. The third column itemizing the current year's budget is followed by the fourth column showing the actual expenditure to date in the current year. This can be useful because the proposed budget for the new year will be prepared before the year-end and this is a chance to highlight how the library is really financially performing and to pinpoint where there may be budgetary concerns. The fifth column shows the proposed budget figures for the new year. At the bottom of the spreadsheet is a 'grand total' line that gives a total figure for each column.

Costing considerations
In preparing the budget the library manager needs to carry out a cost analysis exercise to accurately quantify and cost all the cost areas the budget is required to cover. In the legal sector such cost analysis will need to cover the following:

- *Inflation* – as a large slice of the stock budget is spent renewing existing holdings rather than buying new ones, it will be necessary to factor in inflation quotes on existing required looseleaf and journal stock, and include projected quotes for renewing access to all commercial online subscriptions.

Figure 5.1   Law firm budget proposal

Budget Code	Description	Agreed Budget 2011/2012	2011/2012 Reforecast	2011/2012 Variance	2012/2013 Budget Proposed
	SALARIES				
100-101-000	BASE PAY	£ 150,000.00	£ 145,500.00	-£ 4,500.00	£ 160,000.00
100-102-000	OVERTIME	£ 2,500.00	£ 3,000.00	£ 500.00	£ 3,100.00
	Total	£ 152,500.00	£ 148,500.00	-£ 4,000.00	£ 163,100.00
	HARD COPY RESOURCES				
100-105-600	GENERAL	£ 30,000.00	£ 30,382.00	£ 382.00	£ 33,000.00
100-106-600	COMMERCIAL	£ 13,000.00	£ 10,572.00	-£ 2,428.00	£ 12,000.00
100-107-600	CORPORATE	£ 45,000.00	£ 46,026.00	£ 1,026.00	£ 48,500.00
100-108-600	DISPUTES	£ 20,000.00	£ 20,686.00	£ 686.00	£ 22,000.00
100-109-600	EMPLOYMENT	£ 18,000.00	£ 21,137.00	£ 3,137.00	£ 21,500.00
100-110-600	EUC&T	£ 10,000.00	£ 9,633.00	-£ 367.00	£ 10,075.00
100-111-600	FINANCE	£ 25,000.00	£ 32,226.00	£ 7,226.00	£ 33,000.00
100-112-600	IP/IT	£ 25,000.00	£ 16,459.00	-£ 8,541.00	£ 18,000.00
100-113-600	PENSIONS	£ 5,000.00	£ 4,478.00	-£ 522.00	£ 4,900.00
100-114-600	PRIVATE CLIENT	£ 10,000.00	£ 10,086.00	£ 86.00	£ 10,600.00
100-115-600	PROPERTY	£ 12,000.00	£ 13,145.00	£ 1,145.00	£ 14,000.00
100-116-600	TAX	£ 20,000.00	£ 20,246.00	£ 246.00	£ 21,500.00
	Total	£ 233,000.00	£ 235,076.00	£ 2,076.00	£ 249,075.00
	ELECTRONIC RESOURCES				
100-105-700	GENERAL	£ 350,000.00	£ 357,500.00	£ 7,500.00	£ 390,000.00
100-106-700	COMMERCIAL	£ -	£ -	£ -	£ -
100-107-700	CORPORATE	£ 90,000.00	£ 87,085.00	-£ 2,915.00	£ 88,000.00
100-108-700	DISPUTES	£ 1,050.00	£ -	-£ 1,050.00	£ 1,200.00
100-109-700	EMPLOYMENT	£ 3,500.00	£ 3,330.00	-£ 170.00	£ 4,100.00
100-110-700	EUC&T	£ 5,000.00	£ 4,902.00	-£ 98.00	£ 5,000.00
100-111-700	FINANCE	£ 46,000.00	£ 47,538.00	£ 1,538.00	£ 48,000.00
100-112-700	IP/IT	£ -	£ -	£ -	£ 1,000.00
100-113-700	PENSIONS	£ 22,000.00	£ 22,000.00	£ -	£ 22,000.00
100-114-700	PRIVATE CLIENT	£ 5,000.00	£ 5,000.00	£ -	£ 5,000.00
100-115-700	PROPERTY	£ 750.00	£ 750.00	£ -	£ 750.00
100-116-700	TAX	£ 41,000.00	£ 40,707.00	-£ 293.00	£ 41,000.00
	Total	£ 564,300.00	£ 568,812.00	£ 4,512.00	£ 606,050.00
	OTHER				
100-133-800	SUNDRIES (TRAVEL etc)	£ 9,000.00	£ 7,800.00	-£ 1,200.00	£ 1,950.00
100-134-800	DOCUMENT DELIVERY	£ 2,500.00	£ 4,500.00	£ 2,000.00	£ 2,500.00
100-135-800	COPYRIGHT LICENSES	£ 12,000.00	£ 9,395.00	-£ 2,605.00	£ 11,000.00
100-136-800	TRAINING & MEMBERSHIPS	£ 7,000.00	£ 6,914.00	-£ 86.00	£ 7,000.00
	Total	£ 30,500.00	£ 28,609.00	-£ 1,891.00	£ 22,450.00
	TOTAL COSTS	£ 980,300.00	£ 980,997.00	£ 697.00	£ 1,040,675.00

- Carrying out a *stock audit* – it will help to ascertain what stock and services are required for the new financial year. If there are multiple subscriptions to services, the audit provides a chance to reassess what level of subscription is still needed.
- Parent *organizational plans* – these should be looked at because they may affect stock requirements; for example, plans may have been made to expand or reduce the size of some of the LIS's user groups.
- *New titles and services* being planned – so that their costs can be factored in.

- *IT* – user demand for new or enhanced IT software and hardware in order to access, store and distribute information sources should also be analysed and included in the proposed budget. If they are not to be a part of the LIS budget then their cost implications should be passed on to whichever department is responsible for them.

Budget Presentation

The final budgetary piece of the financial planning process is the budget presentation itself. This is an opportunity to market the LIS service as well as to make a request for funding.

Budgetary timetable
Time plays a critical role in any budget presentation. Whoever is responsible for preparing the budget should be following whatever budgetary timetable is in operation within the organization, and allowing themselves plenty of time to carry out all the cost analysis exercises and audits, as well as writing up the proposed budget itself. When it is presented it may not be approved immediately and so further time will be needed to incorporate any recommended changes to the proposal before it is presented a second time, and maybe even a third time. Getting approval is often a lengthy and frustrating process, particularly when finances are tight and there are other departments presenting their own strong arguments to expand their budgets.

Once the presentations are complete it may take even more time before formal approval is given, particularly if the overall proposed spend exceeds expected revenue or funding levels. Thus, budgets may be returned for more negotiating before final figures are set.

Budget proposal
The written budget proposal itself should include the following sections:

- *Background information* – this should be clear and concise, containing information about the LIS, its role within the organization, agreed goals, mandate and aspirations, all of which should derive from the approved LIS strategic plan. It is an opportunity to reinforce the value of the service to the organization.
- *Overview* – this summarizes specific LIS plans for the period the budget covers. Inflationary trends and any notable changes to purchasing needs that have impacted on the budget should be mentioned, as should brief results of any costing exercises that have been carried out as part of the budgetary process.
- *Budget proposal* (see Figure 5.1 above) – this will be the actual headings and figures themselves and will expand on the *Overview* section. This

section may well be based around detailed spreadsheets outlining all the financial requirements for the coming period, organized under whatever headings and codes the library uses. One-off proposals should be included but kept separate from the normal expenditure budgets. Costs for previous one-off items may well have been budgeted to be paid for over several financial years and so it is important to include any accrued charges. Annual subscriptions that cover two budgetary periods may have part of their renewal costs deferred to the second period and these costs should be included, along with any details on any other LIS expenditure being covered within other department budgets.

- *Phasing* – finance departments tend to split budgets into twelve equal monthly parts or four equal quarterly parts and this will not necessarily reflect LIS real expenditure patterns. Therefore, include any timetable phasing details, highlighting the times when expenditure is likely to be high so that the finance departments are aware and can be prepared.

Budget presentation style
The budget presentation itself can take on many formats, from simply passing on the budget proposals to whoever needs to see them to an in-depth formal presentation. Whatever the format it is an important opportunity to market the LIS and a chance to link the LIS to the business by promoting its services and showing how they support the organization's strategic outlook. It should not just be used as a request for funds.

FINANCIAL CONTROL

Financial control is the third component of financial planning that this chapter will examine. It is chiefly concerned with the practices and procedures that an LIS can use in order to properly manage its income and expenditure. What is required will vary from one library to another but the following three procedures are standard practice for most libraries.

Bookkeeping

Any LIS department needs to ensure it carries out a sufficient level of bookkeeping in order to properly monitor and record its financial transactions. The following are two of the most useful strategies for countering the problems of a busy department.

Problems in tracking paperwork
One of the biggest problems is trying to keep control of the high volume of invoices that law libraries receive. Libraries receive invoices for everything

from pay-by-release updates, to journal renewals, to new stock, to online subscriptions. As many suppliers only offer a 30-day credit system, if payment is not received in time they send out a duplicate invoice. Without a bookkeeping system in place it is easy to process the original *and* the duplicate invoice, especially if more than one person is involved in processing the invoices. If an invoice is not going to be paid within the credit terms then the LIS needs to notify the supplier to prevent any cancellation of service or second copies of invoices.

Another problem is one of paying for goods that have been returned. A lot of book stock is bought on approval, a percentage of which will be sent back. However, returned books often arrive with pre-payment invoices and this creates the risk of these being inadvertently processed for payment. Mistakes can happen.

Other departments' journals, books and online costs can be accidentally assigned to the LIS budget codes by a busy finance department. A bookkeeping system is a useful way to pick this out in that an LIS staff member can be tasked with checking the LIS records against the monthly ledger account report which itemizes what has been debited against all of the nominal codes.

Spreadsheets
Running a bookkeeping system is not a complicated task. In most cases a simple Excel spreadsheet will suffice. This offers the advantages of being flexible and fast, and does all the calculations for you. It is straightforward to use and shows the effects of inflation, as well as recording ongoing actual costs, and financial details on committed expenditure such as standing orders and required renewals.

Library Management System software
Library Management Systems (LMS) usually have a finance module where it is useful to store details of subscriptions and invoices paid. There is often also a facility to allocate these payments to budget codes, which can then be used to produce reports. This is a good way to keep track of what invoices have been paid throughout the year. This information can be used in conjunction with spreadsheets and finance department reports to help with the budgeting process.

Acquisitions Policy

The second practice is to have a clearly laid out acquisitions policy that outlines all of the procedures to follow when ordering material and processing it for payment.

The following checklist covers some of the typical areas that might be included in such a policy:

- Order procedures:

  - Generating orders
  - Placing new orders
  - Renewing existing orders
  - Recording the order
  - Acknowledging receipt of goods
  - Returning goods

- Payment procedures:
  - Recording invoice details
  - How to pay by:

    Cheque
    BACS
    Credit Card
    Foreign Draft

  - Checking monthly ledger

- Contact details:

  - Supplier details:

    Names
    Addresses
    Telephone/email

  - Licences
  - Terms and Conditions
  - Renewal dates

Financial Reporting

The third practice is financial reporting, which needs to be carried out on a regular basis in order to check LIS expenditure and income against budget.

Types of reports can range from a simple monthly list that provides a basic breakdown of current spend and trends in the LIS cost centres, to more in-depth studies that analyse this spend and trends in order to make policy recommendations on future developments. For example, a simple list report might show that a particular supplier's book inflation rate is above the figure budgeted for. With this information, the library manager is able to calculate the overall effect this will have on the budget and then make informed recommendations on what to do.

Figure 5.2   Property expenditure spreadsheet example

Property Item	Actual Expenditure 2010/2011		Agreed Budget 2011/2012		Revised projection 2011/2012		Actual expenditure 2011/2012		Savings/ overspend	
Hard copy: 100-115-600										
Looseleafs - Pay as you go										
Aldridge: Commonhold Law	£	211.75	£	232.93	£	298.68			-£	65.76
Handbook of Dilapidations	£	803.44	£	883.78	£	883.78	£	207.00	£	0.00
Handbook of Rent Review	£	652.19	£	717.41	£	717.41	£	225.00	-£	0.00
Practical Conveyancing Precedents	£	491.26	£	540.39	£	590.00	£	590.00	-£	49.61
Practical Lease Precedents	£	739.20	£	800.00	£	800.00			£	-
Total	£	2,897.84	£	3,174.50	£	3,289.87	£	1,022.00	-£	115.37
Looseleafs - Annual subscriptions										
Commercial Property Development Precedents	£	484.00	£	532.40	£	528.00	£	545.00	£	4.40
Hill and Redman's Law of Landlord and Tenant	£	1,212.15	£	1,078.74	£	1,200.00	£	1,200.00	-£	121.26
Landlord and Tenant (Woodfall)	£	813.00	£	894.30	£	894.30				
Landlord and Tenant Factbook	£	402.00	£	442.20	£	442.20			£	-
Leasehold Law	£	552.00	£	607.20	£	600.00	£	630.00	£	7.20
Precedents for the Conveyancer	£	583.00	£	641.30	£	641.30			£	-
Tolley's Claims to the Possession of Land	£	242.00	£	266.20	£	340.00	£	340.00	-£	73.80
VAT and Property	£	378.70	£	416.57	£	305.76	£	305.76	£	110.81
Total	£	4,666.85	£	4,878.91	£	4,951.56	£	3,020.76	-£	72.65
Serials										
Commercial Leases	£	585.00	£	655.20	£	750.00	£	750.00	-£	94.80
Estates Gazette (sub 1)	£	271.96	£	304.60	£	304.60			£	-
Estates Gazette (sub 2)	£	271.96	£	304.60	£	304.60			£	-
Property Week	£	196.00	£	219.52	£	175.00	£	175.00	£	44.52
Total	£	1,324.92	£	1,483.91	£	1,534.19	£	925.00	-£	50.28
Ad-hoc Book orders										
Unplanned books	£	1,121.54	£	1,750.00	£	1,750.00				
Bohm & Sharples: Land licensing							£	95.00	£	-
Total	£	1,121.54	£	1,750.00	£	1,750.00	£	95.00	£	-
Standing Orders/ Annuals										
Butterworths Property Law Handbook (2 copies)	£	322.56	£	361.27	£	286.00	£	286.00	£	75.27
Directory of Local Authorities	£	121.50	£	136.08	£	142.80	£	142.80	-£	6.72
Law Society Conveyancing Handbook	£	71.95	£	80.58	£	80.58	£	80.58	£	0.00
Total	£	516.01	£	577.93	£	509.38	£	509.38	£	68.55
Supplements										
Reynolds & Clark: Renewal of Businss Tenancies	£	65.00	£	69.74	£	85.00			-£	15.26
Boundaries & Easements	£	65.00	£	65.00	£	75.00			-£	10.00
Total	£	130.00	£	134.74	£	160.00	£	-	-£	25.26
Total HARDCOPY	£	10,657.16	£	12,000.00	£12,195.00		£	5,572.14	-£	195.00
Electronic: 100-115-700										
Law and Practice of Registered Conveyancing - Ruoff and Roper	£	752.00	£	750.00	£	950.00	£	750.00	-£	200.00
Total ELECTRONIC	£	752.00	£	750.00	£	950.00	£	750.00	-£	200.00
Grand Total	£	11,409.16	£	12,750.00	£13,145.00		£	6,322.14	-£	395.00

Levels of reports

Within an organization there will be different structural levels of financial reporting. In a law firm the most detailed level will often be the *transactional listing* which records a department's expenditure and income item by item. Typically, for the LIS department this will be the bookkeeping spreadsheet (see Figure 5.2 opposite). Next level up is the *specific departmental cost centre* which shows the overall cost of a particular cost centre within a department. This is followed by the *total departmental cost centre* which is a combination of the various particular cost centres. This can be followed by a wider *group cost centre* covering, say, the running costs of all of the non fee-earning departments. The final level is the actual *firm-wide total* itself, which covers the firm's total budgetary income and revenue figures. Each level up tends to provide less specific detail but looks at a bigger slice of the business.

Although the LIS department may be less involved with the *group cost* or *firmwide total* financial reporting, it is important its members are aware of financial developments at these levels as it may influence how they control their own LIS finances.

CHARGING FOR INFORMATION SERVICES

Charging for information services is not a new concept. Public and academic libraries have traditionally issued fines for overdue books and for many years library users have paid a small charge to take audio and visual items out on loan.

In the commercial sector there has always been a charge for the LIS in that the library running costs make up a part (albeit a small part) of the fee earners' hourly client charge-out rate.

Rapid development and growing market presence of web-based technology since the late 1980s shifted the concept of charging as a means of small-scale cost recovery to one of making a healthy profit. The reasons for this shift were twofold.

Firstly, as mentioned earlier, the rapid escalation of commercial online information products expanded the trend of organizations having to pay to access information rather than *own* it.

Secondly, developments in technology helped fuel the birth of the knowledge management culture, particularly within law firms who are so knowledge-intensive.

Although some firms still charge for aspects of their information service, since the more widespread introduction of new fee structures in law firms, such as conditional fee arrangements, charging for such services has substantially decreased.

This charging trend was picked up in Hannah Milford's 2004 study *Charging for Information Services in Law Firm Libraries*[3] which showed that nearly three-quarters of respondents to the survey operated as a cost centre only.

The way that online providers charge for access has also had an impact on this trend. They have tended to move from pay-as-you-go charging to annual "all-you-can-eat" charging, which is more difficult to charge back, particularly with the SRA tightening guidelines governing what can be charged for.

NEGOTIATING ONLINE SUBSCRIPTIONS

FIONA FOGDEN

INTRODUCTION

When I first started being involved in negotiating in a large international law firm in 1999, it was the age of books on screen on CD moving over to the internet, current awareness still being partly done by scanning hardcopy and lots of other aspects of information life far more manual than today. It was a time when licences that went with these new online resources seemed a formality and hands-up straw polls in training classes that I ran in 2000 showed that all but a very few of the delegates actually read the contract terms or negotiated a price. It was then a new skill, but in the intervening years it is a skill that has become an element, or in some instances an all-consuming focus, of many librarians at all levels. We should recognize that this could so easily have been different. Procurement of online resources has become something that legal librarians can do well. It is the purpose of this half chapter to build up the skills to ensure that is the case. If we are not careful, if we are unable to demonstrate our worth this element could end up being managed by IT departments, procurement specialists (in or out-sourced) or facilities managers. My reason for laying this groundwork is that the tactics we need to employ, the people we need to engage with and the value we need to demonstrate has changed to be something far more sophisticated than the tinkering around the edges that may have been the norm in the past. Negotiation plus the confidence to talk about content contracts are now fairly common skills required in our constantly changing arsenal of abilities.

This focuses on negotiating online subscriptions, but many of the skills and tips will apply to other arenas of negotiation.

Skills Arsenal Number One – Questions

In negotiating you cannot get anywhere without questions being asked of you and you asking questions of your supplier. Negotiating is about communication, movement in position on both sides and understanding. Questions are an important area in both (or in multiple party or consortia agreements – all the related entities) sides learning about each other. Without communication, a single party in a negotiation risks a number of scenarios:

- Having the upper hand
- The other side having the advantage
- A relationship that is not sustainable due to being one-sided
- Distrust
- Misunderstanding.

It is appreciated that discretion is necessary. It is rarely in your best interests for example to reveal exact details of budget allowances, spend on other resources and many other details. Whilst greater transparency on both sides is part of the objective, commercial realities mean that it would be unrealistic to expect 100 per cent transparency.

Skills Arsenal Number Two – Knowing where You have Wriggle Room

The representative knows their targets, the subscriber the price at which the value which they can gain is exceeded. Dancing about to find the common ground sometimes seems distasteful, but it is not all about money. Value is an area than can create 'wriggle room' in any negotiation. At times where money is paramount, it does not. Questions that can help in negotiating include:

- Can the cost be shared with another department?
- What other business models does the supplier operate that may be alternatives, for example named user with dissemination rights rather than site licence?
- Pay as you go – more relevant to law firms that can recharge than to the government or academic sectors.
- Consortia negotiated licences for the academic sector.

Identifying this ground for yourself is the result of working out the following:

– Most Favoured Position (MFP)

This is the option that is most beneficial to you. It might include a few 'in our dreams' scenarios that you are unlikely to realize.

– Walk Away Position (WAP)

What is the most you are prepared or are able to pay? What are the least amount of users you can manage with? Is your WAP that you must subscribe?[4]

– Best Alternative to a Negotiated Agreement (BATNA)[5]

This is what happens if you cannot come to an agreement. You need to be aware of existing subscriptions and alternative products on the market. It may involve you understanding the consequences of not subscribing, of the services that will be affected, the links you will need to remove from know how systems and a myriad of other issues that can arise.

Figure 5.3   Identifying the common ground for a negotiation

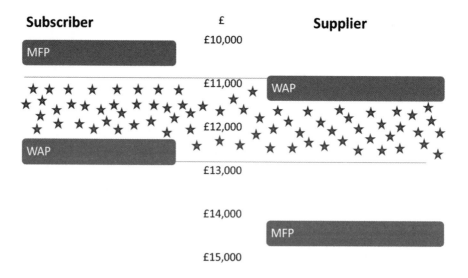

Note: The starred area is the 'common ground' between the subscriber's MFP and WAP and the supplier's WAP and MFP. It is simplified as it only considers the monetary value, but other elements like extra locations and users could be part of the MFP.

There are situations which prevent you from maximizing your MFP, WAP and BATNA and being prepared is key. Many of these come under understanding your contract which is covered later in this section and understanding the needs of your organization and the information market place below.

Skills Arsenal Number Three – Understanding Your Organization, Its Business and Its Needs

There are usually degrees by which an organization needs a product. Understanding whether a product is essential, liked, loathed, a 'nice-to-have' or 'useful-but-could-live-without' can help the negotiator decide on the value of the product and whether that value matches the asking price and terms.

Knowing the strategy of your organization will also help you plan for the future, allowing for growth or contraction in the contract. Understanding the core business will enable you to understand your WAP more clearly. Where your information unit is outsourced and you are negotiating on behalf of a single or multiple entities, explaining to the supplier where relationships stop and start and how far you can take a negotiation are important to manage expectations and avoid frustration if there are delays or you have to refer to someone else. In many outsourced services a negotiator may have remit to do most of the negotiating but one of the steps is to make a final recommendation and so there may be a delay or perceived lack of authority, when in reality it is little different from any other set-up.

You also need to understand additional relationships that may be in place. These might include:

- In an academic environment: sponsorship by the supplier of student places;
- In a law firm: the supplier as a client;
- The organization joint sponsoring a conference with the supplier;
- Authors employed by the organization that write for the supplier;
- Locations of user groups including offshored, outsourced and shared services.

Understanding these added dimensions helps you understand how far you can or cannot push during a negotiation, helps you understand additional stakeholders you may need to consult with and ultimately prevents you looking like an idiot when you cancel something and a client walks away and you lose lots of business as a result.

Skills Arsenal Number Four – Understanding the Supplier, the Product Marketplace and Building a Relationship

Listening is important. Negotiation is not just about what you want. Creating a sustainable relationship with a supplier is the long-term goal. Being aggressive every year will often mean that the supplier's only option is to be aggressive back and start negotiations at a higher price level.

In an ideal situation the same representative and same negotiator deal with successive renewals of the same product. However people change jobs, they get promoted and information about past negotiations gets lost. A subscriber is often impressed by a new representative who has 'done their homework' either via a handover meeting with the previous representative or by visiting the subscriber when accounts change hands. For the organization, keeping a record of previous dealings with the publisher will be invaluable when the internal negotiator or information professional leaves the organization, that way their insights into the relationship can be preserved. Keeping good notes and clarifications about the contract will also prevent misunderstandings in the future.

You also need to have a good idea of what alternatives there are on the market so you may have some relationships that are not current suppliers but may be in the future. Helping you in the negotiation and to build up your MFP, WAP and most importantly your BATNA are:

- What alternative products are there (if any)?
- What makes the product you are subscribing to unique (if relevant)?
- What makes the product valuable to your organization?
- How do different subscriptions overlap with content, either from the same supplier or different suppliers?
- Who are the users of the product – and although it seems unfair to say – not all types of user are equal?
- Are there any other subscription models to the one you have, for example pay as you go vs all you can eat; firm-wide access vs five named users?
- How the product performs, is it reliable, are there faults with it?

Understanding the supplier market, what their tendencies are, what they are renowned for (both good and bad!) will also help you prepare. Where the supplier is new or you have suspicions about their financial health you may want to do a credit rating or director check before agreeing to part with lots of money upfront. This may well help arguments for payments in installments rather than paying upfront.

Where you might be doing something quite new and innovative that involves you investing a lot of time with the supplier and integrating their content in sophisticated ways with other systems, it is all the more essential that you create between you an understanding regarding the longer-term implications of the relationship and agreement about long-term price stability. This doesn't mean you have to sign a contract for five years, but you can at least get written agreement about how pricing will be dealt with in the long term should the subscription continue.

Skills Arsenal Number Five – Understanding the Contract

So far we have talked about suppliers, your organization, knowing what you want to achieve. All this is important when looking at the contract. Getting the right terms in the contract can add or detract to the value of the resource to your organization. For example if you have a service just for library staff but do not have the right to disseminate content from it to others, this may make it virtually valueless to you.

Misusing a contract can also get an organization into serious difficulties and on the wrong side of the law. The example of the *Financial Times* suing Blackstone is just one example.[6]

The contract can actually be a number of documents. You need to ensure you have all the pieces that make up the agreement. Typical names of these documents are order schedule; appendix; online terms & conditions. There may be a reference to another element of the agreement in one document and it is important that you pick up this link. The most common problem is that you might spend time looking at what you think is the whole agreement only to have a reference to 'we reserve the right to change the terms at www. websiteofsupplier.com at any time'.

When you are looking at a contract it is with two broad things in mind:

1. If we cannot change anything in the contract, does this work for my organization?
2. If we can change items in the contract what would these be?

Many suppliers will make amendments to contracts. These may come in multiple forms, either as a side letter, a new version of the contract, as an addendum or similar mechanism.

When looking at a contract the aim is for it to be balanced. If too unbalanced then the supplier may not elect to make the changes or wish you to purchase their product as the risks for them are too great.

Who should read the contract? Even if you have a legal team who are required to read the contract it is essential that someone with an information background reads the contract. This is because you should have a better understanding of how the product is intended to be used, what it should contain and details that a lawyer will not realize are incorrect from your perspective, only from a legal perspective. If you are negotiating for something that is used by a small group of people then it is always worth extracting relevant terms for the users and asking them how they intend on using and sharing the content. This means that when you point out to the users that they are not permitted to do something, the issue does not come as a shock and you have lain the groundwork so that they should know any limitations (where your excellent skills have not managed to negotiate more generous terms that is).

What to look for in a contract – what have you subscribed to?
This may sound obvious, but will you have access to what you think you have agreed to? If the supplier is an aggregator, what recourse do you have if they remove some of the content? If there is no clear indication of compensation or procedures in the event of removed content then consider a take-down clause.[7]

Other things to pay attention to are caps on usage.

What price are you paying?
This may seem simple, but if you have a multi-year deal, check that you are still paying annually. Are there any penalties for use over a certain amount? If you do not notify your intention to cancel by a certain date, is there mention of what price you would be paying next year?

Who are the users and where can they use the product?
Unless the product is for just a few users you need to think about all the different types of 'customers' your service has. Flexible workers, offshored workers, people going on secondment, consultants, maternity cover, visitors, access for subsidiaries and other physical locations may all be relevant. The definition of user is always open to interpretation, the most common confusion being between concurrent usage and named usage, make sure you know and that your users know.

How can the information be reused?
Sometimes this is possible under a category called 'dissemination' or 're-use'. How the information within an online database can be shared amongst interested parties can significantly change the value of the product. Having onerous terms can also make the contract awkward to manage from the point of having to make users aware of the strict limitations and make it difficult to manage risk.

When does the contract run to and is there a notification period?
Is the contract a multi-year one with or without prices for future years? Are there break clauses that would allow you out of the contract? One of the most common ways of restricting your BATNA is to ignore notification periods. Not all contracts contain notification periods, but when they do they usually require the subscriber to notify the supplier an agreed number of days in advance should they wish to cancel. A common time frame is 90 days ahead of the end of the contract. Failing to notify a supplier may not mean you have to renew, they may allow you out of that obligation, but in many instances they will not. Even if you have every intention of renewing, or indeed are obliged to renew for whatever reason, you should agree a price in good time. That way you are more likely to get the best price and the best terms in spite of your alternatives being limited. It is possible to write a letter reserving your right to cancel – this buys you time whilst you come to an agreement. An example of the format of this letter is contained in *Negotiating Licences for Digital Resources* by Fiona Durrant.[8]

What is missing?

Have there been any documents or web terms referred to that you have not seen? Consider potential problems that have been left unmentioned such as the removal of key content, creation of new modules from existing content, increase or decrease in number of users and similar unknowns.

Getting clarity

It may be that you are unclear about what something in the agreement means. In these instances you may not need to change the term, just gain a better understanding of it. Where possible decide what you think it should mean and present that interpretation to the supplier and ask them to let you know if it is otherwise. This tends to speed the process up rather than a 'what does this mean' type of question which always takes longer. Any correspondence on these should be appended to your copy of the contract.

Skills Arsenal Number Six – Being Able to Talk about Money

It may seem odd having this section so far down the list, not that the list is in any order. However it has been placed away from the top on purpose to highlight the fact that while price is important, it is only a small part of the negotiation process. As we demonstrated in the section above, value can be vastly affected by the terms of the contract.

It is also only possible to talk about money when you understand the product, your organization, the contract and the issues surrounding the negotiation as a whole. Often the negotiation cannot be just about money, it is tied up with other elements of what is required such as more users or access for more locations. The best two words to remember are *if … Then …*

For example:

> *If* you can keep the price the same for year two *then* that may attractive;
> *If* you can give access to my marketing team as well, only *then* is the price becoming affordable for us;
> *If* you can come back to us with a closer to what we paid last year *then* we may be able to take this negotiation further.

The communication that takes place is exploring that common ground between what is the supplier's MFP and WAP and what is the subscriber's MFP and WAP. You will have an amount in your budget that you can spend and you may or may not have flexibility to go over this amount. Whilst transparency and openness help a negotiation along, the subscriber would be at a disadvantage if they revealed the top amount that they are able to pay unless by doing so it gets a stratospheric quote back on track.

You also need to be able to talk money with the people internally within your organization. You need to be able to explain the value that the product brings and what functions and work it supports.

Skills Arsenal Number Seven – Knowing When Not to Negotiate

There are often times when it does not make sense to negotiate. There will be various reasons behind this, but it is still important to understand them. This will leave you more time to devote to the important deals:.

- *When the value or increase does not meet your criteria*: you may set yourself guidelines that you don't negotiate on price or anything under a certain amount and you only look at the contract to check that it is workable.
- *When the offer on the table is very reasonable*: let the supplier know that this is the reason you've done it.
- *When you know the only option is to cancel.*
- *If your negotiations last year had an understanding that there would be some pain this year*: let you supplier know that you are only accepting this increase due to a previous understanding and under normal circumstances would delve deeper.
- *Consideration of key relationships*: such as whether the supplier is also a client, talk to the partner concerned if this is the case.

Skills Arsenal Number Eight – Be Organized and Be Innovative

Keep good records about all aspects of your subscriptions. A good place to start is at the end of a negotiation, be the one to summarize your understanding of what was discussed and agreed. Write a letter reserving your right to cancel for high-value contracts and ensure you have a good mechanism for keeping track of contract notification periods and subscription end dates.

In your negotiations be the one to come up with ideas, do not rely on the supplier to find a solution that works for you. It also helps keep things fresh and relevant to your organization. Different ideas will work in different scenarios; just a couple of examples are below:

- *Spread payment monthly* – depending on your financial year you may be paying less than the annual subscription, however look at the long-term picture, it may be creating problems for future years, especially if you have to revert to annual payments for any reason.
- *Include product integration work* – perhaps you have a know how system or single search solution you are planning and the supplier normally charges for consultancy work, you may be able to get this included as part of your agreement.

Skills Arsenal Number Nine – Getting it Right for a New Subscription

When you have a new subscription, as opposed to a renewal it involves a few extra stages in the preparation process. It may be you have a new department so it is totally new, it may be that it is replacing something else.

LOCATING PRODUCTS

Information about what products exist can be gathered from a wide variety of sources ranging from personal experience, approaching publishers, flyers, reading blogs and resources such as Freepint and VIP, attending shows, consulting users within the organization who have worked previously at similar places and consulting other information professionals. When using this latter process, be receptive to feedback from peers as certain information about the product, both positive and negative, will be useful in the negotiation process.

THE TRIAL

Carrying out a proper trial involves a huge investment of time. Most organizations do not have the luxury of unlimited budgets and time. I would recommend not investing the time in a trial unless you have at least an idea of the cost and how it would fit in with your budget. A supplier may try and tell you that they can't begin to give you prices at this stage, but be persistent.

Whilst some quick trials and demonstrations can quickly exclude a product, poorly planned trials can lead to end-users getting 'addicted' to the new product without there being the budget to pay for it. Having end-user addicts can put the purchaser in a weaker position when negotiating as there is not the option of failing to come to agreement without making enemies amongst the addicts. You need to brief anyone involved in a trial about putting feedback through you as a single source so you can get the overview.

Another downside of going into a trial without any planning is that it is beneficial to trial products that perform similar roles at the same time. This avoids end-user apathy of trial following trial, or even the wrong end-user being involved in the wrong trial, and has the benefit of providing benchmarks for each database. Therefore to ensure being in a better position for negotiation it is best to follow the steps below:

- Get some outline information on what the product does and what the product contains;
- Are there any products that perform a similar function that should be trialled at the same time?

- Decide how and by whom the product would be used;
- Obtain a rough price and compare with budget or price of comparative product;
- If the price is not hugely out of reach then arrange a suitable date and length for the trial. Too long a trial and users tend to forget to give feedback, too short and a busy spell might mean they are unable to use the product in the time frame given;
- Decide who should be involved in the trial, are these 'regulars' who can be relied upon to give good feedback or are instructions needed on what sort of feedback is expected from them and by when?
- If the product is complex arrange a demonstration or training session from the publisher for those who are going to be involved in the trial; less complex databases might benefit from an overview by the information professional so it is not oversold. Some people involved in trials may never actually invest time past the demonstration stage and so make decisions based on session alone;
- If trialling more than one product for the same function or similar content, compile a very brief table of the advantages and disadvantages of each product;
- Decide if those involved in the trial should know how much the product costs so they can make a fairer assessment of its value;
- Set a calendar reminder a week before the end of the trial and contact those who have been involved in the trial, asking for feedback;
- Having got some feedback, look at the contract and check that the permissions in it allow the product to be used as desired;
- Note any feedback that might be useful in any negotiation, for example about desired changes to the interface, about performance and so on;
- Record the fact that a trial was undertaken and the outcome and the reasons behind that decision and whether it is something that should be revisited in a few years' time;
- From this point on, armed with sufficient information, the regular negotiation process can be followed.

If it is decided to subscribe this should be done on a timetable that suits the organization. There is little point in starting a subscription if it cannot be used due to lack of training, staff or IT issues. It is not uncommon for subscriptions to commence, only to fail to be used for several months. This under-use can affect everything from usage levels upon which prices might be based, to perception in the organization on how online subscriptions are managed.

SUMMING UP

This isn't just a summary of what has been written here about negotiation – at the conclusion of a negotiation you need to sum up in more ways than one too.

Do some maths, get knowledgeable with an Excel spreadsheet to show clearly what you could have paid if you paid what the supplier asked every time and what you managed to negotiate, pointing out all the detail too.

Summarize what your achievements have been to people internally. Negotiating is something that has demonstrable outcomes and can be measured.

Make a note for yourself of what has worked and what your challenges have been. If there are new challenges, try and work out a solution to mitigate it for next time.

NOTES

1   Basker, J. (1997), 'Resourcing the Information Centre', in A. Scammell (ed.), *Handbook of Special Librarianship*, 7th edn. London: ASLIB, pp. 81–100.
2   McKay, D. (2003), *Effective Financial Planning for Library and Information Services*, 2nd edn. London: ASLIB, pp. 5–12.
3   Milford, H. (2004), *Charging for Information Services in Law Firm Libraries*. University of Sheffield: Department of Information Studies.
4   MFP and WAP are concepts of Michael Taylor Associates, Management Consultant, The Oast House, Horsegrove Farm, Rotherfield, East Sussex. TN6 3LU.
5   Fisher, R. and Ury, W. (1999), *Getting to Yes: negotiating an agreement without giving in*, 2nd edn. London: Random House.
6   'FT sues Blackstone over alleged login abuse', *The Times*, 2 February 2009.
7   Fogden, F. (2011), 'Negotiation of contracts, planning for the unknown with boilerplate clauses', *Legal Information Management*, 11, 1, pp. 27–31.
8   Durrant, F. (2006), *Negotiating Licences for Digital Resources*. London: Facet Publishing.

CHAPTER 6

MANAGING LEGAL INFORMATION PROFESSIONALS

LOYITA WORLEY AND JACKY BERRY

INTRODUCTION

It has often been said that the biggest asset of any organization is its people – its human capital. Profitability is based on the ability of your people, through their expertise and knowledge, to deliver valuable services to your clients whoever they are. Without people the organization would not function, the procedures and processes so often painstakingly created would not be carried out, the technology (usually at some great expense) would not be correctly or sufficiently utilized and the end product might not be of the right quality/quantity to produce a successful business. Although organizations realize that people are its main assets, how many of them go on to nurture their people to develop them into the highly skilled, motivated, professional individuals needed to support their organizations in the challenge to be competitive in the marketplace? To this end, effective human resource management is crucial if you want to maximize the value and performance of your staff especially in a time of continuous change.

This chapter concentrates on this very important aspect of the strategy of any organization – to achieve success the management of staff should be a high priority on an organization's agenda. Here we outline some practical aspects of people management including how to:

- Successfully recruit and attract the best talent;
- Effectively develop and manage employee performance;
- Motivate and reward your employees;
- Restructure and align your resources to meet current and future needs;
- Focus on developing and nurturing your talent for the future; and
- Continue to add and demonstrate value through the HR function.

CHALLENGES

Managing staff in itself can be a challenge, but emerging trends in work practices can add to this. Recent examples of such factors would be increasing globalization, the embedding of information professionals within practice groups, outsourcing and mergers to name but a few.

Globalization

It is not unusual these days to come across information professionals who manage staff both in the office in which they are based as well as in overseas offices. In some cases a manager may never have had a face-to-face personal meeting with their team member. This is perhaps not as shocking as it sounds as technology is now a great enabler with regard to communication and conference calls and video-conferencing makes face-to-face meetings possible even if they lack the personal touch. In these situations it is necessary to be particularly sensitive to language differences as well as local cultural and national concerns.

This is perhaps not quite so extreme when dealing with staff based in one country but spread across many offices, but extra thought still needs to be given to how to manage under these circumstances.

Embedding

Traditionally the library and information centre has been a central resource housing the majority of print materials and information staff. Certain law firms have always followed the 'embedded' route where materials appropriate to a particular practice group or team along with information professional have been physically located with the relevant lawyers and there has been more of this in recent years. The idea being that the physical positioning can nurture a high level of collaboration combined with a deeper understanding of the work carried out and the clients served. By developing the librarian to be an expert in a particular area, they can often become an integral part of the legal team.

As well as benefits this style of working poses challenges in equal measure. There have been cases where the whole idea falls apart when one key individual leaves. Ideally you should have staff at hand to step up when necessary but with staff reductions this is hard to achieve in practice.

It can be the case that there are not enough information staff to permit each practice group to have an allocated staff member and it can lead to duplication with the collection. In addition, it is often harder to provide good training when someone is working by themselves as there is nobody there to offer guidance on research and resources. The management of these roles often lies directly with the practice group leader, sometimes with a dotted line of responsibility to the library, so changing the dynamic of the team and its management.

Outsourcing

Outsourcing is another area that has grown in prominence over the past few years. This could mean that an information team may be staffed by both employees of the firm and of the outsource provider working alongside each other or by the outsourced staff either dedicated to a particular firm or acting as a central resource for several firms. Each of these situations needs to be handled separately from the manager's point of view and the lines of responsibility and management need to be established clearly from the outset.

Mergers

Something that we have seen increasingly in the law firm sector is the merging of firms as a result of the increase in competition. These can be across continents or regional but it is a fact of life that the current economic situation has accelerated and the merger rate is not likely to slow down any time soon. Having said that, there is a high failure rate of mergers and acquisitions, mostly during the integration process. The major causes include bad management, an ill-defined strategy, cultural differences, delays in communication and a lack of clear vision. Therefore, the keys to successful integration processes are a hands-on leadership style, involvement of the entire staff, continuous focus on customers and, most of all, open and honest communication with employees.

Whatever situation you find yourself in when in a position requiring staff management the basic approach is always the same.

CORE ACTIVITIES OF HUMAN RESOURCE MANAGEMENT

Anybody with people management responsibilities has always to be aware of the implications of the legal aspect of their actions; for example, in the fields of equal opportunities, redundancy or age discrimination. Even if a line manager is carrying out the core activities, it is always wise to bear in mind that most human resource actions have underlying legal aspects to them. If in doubt, consult with the experts in the human resource team.

When thinking about managing a group of people, from the outset there needs to be a clear understanding of the core activities of the human resource management process. As managers there firstly needs to be a clear understanding of the strategy of the organization and how people management fits within that strategy. It is very important that the people within any department that is supporting the core function of an organization are in alignment with the overall headcount plan. As stated before, it would be a strange organization that did not believe that people are an essential component of how it fits together. Grant (1998) put forward a theory that an organization would only gain competitive advantage and success if its resources and capabilities were in alignment with its strategy (see Figure 6.1).

Figure 6.1   Resources and capabilities

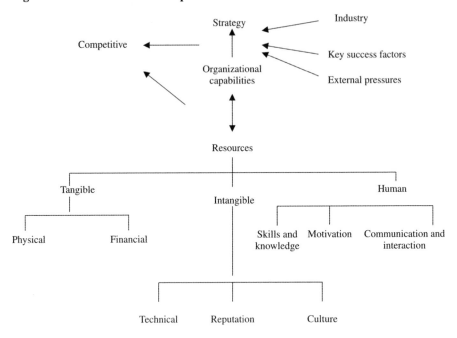

Source: Grant (1998)

Once an organization has determined its mix of resources, taking into account their volume, skills and competencies, then employment of people (in this case legal information staff) gives rise to certain essential duties (see Figure 6.2).

As highlighted in Figure 6.2 the core human resource management process can be seen as a three-stage process:

- *Organizational entry*, which includes role analysis, recruitment, selection, induction, socialization, mentoring/buddying;
- *Organizational performance management*, which includes appraisal, learning and development plans, rewards, personnel management, motivation and coaching;

Figure 6.2   **The core human resource management process within the organization**

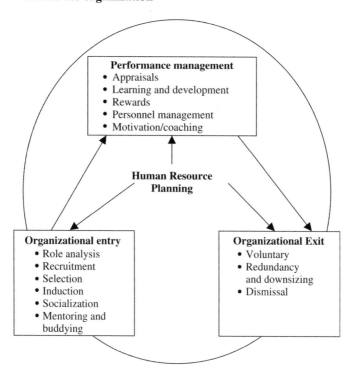

- *Organizational exit*, which includes voluntary exit, redundancy and downsizing and dismissal.

Outside this formal process, the idea of creating a psychological contract with staff is also very important for the relationship with the organization to work. The psychological contract is the tacit or unspoken expectation which an organization has of its employees and the employees have of the organization.

For example, a member of the legal information team may be encouraged by the organization and managers to take on more management responsibilities. Due to his/her increased experience the employee unsuccessfully attempts to gain a position elsewhere. When discovered, the organization then blocks any prospects of gaining a management position internally. The employee feels mistreated and thus the psychological contract is affected. Breaches in the psychological contract can damage relationships and motivation and can lead to conflict. Therefore, sensitivity to the psychological contract is essential and the core functions of managing people should be carried out in ways that grow and maintain good working relationships.

Figure 6.3   Organizational entry: a process model

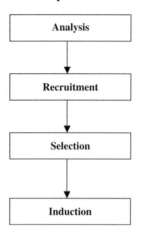

ORGANIZATIONAL ENTRY

The process of organizational entry is one of the most crucial roles that a manager has to carry out. It is not just the financial implications of employing people but also the fact that managers need to employ the right people to become part of a team who will support the competitive advantage of an organization. Assembling the right people in a team may help determine the future viability of an organization. It is also an important role because, as managers, the organizational entry decisions that are made can dramatically alter people's lives. Also, introducing a new person into a team can bring a whole new dynamic to the situation so this stage can have high levels of anxiety attached to it, both for the manager and all the team members. Organizational entry generally has four steps involved (see Figure 6.3).

It is therefore very important that when new employees join, social and professional integration take place as soon as possible within a team to ease what can be an anxious time of change for all concerned. Mentoring and buddying programmes can help alleviate such anxiety and help new staff settle into the ways of an organization more efficiently and effectively.

Analysis

Good analysis is the cornerstone of effective organizational entry and provides a sound basis for recruitment and selection of staff. As can be seen from Figure 6.3, organizational entry is a sequential process and if the analysis of roles is not carried out in an effective manner the whole process could be in danger of falling apart. The first part of any analysis is to understand the strategy of the organization and to identify where roles fit into the big picture and where those roles fit into the short- and long-term plans. The departure of an existing member of staff provides a perfect opportunity to review existing processes and look at possible reorganization or promotion opportunities for remaining staff members. A manager needs to understand the tasks that need to be completed, the skills required to do the work and therefore the roles that need to be filled and how they may change in the long term. A manager must be aware of the environment of the organization and its culture and subcultures as well as the possibility of change and how this may alter roles. Any new headcount request to the organization will not be accepted lightly if there can be no true benefit seen to be gained from the role. A manager needs to have a full understanding of all the roles needed to carry out the strategy of the department and organization. This can be achieved by observing and questioning other members of the team to identify the roles and competencies required to carry out the tasks. Once a role has been identified the manager then needs to write up a job description which can serve as a business case for extra headcount but can also be used to help the future role holder have a better understanding of the role they are required to carry out. This is very important, as potential candidates will question whether the role is right for them and what career opportunities might be available to them. An example of a professional information role within the legal environment can be seen in Figure 6.4. The job description can then be used to identify a set of competencies and skills required which can be applied at the selection stage.

Figure 6.4   Example of a job description

JOB DESCRIPTION

JOB TITLE:	Legal Information Officer
JOB PURPOSE:	To manage know how and information
REPORTS TO:	Head of Information Services
	Partners responsible for Know how and Information
ACCOUNTABLE FOR:	Two Information Officers
MAIN CONTACTS:	Information Officers/Administrators and Managers
	Partners and fee earners in relevant groups
	Professional support lawyers

MAIN DUTIES:

Management of the Information Unit

* Manage and maintain the activities of the information unit on a daily basis; that is, filing, book orders, journal distribution

Enquiries

* Searching hard copy, electronic (for example, Bloomberg, Perfect Information, internet) and know how materials to answer legal, precedent and commercial enquiries in London and other offices

Know How Index

* Gathering, weeding and indexing of information for the Know How Index
* Managing and authorization of records
* Managing the thesaurus locally
* Co-ordination with Information Officers in other offices

Newsletter

- Manage and compile a regular newsletter of current items for internal distribution

Marketing

- Competitor and client intelligence – compiling weekly briefings for distribution to interested parties
- Marketing the services of the unit to fee earners, Information Officers and other interested parties

Training

- Training lawyers and support staff in the use of the information and know how systems

Procedures

- Preparation and management of a procedures manual
- Responsible for a collection development process and policy

Budget/Business plan

- Administer and set the information budget where appropriate
- Maintain charge-back procedures for electronic databases
- Work with PSLs to prepare and manage the business plan

ADDITIONAL DUTIES:

- Assess relevance and usefulness of know how when fee earners leave the firm
- Attendance at relevant fee earner meetings such as Prayers, Group lunches
- Attendance at relevant Know how and Information department/business service meetings; for example, Indexing group, department team meetings, monthly business services meeting
- Other firmwide know how and information projects and other ad hoc projects across the firm

PERSON SPECIFICATION:

Attainments

- Graduate with information qualifications
- Candidate with at least 2–3 years' experience in a legal or financial information background. Ability to organize and manage information both in hard copy and electronic formats

- Computer literate with online database experience
- Ability to train users in the use of information sources
- Ability to work independently and as part of a team
- Strong service orientation and good communicator. Good interpersonal skills and ability to relate to all levels of staff
- Pleasant, outgoing personality

Recruitment

Once the analysis stage is complete, the next stage is the actual recruitment of staff and attracting a pool of candidates that meet the requirements of the job description. From a career development and motivational point of view it is always wise to attempt to recruit legal information staff internally first. This will allow the organization to retain the skills of internally grown staff and reap the benefits of both the time and financial commitments in training and developing staff. In most large organizations, the human resource department will have a policy for advertising internal vacancies, usually via their intranet. This also has the added bonus that all staff in the organization will see the advert and a candidate may be located through this network.

If no internal candidates are found to be suitable, a decision has to be made to attract a pool of candidates from the external market. This can be done by using job lists, specialist employment agencies or executive search consultants. New employees can also be located by using the networking capabilities of the team, which is a useful way to keep recruitment costs down to a minimum.

In-house management of the recruitment of external candidates can be a very time-consuming process although at times it can be the best option; for example, when an unskilled job needs to be filled that can be advertised quickly and cheaply in the local press. However, generally advertising an available job means an expensive advert in a suitable publication with a closing date some weeks away and the possibility that many applications will arrive which will take time to deal with.

Using specialist employment agencies helps avoid the pitfalls of carrying out the process in-house. Agencies such as TFPL, Sue Hill Recruitment, Glen Recruitment and many others specialize in helping candidates in the information profession gain access to roles within organizations across all sectors, including private, public and governmental. The process tends to be much speedier and more efficient than carrying out the process internally. It is also very useful to build up a rapport with the agencies to enable them to understand your recruitment needs and to gain an understanding of how the organization and the legal information department operate. Keeping the communication lines open with the agency chosen is vital to the process.

Executive search consultants, otherwise known as 'head-hunters', can be used, especially if a senior or high-profile role needs to be filled. However, this method of recruitment can be very costly in both time and money.

Overall, when thinking about the recruitment process, the following points need to be taken into account:

- Can the role be filled by an internal candidate?
- Do we have the money to pay for the recruitment costs if an agency or consultant helps the organization recruit?
- What information needs to be given to candidates and agencies to enable them to make an informed decision about their choice to apply for a job within the organization?

Selection

Once the most suitable recruitment process has been chosen, the selection process needs to be started. Whether an organization is recruiting internally or externally, a suitable pool of candidates will have supplied their curriculum vitae (CV), a covering letter, and/or an application form. This information needs to be compared to the job description for the role and the selection criteria to make an informed decision about which candidates should be invited for an interview. Once the most suitable candidates are identified, a method of selection needs to be chosen to identify the person-role fit. The most common method of selection is the interview process but some organizations do use other methods such as personality tests, intelligence tests and attendance at assessment centres. Alongside the interview process it is also a good idea to set candidates a case study related to the role applied for or indeed asking them to give a short presentation on a particular topic that they could be involved with in the role. An example of selection criteria, both essential and desired, is outlined in Figure 6.5 opposite.

Interviews can be very useful in assessing personal characteristics such as interpersonal skills, social interaction, communication skills and general practical intelligence. Interviews are also a good opportunity to sell the organization and the job on offer and for negotiating terms and conditions. It is important at this stage that the psychological contract between a candidate and the interviewer is formed. It is therefore ideal for managers to be trained in interviewing skills by their organizations. The main weakness of an interview is whether the process accurately addresses the ability of an individual to carry out a role and their possession of the relevant experience and skills. This can be difficult to establish during the course of an interview lasting an hour or so.

Figure 6.5 Selection criteria

Characteristics	Essentials	Desirable
Qualifications	Degree qualification in information science	
Work attitudes	Independent worker, organized, meticulous, responsible and reliable Also needs to be a confident, flexible self-starter	
Computer literacy	Proficient user of internet and online databases such as *LexisLibrary* and *Westlaw UK*	
Language ability	Fluent in the English language	
Interpersonal skills	Outgoing and able to get along well with fellow colleagues	
Subject knowledge		Background in legal information management and research

Induction

Once a suitable candidate has been selected and the job offer accepted, the human resource department will have to deal with the legal formalities such as taking up references and agreeing the relevant terms and conditions for the role and confirming a start date. The candidate is then ready to join the team. It is at this stage that any new member of a team will feel anxious about the changes that will be happening to them. It is therefore very important that managers try to ease the anxiety as best as can be achieved within the first few weeks of joining. A good way to do this is by carrying out an induction process, which will enable the newcomer to feel at ease with the new organization and environment and have a better understanding and working knowledge of their role. Most organizations will offer a firm-wide induction, which could include the following topics:

- the firm and its strategy
- information and benefits
- health and safety
- how the business works
- a tour of the building
- overview of departments in the organization
- career development
- technology at the desktop
- meeting key people.

Once a newcomer eventually joins the legal information team, a further induction should take place to familiarize the individual with their own job. The following topics should be addressed with any new member of the legal information team:

- how the role fits into the organization and team
- daily tasks involved with the role
- a skills audit to identify training and development needs.

Socialization, Buddying and Mentoring

An induction process will certainly help alleviate a newcomer's anxiety but it tends to be a formal process. A new member of staff also needs to feel that they are part of a community and needs to form relationships quickly. They also need to understand the reality of how an organization and department works; for example, who they go to if they have a personnel issue, where to go for stationery and so on.

Thus, socialization is very important in the first few weeks. A good way to help this is by providing a 'buddy' for new staff in the short term, say three months. A new member of the team can be paired with an established member of staff to help them learn the ropes, or 'how we do things around here'. Ideally, it should be a peer member of staff or lower member of staff. The emphasis being on a friendly face who can help with practical issues and, ideally, any discussions should take place in a social environment, either in-house or externally. In the longer term, it may also be worth investigating a mentoring process.

This approach to people development introduces an independent and objective source of help that is outside the line management relationship. It is a confidential, one-to-one relationship, which exists to help the 'mentee' make decisions to enhance their progress towards specific goals. A mentor will also help the mentee with work-related support and provide advice and experience and a listening ear. Mentoring provides benefits for both mentors and mentees.

The mentee has the benefit of a confidential and respected guide to help them through their work and career, and the mentor has the opportunity to help others more junior than themselves to grow and develop at work. Mentoring relationships can reap rewards for all involved.

As has been stated, the process of organizational entry is a complex one and should be planned very carefully if the correct resourcing and skills set is to be achieved for both the organization and department.

ORGANIZATIONAL PERFORMANCE MANAGEMENT – INVESTING IN HUMAN CAPITAL

Of course, once a new employee is settled into the department and role, they will still need support and efforts should be made to continue to develop the individual throughout their time with the organization. Any organization who takes its responsibilities to its staff seriously will have systems and processes in place to assess the extent of employee contribution and to promote continuous high performance. Most legal information professionals will be working in an environment that is not solely that of their own profession – individuals will have secured roles in law firms, academic environments or specialist organizations that are environments mainly for other professions and it can at times be difficult to offer a clear career development path in these circumstances. However, it is the responsibility of a manager, working alongside the human resource department, to manage performance and develop individuals to enhance their careers to the greatest extent possible. To be successful, managing performance and career development need to have the following elements:

- a culture which promotes challenge and responsibility, thus enhancing motivation;
- processes and systems that clearly support the strategic direction of the organization;
- a career framework in which employees can develop and progress;
- focused training to support learning and development;
- feedback mechanisms to monitor progress;
- equitable remuneration structures.

Appraisals

Performance management is one of the core functional duties delegated to line managers. Part of that process is the use of performance appraisal to assess the performance and development of staff. Appraisals help recognize an individual's performance and assess the work that has been achieved over a period of time, identify what is expected over the coming year by setting clear objectives that support the strategy both of the department and organization and identify strengths and areas for development in order to support career development.

This process should be seen as a continual loop of development and improvement that connects an individual's performance with the strategy and business plans of the department and organization (see Figure 6.6).

Performance appraisals have many aims, which are identified in Figure 6.7.

Figure 6.6   Elements of performance management systems

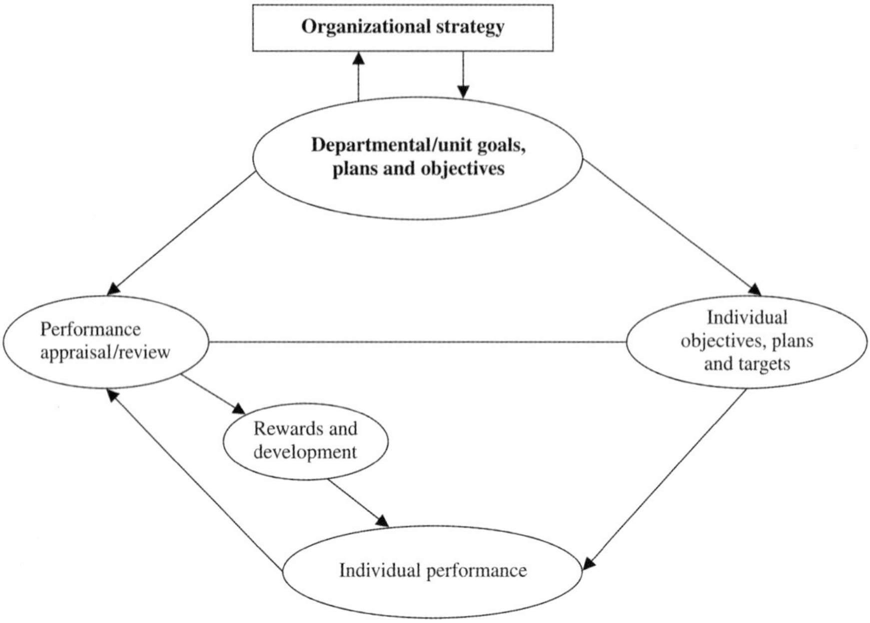

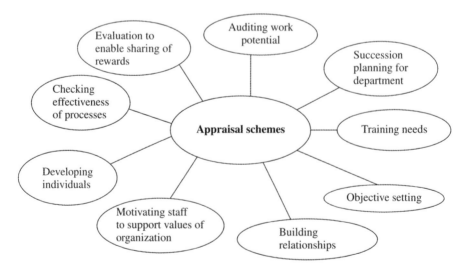

Figure 6.7   Functions of appraisal schemes

Performance appraisal generally takes place on an annual basis but it is always wise to carry out regular updates, possibly quarterly but definitely at the half-year stage to check performance and identify which objectives are on target to be achieved or need to be amended. This is crucial if any major changes have taken place within the department or organization. Sometimes objectives set at one point in the cycle can become completely unachievable due to circumstances beyond an individual's control. When appraising an individual the areas that need to be looked at will vary from organization to organization. However, for a legal information professional the following areas should be taken into account:

- Technical/professional skills – is the individual competent in using an organization's technical systems plus the specialist technical databases required to carry out their roles; for example are they expert/less expert in using all the various databases?
- Provision of service – does the individual deliver excellent service to the internal clients, inspiring confidence and building relationships with staff at any level (that is, from junior members of staff through to managing partner)?
- Commercial and organizational awareness – does the individual have an understanding of the 'bigger picture' (which is important if a high-quality excellent service is to be achieved)?
- Resource, work and financial management – where applicable, does the individual manage their resources in a well-organized and time-efficient manner?
- People skills – does the individual work well within their team and also as an individual and are they able to communicate well, applying good interpersonal skills at all times?

Another important part of the appraisal process is to set objectives which identify tasks that need to be carried out for the following year in support of the strategy of the department and organization but which also identify gaps in training and development that could prevent those objectives being met. When setting new or realigned objectives it is important that they are SMART, that is, Specific, Measurable, Achievable, Realistic and Timely. If objectives are not SMART then an individual can feel overwhelmed and anxious, especially if the objectives are felt to be unachievable and unrealistic. The manager's role is vital in negotiating with the employee so that objectives set are agreeable to both. The manager and individual can then monitor the objectives throughout the year for progress.

Although performance appraisals are an important part of the core human resource process, there can be problems with them. Some of the issues are identified below:

- Members of staff who have been in an organization for some time will find them somewhat tedious – a bureaucratic process undertaken for its own sake.

- Members of staff can get very anxious regarding appraisals.
- Managers may ignore objectives and outcomes of appraisals, which enhances the belief by some employees that appraisals are just a bureaucratic formal paper exercise.
- Ill-informed assessors – it may be that the person appraising an individual is doing so purely because of their job title. They may not have the full knowledge of an individual's performance and progress to make an informed judgment. This can cause resentment with staff.
- The belief that an individual's performance is influenced by personal relationships with the appraiser both from a negative and positive stance. An appraisal process needs to be as objective as it possibly can be.
- Appraisees sometimes feel that they have to over-extend themselves to impress the appraiser. This can lead to stress and possible underperformance as the over-commitment throughout the year becomes apparent. If the appraiser knows the appraisee well, this over-commitment should be balanced at the interview.
- Comments can be made at the interview regarding an appraisee's performance that are a 'shock' to them. Any message on performance should be filtered through to the individual throughout the year. The interview should not be seen as the opportunity to raise poor performance issues. The idea is to comment on the work carried out over the period under review and constructively move forward.

Although these issues are important to bear in mind, appraisals are still seen by most organizations as an important process in human resource management. The interview is crucial to the process and it is an opportunity to re-establish a rapport with staff. The key to an interview being successful is twofold. Be prepared and know your staff and their roles and achievements well. As a manager you need to put staff at ease, as they may be feeling anxious: show respect, be warm, empathetic, open and supportive. Always give examples to support comments made and be constructive rather than destructive. However, always be sure that any praise given is genuine. If successful an individual will feel that the appraisal process and interview has been worthwhile and they will feel motivated and enthused to continue operating at a high level of output.

Learning And Development

One of the key elements to an appraisal process is identifying any learning and training development requirements for individuals to support and help them achieve their objectives and develop them in their careers. Most organizations have training departments which identify the core training required for all their staff to maximize their effect on the business. Some examples of core training may include project management skills, meeting skills, presentation skills, negotiation and influencing skills, time management, interviewing skills or team leadership. This will, of course, depend on the size of an organization and its overall strategy but as information managers it is vital that legal information staff are given the opportunity to partake in such organizational core skills training.

Most organizations will also understand the need for specialist departments, such as a legal information department, to offer training which is of a specialist nature. This can be offered both internally by the department itself and externally. Again depending on the size of the department there could possibly be an experienced team of legal information professionals that could offer internal training to the less experienced members of the team. An example of such training could be as identified in Figure 6.8.

Figure 6.8   Examples of training offered by 'experts' in own legal information department

In-House Training Courses

Category	Training
Information Skills	
	Enquiry Management
	Legal Research
	Company Information
	Thesaurus Construction
	Copyright
	EC
	Tax Information Sources
	Cataloguing and Classification
	Deals Research
	Specialist Finance Sources
	US Information Sources
	Sector Analysis
Management Skills	
	Budget Management
	Organizational Insight
	Creativity and Problem Solving
	Communication Skills
	Training the Trainer
	Mentoring
Systems Training	
	Bloomberg
	Legal Desktop Sources
	General Desktop
	Intranet

At times, training requirements will be identified that cannot be offered internally and external providers then need to be sought. Such providers as TFPL, ASLIB, CILIP and other specialists offer training courses directly aligned to the requirements of the profession. These courses include research skills, records management, knowledge management, copyright law and many more.

Once a member of the team has attended an external course it is always useful for them to give a presentation to the rest of the team and/or write a report on their experiences. This then allows others to benefit from the learning of the attendee. It is also a good idea to place any written documentation and handouts from courses into a shared library area of the department. Another advantage of this reporting back is to assess whether the course should be attended by any other team members. Many providers will also offer external courses in-house and this can be a way of keeping the costs down.

Continuing professional development

CPD is another important aspect of learning and development and can be easily organized within a legal information department. This can help to raise the profile of individuals and the department. It helps put staff in the driving seat of their careers, gives them control, job satisfaction and a sense of professionalism.

The CPD programme can operate on a similar basis to a lawyer CPD programme where certain activities, both internal and external, have CPD points attached to them. An individual legal information professional keeps a record of training and development activities and accrues CPD points. This again is a valuable process in analysing and recording professional development to support the appraisal process and also the department and firm. An outline of a CPD programme is identified in Figure 6.9 below.

Figure 6.9   Example of allocation of hours to be achieved for CPD

In-house	CPD hours	External	CPD hours*
Information lunches	1	Electronic system training	3 or 6
Retreat	8	ASLIB courses/functions/ committee work	3, 6, 12
Non-group meetings	.05	TFPL courses/functions/ committee work	3, 6, 12
Stand up briefings	.05	BIALL courses/functions/ committee work	3, 6, 12
Trainee lectures	1	CILIP courses/functions/ committee work	3, 6, 12
Presentations/delivery/ preparation	3	CLIG meetings/functions/ committee work	3, 6, 12
Training sessions to groups, individuals, etc.	1	SLA meetings/functions/ committee work	3, 6, 12
Group lunches	1	Weekend courses – work related	6, 12
In-house courses	3, 6	Writing articles for journals	4
Special projects/meetings	1	Attending exhibitions – work-related	1–6
Chartership meetings	1	Committee work	1–6

Note: Allocation of hours for activities both in-house and external:
* 3 hours is half a day, 6 hours is one day and 12 hours is 2 days

Legal Information Department
CPD programme for legal information staff CPD hours to be achieved for different categories of staff from May 2010 to April 2011: Information Managers – 60 hours, Information Officers and graduates – 48 hours, Information Administrators – 24 hours. Each individual member of staff to keep record of CPD hours.

The hours stated are the minimum number to be achieved. Each individual information officer has different requirements for CPD and the number of hours achievable may be far less than the number quoted.

Continuing professional development is also a crucial development process for information professionals who wish to attain chartered status with CILIP, the Chartered Institute for Library and Information Professionals. There are many schools of thought on whether chartering with the profession is necessary. Often it is heard amongst information professionals who work in the legal sector that professional development and chartership with CILIP is '... not worth having'; 'I don't need it to work in commercial/legal organizations'; 'It's only for information professionals in the academic and public sectors'; 'I've been successful without it'; 'What is the point?'; 'It's not for me'. So why charter? Whatever sector the information professional occupies, chartering is supporting the code of professional conduct of CILIP. It also gives individuals personal satisfaction at achieving the qualification and helps their own assessment of development. It can help with promotion and career opportunities, especially if people wish to move from sector to sector. It provides a sense of professional pride, involvement and awareness of the profession and, of course, academic credits to attach to your name. There are several ways to charter with CILIP but an added value of writing a professional development report is that it can be used for the annual appraisal, as it becomes a record of an analysis of individual training needs, a preparation of objectives for the future and an evaluation of progress.

Other methods of learning and development
As a manager of legal information staff the responsibility of developing and identifying learning and training opportunities can often fall at the manager's feet. A manager will know the roles of the staff and their work commitments and have appraised their development and achievements. Managers should be aware of the following:

- They themselves act as a role model. Staff will often adopt many of the practices and attitudes of a manager. So, if a manager takes training and development seriously then so will the team.
- On a day-to-day basis a manager will offer guidance and advice as part of their own role.
- A manager can affect opportunities for development by identifying new areas of work and extending an individual's responsibilities.

- A manager is a gatekeeper for external training especially if a cost is involved.

Staff development does not always have to be a formal activity. Much development and training is done on the job and can be personal development, such as increasing self-confidence, greater self-awareness, team working or organizational understanding. On-the-job training works where encouragement is to the fore and mistakes are allowed to be made. Risks in developing individuals will only work well if there is a culture of trust and openness.

Individuals have to make mistakes sometimes to know that eventually a task will be successfully achieved. This is where reflecting on learning is crucial to understanding what has been learned and identifying how things can be improved the next time round. Coaching is a good way of offering on-the-job training. It offers the opportunity of transferring knowledge and skills from a more experienced person to a less experienced one. Shadowing a more experienced person is another way of learning from an experienced person. A useful way of thinking about coaching is to imagine a strong piece of rope attached between the manager and the member of staff needing coaching. As the member of staff learns from the more experienced person the rope becomes thinner, eventually becoming just a thin piece of elastic. At this point the member of staff has gained experience but always knows that the thin piece of elastic can turn into the strong rope again as required. This type of learning can of course be time-consuming but if recognized as a valuable part of developing people it will add value to the team and the organization as a whole.

Another mode of staff development is job rotation, which encourages members of a team to be able to work proficiently in each other's jobs, thus creating greater flexibility and skills within the team as a whole. This would only work if a team was of a certain size and fitted in with the culture and structure of an organization.

Rewards

In agreeing to work for an organization an individual is agreeing to exchange their skills set and their effort for reward. Reward can be seen as two different types, one intrinsic and the other extrinsic. Extrinsic rewards are the most obvious to the individual; for example, the pay an individual receives for the job carried out, the social rewards such as praise, recognition and responsibility, the added rewards such as health club membership, health-care costs and so on. Intrinsic rewards are from doing the job itself, for example self-satisfaction and motivation.

So, rewards can be multi-faceted but pay, which is seen by most individuals as the key reward, is of course very important. It can give individuals a certain lifestyle that they aspire to but also it is a measure of the value that an organization places on an employee. It seems a very simple equation – an employee offers their service to an organization and the organization pays them in return. But generally the issues surrounding any reward system are fraught with issues and can be very complex. Most reward systems are designed to achieve the following:

- attract suitable employees from the marketplace
- retain valued employees
- encourage employees to achieve their objectives
- encourage the development of skills
- recognize the contributions people make to the organization
- align the interest of employees with the success of the organization.

Pay and reward systems can be a very emotive topic amongst team members and to offer a 'fair and just' system can be very difficult for any manager. To achieve this a manager must take into account the following issues:

- The system of pay should be competitive with the outside market to set the correct level for the skills required of individuals to carry out their roles. Many organizations will use outside consultancies to ascertain this, so most managers will be working within a framework that has already been set by their organization.
- To support any system of pay, especially if it is set by the organization, the information manager should be aware of the information employment market themselves. This can be achieved by talking with the specialist recruitment agencies within the information world. There are also salary surveys produced by the British and Irish Association of Law Librarians (BIALL) annually and CILIP which give an indication of the salary levels in the legal market for information professionals. These of course can only be used as a guideline as not all information professionals in the legal market submit their information to these surveys.
- Monitoring the market should also be achieved by keeping an eye on adverts in specialist journals (such as CILIP), the general press and the various e-mail lists and BIALL Job Board. Over time this can give a good indication of what the market is paying for information levels in differing areas and skill sets.
- General networking amongst colleagues within other similar types of organization can also be a useful tool in ascertaining levels of pay and increases annually. This of course depends on the confidentiality of such information but if the network is strong and there is a high level of trust amongst individuals, then this could be a good method.
- Organizations should pay individuals at a level that is both sufficient to attract but also retain their employees. As stated before, this seems a simple equation but when managing teams of people the element of motivation is very high on the agenda. Pay can either be seen as a huge motivator for

staff or in fact a demotivator if the system, levels and increases are deemed 'unfair'. It is also important that all staff are seen to be treated in a similar way or again the process will be deemed 'unfair'.

- Another area that can be fraught with issues is if an organization pays an annual bonus related to performance. Again most organizations will have a system in place for the process and the manager must have a clear understanding of how this works for the department and individuals to enable it to appear 'fair'. But it would be wise to remember that 'fairness can be in the eye of the beholder'. Whatever system for rewards is in place, at some point in time an individual may become demotivated and unhappy.

Personnel Management

Another very important responsibility for any information manager is dealing with personnel management issues. This can be very time-consuming, often becoming a regular task that can sideline other responsibilities. Thus care and understanding in dealing with such issues and knowing when to pass them on to a human resources specialist is crucial. Otherwise the amount of time spent sorting out such issues could turn an information manager into an HR manager.

Most organizations will have a staff handbook that outlines general rules, regulations and processes that each individual within an organization should adhere to. This will cover such items as:

- terms and conditions – absence (sickness, holidays), general hours of work, contracts, overtime;
- financial rewards and benefits – salaries, pensions arrangements, season ticket loans, life assurance, health insurance, gym memberships;
- policies – compassionate leave, equal opportunities, disciplinary rules, grievance procedures, health and safety.

Even with such information available there will be times when general personnel issues will arise with legal information staff that managers will have to deal with themselves. These could include poor or underperformance, relationship problems between members of a team, general misconduct, harassment or stress. Some pointers for dealing with such issues are:

- Make sure you have built up a rapport with the team to enable them to feel comfortable discussing problems. An open-door policy is always top of the agenda.
- Be firm but fair in the approach taken. Never skirt around an issue and don't be afraid to tackle a problem with a member of staff. Most people will respect this approach. It saves time in the long run and an individual will know where they stand.

- Help the individual to work out a solution themselves. Be very wary of giving answers and solutions. If this approach is taken then a manager can be overstressed by taking on the problems of all team members themselves.
- Always think of problems as issues that need to be resolved with an individual and can constructively be discussed so that an individual can move forwards. It is a manager's responsibility to develop an individual even in times of stress and worry.
- Be aware that some issues may be beyond your competence as a manager and the support of a professional HR person is needed. This is important to recognize, otherwise a manager could find themselves in very difficult situations where their knowledge is limited and information and advice given to an individual could be legally wrong, for example on harassment issues.

ORGANIZATIONAL EXIT

The last phase of the human resource management cycle (see Figure 6.2) is managing the exit of staff from the organization. It can also be the most difficult and stressful process, depending on the nature of the exit. Whether the exit is related to leaving the organization voluntarily, to redundancy and downsizing, to retirement or to dismissal, it can be a traumatic time for both individuals and the organization as relationships and teams are broken and working practices change. The motivation of remaining staff can be affected dramatically. Exiting an organization can be one of the most significant phases in an individual's life.

Although it is a very important phase, most organizations and managers generally do not deal with exit in an effective way. This is mainly due to the fact that any exit will have a certain amount of emotion attached to it and some managers will find this very difficult to deal with. Any aspect of exiting an organization will have a large element of change attached to it and managing this change is crucial if the remaining team are to move forward effectively. This is particularly important where a downsizing has occurred, as team members remaining could suffer from 'survivors' syndrome' and the related guilt attached to the fact that they are still in possession of a job. Another important aspect of people exiting an organization is that a lot of knowledge could walk out of the door with them. It is thus very important that mechanisms are put in place to capture that knowledge before an individual departs.

Leaving the Organization Voluntarily

Many exit instances arise because the individual chooses to leave an organization voluntarily; perhaps with a change of personal circumstances, to pursue other activities, a more responsible position within another organization or to retire. It is very important to have an exit interview at this stage to ascertain the employee's reasons for leaving and to learn from their experiences within an organization. With retirement it can be stressful to go from full-time working to no work at all and if possible a phased approach should be investigated with perhaps the possibility of keeping staff on short- or fixed-term contracts to help them deal with the major change in their lives.

Redundancy and Downsizing

This is an area that needs very careful and sensitive managing. Most organizations will put a process in place if it is deemed necessary to follow through a redundancy programme. Interestingly, as stated at the beginning of the chapter, most organizations believe that people are their greatest asset so individuals find it very difficult when their employer acts in an apparently counter-productive way. That said, most managers will be aware of the bigger picture affecting an organization and at times the process of downsizing may have to be undertaken. The key element is to try to alleviate any unnecessary stress that may occur with team members and be as open and honest in communicating the process as far as sensitivity and legal aspects of the process allow. Dealing with the downsizing 'survivors' guilt' can be a huge issue for managers. Again, communication and listening to employees' fears and emotions are crucial if the team is to be motivated to move forward.

Dismissal

At some point as a manager, dealing with disciplinary issues may be necessary. As stated above most organizations will have a process in place for disciplinary issues and these should be followed with advice from the human resources expert. In the first instance, if an issue has arisen, a manager may need to have a counselling-type interview with an employee, which hopefully may avert any further action. If further action is required and the disciplinary process is put into place, it could be wise to have a third party present at any meeting. The final decision for dismissal would not be solely the responsibility of a manager but carried out in alignment with the human resources department. The manager's role would be very important in making sure the team's morale was kept buoyant once the process had been completed.

For whatever reason an employee leaves an organization, their experience will go with them. It is wise therefore that this is captured during the working life of the employee. This 'knowledge harvesting' is crucial if the department is to continue offering an efficient and effective service after an employee has left. Therefore practices and procedures need to be put into place and be reviewed on a regular basis to ensure business continuity.

SKILLS REQUIRED TO MANAGE LEGAL
INFORMATION PROFESSIONALS

Having identified the key elements of the human resource management process, this section identifies some key skills required to manage legal information professionals. As can be seen, the role can be complicated and full of emotional pitfalls. To help people meet their full potential, which in turn supports the strategy of an organization, a lot of work needs to be carried out to motivate and drive them forward. Most managers in organization arrive at their positions by default. They are excellent in their day-to-day technical roles and are thus promoted to manage. However being an excellent information professional does not necessarily mean that management skills come naturally. There are indeed many skills needed to make a team perform together and as individuals.

Leadership

One of the key skills required to manage legal information professionals is leadership. There has been much discussion in the management press regarding the differences between a manager and a leader. Can a good manager be a leader as well and vice versa? Figure 6.10 identifies some key elements of both managers and leaders as suggested by Bennis (1998).

Figure 6.10   Managers versus leaders

Managers	Leaders
• are driven by context	• master their context
• administer	• innovate
• maintain	• develop
• focus on systems	• focus on people
• rely on control	• inspire trust
• take short-range view	• take long-term perspective
• ask how and why?	• ask what and why?
• keep an eye on bottom line	• keep an eye on horizon
• imitate	• originate
• accept the status quo	• challenge the status quo
• do things right	• do the right thing

Source: Adapted from Bennis (1998)

Nurturing and Emotional Intelligence

Another key skill when managing people is the ability to nurture staff and help them grow in their roles. This can be achieved by coaching and mentoring staff and passing on experiences and knowledge that will help staff develop. To be able to do this effectively, managers need to have emotional intelligence. They have to be self-aware, have good self-management, be socially aware and have excellent social skills. These are difficult skills to identify and deliver but an excellent manager and/or leader will need these skills if they are to be effective and not just successful in their roles. Figure 6.11 identifies some of the key elements of emotional intelligence and some related skills.

Figure 6.11   Elements of emotional intelligence

Elements of emotional intelligence	Skills
Self-awareness	• emotional self-awareness – ability to read and understand your own emotions as well as recognize their impact • accurate self-assessment – realistic evaluation of strengths and limitations • self-confidence
Social awareness	• empathy – skill at sensing other people's emotions and understanding their perspective; the ability to 'put yourself in other peoples' shoes' • organizational awareness – ability to read the currents of organizational life, navigate politics • service orientation – ability to recognize and meet customers' needs
Social skills	• visionary leadership – inspire with a compelling vision • influence – ability to use a range of persuasive tactics • developing others through feedback and guidance • communication skills – listening and communicating clearly • change catalyst – initiating new ideas and leading people in a new direction • conflict management – ability to de-escalate disagreements and bring resolution • building bonds – cultivating and maintaining a web of relationships • teamwork and collaboration – competence at promoting cooperation and building teams

Communication

Communication skills are crucial if emotional intelligence is to be achieved. Conducting any form of relationship within the workplace implies communication with people. All communication is important, whether it be formal or informal, but the better a communicator a manager is, the better the relationships with a team will be. Although as human beings we communicate every day of our lives, it can be fraught with pitfalls. What a manager believes has been communicated can at times be misunderstood or received in completely the wrong way. This can cause demotivation, hidden agendas, 'Chinese whispers' and upset.

The main reason for communication to go awry is distortion of the medium that a piece of information is communicated through. This can be viewed as a technical process as identified in Figure 6.12 below.

Figure 6.12   Communication as a technical process

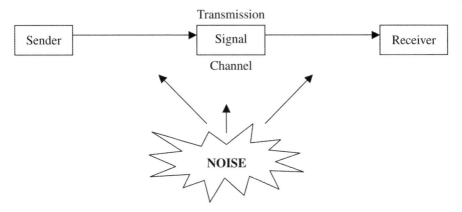

This technical process can be used as a basis to understand how as human beings we communicate with each other. A sender of a message frames the information they wish to communicate and chooses a medium via which it is communicated; for example, face to face, e-mail, telephone, text and so on. This intended message may be affected by the beliefs and values of the sender as well as other messages already forming in their brains. So what they think they are communicating may be affected by other things. Once the receiver has taken on board the communication it will be filtered by that person: they in turn have a set of beliefs, values, doubts and fears and may 'misinterpret' the original communication. Also, before the message reaches the receiver, it may have been distorted by 'noise', for example too much information already being received by the recipient, open-plan offices and so on. Thus messages can be received in a completely different way from how the sender had first framed the communication. Feedback is a good technique to make sure that the receiver has interpreted the message in the correct way. This can help alleviate any miscommunication issues.

Generally communication should be carried out in an open, honest, supportive climate where staff feel comfortable that they can ask questions if anything communicated to them is not understood or they feel that it is not correct. The team will then feel trusted, secure and confident in their roles, the team, department and organization as a whole.

Motivation

As a manager it is important that circumstances and an environment are created that motivate the team who are being managed to increase productivity and efficiency. This in turn supports the strategy of an organization and helps to achieve competitive advantage. There are many theories of motivation but they tend to fall into the following categories:

- Satisfaction theories – the belief that a satisfied worker is a more productive worker. A.H. Maslow (1970) suggested that there are five levels of need that influence an individual's behaviour: he put these into what he called a hierarchy of needs (see Figure 6.13).
- Maslow's theory is a useful starting point in assessing ways in which to motivate particular individuals in the workplace. If an organization provides rewards and/or incentives to enable them to satisfy their needs then they will be motivated.
- Incentive theories – workers will increase their efforts to gain a reward.
- Intrinsic theories – someone's reward is the satisfaction of a worthwhile job.

Figure 6.13   Maslow's hierarchy of needs (1970)

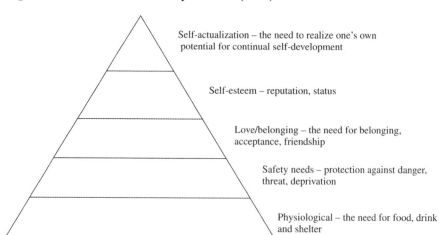

Self-actualization – the need to realize one's own potential for continual self-development

Self-esteem – reputation, status

Love/belonging – the need for belonging, acceptance, friendship

Safety needs – protection against danger, threat, deprivation

Physiological – the need for food, drink and shelter

There are other aspects of people's lives that affect their motivation. Individuals belong to many organizations – not only in work but in the family and social environment. These may have a huge effect on someone's motivation and their need to achieve and aspire towards success. But it is not necessary for one part of this to meet the whole of the motivational needs. Certainly in law firms, considering the diversity of personnel to run an organization (from partners to staff who work in the information department), their motivational requirements can also be very diverse. Some examples of motivators are:

- high pay – a level of pay that will be above average and increase at a higher rate than the cost of living;
- advancement – the opportunity to improve oneself;
- congeniality – working with people in a team who work together well and are friendly and approachable;
- autonomy – being able to set objectives, plan workload and to have control over how to carry out one's role;
- security – an assurance of continued work and a comfortable retirement;
- responsibility – the opportunity to make decisions and to be accountable for results and to have a responsibility for some of the firm's resources, such as people, money;
- status – recognition by others of the importance of a role within the firm;
- achievement – the opportunity to solve problems and being able to see the outcome of efforts made.

Just as importantly as motivating staff it is very easy to demotivate them. Some common demotivators are listed below:

- being given poor-quality, boring work all the time
- being treated as a subordinate
- always being criticized and never praised
- stifling of independence and creativity.

Although a manager can support a team and motivate them to the best of his/her ability with the resources and processes available, to allow this to happen it has to be apparent to staff that self-motivation is also a key to success.

CONCLUSIONS

This chapter started with the preface that people are the biggest asset belonging to an organization. To support an organization in obtaining the right people and then developing them and motivating them to deliver a high-quality, efficient and effective service, the role of an information manager is crucial in the process.

This in turn will help the organization achieve its goals and gain competitive advantage in the marketplace. The organization will then be enabled to reward and remunerate its employees for their efforts. Although the chapter has outlined the very important role of the information manager in this mission, it is also the responsibility of each legal information professional to take control of their own careers and motivation as far as they can. An information manager who has the skill set to support their staff in their goals will achieve a successful team. If he/she remembers to listen, communicate and empathize with staff, an information manager will be able to maintain a high-quality team of individuals that an organization respects, requires and rewards.

CHAPTER 7

COPYRIGHT AND DATA PROTECTION

CHRIS HOLLAND

INTRODUCTION

This chapter is intended as a broad overview of copyright and data protection and is not a comprehensive guide. It is important to note that nothing in this chapter is intended to be legal advice and that the author is not legally qualified, although he does have experience of dealing with copyright issues over a number of years while working as a legal information professional at the Law Society of England and Wales and at a large city law firm. The author is also the BIALL representative on the Library and Archives Copyright Alliance (LACA). I should acknowledge that have learned a great deal about copyright from my fellow members of LACA, for which I am grateful. At the end of the chapter there is a short bibliography and a list of useful websites which the reader looking into any specific issues in more depth may find useful.

Copyright and data protection are both about complying with the law but from the perspective of law librarians it is also about practical risk management. The important question is what can I do to reduce and manage any risk to myself and the organization I work for? In relation to copyright this leads to many more specific questions: What activities by my library users do I need to be concerned about? What copying activities can I obtain a licence for? What licences do I need? What guidance do I need to provide in the library? What records do I need to keep? Copyright is a complex area and it may not be possible to reduce the risk to zero, but you can do a lot to promote compliance and reduce the risk to a minimum.

THE REASONS FOR COPYRIGHT

The economic rationale for copyright is that it establishes a limited monopoly for creators of 'literary, dramatic musical and artistic works' in order to encourage those creators to continue in their creative activity for the benefit of society. There is also the strong ethical argument that creators are entitled to profit from the fruits of their labour. In practice that means placing legal restrictions on what others can do with their works. Monopolies are often thought of in a negative light as they do not encourage free competition, but copyright is a special case.

Ideally there should be a balance: copyright should offer sufficient economic incentive to creators of original material and to those who enable them to publish and exploit their works, but not too strong a monopoly which will have negative effects, such as stifling creative reuse of Copyright material. An example might be the back catalogues of record companies containing sound recordings which others wish to publish but are unable to obtain permission to do so.

It follows that copyright needs to be limited and the main limitations on the monopoly are the term or duration of copyright and the exceptions in the law which allow acts in specific circumstances which would not normally be permitted.

UK LEGISLATION

Copyright legislation in the UK has a long history: The 'Statute of Anne' of 1709 was the first Act of Parliament devoted to copyright. The main current piece of legislation is the Copyright, Designs and Patents Act 1988 (CDPA). It has been amended numerous times and EU law has played an important and increasing role in shaping UK legislation and in developing case law. Some of the most significant amendments to the CDPA stem from the implementation in the UK of the European Union's Copyright in the Information Society Directive (commonly referred to as the Information Society Directive or the Copyright Directive (Directive 2001/29/EC)). It should be borne in mind that some important concepts are not defined precisely in legislation and subsequent case law is very significant in understanding copyright law.

Copyright is a right which in UK law arises automatically in respect to original literary, dramatic, musical or artistic works, sound recordings, films and broadcasts. There is no requirement to register copyright although it is common practice to attach a copyright statement to a published work. 'Literary works' covers a wide and diverse range of material including emails and computer programs as well as novels, legal texts and poetic works. Most of the materials which law librarians keep in their collections will be included under 'literary works' for the purposes of the legislation. This would for example include law reports, legal texts and transcripts of cases, whether published in print or in electronic form.

WHO OWNS COPYRIGHT?

The creator of a copyright work is in general the first owner of the copyright, but in practice it is often transferred to others (sold, donated, bequeathed and so on) and is quite likely to belong to the publisher in many cases. Often there is no easy way of determining this without some research. If a creator produces a copyright work in the course of employment then depending on contracts, the employer is likely to be the copyright owner. (CDPA 11 (2))

WHAT ACTS ARE RESTRICTED BY COPYRIGHT?

Section 16 of CDPA lists those acts which are restricted and which are the exclusive right of the copyright owner:

- Copying
- Issuing copies to the public
- Renting or lending to the public
- Performing or showing the work in public
- Communicating the work to the public
- Making an adaptation of the work to do any of the above with the adaptation.

As legal information professionals our main concern will usually be copying. The idea of performing a legal text on stage is an intriguing one, but not a likely occurrence.

COPYRIGHT TERM OR DURATION

The copyright term for 'literary, dramatic musical and artistic works' is the lifetime of the creator plus 70 years (that is, 70 years after the year in which the creator dies). As legal information professionals, that is the term which will apply to the vast majority of works which we deal with and which we hold in our collections, whether print or electronic. There is also a copyright in the typographical arrangement of a published edition of a work, which lasts for 25 years from the date of publication. Sound recordings and audio-visual products such as films are also protected by copyright but the rules about term are different and more complex. As they are less relevant for law librarians I will not attempt to cover them here.

COPYRIGHT IN DATABASES

It should be noted that 'databases' as defined in CDPA 3A enjoy separate protection introduced by the Copyright and Rights in Databases Regulations 1997 (SI 1997 no 3032), also known as the Database Regulations. These regulations serve the purpose of implementing in the UK, Directive No. 96/9/EC on the legal protection of databases. As in many areas of copyright law the subsequent case law plays a vital role in interpreting the meaning of the law.

SUBSTANTIAL PART

Copyright in a work is only infringed if the act relates to the whole or a substantial part, as stipulated by CDPA 16 (3) (a). Therefore copying a part of a work which is not substantial does not infringe copyright. There is a long history of case law on the question of what constitutes a 'substantial part' and it is clearly not safe to assume that because an extract from a work is short, that it is therefore not substantial. In practice the courts will look closely at the significance of the extract in the context of the whole work and at considerations of quality (as opposed to quantity). It would generally be unwise to rely heavily upon the assumption that an extract is not a substantial part without further consideration.

FAIR DEALING AND EXCEPTIONS TO COPYRIGHT

'Fair dealing' is a term which plays an important part in the CDPA in the context of acts of copying which may be permitted within the law. Broadly, it is what can be done with a copyright work without infringing. Fair dealing is used as an umbrella term which covers any acts of copying which fall within one of four specific exceptions to copyright listed in the CDPA. One should bear in mind that fair dealing is not some form of licence to copy. It is really a defence which can be used for acts which fall into one of these categories.

Despite its importance, there is no definition of fair dealing in the legislation, although there are examples of what does not qualify as fair dealing. It makes its appearance in Section 29 of the CDPA, which is headed 'Research and private study'.

> *Fair dealing with a literary, dramatic, musical or artistic work for the purposes of research for a non-commercial purpose does not infringe any copyright in the work provided that it is accompanied by a sufficient acknowledgement.*
> *CDPA 29 (i)*

The following subsection goes on to state that fair dealing in the same class of works for the purposes of 'private study' also does not infringe copyright subject to the same conditions. Section 30 of the CDPA covers the other situations to which fair dealing may apply: criticism, review and news reporting.

One should note that just as fair dealing is not defined in the legislation, neither is 'non-commercial purpose'.

Fair Dealing And Library Privilege

A level of protection for librarians and archivists in 'prescribed libraries' and the staff of those libraries generally is provided by Sections 37 to 44A of CDPA.

They are provided with a means of supplying copies from copyright works to their users while protecting themselves from charges of copyright infringement as long as they comply strictly with the statutory requirements. The main points (not a comprehensive list) are:

> They must obtain a signed declaration that the copy is required for purposes of non commercial research or private study. (echoing the wording of CDPA Section 29, see above)

They must have no reason to think that the material details of the declaration are false.

As long as they comply with the requirements, then the liability for any infringement (if for example the library user has falsified their intentions on the form) sits with the library user. See CDPA 37 (3).

Pointers About Fair Dealing in CDPA

Another interesting aspect of Sections 37 to 44A of the CDPA is the light they shed on what might qualify as fair dealing. It is very clear from Sections 38 and 39 that only one copy of an item can legitimately be supplied to the library user. In terms of extent, only one article may be supplied from a periodical and in relation to published editions of other literary, dramatic or musical works, 'no more than a reasonable proportion of any work', CDPA 39 (2) (b). See also the section on CILIP guidance below.

Prescribed Libraries

More details on 'library privilege' as it is sometimes called are given in the Copyright (Librarians and Archivists) (Copying of Copyright Material) Regulations, SI 1989/1212, including the scope of the term 'prescribed libraries'. Prescribed libraries include: local authority libraries; government libraries; the legal deposit libraries; school and academic libraries and also:

> Any other library conducted for the purpose of facilitating or encouraging the study of bibliography, education, fine arts, history, languages, law, literature, medicine, music, philosophy, religion, science (including natural and social science) or technology, or administered by any establishment or organisation which is conducted wholly or mainly for such a purpose. (SI 1989/1212, Schedule 1, Part A, S6)

It is important to note that while this definition seems very wide in the range of libraries which are included, any library which is run for a profit is explicitly excluded.

A template for the form which the library user should be required to sign when requesting a copy is included as Schedule 2 of SI 1989/1212.

CILIP Guidance on Fair Dealing

The Chartered Institute of Library and Information Professionals (CILIP) make two posters available on their website which can be used to display in libraries to provide information for library users. The 'gold' poster is designed to be of assistance to users of self-service copying facilities in the library from print originals. This is a summary of its guidelines:

- Single copies only
- Digital copies must not be placed on a network
- One article only from a periodical
- Only one chapter or 5 per cent of any other work
- Only for purposes of non-commercial research or private study.

This poster is widely used and the guidelines correspond with similar guidance given in other sources in the past.

Other Exceptions under CDPA

Apart from fair dealing there are many other specific exceptions listed in the CDPA. The fair dealing provisions are comparatively broad in scope compared with the other exceptions, which only apply in very specific circumstances. I will mention only some of these exceptions which are more obviously relevant for legal information professionals here.

Temporary Copies which are an Unavoidable Part of an IT Process

This is a later amendment to the CDPA to make allowance for the fact that any processing of a file by computer creates temporary copies, which could be 'infringing copies' without this amendment. The making of temporary copies of a literary work as an unavoidable part of the process of transferring the work electronically and which has no independent economic significance does not infringe as long as the use being made of the work is in itself lawful. This is contained in CDPA 28A and was introduced by SI 2003/2498 implementing one of the exceptions included in the Copyright Directive. This exception does not apply to computer programs and databases.

Making Accessible Copies By or For the Personal Use of a Visually Impaired Person

The Copyright (Visually Impaired Persons) Act 2002 inserts new provisions 31A to 31F into the CPDA which provide an exception which enables copyright works to be copied, if necessary the whole work, in order to produce an accessible copy. This is a valuable facility for those with visual impairments, but it is subject to a number of conditions, which should be read closely. For example the exception does not apply if an accessible version of the work is available commercially.

The Copyright Licensing Agency also offers a Print Disability Licence Scheme, which at the time of writing is not subject to licence fees and which may be more convenient in some cases than relying solely on the statutory exception. Under CDPA 31D the exemption for 'approved bodies' (an educational establishment or a body that is not conducted for profit) to provide accessible copies of copyright works which they hold does not apply if a suitable licence scheme is available.

COPYING FOR PURPOSES OF PARLIAMENTARY OR JUDICIAL PROCEEDINGS

The exception for parliamentary or judicial proceedings is to be found at Section 45 of the CDPA. This is of obvious relevance for legal information professionals:

1. Copyright is not infringed by anything done for the purposes of parliamentary or judicial proceedings.
2. Copyright is not infringed by anything done for the purposes of reporting such proceedings; but this shall not be construed as authorizing the copying of a work which is itself a published report of the proceedings.

COPYING BY LIBRARIANS OR ARCHIVISTS: REPLACEMENT COPIES OF WORKS

There is also a limited exception for the librarian or archivist of a prescribed library or archive to make a single copy of a work in the permanent collection in order to preserve or replace that item by placing the copy in its permanent collection in addition to or in place of the original. See CDPA Section 42.

WHEN THE EXCEPTIONS DO NOT HELP

If you need to copy or reuse a copyright work in circumstances not covered by the statutory exceptions, there are other avenues for doing so legally. There are licensing organizations which are able to sell you a licence covering a range of copying activities. Alternatively, as long as you are able to identify the owner of the copyright you can of course apply to them for permission to use their work in the way you intend.

THE COPYRIGHT LICENSING AGENCY

The Copyright Licensing Agency (CLA) was established in 1983 and is jointly owned by two rights holder organizations: the Authors' Licensing and Collecting Society Ltd and the Publishers' Licensing Society Ltd. Its purpose is to develop and promote collective licences and to collect licence fees and distribute them to copyright owners. They are also able to license copying of artistic works on behalf of the Design and Artists Copyright Society Ltd. The CLA is a prominent member of the International Federation of Reproduction Rights Organisations (IFRRO).

The CLA offers licences to copy from a very wide range of print publications, including books, journals and law reports. These licences now include the making of digital copies from print sources. Some publishers choose to exclude all of their publications or specific titles from this scheme and there are lists of those exclusions on the CLA website. The range of licences available includes a higher education licence, which is relevant for academic law librarians and a Law Licence, which is geared to the needs of law firms and barristers chambers. The Law Society and the City of London Law Society have played an active part in negotiating suitable terms for the Law Licence with the CLA.

In a new departure, the CLA has recently started to offer a licensing scheme for the copying of digital material from web sites (born digital content) and it will be very interesting to see how this develops. Those websites covered by this scheme will carry easily recognizable symbols. An updated Law Licence, including licensing for copying digital material was launched in 2012.

THE NEWSPAPER LICENSING AGENCY

The Newspaper Licensing Agency (NLA) offers a variety of licences to licence copying from newspapers, including since January 2010 copying content from newspaper websites. It is owned by the UK's large national newspaper groups and collects licence fees on their behalf. Among the licences on offer are a professional partnerships licence, which is geared mainly at the legal sector, a business licence and an educational licence. It also offers licensing to commercial web aggregators and their clients. Business subscribers to press monitoring services need to be aware of the copyright restrictions which apply to the content they receive from the agency.

CROWN COPYRIGHT, REUSING GOVERNMENT CONTENT

Crown Copyright is managed by the Controller of Her Majesty's Stationery Office, and this function is now part of the National Archives. A vast range of government copyright and database right material is available under the terms of the Open Government Licence, under which: 'The Licensor grants you a worldwide, royalty-free, perpetual, non-exclusive licence to use the Information ...' The conditions are very simple:

> *The information can be copied, published, adapted, distributed and exploited commercially. It can be combined with other information and included in your own product or application. The requirements are mainly proper attribution, no misrepresentation of the information or claiming official status or support for your own works, do not infringe other legislation such as the Data Protection Act in your reuse of the information.*

Policies on licensing the reuse of public sector information are guided by the UK Government Licensing Framework, details of which can be found on the National Archives (TNA) website, along with further information on the Open Government Licence. It is interesting to see that the terms of the Open Government licence '... have been aligned to be interoperable with any Creative Commons Attribution Licence'. See below for further information on Creative Commons.

COPYING FROM DIGITAL CONTENT

If your organization subscribes to electronic information services, whether they are e-books, electronic journals or online databases and so on, what you can legitimately do with that content will be governed primarily by your contract or licensing agreement with the supplier rather than by general copyright law. It is vital that before signing up to any agreement you examine the permissions included and negotiate further with the supplier if they are not clear or the licence does not cover an activity which is important for your organization.

There is also of course a wealth of useful content freely searchable and viewable on the internet. If you want to copy or reuse that content, however, the copyright implications must be considered. The first place to check will usually be the website itself. Does it carry a statement with the wishes of the copyright owner? What restrictions do they place on the reuse of their material? Do you need to request their permission? You may be required to click your acceptance of terms and conditions in order to access material on a website, in which case you are bound by the conditions you have agreed to. If there are no stated terms and conditions on a website, it does not follow that you can do whatever you wish with the content and in those circumstances you may have to contact the owner. It is particularly important to obtain permissions for any third party material you plan to make available on an internet or intranet page.

The CILIP blue poster (one of a pair – see the description of the gold poster under 'fair dealing') is designed for display in libraries to inform library users about copyright issues in copying from websites (or other digital sources). It can be found on the CILIP website.

Linking to the content of other websites from your own site also has copyright implications and you should consider whether you have permission to do so in specific cases and consider seeking permission if uncertain.

Naturally content which is accessible on the internet can take many forms and different types of copyright will apply, depending on whether that content is textual, graphic, video or a sound recording.

CREATIVE COMMONS

Many owners of web content now use the Creative Commons (CC) symbols, which offer an easily recognizable, standardized way of indicating what the rights holder is happy for you to do with their material and which actions they choose to exclude. It is essentially a form of licensing for online content, which is freely available to anyone who wishes to use it, from individual members of the public to international organizations. It is used mostly by rights owners working in a non-commercial context, who are happy to make original content available for others to use, as long as their wishes regarding its reuse are respected. It can be seen as a compromise which protects the owner's rights without asserting the full restrictions of copyright law. Organizations as diverse as Wikimedia, the White House and the British Library have made use of Creative Commons licensing.

DIGITIZATION OF CONTENT FROM PRINT SOURCES

The fact that content can be digitized and made available in electronic form so readily causes concerns for rights holders and understandably so, although this activity is included in defined circumstances in some of the CLA's licences.

In recent years a number of large-scale and ambitious digitization projects have emerged. There is the Europeana project set in motion by the European Commission with the intention of creating a vast digital library with contributions from the collections of some 48 nations. In the USA the Google Library project, which set out to digitize the collections of about 40 major libraries ran into controversy with rights holders over copyright issues which became the subject of a class action by rights holders. In the case of European libraries, such as the Bodleian, only out of copyright works were in scope for the Google Library project. By contrast the digitization of US libraries included out-of-print works which are still in copyright. Attempts to reach a settlement with rights holders, which could have major implications for US copyright law are now facing further legal issues. Despite the legal complications, Google has established itself as a major player in terms of book digitization because of the scale of the Google Library project. It is estimated that some 30 million works have been digitized.

ORPHAN WORKS

These large scale digitization projects like Europeana and Google Library have brought the copyright problem of 'orphan works' to the fore. This is the problem of works which are still in copyright or likely to be so, but the current owners of the rights cannot be identified or located. This puts a practical difficulty in the way of seeking permission. This can be an issue for any scale of digitization project, but the larger the scale the greater the headache, as diligent research into ownership for every orphan work becomes a massive task and most likely beyond the resources of the project. Both the UK government and the European Commission have become concerned about the issue of orphan works (see Hargreaves Review below for recent UK developments).

THE INTELLECTUAL PROPERTY OFFICE

The Intellectual Property Office is the UK government body responsible for copyright policy and is part of the Department for Business, Innovation and Skills. The IPO website, www.ipo.gov.uk is a valuable source of information and official advice on copyright issues.

EUROPEAN UNION

Copyright is an area of law with well developed EU legislation which has a strong influence on UK law. Of particular importance is the Copyright Directive, Directive 2001/29/EC on the harmonization of certain aspects of copyright and related rights in the information society. These are some of the specific changes which result from the implementation of this directive in the UK by the Copyright and Related Rights Regulations 2003 (SI 2003/2498):

- The narrowing of the previous exception for research to the current wording 'Research for a non commercial purpose', which was obviously very significant for any organizations working in a commercial context which previously relied upon this exception.
- The introduction of an exception for incidental and unavoidable copies resulting from IT processes, CDPA 28A.

- Making interference with technological protection measures, designed to protect copyright in a work, illegal. See CDPA 296 and following sections.

The jurisdiction of the European Court of Justice also applies to copyright cases and the decisions of the court can be very significant for UK law.

INTERNATIONAL ORGANIZATIONS AND TREATIES

The UK is party to a number of international treaties related to copyright which have an influence on UK copyright law. The Berne convention of 1886 (The International Convention for the Protection of Literary and Artistic Works) is particularly influential as a source of copyright law. It is for example the source of the Berne three step test which is applied to statutory exceptions to Copyright within the EU Information Society Directive, Article 5 (5), 'The exceptions and limitations provided for ... shall only be applied in certain special cases which do not conflict with a normal exploitation of the work ... and do not unreasonably prejudice the legitimate interests of the right holder'.

Also very significant are the Universal Copyright Convention (UCC) established under the auspices of UNESCO in 1952 and the Agreement on Trade Related Aspects of Intellectual Property Rights (TRIPS), which was established by the World Trade Organization.

RECENT COPYRIGHT DEVELOPMENTS: THE DIGITAL ECONOMY ACT 2010

The Digital Economy Act (DEA) was passed in April 2010. It covers a range of technology-related topics including a determined attempt to address the issue of online copyright infringement by establishing an entirely new regulatory framework to be administered by Ofcom. For this purpose the DEA inserts new sections into the Communications Act 2003. The main target is clearly the types of infringement perpetrated by the sharing of illegally copied music and games via the internet, P2P file-sharing. It creates new duties for Ofcom as the regulator and also for Internet Service Providers (ISPs). The ISPs will have a duty to maintain details of apparent infringements reported to them by rights owners and will also have a duty to notify subscribers suspected of those infringements. The initial record-keeping will be based on internet protocol addresses and therefore not disclosing individual subscribers' details, but there is provision for copyright owners to apply for a court order to obtain individuals' details in serious cases of alleged repeated infringement. Ofcom have produced a draft Initial Obligations Code as required by the DEA for the full implementation of its provisions, but the code is yet to be approved and activated.

This is of interest as a new departure in tackling online copyright infringement but also of concern to librarians because the vague definitions of the DEA leave the door open for libraries offering internet access to their library users to be classified as internet service providers and therefore subject to the complex and expensive reporting requirements of the DEA. It seems likely that this is an unintended consequence of the legislation and the issue may be addressed at the time of detailed implementation of the scheme (assuming this happens). The government has recently followed up with a statement of intent to proceed with implementing an amended Initial Obligations Code, with some changes to the costs regime. This follows a largely unsuccessful judicial review of the DEA brought by BT and TalkTalk. See Government Response to the Hargreaves Review of Intellectual Property and Growth, 3 August 2011, IPO.

HARGREAVES REPORT

In May 2011 Professor Ian Hargreaves presented his report, 'Digital Opportunities: an independent review of IP and growth' which was commissioned by the prime minister in November 2010. Hargreaves was tasked with looking at the UK's Intellectual Property regime with a view to recommending changes to those features which impede economic growth. It was designed to be a firmly evidence-based review, not to be influenced unduly by the lobbying of powerful interest groups.

Hargreaves is very concerned about the role of existing copyright law in relation to the rapid developments in internet-related technology: 'Digital technologies are based upon copying, so copyright becomes their regulator: a role it was never designed to perform' (Hargreaves, 1.18).

Hargreaves recommended some ambitious reforms in the area of copyright to make the UK economy as competitive as possible for the digital age, and these recommendations have largely been taken up by the government in principle. The Gowers Review of Intellectual Property was an independent review of UK intellectual property (IP) commissioned by Gordon Brown, focusing on UK copyright law that was published in December 2006. The review concluded that the UK's intellectual property system is fundamentally strong but made 54 recommendations for improvements:

- Legalize format shifting for personal use.
- Digital Copyright Exchange – an efficient market in rights clearance.
- A scheme for freeing up 'orphan works' which cannot currently be reused.
- Introducing a requirement for codes of conduct for collecting societies on a voluntary basis but also with a statutory backstop if required in specific cases.

- Widen the exception for non-commercial research to cover text- and data-mining.
- Widen the exception for library archiving.
- Introduce an exception for parody.

See the IPO website, www.ipo.gov.uk, for further information. Only time will show to what extent these initiatives are developed in ways which affects the professional lives of law librarians.

UK CASE LAW

We have noted the importance of the courts in developing copyright law but this is not the place to go into any detail. However you may wish to look at the topical example of *Newspaper Licensing Agency & ors v Meltwater Holding BV & ors* [2011] EWCA Civ 890, which deals among other things with what constitutes a substantial part and whether a headline can be a literary work in its own right in the context of internet-based media monitoring services. See Pedley 2008 and also Padfield 2010 for discussion of some of the case law touching on specific copyright issues.

DATA PROTECTION

The primary purpose of the data protection legislation is to provide rights and safeguards for the individual citizen with regard to the collection, storage and use of their personal data by organizations. The principle piece of legislation concerning data protection in the UK is the Data Protection Act 1998 (DPA 1998). The DPA 1998 implements the European Directive on the processing of personal data and the free movement of such data, Directive 95/46/EC.

DPA 1998 1 (1) of the act, which defines some of the basic concepts of data protection, defines 'personal data' as follows:

> ... *data which relate to a living individual who can be identified –*
> *(a) from those data, or*
> *(b) from those data and other information which is in the possession of, or is likely to come into the possession of, the data controller, and includes any expression of opinion about the individual and any indication of the intentions of the data controller or any other person in respect of the individual.*

There is also a more specific category of 'sensitive personal data' which is dealt with in Section 2 of the DPA 1998 to which different rules apply. Sensitive personal data includes information such as racial or ethnic origins, political beliefs, trade union membership, health, sexual life, information relating to offences or alleged offences.

INFORMATION COMMISSIONER'S OFFICE

Data controllers have a number of obligations under the DPA 1998 including registering as such with the Information Commissioner's Office (ICO). The web site of the ICO describes its role as follows:

> *The Information Commissioner's Office is the UK's independent authority set up to uphold information rights in the public interest, promoting openness by public bodies and data privacy for individuals.*

Its responsibilities also include administering the Freedom of Information Act 2000. The eight data protection principles define the way in which personal data should be stored and processed by data controllers and they are contained in DPA Schedule 1 (1). They provide general guidelines rather than prescriptive detail. They are reproduced here because they are so central to responsibilities under the DPA:

"The principles

1. Personal data shall be processed fairly and lawfully and, in particular, shall not be processed unless –

   (a) at least one of the conditions in Schedule 2 is met, and
   (b) in the case of sensitive personal data, at least one of the conditions in Schedule 3 is also met.

2. Personal data shall be obtained only for one or more specified and lawful purpose, and shall not be further processed in any manner incompatible with that purpose or those purposes.

3. Personal data shall be adequate, relevant and not excessive in relation to the purpose or purposes for which they are processed.

4. Personal data shall be accurate and, where necessary, kept up to date.

5. Personal data processed for any purpose or purposes shall not be kept for longer than is necessary for that purpose or those purposes.

6. Personal data shall be processed in accordance with the rights of data subjects under this Act.

7. Appropriate technical and organisational measures shall be taken against unauthorised or unlawful processing of personal data and against accidental loss or destruction of, or damage to, personal data.

8. Personal data shall not be transferred to a country or territory outside the European Economic Area unless that country or territory ensures an adequate level of protection for the rights and freedoms of data subjects in relation to the processing of personal data."

Section 7 of the DPA deals with the rights of data subjects to request and receive personal information about them which they believe to be stored by a data controller. Responding to 'subject access requests' is an important duty of the data controller under the DPA.

The website of the Information Commissioner's Office, www.ico.gov.uk, is a very good source of further information on rights, duties and procedures under the DPA 1998. It should prove useful for data controllers and data subjects. As with copyright, case law plays a vital role in determining the meaning of the law. For example the decision by the Court of Appeal in Durant v. Financial Services Authority [2003] deals with the meaning of 'relevant filing system', which affects the question when data in manual filing systems falls within the scope of the DPA 1998.

The Information Commissioner is also responsible for enforcement functions under the Privacy and Electronic Communications (EC Directive) Regulations 2003, SI 2003/2426, which implements the Directive on Privacy and Electronic Communications, Directive 2002/58/EC. These regulations deal with the use of 'electronic communications networks' for direct marketing purposes, among other topics. This represents a significant area of the Information Commissioner's activities.

CONCLUSION

It is fair to say that as legal information professionals we are very likely to be closely involved in formulating and implementing policies around copyright and taking related risk management decisions. This is now a central part of our skill set. Formulating a central copyright policy, based on an audit of the organization's requirements is a good way to start, which can also be used as a basis for deciding what licenses might be required.

We may also find ourselves with responsibility for data protection issues. In this case also a central policy for the organization is essential. This needs to be linked to a comprehensive understanding of the types of records kept by the organization, with security, retention and disposal policies agreed and implemented by all concerned in processing personal data.

USEFUL WEBSITES

Authors' Licensing and Collecting Society: www.alcs.co.uk
British Copyright Council: www.britishcopyright.org
Chartered Institute of Library and Information Professionals: www.cilip.org.uk
Copyright Licensing Agency: www.cla.co.uk
Creative Commons UK: www.creativecommons.org.uk
Europeana project: www.europeana.eu
Information Commissioner's Office: www.ico.gov.uk
Intellectual Property Office: www.ipo.gov.uk
Libraries and Archives Copyright Alliance: www.cilip.org.uk/laca
National Archives: www.nationalarchives.gov.uk
Newspaper Licensing Agency: www.nla.co.uk
Publishers' Licensing Society: www.pls.org.uk

CHAPTER 8

KNOWLEDGE MANAGEMENT

ANN HEMMING

Since the first edition if this book, it's fair to say that we have experienced an unprecedented period of change in legal service provision.

We are still waiting to see what impact alternative business structures will have on law firms, still working through the implications of outcomes-focussed regulation and of course looking at a period of exceptional change in higher education, with many changes anticipated in the way law will be studied and accredited. Add to this the continuing impact of the changed financial landscape, which is having a greater effect on the legal industry than many of the previous recessions. What else has changed dramatically? Of course it is our use of technology which is continuing to change the way we do business, communicate, learn and acquire knowledge.

So how to explain knowledge management in 2014, what are the most successful strategies, what can technology do to help and how can you make sure that you are developing a sustainable strategy for the benefit of the business?

KM is not a difficult concept. The drive for KM is basically about not reinventing wheels. Firms have a vested interest in making sure that by sharing knowledge they improve efficiency. The knowledge becomes the organization's asset rather than an individual's (that will leave if they do). It is about efficiency and profitability and therefore is tied to the bottom line of any business.

What is difficult is the implementation. There are a range of cultural issues that underpin a KM strategy. To make KM work you need to understand the existing cultural barriers in your organization. So although the basic concepts and principles are worth understanding, to implement KM will mean paying attention to the particular culture of your firm and the teams you are working with. If you are working with a team of highly skilled individuals who work relatively autonomously, then clearly your approach will be very different to that you would take working with teams dealing with commoditized or process work. Whatever the team, KM implementation invariably involves a change management programme and, as with any change process, this is often painful.

What role does the Library and Information Service have as part of the KM strategy? Librarian/Information staff (LIS) are an integral part of the KM investment the firm is making. They manage an expensive and vital resource and the way that the library is organized should be built into the KM strategy.

What knowledge do firms need to manage? When trying to set your KM strategy it is quite often a good idea to map your know how initiatives against a simple grid. It can help you have conversations with the key stakeholders in the business and agree where priorities should be set for actively creating, capturing, maintaining and sharing knowledge. In the simplest terms this can be charted into 4 quadrants.

Figure 8.1   Know how initiatives grid

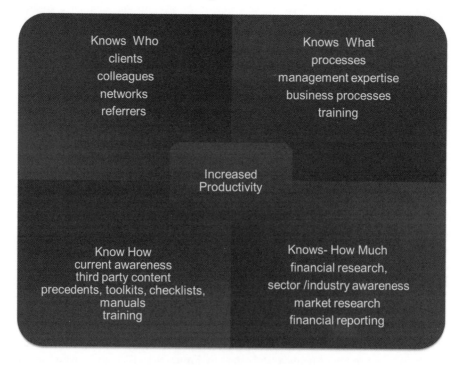

I have used this simple grid with many firms as a way of charting what initiatives they currently have for maintaining knowledge and identifying the biggest gaps. Although as LIS staff, we will tend to gravitate towards bottom left quadrant (the capture and collection of precedents and other documents), it is worth remembering that actually that is only one small part of the knowledge that needs managing in an organization. Each quadrant is important, particularly in a knowledge business such as law. In each quadrant, managing knowledge can benefit from an information professional's skills in analysis, organization and categorization of knowledge assets.

It is vital that the firm knows how profitable the business is, how teams are performing and can spot trends and opportunities as soon as possible. This sounds easy, but is actually very difficult to achieve. Firms are investing a lot of resources in getting better business intelligence from their financial systems, analysing what is the most profitable work that they do – and spotting any shortfalls in resources or trends in billing that may affect profitability.

Similarly in a modern law firm, where so many processes are automated and so much of the work is subject to detailed procedural scrutiny, it is important that the knowledge around 'how we do things round here' is maintained. This know how may take the form of manuals, procedures policies, training and IT systems (such as case management and document automation applications). These are all designed to systematize work, to make it easier and quicker to produce consistently high-quality work for clients at competitive prices. Even in complex legal transactions, some elements of the work will be routine and capable of being systematized. Automation will allow the firm to delegate work and do it more profitably.

Know who is also critical. As firms grow in size and have an increasingly mobile workforce, it is difficult to know who all the internal experts are. This is vital for building trust and teams that can cross-sell expertise to clients. It is also becoming a standard that firms will have quite complex team structures so that they can service clients in a particular industry sector, or respond to complex tenders for multi-file work. In order to do this, lawyers need to know who has the relevant expertise, who has done the latest deals and who is actively involved with their clients and contacts. Lawyers also need to know who their clients are, what they are interested in and all the complex interrelationships that help to build a good service. Firms have invested heavily in CRM systems to 'harvest' contact information from individual e-mail accounts, and to gain as much information about colleagues and contacts as possible. Some firms are also now developing their own internal 'Facebook'-type applications to allow internal experts to publicize their expertise and relationships.

The growth of the use of social media within organizations has a huge potential benefit for connecting know how and internal experts and should also been seen as a resource that the information professionals can harness as part of a KM strategy.

If we now review the know how element of this quadrant, this describes the means of collecting, organizing, maintaining and developing the technical (legal) knowledge of the business. This is traditionally the area where knowledge workers, LIS and Professional Support Lawyers are most heavily (although not exclusively) engaged in KM.

So although I will spend some time discussing the capture of know how, do remember that KM needs to be applied to all areas of the quadrant and that LIS staff have skills that can be applied to projects in any of the four quadrants.

Because of the increased use of technology to analyse and then systematize processes you will increasingly find that a KM initiative will involve capturing and using knowledge from all four quadrants.

If you are starting to read around on the subject, then a very good resource is the *Complete Idiot's Guide to Knowledge Management* (Rumizen 2001): although this is now quite old it still has a lot of sensible advice.

Rumizen defines KM as follows:

> *... knowledge management is the systematic process by which knowledge needed for an organisation to succeed is created, captured, shared and leveraged.*

The key points of this definition are developing *systems* that actively support KM and developing *processes* to capture and share that knowledge.

Initial capture requires a lot of individual planning and thought. It is worth acknowledging the cultural tensions in KM at the start of any project. Lawyers are still measured by and large on individual performance as well as team measures. They are trading in their own hard-won knowledge and there is a natural and understandable desire to protect that intellectual capital as part of their professional profile. However for the firm, the reality is that one individual can only achieve so much in terms of profit, revenue and sustainability. For the firm, it is important that knowledge is shared and becomes part of the organization's capital. It means tasks can be completed more profitably, with less risk and can be delegated to more junior staff, to help increase their knowledge and to improve profitability.

For a very practical analysis of these tensions, and strategies to harness knowledge, *Effective Knowledge Management for Law Firms* (Parsons 2004) will give you an excellent overview of the issues to consider when setting and delivering a knowledge strategy.

These issues are not new; law firms have always managed their knowledge. Both the legal profession and legal education are based on the apprenticeship model. Trainee solicitors and juniors work with their peers to gain experience and knowledge so that it is retained within the organization. Successful firms develop sophisticated training programs and, more recently, tools to facilitate knowledge transfer and to retain as much knowledge as possible within the organization. This then creates a virtuous circle as the firms with the best training and know how attract the best talent and are able to grow their business and develop their competitive advantage.

THE KM STRATEGY

Given that managing knowledge is at the heart of the law firm business, why do you need a separate KM strategy? The main reason is that you need to identify and articulate the main goals that will give benefit to your firm. It is also important to get senior management buy-in and sponsorship. There will be huge differences in approach depending on the type of firm you work for. So if you are setting or updating a KM strategy, your first step should be to understand the firm's business strategy and where the main priorities lie. If you are reasonably new to law firms, then I would recommend taking the time to read some of the main works your managing partner is likely to have on his/her personal bookshelf. Nick Jarret-Kerr's book *Strategy for Law Firms: After the Legal Services Act 2007* (Law Society 2009) is a good starting point and Nick also maintains an excellent blog. Most law firm managers have also read Richard Susskind's book the *End of Lawyers?* (OUP 2008) and it is worth making sure you understand the predictions Richard makes, even if you don't agree with them. His main premise is that because of the rise in technology and commoditization, the way legal services will be delivered in the future will change fundamentally. We are already seeing evidence of this shift – at the time of writing the emergence in the legal market of large corporates offering legal services (the Co-operative for example) is inevitably going to affect the whole industry. So as first steps it is worth reviewing what your firm is trying to achieve. Is it developing a lot of commoditized work, or is it looking to develop high net worth niche services? Is it aiming to be a full service firm, or specialize in certain disciplines and service areas? Are there specific risks to your business from competitors or because it needs to develop new expertise? Your strategy is best developed as part of the main business planning cycle, referenced back to the firm strategy and then revised by reviewing the individual business plans of the business units.

AUDITING YOUR KNOWLEDGE MANAGEMENT RESOURCES AND PROCESSES

Most of the textbooks on knowledge management will recommend that you undertake some kind of knowledge audit and that you repeat the process at regular intervals. The reason for an audit is similar to a stock review. You need to find out what gaps you have in your KM strategy and prioritize your activities. You also need to do regular reality checks on your plans and processes.

Knowledge audits can take many forms, but the most successful are very targeted and focussed. Work with a specific team to understand the way they work, shadowing is often a good way to start, and then look at the information they need to access over and over again. Is this know how easy to find, is it capable of being made readily available and are documents easy to complete? Breaking down a legal process or transaction into its constituent activities and outputs allows you to 'audit' and identify gaps and also process improvements. Once you have found these gaps then you can start to build tools and resources to make the improvement. LIS has a key part to play and skills that can be used as part of the project team working on these initiatives. They are likely to be able to spot trends and to analyse audit results. They will also know the internal experts who can help develop solutions. LIS are also good at organization and can help keep projects on track.

In such a fast-moving market, you should regularly review your methods and the knowledge you are managing. Is it still as valuable to the organization, is it being reused and are there alternative resources now available that devalue an internal knowledge capture effort?

For a useful article on knowledge audits, read 'Unlocking Potential' by Graeme Burton in *Inside Knowledge* magazine (Volume 10 Issue 4, December 2006/ January 2007).

Practical Law Company (*About Practical Law Company* 2010) have also produced a useful audit of KM in law firms after interviewing a number of their key client firms.

DEVELOPING YOUR KM INITIATIVES

So having worked through the strategy, you understand the culture of the firm and the business priorities. You have completed an audit and have articulated where the knowledge gaps are and identified a list of priorities to improve knowledge management in the firm. The next step is to agree your plans and the tactics for successful delivery and get the endorsement of your colleagues and management. At this point, it is worth looking at what other initiatives are planned within the business and the level of resources available. With the current restrictions on budget and manpower it is very important to apply good project management principles to your KM initiatives. This simply means making sure you balance time, resources and quality. You will not be working in a vacuum; your lawyers will have been managing their knowledge for years. No law firm would survive if they did not have some means of managing this combined and cumulative knowledge. A successful KM policy will leverage existing best practice and 'showcase' projects to build on the existing initiatives in place.

You may also feel that technology is not the right place to start: if you have limited resources and one of your priorities is to improve the 'Know-who' knowledge in the business, then supporting 'tacit' sharing of knowledge by organizing regular team briefings, seminars and know how sessions may well be a good way to start the process. If you have some 'stars' who need to promote their know how but have limited time, they may well find a blog is a good way to informally document what they are doing.

THE KM ROLES AND RESPONSIBILITIES

So far I have written this chapter assuming that you will be able to take a lead role in your KM strategy, which may not be the case. Whatever your role is, as part of the KM team you will be working with colleagues from across the business. Professional Support Lawyers, HR staff or a range of different business leaders may own the strategy in your firm. KM organization in law firms varies enormously and there is no good or bad organizational structure; the key is to understand what the strategy is and then make sure that you are supporting and providing real value in its delivery. For more on the role of the law librarian in KM strategies, Steven Lastres has written a very good article '*Aligning Through Knowledge Management* Information' (Lastres, June 2011). The fact remains that the library and legal information resources that the firm invests in form a significant part of the KM budget. The external knowledge resources you procure, from services such as PLC and Lexis PSL, offer an increasing amount of outsourced knowledge management and will be part of the whole KM strategy. Similarly, the way that the library organizes and distributes information resources should dovetail with the other KM collection and organization activities within the business; LIS staff provide an incredibly valuable KM role. The information professional is expert in a range of KM skills.

I will just list a few areas where LIS impacts on KM strategy:

- Resources: LIS are skilled at locating and evaluating information resources. As the pressure to extract best value with limited budgets increases, it is very important to make sure that your internal KM activities are focused on 'crown jewels', that is the management of knowledge that is unique and of high value. Librarians can help by demonstrating what is commercially available and making sure that lawyers are not reinventing the wheel when they create their internal know how.

- Organization: LIS have excellent skills in classifying and organizing resources into meaningful groupings so that they can be retrieved easily. These indexing and organizational skills are highly valuable when managing all sorts of information resources across the business.
- Audit and review: LIS are very aware of the need to maintain resources and audit for out-of-date or redundant materials. In the legal environment, this is vital to reduce the risk of out-of-date materials being used. Maintenance is at the heart of knowledge management and can be where many internal systems fail as not enough attention is paid to the regular review and removal of out-of-date materials.
- Promotion and user education: LIS play a key role in promoting best practice in the use of information. Expertise in search and retrieval skills is more important than ever given the explosion in available information. Their skills in advising on technology solutions to improve search and retrieval, as well as their role in user education should not be underestimated.

MANAGEMENT OF THE KM AND LEARNING AND DEVELOPMENT FUNCTIONS

In KM projects, the general advice is to keep decision-makers to a minimum. Ownership has to be encouraged, therefore representative lawyers from each department or work group will be required, but they should be there for help and advice – not to make the final decisions. In the senior KM structure it is important to have managers with an overview who can see the whole picture and not just the needs of their own particular department. In some firms, Learning and Development (L&D) and KM are managed separately, however in the firms with some of the best KM initiatives, the two work holistically, with the L&D activities and strategy generating KM content and the KM strategy identifying the need for additional L&D, while both are assessed as part of the firm's competency framework and individual performance. As online learning tools become more prevalent, the distinction between KM and L&D becomes even more blurred.

OTHER KM ROLES IN THE BUSINESS

There are some projects that fit closely with the LIS remit, but you can also transfer your skills to take a leadership role in delivering your KM strategy and there are many examples of librarians taking on that mantle. This will depend very much on your own personal preferences and the opportunities available to you. It is also important for you to remember that the KM strategy is very much a collaborative exercise and will involve a much broader team than just the information professional. It will inevitably involve Information Technology and it is essential to not only develop your own knowledge of IT resources, but to develop good working relationships with the IT team.

You will also have to build relationships with the HR and Learning and Development functions within your firm. If you want to encourage lawyers to contribute their know how to the firm, then these behaviours need to be recognized and rewarded and your HR team is best placed to make sure that this is embedded into the firm culture. The training team are also deeply involved, and having a close working relationship with them works both ways: librarians can identify new areas of law that require training, while L&D can also identify who are the internal experts that need to be encouraged to contribute.

I will also mention the business development team (BD) as part of the KM structure. BD will be working with lawyers to identify new products and strategies to bring to market. They are also involved in creating knowledge resources, and also need access to a complex array of business intelligence. LIS can play a key role in supporting the BD activities of the business. Finally, the most important members of the team will be your lawyers. Making sure that you have the commitment of the partnership to your strategy is the most important component for ensuring success.

Professional Support Lawyers (PSLs) and Legal Departments

Many larger firms have Professional Support Lawyers who are the 'front line' KM workers. You will need to agree where your role ends and the PSL role begins; traditionally there has been tension around some services, notably current awareness and where responsibilities lie. The PSL role will vary from firm to firm, but the most successful PSLs have taken a strategic role in developing and supporting client-specific know how and business development initiatives. They will be involved in the creation and collection of know how, but the service works best where there is a good understanding of the different roles of LIS and PSL. Your relationship with the legal departments also needs to be kept under close review. As legal work becomes more and more specialized, some LIS teams have developed specific practice area expertise and may even take on more of a traditional PSL role. There are many opportunities for the information professional who can develop these skills (in both legal and in industry sector knowledge) to make a huge contribution to the KM initiatives in their firms.

Outsourcing

PSL and LIS roles have been further complicated by the rise of outsourcing of some knowledge (and library services). PLC has now become well established as an outsourced resource that supplies a lot of the current awareness and standard documents that many departments need. Firms have taken a strategic review of their internal investment as a result and some firms (Freshfields being a notable example) have decided that the majority of know how work can be done by an outsourced provider. Lexis have also entered the market with their PSL product, offering lawyers and law firms access to large teams of Professional Support Lawyers whose sole function is to create and maintain knowledge resources.

As global legal outsourcing continues to advance, more firms are likely to review their in-house investment and already we are seeing some firms outsource some of their KM and library functions, either onshore or to offshore teams, CMS Cameron McKenna being an example. This presents the LIS staff with both opportunities and challenges. Becoming part of an outsourced library function may offer you greater scope and support to further your career, however inevitably it can also lead to a reduction in available roles within law firms.

ENCOURAGING A KNOWLEDGE SHARING CULTURE

There is a perennial problem in encouraging lawyers to share their know how. Lawyers are unlikely to see this as a top priority unless the firm makes it clear that it is regarded as part of the expected behaviours. It is also important to make sure that lawyers feel that there is a personal benefit in sharing their know how. The most successful KM strategies link advancement and reward to the contribution of know how. But this has to be handled very carefully; simply giving lawyer's quotas for KM contribution does not provide the right incentive.

Therefore most firms provide targets for contribution and have a system for measuring the quality and value of the resources being created and link their reward and advancement structures to measures of KM activity. Many firms have also linked their KM and risk management strategies to 'add teeth' to their KM policies.

To encourage the desired behaviours, firms tend to put in place some guidelines about the types of KM activities that are expected of fee earners. In some firms know how itself is also set a value (normally based on the complexity of the item, the reuse potential and activity) and the reuse of the item is monitored as part of the ongoing audit processes. This can help a firm to continually appraise the know how activity and gain additional information on the value of their investment.

MANAGING KNOWLEDGE RESOURCES AND DISTRIBUTION

The traditional way KM is captured is to have some form of submission, approval and publishing process. This may be manual or a simple e-mail form or it may be more complex and automated, sometimes embedded within either your Document Management System (DMS) or portal/intranet. (I am leaving to one side for the moment how you actually get lawyers to submit or contribute to know how. This has always been an incredibly difficult process and recent technology initiatives are making some headway in relieving this burden.)

Taking a standard contribution process, a lawyer will normally submit their item to some form of 'Controller' – this may be a PSL, an information professional or a lawyer tasked with this duty. The role of the controller is normally to review the item, make sure it is of suitable quality – possibly canvass approval from others within the business and check how it relates to other know how items. The Controller normally then adds additional metadata (keywords, document types and review dates for example) and any 'health warnings' on the reuse of the item. The item is then normally 'published' either within a document management repository or file system/intranet or portal.

Any know how that is selected for retention will need to include information about why it is being retained and should be used; this is part of the editorial process and is normally part of a 'profile'. Lawyers need to know at first glance why the document they have retrieved is good know how and how it could be relevant to their situation. It should differentiate a maintained document from standard matter documents and should 'rank' know how as more significant in search results. Describing the document in great detail is not necessary, but ensuring maintenance is important for risk management and quality control. However lawyers do not want to or have time to do any laborious form-filling when submitting know how. They simply need to explain why a particular item is considered good know how. If they cannot do that, then it probably should not be stored. A policy on what know how is to be retained, an editorial workflow and an easy submission method are vital to the success of a know how project.

Content management is where most knowledge management projects flounder. If the content is not maintained it becomes useless and potentially dangerous. The ability to store and search all documents is useful but carries risks if information is used out of context. It is imperative that lawyers can easily find out if know how is still accurate, particularly as the pace of change increases. A disposal and 'weeding' policy is essential, technology can now be used to monitor usage of know how and to enable users to add ratings or comments and this can then help the KM managers review their content. It is necessary to make decisions about what know how is going to be kept and what is outsourced, how valuable it is, how much it will be reused and therefore the effort that should be invested in the collection and this needs to be part of an ongoing maintenance process. This normally translates into the team or department strategy and should be actively managed to make sure a know how collection is 'crown jewels' and not low-value content; or in some cases simply an attempt to recreate what is available in online databases of articles and precedents (such as Westlaw UK, Lexis and PLC). Integration of external resources can also help with maintenance – Lexis and Justis for example have developed tools which allow users to interrogate internal know how as it is accessed and see immediately if there are any case or legislation references that need reviewing. Content management strategies also need to ensure that business rules regarding issues of confidentiality, and ethical walls, are adhered to. Some documents must be protected, but a profile may be of more general availability. Copyrighted documents may be treated in the same way. As soon as some parts of the KM store start to have limited access then this can impact back on your KM strategy as parts of the organization try to restrict access to their know how either because it is deemed confidential or because they fear 'dabbling' in their area of expertise by others in the business.

More recently technology has offered new ways to manage know how content. As firms introduce more social media tools, some legal departments are finding that where the emphasis is not on retention of precedent materials, introducing a blog or wiki that lawyers can contribute to can be a more flexible and dynamic means of sharing know how. Many projects are now starting to use these technologies; however the simple rules around retrieval, organization and ensuring that information is current will remain.

Multimedia content is also being used to share knowledge; this may be podcasts, webinars, e-learning materials or audio files. The same principles apply to multimedia content.

TECHNOLOGY AND KM

Although KM should not be seen as an IT initiative, it is inevitable that the organization of your knowledge resources will be handled to some extent through technology.

If you ask most lawyers how they want to access their know how they will probably refer to Google. Lawyers have to use a huge array of software and want something that will fit into the way they currently work and make their lives as easy as possible. Unfortunately this means a lot of hard work for the IT and knowledge professionals.

The LIS team will need to have a really good relationship with their IT departments and make sure that their IT colleagues understand the library's requirements; similarly it is well worth understanding what the IT department's strategy is. A new version of the document management system or a new version of Microsoft may offer you new opportunities to develop KM interfaces. It is also worth while keeping up with latest trends in legal technology. Reading the *Legal Technology*

Insider (http://www.legaltechnology.com/) is a quick and easy way of keeping up to date.

LIS staff are also often at the forefront of spotting new technologies that can support knowledge sharing. Many have pioneered the use of social media within their firms and have worked closely with IT to develop new and innovative tools to support KM.

Traditionally knowledge resources are indexed and identified through the use of taxonomies, either developed by the firm or via an expert third party, such as PLC. Knowledge resources also need to have metadata (information about the information) to enable lawyers to understand how to use documents, when they were created, who by and so on. Although it has become much easier to automate the allocation of metadata and taxonomies, in most firms there still has to be some manual intervention in order to maintain and index know how.

The debate over whether to simply use a search engine to access know how, or whether a more structured means of storage and presentation is necessary has been a hot topic for many years. Search technology is evolving so that it can now make assumptions about documents, can categorize and 'cluster' and can also 'learn' from examples what to include in search results and how to rank findings. Although this does cut down on the need for documents to be organized and profiled, organization of internal know how is still important for quality control purposes. Some firms are now also indexing external content and presenting that back as part of the search results. Enterprise search or federated search offers new opportunities to pull together different sets of data from different systems to present powerful new 'mash ups' that can enhance knowledge sharing. An example of this would be a topic search that will find know how documents, details of staff who have currently got matters relating to that topic, external research resources and which clients the firm currently provides advice to on that topic. Search technologies and taxonomies fall very squarely within the expertise of the information professional and you can make a really valuable contribution to the development of effective tools for distributing know how to lawyers. Even if your budget does not stretch to some of the more sophisticated search tools, there are a lot of very simple ways of organizing information and linking it together to provide really effective and powerful resources.

DOCUMENT MANAGEMENT, INTRANETS AND PORTALS

Although search is important, you will also want to provide specific views of your know how in the firm document management systems, intranet or portal. Having a good firm-wide taxonomy can help you automate this process, making it easy to deliver targeted content to teams and individuals based on their interests and areas of expertise. Recently many firms have started to develop portals that provide views into their document management systems, financial systems and other core systems to provide both team and personal views – effectively a one-stop shop for the lawyer. The LIS staff often play an important role in managing and maintaining these systems. LIS staff can often be involved in the development and maintenance of taxonomies and in the whole content management process. They will often manage the distribution of key content such as links to websites, current awareness news feeds and many other sources of information. Some LIS also become involved in the development of document retention and records management policies that underpin the management of information in the business.

The next section gives a case study of just such a project.

CASE STUDY

This was a KM project for a law firm with 250 lawyers, and was project managed by the head of KM. The core project team also included one PSL, a senior partner, the head of BD, Finance, HR and IT. The broader project team included a PSL and the intranet administrator (a librarian). The team worked together to identify the requirements for a new portal, to be built using SharePoint 2010. The requirements consultation involved interviews and workshops, as well as a thorough review of their current intranet and KM content in their document management system and library database. It also looked at the external resources the firm used.

The team then drafted up a requirements document and sent a proposal to the management board for investment in the new portal. Following a procurement exercise, the team then worked with a supplier to develop a new, personalized portal which would integrate many of the firms' disparate information resources.

The team worked through a huge 'wireframing' exercise, developing detailed views of content for personal, team, firm and office views.

The LIS team were responsible for much of the auditing on the existing intranet content that needed to be either transferred or archived, and for the development of the specific taxonomies that underpinned the development of the system.

The LIS team also advised the finance and BD teams on the taxonomies to use to integrate content from their systems so that the portal could display client and sector views that displayed information from both systems to the end-user.

The portal was piloted with lawyers from each of the practice groups, plus the PSL and the LIS staff supported the review of end-user testing. The LIS team were also given a central role in managing the publishing of KM content within the portal, being able to manage the distribution of news, useful links sections and RSS feeds to the different pages.

The LIS team and the IT department worked very closely throughout the whole project, developing the original budget, making presentations and consulting widely within the business.

Because of the personalized nature of the service, lawyers can now log on to views of their clients and matters and have a dedicated know how section of their portal. This know how section targets KM materials contained in their document management system along with library information and external content from their favourite resources.

Client and sector views of information are also available, this pulls together financial information, expertise and documents to help lawyers get a better understanding of 'who is doing what for whom' and also gives senior management improved information on financial performance.

Due to the specialized legal work, very specific taxonomies were drawn up with assistance from the PSL, but in the majority of cases, the information professionals were able to advise on the use of a standard taxonomy maintained by a third party vendor to cut down on administration and maintenance. The portal views prompted the LIS staff to have discussions with each of the practice groups and helped them audit their know how content, in some cases making decisions to stop maintaining their own know how and use third party products instead. The LIS team helped the practice groups formalize this by drafting a charter of what content would be maintained and would be collected and used. Much of the know how contained within the portal is now supplemented with eternal resources. Integrated views of library and KM contents help PSLs maintain their collections.

The LIS team were also involved in improving the staff directory information, helping to develop views that showed expertise through referencing the work types that lawyers had applied to their matters.

The whole process has raised the profile of the LIS team, demonstrated their skills to the business and helped them to develop new working relationships with others from both support and practice groups.

CONCLUSION

Technology is a great enabler and can help the LIS team move out of traditional library roles and apply their skills in a much broader setting. However KM is not an IT project and making IT the centre of any initiative is not the best way to go about it. KM projects need to balance the needs of the business, the time pressures of staff and never underestimate the effect of cultural pressures on any initiative for change.

KM projects also require you to develop excellent communication skills, and LIS staff are often translators having to help lawyers and IT understand each other's specialist languages. They also have to be diplomats; sometimes getting agreement on KM can feel as though you are trying to establish a peace treaty at the UN.

However getting involved with KM is an opportunity for you to get a much better understanding of the business you work in. LIS skills and expertise can really help prioritize KM work; LIS staff already work closely with their lawyers and have a good understanding of what information they need. LIS staff can help to build connections between people and information and this is really at the heart of good KM. For your own career it is important that you understand and get involved in KM projects. They will be happening in your firm and you need to take the opportunity to get involved. They are fascinating and frustrating in equal measure but are also at the very centre of an information professional's personal development.

CHAPTER 9

COLLECTION MANAGEMENT

CONTRIBUTORS:
DIANA MORRIS
LESLEY YOUNG
CHRISTINE MISKIN

CATALOGUING AND CLASSIFICATION

DIANA MORRIS

CATALOGUING

Many people assume that traditional cataloguing is no longer relevant in the age of the internet and some library schools devote very little attention to what was once regarded as a core skill of the profession. However, law books and other materials are still being published and bought in significant numbers in hard copy and Google is not going to help anyone locate them on the shelves of a law library. Some sort of catalogue is needed which users can search by means of a number of different access points, whether it is title, author, subject or something else, to find the material they need, and someone has to create the catalogue entries. The old 5 x 3 card catalogue filed in wooden cabinets is pretty much a thing of the past now, but there are in use any number of electronic library management systems with cataloguing modules which store the same information, albeit entered differently, via an onscreen form.

Cataloguing for Users

The most important thing about a catalogue is that it should help the library's users find what they need, as quickly and easily as possible. It sounds obvious, but it is easy to get carried away with the detail and forget this; a catalogue full of bibliographic detail may be professionally satisfying but, if it obscures the information users are looking for, it is pointless. It is also important to bear in mind who you are cataloguing for: the users may be judges, barristers, solicitors, trainee solicitors, students or a combination of these, and this is likely to affect cataloguing policy in some areas, such as choice of subject terms or the amount of descriptive material included. There are however two essential features of a law library catalogue whoever the users are: first, there should be as many access points as possible to facilitate fast retrieval; and second, the collection should be kept up to date with new material being catalogued as soon as possible. This is of course particularly important with legal materials where out-of-date information can be positively dangerous.

Cataloguing Legal Materials

Legal materials fall into two main categories: primary and secondary materials, each of which present their own cataloguing challenges. Primary materials consist of case reports and statutory materials which, when supplied in hard copy, are usually received as serial publications, often cumulating into annual volumes. The *All England Law Reports*, for example, are issued in weekly parts and cumulated into a number of bound volumes for each year. How should such a publication be catalogued? One option would be to have a single catalogue entry for the series with open dates. If a library management system is being used in which the catalogue is linked into the circulation system, each volume needs to be recorded uniquely within the entry so that it can be loaned. If there is no link to a circulation system, then a very simple catalogue entry is probably sufficient, with basic bibliographic information and indicating where the series can be found on the shelves, but not much more. If no hard copy primary materials are held at all, then the catalogue entry would simply refer to the online services and indicate how they can be accessed.

Some people may question whether primary materials need to be catalogued at all, particularly statutes. There is after all very little to put in the entry, and a large collection of bound volumes of statutes would be very visible in a library's legislation section. There are however good reasons to do so, apart from simply having a catalogue that is a complete record of your collection. The first is that there may be several series of statutory materials (for example that of the Incorporated Council of Law Reporting, as well as the Queen's Printer's version) which need to be distinguished. Another is the same point made above with regard to the *All England Law Reports* – if individual volumes of statutes are to be loaned using an electronic system, they will need to be in the catalogue.

Cataloguing secondary materials is more complicated. They consist of such publications as textbooks, journals, official reports, commentaries, digests, and series such as *Halsbury's Laws*.

Textbooks may be straightforward, but often are not. They may be in the form of looseleaf encyclopedias with regular updates, annual handbooks or bound volumes with irregularly published cumulative supplements. There are also some works supplied in mixed format with bound and looseleaf volumes, or bound with a CD ROM included. It is usual to have a single catalogue entry for such publications while making it clear what all the different elements are and how they are connected so that users can decide which of them they need for a particular task. However, if superseded editions are kept on the open shelves they should probably have separate catalogue entries to avoid confusion with the current editions.

Journals will normally be catalogued in the same way as law reports (see above), while official reports, commentaries and digests will be treated the same as books. There are however a number of multivolume series found in most law libraries which can present some problems. These may include *Halsbury's Laws*, *Halsbury's Statutes*, *Halsbury's Statutory Instruments*, the *Encyclopedia of Forms and Precedents* and *Atkin's Court Forms*. These can be problematic because they include at least two physical formats (bound and looseleaf volumes), and possibly a third (electronic), as well as three different publishing cycles (irregularly published replacement bound volumes, annually published index volumes and looseleaf updates), and cover the full range of legal topics. To take one as an example, *Halsbury's Laws* could be catalogued in a number of different ways: there could be a single catalogue entry with a full description of each element and each volume separately listed within it for lending purposes. This would lead to a very large catalogue entry as there are around 60 volumes which may be an issue, depending on the library management system used. Alternatively there could be an entry for each volume, to enable subject searching. This would lead to many more records, but each one would be much smaller. If there is no link between the catalogue and the library's circulation system the decision could be taken, as with statutes, not to catalogue it at all, particularly if it is a small collection and *Halsbury's Laws* is prominently displayed within it.

What to Include

So what should a typical catalogue entry include? This will of course vary depending on the type and size of library, its users and the publication being catalogued, but there are some general principles to keep in mind. The title is obviously important in any catalogue entry, but particularly for law books where an original author is often incorporated into the title and the names of authors of later editions are unfamiliar to users. One of the most obvious of these is *Chitty on Contracts*, now in its 30th edition, the original author of which, Joseph Chitty, died nearly two centuries ago. Other essential elements are author or editor, publisher, year of publication, shelf location and subject. These are probably the minimum required to accurately identify a work and, apart from year of publication, will be access points for searching. In addition, it could be useful to include the number of pages, to make it clear whether the item is a lengthy work or a pamphlet, as well as the edition, ISBN, physical description (looseleaf, hardback and so on) and a notes field, where any information of value to the user can be recorded in free text.

Cataloguing Standards

To ensure consistency of policy over the years and between different cataloguers, it is essential to follow some sort of cataloguing standard, of which the most commonly used one is the *Anglo-American Cataloguing Rules*, Second Edition (AACR2). This is a detailed and weighty tome and many libraries, particularly those in law firms, may feel that it is far more detailed than is necessary for their collections and prefer shorter entries, designed to suit their users' particular needs. However, every library should have their own cataloguing manual, whether they are using AACR2 or not: if they are using it, the manual will be used to record the circumstances in which their own practice differs from AACR2 and to record local information such as format of shelf references. If they are not using it, the manual will record details of their own policy in all areas. In the days of the card catalogue it would probably be considered quite brave (or foolish) to design your own cataloguing rules, but now that most cataloguing is done via an onscreen form it is much easier; the software used will most likely be programmed to produce the desired display in the catalogue automatically as well as to help ensure consistency in fields such as author and publisher by means of authority lists. Many of the rules will therefore be built into the system and will not need to be remembered by cataloguers or set out in a manual.

Any library which is part of a bibliographic network, which wants to download MARC records, or whose catalogue is routinely accessed and searched by outsiders, really must use AACR2, as it is the international standard. Others may feel that although it is too detailed for their needs, its principles are a good basis for their own rules. For these reasons there follows a brief description of the basics of AACR2, highlighting one or two areas which present difficulties for those cataloguing law publications.[1]

AACR2

The basic structure of AACR2 is in two parts – description and access points. Description consists mainly of copying information as it appears in the publication. Where the information is taken from and how strictly it should be transcribed varies depending on the area of the record. The title, for example, should only be taken from the title page whereas information in the notes area can come from anywhere, including from outside the publication itself. When it comes to transcription, the title should be reproduced exactly as it appears on the title page, while the publisher's name should be in the shortest form possible while remaining internationally identifiable. There is no discernible logic behind these rules or principles to be applied – cataloguers simply have to familiarize themselves with them.

The descriptive format is as follows:

> Title proper [general material designation] = parallel title: other title information/first statement of responsibility; each subsequent statement of responsibility. – Edition statement/first statement of responsibility relating to the edition. – Material (or type of publication) specific details. – First place of publication etc: first publisher etc, date of publication etc. – Extent of item: other physical details; dimensions. – (Title proper of series/statement of responsibility relating to series, ISSN of series; numbering within the series. Title of subseries, ISSN of subseries; numbering within sub-series). – Note(s). – Standard number.

This looks very long and involved, but in practice not all these elements will be relevant to every publication, and any library may choose to simplify or shorten it. A description for *Chitty on Contracts* for example, might look like this:

> Chitty on contracts. – 30th ed./[general editor: H.G. Beale]. – London: Sweet & Maxwell, 2010. – 2 vol. – v. 1. General principles; v. 2. Specific contracts. – ISBN 978184038661.

This excludes details of pages, dimensions, series and previous editions, but for many libraries will be quite sufficient as it provides all the essential information needed to identify the work. This brief entry conforms to the order of fields and punctuation given above, but any library which does not exchange records with other libraries does not need to follow this format at all.

Access points are the means by which users find publications, however they may have been described. This means that the decisions made about them are arguably more important than those of purely descriptive fields, as they can make the difference between users finding and not finding what they are looking for. AACR2 presents a number of problems for those cataloguing law books. One of these arises from the fact that many well-known legal textbooks incorporate the original author's name in the title, by which they are universally known. These include *Chitty on Contracts* (see above), *Clerk & Lindsell on Torts*, *McGregor on Damages*, *Gatley on Libel and Slander* and many others. AACR2 states that the main entry should be under the current author and only under the title when no author is given on the title page; this would lead to the main entry for these works being made under a name no one has heard of. The difference between a main entry and an added entry may not matter in an online catalogue as both will be picked up in any search; however it will matter if your catalogue generates lists of new acquisitions where each item is only listed once. Clearly common sense dictates that in situations like this the rule in AACR2 should not be followed.

Another problem arises when publications change title, often when they are taken over by another publisher. Many Butterworths publications, for example, have the word 'Butterworths' at the beginning of the title, which obviously had to be dropped from the titles of those works which were taken over by Tottel (now Bloomsbury Professional). The title as given on the title page ought to be the one used, but in the case of looseleaf encyclopedias where the original binders are still in use it makes more sense to stick with the original title, at least for the main entry, as long as the change is indicated in the notes.

Note that two of the essential elements of a basic catalogue entry mentioned in *What to include* do not appear in the descriptive format given above. The first of these, shelf location, provides the link between the catalogue entry and the physical item and so must be present on every catalogue entry. It is not included in the descriptive format above however as it is not an integral part of the publication itself but is a locally assigned access point. It could be a class mark, in the case of textbooks, or a reference to a particular shelf or area of the library. There could also be two separate fields for class marks and shelf references, with shelf references perhaps being assigned at copy level, where different copies of the same publication are held at different locations. Those adhering more or less strictly to AACR2 would probably add this field at the end of the description, but it could go anywhere where it could easily be seen. The same applies to subject terms: these are not part of the description as they are assigned locally, but they are a vital access point.

RDA

AACR2 was first published in 1978 and has since been widely used in the creation of millions of bibliographic records. However, continuing revisions have made it very complex and unwieldy and it struggles to deal with an ever-increasing number of digital formats and publication practices. A draft third edition was abandoned in 2002 in favour of an entirely new approach, and *Resource Description and Access* (RDA) was launched in the summer of 2010 as an online product called the RDA Toolkit.

RDA retains many of the AACR2 principles, but, crucially, instead of having media-specific rules RDA has single rules that can be used for any type of resource. It has also removed the Anglo-American bias of AACR2 to a large extent and is designed to be compatible with other standards based on internationally agreed principles.[2] Although larger libraries in the UK have recently implemented RDA in their cataloguing procedures, the extent of take-up in smaller libraries is yet to be seen.

CLASSIFICATION

A good catalogue will describe accurately a library's materials and provide numerous access points for searching, but it cannot determine how to order those materials on the shelves. Most law libraries use some type of classification scheme to organize their materials, whether it is a published scheme such as Library of Congress, Dewey Decimal Classification or *Moys Classification and Thesaurus for Legal Materials*, a scheme developed in-house or simply a system of broad subject groupings. Such schemes are normally used only to classify textbooks, however, as the distinctive nature of legal materials does not lend itself to a single principle of organization.

Principles of Organization

The basic principles of organization in a law library are by jurisdiction, form and subject.

Jurisdiction
Unless a library contains only English materials, most users will expect materials concerned with one jurisdiction to be arranged separately from those concerned with others. A case could be made for grouping books on common law topics together regardless of jurisdiction; an academic researcher, for example, might expect to find all books on contract together whether they came from England, Australia, or some other common law jurisdiction, but in practice this rarely happens.

Form
As noted above, legal materials fall quite naturally into primary materials (legislation and case reports) and secondary materials (journals, government and other official publications and textbooks and so on). Most law libraries file by this arrangement with a slight variation, so that legislation is shelved with the relevant indexes and other finding aids, while case reports are filed with their associated case digests and citators. So, for example, *Halsbury's Statutes* and *Halsbury's Statutory Instruments* will be filed in the legislation section, and *Current Law* and the *Current Law Citator* will be with case reports. This will be followed by official publications, filed by issuing department or series, and journals filed alphabetically by title, leaving only textbooks to be subject classified.

Subject
It is possible to file specialist journals or official publications along with textbooks in the same subject area. Libraries with a large amount of company law material could for example file *Butterworths Company Law Reports* with *The Company Lawyer* next to company law textbooks, but this can become very complicated and is probably best avoided. Arranging textbooks on the shelves however is almost always done by subject. Small libraries may find it sufficient to arrange their books under broad alphabetical headings with prominent shelf labels, but this is unlikely to be practical for large collections. Use of a classification scheme which allocates a quite specific classmark to be displayed on the book spine enables it to be found quickly and, just as importantly, for it to be shelved correctly when returned. Prominent shelf labels can and should still be used to facilitate easy browsing,

but as these will not be in alphabetical order a synopsis of the scheme used, also prominently displayed, will help guide users to the relevant shelves.

The decision on which principle of organization to use first will depend on the size and content of the collection. While an arrangement by subject will almost always come last, the decision on whether to organize by jurisdiction or form first will depend on the amount of foreign material held; if it only amounts to some textbooks and maybe a series or two of case reports, then it probably makes sense to file by form first. In this case a series such as the *Australian Corporation and Securities Reports* would be filed alphabetically by title with other law reports series, separately from Australian law textbooks which would be classified with other textbooks. Libraries with large foreign law collections are more likely to keep the materials for each jurisdiction entirely separate, using the form/subject arrangement for each one.

Classification Schemes

The most commonly used published classification schemes used in law libraries are Library of Congress (LC), mainly in academic libraries, and *Moys Classification and Thesaurus for Legal Materials*, mainly in law firm libraries. Dewey Decimal Classification (DDC) is also used, and a sizeable number of law firm libraries use schemes developed in-house, a trend that seems to be growing.[3] The disadvantage of using general schemes for law collections is that you can only use one small part of it for the whole collection, which may lead to insufficient specificity or some very long shelf marks. The usual reason for their use is that other libraries or collections within a university or college are also using them, leading to a uniform approach. The Moys scheme, currently the only one published specifically for law, provides notation to fit in with both Library of Congress (K) and DDC (340).

Schemes devised in-house have the advantage of flexibility and relevance, being designed for a particular collection, but they can also appear rather amateurish and inflexible, unreceptive to new legal concepts and subject areas, unless devised by someone with a great deal of experience.

Libraries which choose to use an alphabetical subject arrangement rather than a formal scheme will need to decide how broad or narrow the divisions should be and whether to subdivide them. For example, there could be a category of 'finance' with books on banking, investments and financial services filed alphabetically by author. Alternatively, there could be a category for books on finance in general, followed by separate sections for banking, investments and financial services. One of the problems with this is what to do when there is only one book on a subject; the temptation would be to create an unhelpful 'miscellaneous' section, which should be avoided if at all possible. For anyone needing to arrange a small collection from scratch, there are a number of places to find a list of topics, such as the subject headings used by *Halsbury's Laws*, or those used in the legal publishers' and bookshops' annual printed catalogues.

If a library's users are very familiar with their subject areas and the books available in them, the simplest and most user-friendly arrangement might be alphabetical by author, an approach favoured by the Inns of Court. This arrangement does not of course allow meaningful subject browsing, but if someone is looking for a particular title they can find it without needing to know the subject area it has been classed under or the classmark. There is the problem of books which have editors or several authors and those known more commonly by their titles, but a good catalogue ought to overcome this.

DEVELOPING THE COLLECTION AND MANAGING THE SPACE

LESLEY YOUNG

The manner in which a collection is developed and maintained will depend on the type of library and the requirements of the parent organization and its users; there may also be external standards which must be taken into account. The library must ensure that it meets current needs and is sufficiently flexible to anticipate and provide for future developments. It should fulfil these aims in the most efficient and economic way possible. It is a good idea to have a clear public statement of what the library collects and how it is made available in order to ensure consistency in practice and to make users, colleagues and other libraries aware of what the library can provide. This should be reviewed regularly to ensure that it continues to reflect the library's purpose.

Three main issues will be considered here: the purpose of the collection in particular the relative emphasis between building a permanent collection and providing a service that meets the immediate needs of the users; the budget, especially the competing requirements of monographs and subscriptions; and space, balancing the relative demands of print and electronic storage along with other needs.

COLLECTIONS AND SERVICES

Libraries are no longer simply defined by the size of their collections but by their ability to meet their users' needs as efficiently as possible from any source.

Some libraries may have a closely defined user base and maintain small, tightly focussed collections supplemented as required by inter-library loan or an external document supply service. Such collections are more likely to have an emphasis on online databases rather than printed volumes. Other libraries fulfil a wider, more custodial role and maintain large historic research collections alongside electronic resources which may supplement or duplicate the print material. Increasingly they are making their collections more widely available by digitizing older material and providing access to it through the online catalogue or the website.

In spite of the fact that law was one of the earliest disciplines to develop electronic databases in the early 1970s, most law libraries are still 'hybrid' with a mixture of print and electronic resources. Each library has to decide on the correct balance for its collection, taking into account the relative importance of ease of searching and the permanence of the collections.

Some types of legal research are better conducted electronically and the print titles are barely used. This is particularly evident with citators, journal indexes and general reference titles where currency and speed is important. Some electronic resources directly reproduce the print but with added benefits such as effective searching, greater currency (although not always), the ability to download and reuse, for example forms and precedents that can be customized. Others are designed to take full advantage of the format and display the content in a way that bears no relation to the way in which print resources are presented.

PRINT RESOURCES

The issue of permanence is closely related to format. In general, the most permanent formats are non-electronic, that is print or microform. Looseleaf is not a permanent format since pages are discarded during the updating process and the title will reflect the current situation. Successive hard bound editions do provide historic snapshots of the law current at that time. Print resources are still preferred by many users conducting in-depth research or where they need to obtain an overview of a subject with which they are unfamiliar. With a few exceptions, such as small teaching collections in academic libraries or particularly fragile material where a surrogate is available, any user once admitted to a library may use all of its print resources.

Microform

Microform, both 'film and 'fiche, is in general less popular with users because it can be difficult to use. It requires specialist equipment to access and the quality of the reproduction is often poor. It can be damaged if not stored correctly and can easily be misfiled and lost.

ELECTRONIC RESOURCES

The main issues with electronic formats in general is that, unlike print, the library is no longer sure that the content subscribed to will continue to be available nor is it fully in control of who can access it. The licence may be very restrictive, or it may prove prohibitively expensive for the library to negotiate a licence that permits access to all of its users, regardless of their status and physical location.

The earliest electronic resources were available on CD ROM and later DVD and both have now largely been overtaken by online. Although they offer the user some of the advantages of online with the added benefits of portability and usability where online connections are not available, licences often restrict use to a single work station and do not permit networking. There are still a few current titles that are only available in this format and publishers continue to issue them as accompaniments to books since they are a cheaper way of providing large amounts of additional material. There is a body of historic material not available in an alternative electronic format. However as work stations are upgraded to allow full use of sophisticated online resources, there are fewer machines capable of playing them and the content will be lost.

Online collections are for the most part rented rather than owned by the library. If the library stops subscribing, users will usually lose access to everything. If the subscription is restarted, they can access everything available on the database at that point. If the library cancels a print subscription it will still have the material it has already paid for. If the library restarts the subscription there will be a gap in the holdings which the library can only fill by paying separately for the missing volumes. The content is subject to withdrawal or change. The provider may not own the content and could lose the right to make some of it available. Increasingly content owners are choosing to withdraw their material from large aggregated databases in order to make it available on their own platforms. In these situations, the library will have to take out an additional subscription if users need to continue to have access to that material. It may be possible for the library to purchase electronic content outright and pay an access or platform fee to the provider. However, if it then stops paying it may no longer have access to the interface and the content will be virtually unusable without additional software which the library may not have the money or the expertise to provide. In the academic world there are various initiatives such as JSTOR, LOCKSS or Portico which aim to preserve electronic journals.

BUDGET

All collections budgets are under pressure. In many libraries general economic conditions have meant that budgets have been severely cut or at best not increased in line with inflation. Price inflation within law publishing consistently appears to be several percentage points higher than the general rate. Successive increases in VAT have resulted in instant price rises before general inflation is taken into account which is particularly serious for libraries with a large proportion of electronic resources. Law is increasingly international in scope and those libraries with significant foreign and international collections have been badly affected by currency fluctuations which make it difficult to control expenditure.

Sources of Supply

The decision on where to purchase is an important one as it will determine how effective the library is at making its budget stretch further. The library can choose between purchasing direct from the publisher/content owner, or from an intermediary such as a library supplier (for print monographs and e-books), subscription agent (for serials, book continuations and increasingly e-books), aggregator (for large collections of electronic resources) or bookshop. The library's parent organization may have supplier agreements in place which limit choice and many academic libraries are part of regional consortia which have negotiated favourable terms with suppliers. The library will need to decide which type of vendor will provide the most relevant service.

The bigger law publishers are set up to supply their own titles direct to libraries and their staff should be familiar with their publishing output and provide information on upcoming titles of interest. If the library purchases a large number of the publisher's titles, it may be possible to negotiate an agreement whereby in return for payment up front the library is protected from unexpected price increases over an agreed period. This helps with budget planning although the library will be restricted in its freedom to implement cancellations. Some are part of bigger transnational organizations and can supply titles from their sister companies overseas and invoice in sterling. They are not always as familiar with overseas titles as with their UK output but they can act as intermediaries.

Library suppliers and subscription agents have relationships with a wide variety of UK and foreign publishers and often have offices overseas. They can provide consolidated invoices in an agreed currency; offer discount for early payment of online subscription invoices; and provide consolidation and 'shelf ready' services which reduce the time spent by the library on processing and claiming material. In some cases libraries can configure their acquisitions systems and procedures to exchange bibliographic and payment information electronically and so reduce duplication in creating records.

Bookshops play a much smaller role in library supply than they once did but there are still law bookshops around which provide a specialist service and expertise and may be able to supply urgent items within hours.

Subscriptions

The largest proportion of the law library's collections budget will be spent on subscriptions and standing orders because of the serial and continuing nature of much law publishing. Legislation, law reports and journals are all obvious examples but many books are effectively subscription-based as well. Many of the 'classic' texts are published in frequent editions with supplements between editions. Updates for many looseleaf titles are received on standing order (and in addition take up a lot of staff time to file). The costs for these updates and editions are unpredictable since they vary greatly in frequency and size. Most databases are only available on subscription and even if they are purchased outright, the library may still have to pay an annual access fee to the publisher. Similarly individual e-books will normally require an access fee based on a set period or set number of uses so even some monographs are now effectively only available on subscription.

Strategies to Make the Budget Go Further

These ongoing commitments make it difficult for the library to ensure that there is a sufficient budget allocation for the purchase of monographs when needed. They also mean that the library cannot always alter course quickly as user needs change or budget cuts require savings to be made. Subscriptions tie the budget up for at least a year although standing orders can normally be cancelled relatively quickly. Contracts and licences for online resources often require several months' notice to cancel. Supplier agreements that commit the library for a fixed period reduce flexibility still further.

There are a number of strategies that a library can adopt to ensure that the collections budget continues to provide for users' needs and preferences although not all will be appropriate for every library:

- Compare large databases to identify overlapping content and try to remove duplicated material from one of the subscriptions;
- Subscribe to specific subsets of large databases or put together a tailor-made collection relevant to the users' interests;
- Check for overlap between print and electronic holdings; consider if it is necessary to subscribe to both formats;
- Monitor usage statistics and use the information to ensure that the library subscribes to electronic resources that are needed;
- Purchase paperback rather than hardback titles if use is not likely to be heavy;
- Identify an acceptable hardback alternative to a looseleaf title;
- Replace a looseleaf work every couple of years instead of buying the updates where currency is not a major issue for the users and the main work is cheaper than the updating service;

- Rely on free electronic resources where the content is likely to be available long term and is authoritative and authentic – increasingly, official websites of government departments and international organizations carry statements of authenticity and provide documents in pdf;
- Explore collaborative partnerships with other libraries. It may be possible to organize reciprocal access for readers; share electronic subscriptions; agree who should specialize in particular subjects or jurisdictions; agree who should purchase particular expensive print titles.

Other Calls on the Budget

Maintaining an electronic collection whether online or on CD requires expenditure on equipment, software, networks and technical expertise to maintain access. The infrastructure must be renewed every few years in order to ensure that the resources are still accessible as providers continually enhance their products with new features and migrate to more sophisticated platforms.

SPACE AND STORAGE

Competing demands on space within organizations mean that increasingly the library must justify the amount of room it occupies. Recent major refurbishments in all types of library have included the reorganization of existing space to meet the need for more office, teaching, private and group study and social space within the library in addition to the growing needs of the collections themselves.

Print, microform and electronic formats each have their own requirements that affect the way in which library space must be organized and there are a number of strategies that can be adopted. Reformatting collections is probably the most popular in many libraries. Some years ago this would have involved replacing print material with microform. This is still an option as the storage cabinets are very space efficient.

Electronic Collections

Electronic collections are ideal for libraries developing new collections within existing space or coping with a reduction in shelving. However, they have their own particular requirements such as power points in the right place, sufficient work stations to meet user demand, server rooms, printers, cabling and WiFi which can be difficult to set up in older buildings.

Print Collections

More commonly libraries are now replacing print with online not only to save library space but also to meet user demand for access to resources away from the library and at any time. The electronic availability of heavily used sets of law reports and journals makes it possible to reduce the number of print copies held. Converting looseleaf print subscriptions to online equivalents offers several benefits in addition to reducing the amount of space taken up by bulky binders.

Print collections are expensive to maintain in terms of space particularly in libraries which must provide historic collections in addition to current resources. The way in which shelving is configured and volumes are organized can help to maximize space usage although the library must balance this with ease of use.

A classification scheme can help users to find their way around a large collection more easily and allow for browsing, but classified collections take up more space than those organized more simply. If the law collection is part of a larger multidisciplinary library this decision may be made elsewhere. Arranging volumes by height, that is, in two sequences, is a more efficient use of space than keeping everything in a single sequence, but it can make it harder for users to find the volumes they require. Binding loose issues of serials will save on space and has the added benefit of making the paperbound parts more durable and less vulnerable to loss. However this does have additional budget implications for the library.

Mobile or compact shelving can double the amount of shelf space available compared with fixed shelves but it is not practical for high-use collections, requires reinforced flooring and once installed will mean less flexibility in the use of the space. It is, however, ideal for closed access storage which is often in a basement area.

Volumes stored in closed access can be shelved more densely but the library will need to decide what the balance between open and closed access should be taking into account users' needs. In general it is less satisfactory for users since it prevents them from browsing the collections and staff intervention is required each time a title is needed. Closed access volumes kept onsite, in the same building as the library, can be provided almost on demand but if the volumes are stored elsewhere it may take hours or even days to retrieve them for use. Environmental conditions in closed access areas can be more tightly controlled and therefore protect volumes from the damaging effects of dust, light and extremes in temperature and humidity. Suitable candidates might be:

- old, rare or fragile volumes
- superseded editions of monographs
- sets of older journals or law reports in a little researched subject
- titles held electronically
- superseded consolidations of legislation.

The ultimate way of dealing with pressure on space is to withdraw print material from the collections. As user needs change and access to electronic resources becomes more reliable, libraries may be able to identify suitable categories. In particular the number of copies of legislation, law reports or journals can be reduced as print use decreases. If libraries wish to be cautious they can put such material into closed access storage to see if the material is requested and then withdraw it after they are satisfied that it is not. It is unlikely that such material can be sold although there are second-hand law book dealers who can be consulted. Material can be offered on appropriate discussion lists or via the BIALL duplicates exchange scheme. Companies such as Anybook.biz will collect unsorted material for sale and return a percentage of the proceeds to the library. There are various charities such as Book Aid International or the International Law Book Facility which send selected books and serials to overseas libraries. Some academic libraries participate in the UKResearch Reserve which aims to ensure that there will be three print copies of serials (monographs may be included later) available in the UK allowing other libraries to withdraw their sets.

TAXONOMIES AND INDEXING

CHRISTINE MISKIN

TAXONOMIES

A well-constructed taxonomy allows maximum exploitation of an organization's knowledge assets. As a component of the information architecture of the digital information environment, the taxonomy will make that information both useable and accessible. It will allow interoperability, linking and exploitation of data held in disparate databases. For example in a law firm, a corporate taxonomy will enable access to the firm's marketing, know how, client relationship and document management systems, and allow linkage to the intranet and website. In the academic environment taxonomies are embedded in many of the legal and business databases including Westlaw, Lexis and PLC.

WHAT IS A TAXONOMY?

Taxonomy is the science and practice of classification and the term derives from the Ancient Greek *taxis* (arrangement) and *nomia* (method) and was originally used in scientific disciplines, but is now applied to widely disparate bodies of knowledge. A taxonomy in the information field is a form of controlled vocabulary. It normally consists of a set of terms which are related to each other in hierarchical, or parent-child, arrangements. They should be distinguished from ontologies, 'which are models for describing the world and consist of a set of types, properties, and relationship types' (see further, http://dictionary.reference.com/browse/ontology). The ontology has moved into law with the advent of the semantic web and AI research (Vyner 2010).

Folksonomies are a recent development of taxonomies and are created by both users and authors of electronic material. Keywords or tags are assigned to pieces of data in an uncontrolled way and they can be used by other searchers (for a definition see http://vanderwal.net/folksonomy.html). Thomas Van Der Wal is credited with originally naming and defining them. They began to emerge in 2004 and the process is also known as social tagging, social bookmarking and social indexing. Software to manage tagging has been written and sites such as Delicious (http://www.delicious.com) and Flickr (http://www.flickr.com) use them.

There is a close connection between taxonomies and thesauri. The latter are another type of controlled vocabulary, where terms are grouped together so that existing relationships between concepts are made explicit and they have been in existence for a long time. The original Legal Information Resources *Legal Thesaurus* is a good example. It was devised in the mid-1980s to index a large database of journals consistently (*Legal Journals Index*). Within the legal information world, the term 'thesaurus' has now generally been superseded by the term ' taxonomy', though the distinction between the two continues to be blurred: the latter became widely used in the late 1990s with the advent of the web and is normally understood to describe general methods of organizing information using forms of controlled vocabularies.

PUBLICLY AVAILABLE LEGAL TAXONOMIES

There are several published legal subject taxonomies available both here and in the United States, some can be licensed but most have to be paid for. The Taxonomy Warehouse website (http://www.taxonomywarehouse.com) provides useful listings which include detailed information about format, number of terms, fees and licensing information.

The *Legal Taxonomy from Sweet & Maxwell* (http://www.sweetandmaxwell.co.uk/ legal-solutions/legal_research.aspx) is an extremely complex product, based on facet analysis. It contains the keywords assigned by Sweet and Maxwell editors to many of their products, including *Legal Journals Index* and supersedes the original *Legal Thesaurus* (Duffield et al. 2010). It is available to subscribers as a desktop tool, the Taxonomy Viewer, which can be downloaded to view and use the taxonomy, which is regularly updated (Scott and Smith 2010).

PLC (Practical Law for Companies) maintains taxonomies to access both PLC content and their own legal content, which is available to subscribers to download for their internal use (http://www.practicallaw.com/0-382-2401).

The Integrated Public Sector Vocabulary (IPSV) (http://doc.esd.org.uk/IPSV/2.00.html) is a controlled vocabulary for use with subject metadata. Dextre Clarke (2007) provides an insight into the building of the vocabularies. The e-Government Metadata Standard (e-GMS) version 3.1 requires the use of at least one IPSV term for all UK public sector information resources that are to be shared with the public, businesses or other public sector bodies. IPSV is fully compliant with ISO 2788 and BS 8723 and an example of its use is given in Jordan and Lippell (2010). Responsibility for updating has passed from the Cabinet Office to The National Archives but is subject to budgetary restraint.

CORPORATE/ENTERPRISE TAXONOMIES

Several law firms now have corporate or firm-wide taxonomies, some of which are based on existing taxonomies such as the original *Legal Thesaurus* or the Tikit standard taxonomies mentioned above.

If the latter are used, the normal practice is to adapt the various segments of the taxonomies to the firm's data sets, using the standard as a framework to ensure all legal areas are covered. The main segment is a legal subjects list. The taxonomist will decide which areas apply to the firm's work and alter the taxonomy accordingly. For example, a firm specializing in banking law, but undertaking no family law, may need to supplement the standard list of banking terms but omit the family law section.

Other taxonomy segments which can be tailored for use include language, work type, practice area (often very specific to the firm), jurisdiction and industry/sector. The latter can be based on the Standard Industrial Classification with terms being added or deleted as necessary.

Other firms have invested huge resources into compiling their own taxonomies from scratch, with mixed results see Murty (2005). Self-built taxonomies have probably come of age within the largest organizations. The advent of the recession and the much harsher fiscal environment in which the profession finds itself means that such large-scale projects are becoming rarer. Organizations are beginning to implement enterprise search systems which will search across all databases and frequently contain both taxonomies and taxonomy building and management software. See the section on Automated Indexing below for more details.

TAXONOMY PLANNING

Building a taxonomy is an extremely difficult and intellectually challenging job and is not to be undertaken lightly. It is recommended that before embarking on such a project all existing taxonomies in the field should be considered for use to avoid reinventing the wheel. There should always be high-level management support for such a project, as it can easily be time-consuming and extremely costly and may not deliver the required solution. It will also need buy-in from all departments of an organization, not just the information department. Project planning should include focus groups to try to identify the terms to be included in the taxonomy. Such a project was described by Jacob and Barker (2010) and see further Lambe (2007).

TAXONOMY CONSTRUCTION

Who Should Build a Taxonomy?

It cannot be emphasized too much that information professionals are the ideal people to construct taxonomies, because of their training in the principles of information retrieval. In a law firm, professional support lawyers should be consulted for their in-depth knowledge of how the firm categorizes its precedents and other internal documents, but they should not be involved in the actual taxonomy construction

Building a Taxonomy

When constructing a taxonomy we are deriving a structured list of terms which are regularly used to describe the content of documents that are held within knowledge management and other database systems. It will be used for two purposes: for indexers to index the contents of documents accurately and for searchers to retrieve documents which are relevant to their current research or enquiry. To provide the maximum number of documents to match the searcher's enquiry directly, without huge numbers of false hits, there are certain principles to be used when constructing taxonomies. These are clearly explained in Aitchison, Gilchrist and Bawden (2000). Because law is such a clearly defined subject without the number of soft terms which exist in the social sciences, for example, it is reasonably easy to build up a list of terms. These can be based on existing lists and also incorporate terms peculiar to the organization. Facet analysis is recommended for the underlying framework of the taxonomy but rigid adherence to its techniques is not essential, as what started out as a small and simple project could result in an extremely unwieldy, difficult to display monster.

There are international standards in existence relating to thesaurus and taxonomy construction and they have been recently reviewed by Dextre Clarke (2010).

ISO 2788 and 5964 were replaced in 2011 by ISO 25964-1:2011 *Thesauri and Interoperability with Other Vocabularies*, which gives recommendations for the development and maintenance of thesauri intended for information retrieval applications. It provides a data model and recommended format for the import and export of thesaurus data and is applicable to monolingual and multilingual thesauri. It is not applicable to the preparation of back-of-the-book indexes. Principles within the Standard relate to the use of compound terms and how they should be divided (or factored). The Standard also explains the nature of relationships between terms which must be hierarchical, associative or equivalent (parent/child; related or synonyms). The taxonomy should also include scope notes giving guidance on the meaning and potential usage of terms where necessary. This helps the indexer enormously and will provide added consistency of term usage.

It is possible to attend courses on taxonomy construction run by ASLIB (http/www.aslib.com/training/index.htm and TFPL http://www.tfpl.com/training). These courses are run by experts and include practical exercises. Courses run by commercial organizations will almost certainly be more expensive.

SOFTWARE FOR TAXONOMY CREATION AND MANAGEMENT

Probably the most commonly used software for the initial planning and construction of a simple taxonomy is Microsoft Excel, as it is possible to represent easily several levels of hierarchy on a spreadsheet, which can be saved as a CSV (comma separated values) file. This will allow it to be exported to other software. More complicated taxonomies are not suited to such a method and once lots of non-preferred terms, scope notes and multiple hierarchies appear, proper taxonomy software should be used.

A specialist software package for legal and business taxonomies is supplied by Tikit as part of their Classification Manager software. Other packages in common use include MultiTes Pro (http://www.multites.com/index.htm).

More expensive products include Schemalogic (http://www.schemalogic.com) which offers a suite of taxonomy management programmes, including a metadata management tool which can be used with Microsoft Sharepoint 2007 (http://www.schemalogic.com).

Synaptica also offers enterprise search software: see post under enterprise search software (http://www.synaptica.com). SoutronTHESAURUS is offered by a UK company (http://www.soutron.com).

In the field of ontologies, Smartlogic, a UK-based company, produces both an ontology manager and classification and taxonomy tools in its Smartlogic

Semaphore package which is used by some law firms. Its products are international standard compliant (http://www.smartlogic.com/home).

Another tool which attempts to capture more than just hierarchies but will include other categories, attributes and so on, and which is closely related to ontology creation, is known as 'mind mapping' or 'concept mapping' software. Wordmap is a vendor in this field (http://www.wordmap.com).

Some of the latter packages are also closely associated with enterprise search systems mentioned in the Automated Indexing section.

Leonard Will produces a comprehensive list of such packages, with contact details and descriptive notes, on his website (www.willpowerinfo.co.uk).

TAXONOMY IMPLEMENTATION AND DISPLAY

The types of taxonomy display are many and varied. If the user is a searcher and not an indexer then a simple layout without added functionality is preferable. This should be discussed with the stakeholders within the organization before a decision is taken. If the user is an indexer or taxonomist using it to index content then a more sophisticated display and functionality can be made available to them. It is recommended that the number of top terms should be restricted to allow for full display. Most law firm taxonomies limit the number to about 30 to ensure they can be accessed easily. For a full discussion of the options see Hedden (2010).

USER TRAINING

The importance of user training cannot be over-emphasized as it is here that the functionality of the software can be fully explained and optimum searching strategies can be explored, to ensure users get full value from the organization's data resources.

MANAGING THE ONGOING PROCESS

A taxonomy is a dynamic tool and this is particularly true in the legal field where changes in the law produce new terms on a regular basis. An information department professional should be appointed as the taxonomy expert. He/she should have been sent on relevant courses and have an intimate knowledge of the firm's business and information systems and requirements. He should also possess excellent interpersonal skills, as what would normally be perceived as an entirely non-contentious area of a firm's work can easily become politicized.

Taxonomy by committee is never recommended. Bergman (2010) has written a case study of Clifford Chance's taxonomy management processes. The buy-in of senior managers and partners is essential to the process as is a sensible budget allocation.

INDEXING

Indexing is the art of applying terms to books and documents to describe their contents accurately and will frequently involve the use of taxonomies and other structured/controlled vocabularies. We are not concerned here with back-of-the-book indexing. Booth (2001) provides an excellent introduction to the subject.

MANUAL INDEXING

Manual indexing may include the use of keywording, tagging, subject heading assignment, authority files and metadata applications. Some of these terms are interchangeable. For example keywording may involve the use of a taxonomy, but may also use an uncontrolled vocabulary. Authority files are lists of, for example, organizations, names, countries and so on which ensure uniformity of term use. Metadata is often described as 'data about data' and can include additional information to keywords, such as author; title; date. There are standards relating to metadata use known as the Dublin Core (http://dublincore.org/).

Because of the great variety of legal materials, different indexing principles and techniques may need to be applied to indexing a statute, for example, than indexing a law report. Booth (2001) gives some guidelines in her section on Subject specialisms.

AUTOMATED INDEXING

This is a rapidly developing field and includes a number of techniques and software. It is obviously more practical than manual indexing for use where large volumes of data are involved, but it will not offer the same precision of recall as manual indexing, particularly in the legal field. It works well in areas of fast moving changes in content such as news and consumer-related databases. Software is becoming more sophisticated and much of it now utilizes taxonomies, including automated tagging and automated categorization systems. The latter involves material that already has some metadata assigned to it. Large internet search engines do not necessarily use taxonomies but rely on algorithms.

ENTERPRISE SEARCH SOFTWARE

Large, commercially available enterprise management software has been available since about 2000 and will manage multiple databases. The software includes automated tools and can be extremely costly. Many of the companies are US-based and the most well known include Data Harmony (http://www.dataharmony. com) and Synaptica (http://www.synaptica.com). Recommind Decisiv Search is used by Clifford Chance for searching across multiple global databases (see case study at http://www.recommind.com). Autonomy (http://www.autonomy.com) is used by a few firms and IDOL is an 'Autonomy Lite' package which is used in the iManage document management system, owned by Autonomy and is therefore much more widespread. Some firms also use FAST (www.searchtechnologies. com) and Solcara (http://www.solcara.com) is used particularly by smaller firms. For example, one large law firm uses FAST to search their know how system and Solcara to search across four information portals, both services running via their NavigatoR interface. This removes the need for fee earners to remember which database they should be searching and works very well.

SOURCES OF FURTHER HELP

Unsurprisingly, there are few organizations devoted specifically to taxonomy work. ISKO the International Society for Knowledge Organisation (http://www. isko.org/) has a UK branch which holds occasional seminars on taxonomy and indexing. The Society of Indexers is very active in the indexing field, running courses and conferences and publishing a journal, *The Indexer* (http://www. indexers.org.uk/). Some years ago it published a *Guide to Legal Indexing* by Betty Moys (1993). The Cataloguing and Indexing Group is a special interest group of CILIP (see Coburn (2010) for details).

An annual taxonomy bootcamp is held in Washington DC and has some extremely interesting sessions (http://www.taxonomybootcamp.com/2011/).

There are also specialist blogs devoted to information retrieval issues including taxonomies and indexing.

NOTES

1 For a more detailed discussion on cataloguing legal materials using AACR2 see Holborn, G. (2010), 'Cataloguing: AACR2 and all that', *Legal Information Management*, 10(1), 18–23.
2 For further information about the replacement of AACR2 by RDA see Chapman, A. (2010), 'The case of AACR2 versus RDA', *Legal Information Management*, 10(3), 210–213.
3 See Brett, R. (2008), 'Classification practice in law libraries: a brief survey', *Legal Information Management*, 8(1), 61–3.

CHAPTER 10

E-LEARNING AND VIRTUAL LEARNING ENVIRONMENTS

ANGELA DONALDSON

INTRODUCTION

Because of the nature of the subject matter of this chapter, the focus is on academic environments, rather than commercial legal information services, but many of the points discussed may be equally applicable in the commercial sector. Hemming (2008)[1] discusses a number of surveys conducted in law firms, which show that many law firms are actively investing in e-learning as a means of training their staff, so while the examples considered in this chapter are taken from higher education institutions, there is no reason why the principles could not be applied to the law firm sector.

WHAT IS E-LEARNING?

E-learning will mean many different things to different people, and there are many different definitions of the term. Given the rapidity of change within the sphere of educational technology, it is interesting to compare definitions from some years ago with more recent ones.

In 2002, Allan[2] defined e-learning as:

> *Elearning involves learning that is delivered, enabled or mediated by electronic technology, for the explicit purposes of training and/or education. It does not include stand-alone technology-based training such as the use of CD-ROMS in isolation.*

This definition could be read now as one which puts more emphasis on the technology concerned and less emphasis on the learning, and possibly at that time, that was the prevailing view. Many a lecturer in that period may well have felt that by making an electronic copy of his lecture slides available to his students he was adequately fulfilling his institution's e-learning requirements. Now the definition of e-learning is much broader, and another term, blended learning, which combines traditional and online teaching, has also become much more commonly used and embraced:

> *The term 'e-learning' can now sometimes be too narrowly defined to describe fully the widespread use of learning technology in institutions. We think it is more appropriate to consider how institutions can enhance learning, teaching and assessment using appropriate technology. HEFCE (2009)[3]*

> *E-learning can be defined as 'learning facilitated and supported through the use of information and communications technology'. It can cover a spectrum of activities from the use of technology to support learning as part of a 'blended' approach (a combination of traditional and e-learning approaches), to learning that is delivered entirely online. Whatever the technology, however, learning is the vital element. JISC (2011)[4]*

> *Blended learning is the thoughtful fusion of face-to-face and online learning experiences. The basic principle is that face-to-face oral communication and online written communication are optimally blended into a unique learning experience congruent with the context and intended educational purpose. Garrison and Vaughan (2008)[5]*

These later definitions identify the learning element as the most important part of the activity, with the delivery methods used being seen as secondary to the learning received.

WHY USE E-LEARNING?

Most universities will have either an e-learning policy or strategy, which academic staff will be expected to engage with. Such a policy may well include a set of minimum standards, which staff will be required to meet in regards to their e-learning provision, as well as the capacity for exceeding those standards. So although it could be argued that many academics and librarians have no choice in whether or not they engage in e-learning, there are other reasons cited for why institutions have adopted e-learning as a primary delivery method. The UCISA Survey (2012)[6] cites enhancing the quality of teaching and learning, and meeting student expectations as the two key drivers behind e-learning. The JISC Student Expectations Study (2007)[7] found that prospective university students wanted technology to:

- support established methods of teaching and admin;
- act as an additional resource for research and communication;

- be a core part of social engagement and facilitate face-to-face friendships at university.

Interestingly, the study also found that students suspected that if all learning is mediated through technology, this will diminish the value of the learning. So it would appear from the JISC Student Expectations Study that students would prefer a blended learning approach, with face-to-face contact backed up by appropriate online materials.

In preparing e-learning materials, the same pedagogical principles need to be applied as when preparing face-to-face teaching materials. The intended learning aims and outcomes must be the guiding factor and the technological elements should be selected to support, enhance and deliver those outcomes, rather than to show off one's technical ability and knowledge. Students will easily see through any such materials without a sound pedagogical core, as this quote from the JISC Student Expectations Study shows:

> *When discussing Second Life, students felt that games and virtual worlds as part of learning could easily become 'tragic' – technology being used for its own sake, and used rather childishly. They would need to understand the educational benefits of virtual worlds or games, it is not enough that they are simply 'new'.*

Learning Styles

Hartley (1998)[8] defines learning styles as the ways in which individuals characteristically approach different learning tasks. There is a wealth of literature available in the field of learning theories and styles, which it is not possible to do any more than skim the surface of here, so individual research is strongly recommended if you want to find out more about this subject.

Honey and Mumford (1982)[9] identified four different learner styles:

- activists – prefer to learn by doing, rather than reading or writing;
- reflectors – stand back and observe the big picture, analyse things before acting;
- theorists – like to adapt and integrate their observations into frameworks, take a logical step-by-step approach;
- pragmatists – enjoy problem-solving scenarios, where new ideas or theories can be put to the test.

Learners however rarely fit wholly within one category, as Pritchard[10] confirms:

> *The four basic types of learner, as characterised by preference for active, reflective, theoretical or practical learning, are clearly different one from the other, but most learners are not extreme examples of just one preference. Most people have characteristics of all four dimensions.*

The field of neuro-linguistic programming has identified three particular learning styles (Pritchard):

- Visual learners – prefer to learn by seeing. They have good visual recall and prefer information to be presented visually, in the form of diagrams, graphs, maps, posters and displays.
- Auditory learner – prefer to learn by listening. They have good auditory memory and benefit from discussion, lectures, interviewing, hearing stories and audio tapes.
- Kinaesthetic learners – prefer to learn by doing. They are good at recalling events and associate feelings or physical experiences with memory. They enjoy physical activity, field trips, manipulating objects and other practical, first-hand experience.

The Myers-Briggs Model uses psychological terms to describe learner styles, defining eight different types (Pritchard):

- *extroverts* – are happy to try things out and focus on the world of people;
- *introverts* – are more likely to think things through and to focus on the world of ideas;
- *sensors* – tend to be practical and detail-oriented, and focus on facts and procedures;
- *intuitors* – are imaginative, concept-oriented and focus on meaning;
- *thinkers* – are sceptical, and make decisions based on logic and rules;
- *feelers* – are appreciative and tend to make decisions based on personal and more humanistic considerations;
- *judgers* – set and follow agendas, and seek closure and completeness even without having the full picture;
- *perceivers* – adapt to changing circumstances and will defer completion until more is known.

It is also helpful to have a basic understanding of deep and surface learning, and the following table is adapted from one available on the HEA's Engineering Subject Centre's website:[11]

	Deep learning	**Surface learning**
Definition	Examining new facts and ideas critically, and tying them into existing cognitive structures and making numerous links between ideas.	Accepting new facts and ideas uncritically and attempting to store them as isolated, unconnected, items.
Characteristics	Looking for meaning. Focussing on the central argument or concepts needed to solve a problem. Interacting actively. Distinguishing between argument and evidence. Making connections between different modules. Relating new and previous knowledge. Linking course content to real life.	Relying on rote learning. Focussing on outwards signs and the formulae needed to solve a problem. Receiving information passively. Failing to distinguish principles from examples. Treating parts of modules and programmes as separate. Not recognizing new material as building on previous work. Seeing course content simply as material to be learnt for the exam.

Other approaches to learning include behaviourist and constructivist, which are described by Brown (2004)[12] as:

- Behaviourist: building connections between stimuli and responses, task analysis and reinforcement. Relevant to course design, instruction and assessment.
- Constructivist: learners build schemata that enable them to construct meaning and understanding. Implications for teaching are to help the students to develop more sophisticated concepts through the use of discussion and study tasks.

With so many different theories of learning and learning styles to be aware of, one could be forgiven for feeling overwhelmed at the prospect of creating e-learning materials. But some comfort can be taken from the results of a survey of the relationship between student learning style and VLE use, carried out at Kingston University (Heaton-Shrestha et al. 2007),[13] which produced two reassuring findings:

- In the 'blended' environment of VLE and on-campus learning provision, the wider range of options seemed to allow learners to tailor their studying to their preferred learning style.
- The VLE disadvantaged neither students with non-conventional styles nor those with more conventional styles, but could benefit a diversity of styles by providing a greater range of options for learning and studying.

The message coming through strongly from the literature is that by using a variety of tools and techniques in your learning materials, you will be more likely to appeal to a wider number of students.

Stakeholders in the e-Learning Process

E-learning will involve staff from a whole range of different university departments, all with a variety of different skills to contribute. Becoming involved in e-learning can be an opportunity not only to develop one's own IT and digital literacy skills, but also to cultivate important and valuable links with other staff elsewhere in the institution.

Learning Technologists and Educational Developers

In recent years, most universities will have seen the addition of learning technologists and/or educational developers to the support network available to teaching staff, sometimes based within the library and sometimes based in a more central academic support department. Their main role is to support staff in the development of technological enhancements to their teaching and their skills and knowledge can be invaluable. The Association for Educational and Communications Technology redefined its definition of educational technology as a profession in 2007 to read:

> *Educational technology (also called learning technology) is the study and ethical practice of facilitating learning and improving performance by creating, using and managing appropriate technological processes and resources. Januszewski and Molenda (2007)*[14]

The ALT (Association for Learning Technology) states its purpose as: to ensure that use of learning technology is effective and efficient, informed by research and practice and grounded in an understanding of the underlying technologies, their capabilities and the situations into which they are placed.

Learning technologists and educational developers will possess a different skill set to that of the academic librarian, and will have a wide knowledge of the various software tools and processes available to support e-learning. They can help you bring an idea to life, through selection of appropriate delivery tools, thus improving your own skills at the same time.

Find out more:
- Association for Learning Technology (www.alt.ac.uk) – the website contains publications, details of events and webinars, a quarterly newsletter and RSS feeds

Librarians and Information Professionals

Along with the more traditional activities that one associates with the role of a librarian or information professional, teaching and training is playing an increasingly larger part in that role. The fact that librarians act as teachers for a large proportion of their time is becoming more recognized and accepted, through the gaining of appropriate teaching qualifications (such as the PGCHE). The decision to gain these additional qualifications can be either an individual decision, or at the behest of one's employer, where that employer obviously values the teaching role of the librarian.

Legal information skills is the obvious area in which one might expect a legal information professional to be involved in e-learning, but beyond the subject specific there are opportunities to develop educational resources in other areas, such as more generic information literacy skills, referencing and plagiarism.

> *Find out more:*
> - SCONUL (Society of College, National and University Libraries) (www. sconul.ac.uk) – the website contains publications, details of events and statistics.
> - Librarians as Teachers Network (http://latnetwork.spruz.com/) – network supporting librarians in their teaching activity, with a blog, forums and details of events.

BARRIERS TO INVOLVEMENT WITH ELEARNING

Although it has already been stated that many higher education institutions will have a policy on e-learning, and will expect its staff to participate, it should also be acknowledged that there are a number of obstacles, both real and perceived, which will need to be overcome before e-learning is fully embraced by all.

Time

The first of these obstacles is time, both in terms of time needed to learn how to use new software and/or the virtual learning environment, and in terms of the time needed subsequently to create and maintain learning objects. There is no getting away from the fact that a certain amount of time is needed to learn the skills necessary to exploit the various e-learning tools. Many academics, while appreciative of the advantages of interactive learning objects, cite the reduced hours allocated to them as the main reason why they are still only at the basic level of uploading Word or Powerpoint documents to the virtual learning environment and nothing more. If an institution wants to be seen as in the vanguard of e-learning, then it will have to recognize the time issue and allocate appropriate hours to its staff. O'Neill, Singh and O'Donoghue (2004)[15] recognize this fact:

The implications of e-learning for lecturers are significant and should not be overloaded by institutions implementing such programmes. Lecturers must be provided with sufficient time and resources to ensure that online courses are suitably developed and implemented to meet the needs of students.

Once the basic skills have been acquired, then the time involved in planning and creating an actual learning resource can vary in just the same way as creating a face-to-face learning activity. Learning repositories (see elsewhere in this chapter) could be investigated as a way of saving development time, as it may be someone else, either at the same or another institution, has created an open educational resource which can be either used as it is, or adapted to reflect local changes, with minimal time and effort required. Academic law librarians who may not be working under the same 'allotted hours' scheme as lecturing colleagues, may also be able to assist their teaching colleagues in the creation of learning resources.

Cost

The second obstacle is the perception that e-learning is expensive if it is to be done well. As with most things, it is possible to spend vast amounts of money on e-learning, but more money spent does not necessarily equate to a better product at the end of the process. For example, an institution could spend tens of thousands of pounds (if not more) equipping a state of the art recording studio to produce top quality videos, when very creditable and watchable results can be produced using handheld DVD recorders and basic editing software. MP3 voice recorders can be purchased for under £30, giving a simple way to record voiceovers onto a slide presentation, or a straightforward audio file, either as a podcast or as audio feedback. Similarly, webcams are available very cheaply, offering the option to produce video files quickly and easily.

If your institution employs learning technologists or educational developers, then they would be useful people to consult before purchasing (or requesting purchase of) any equipment. In the absence of such specialists, IT and computing services staff may be able to advise or you could look at the ALT website (www.alt.ac.uk) or seek advice from other professionals via one of the many e-learning technology-related e-mail lists available, through organizations such as JISCMAIL (www.jiscmail. ac.uk) or MAILTALK (www.mailtalk.ac.uk).

Training and Support

Training in the appropriate selection and use of e-learning tools is another area which needs to be addressed and embraced by institutions serious about their e-learning goals. Copeland[16] identified this issue back in 2001:

Effective distance learning will not happen unless students and staff receive proper training in the use of technology. At the moment, computer-mediated

*learning is confined largely to enthusiasts for new media. If online provision
is to become a key element in universities of the future, employers will need to
provide a major programme of staff development and training.*

More than 10 years have elapsed since Copeland's quote above, but the statement
is still as relevant today – technology enthusiasts still lead the way in developing
and promoting e-learning within institutions, and employers still need to provide
major staff development and training programmes to enable the less enthusiastic
to catch up.

Technical support needs to be available for e-learning activities so that staff
aren't put off and can work through any problems to a successful conclusion.
How this support is provided will differ from institution to institution. One
obvious way to provide support for e-learning is by using e-learning methods
themselves. Many virtual learning environments will have staff development
areas within them, with modules or programmes aimed at assisting academic and
other staff to get the most out of e-learning tools. Not only are these an excellent
way to deliver support at the point of need, but they can also be used to showcase
a variety of different e-learning tools.

Access to Equipment

The issue of access to equipment, both in terms of hardware and software, can
often be the deal breaker when it comes to engaging with e-learning. In short,
in order to be able to create learning objects and fully exploit the range of
technologies available, you need a PC of a sufficiently high specification to run
the various software packages, and you need licences for the software packages
themselves. These two apparently simple requirements can be major stumbling
blocks within a university setting, for a number of reasons.

In the current financial situation, it is not uncommon for student PCs to
be prioritized in the upgrading schedule, and for the old student PCs to be
redeployed as staff machines. This can mean that staff rarely have the latest,
top of the range PCs, with the capacity to cope with a range of software
applications. Having a PC of a high enough spec is crucial if people are to
be engaged in e-learning, as there is nothing more likely to put someone
off than waiting an age for the computer to process their activity or,
worse, the computer constantly crashing. If an institution is serious about
its e-learning policy, then it will need to recognize that investment may
be required in staff hardware and software in order to reach its goal. For
students wishing to purchase their own personal laptop or other device, an
institution cannot dictate which equipment they should purchase, but merely
recommend an ideal spec to be considered which should minimize potential
frustration arising through technological problems such as malfunctioning

hardware, software configuration, slow or down servers or busy signals (Volery and Lord 2000).[17]

Licences for software packages can also be problematic. Again, given the size and scale of the average university, there are often policies in place regarding which software packages are licensed for general use by staff. Requests for licences for new software products may need to be submitted to a central IT department for purchase consideration, which may or may not be granted. So it may be that an institution has a licence for one particular screen-capture tool (possibly deemed the product most likely to suit the requirements of the greatest number of staff), and will not support licences (individual or otherwise) for a different screen-capture tool, even though there may be strong evidence to support the use of the second product in particular circumstances. This is not to say that there is no point asking for the tools required, but a request supported by a strong business case outlining the advantages of the new package as opposed to the existing software may have more chance of success.

Many software packages offer basic versions of their product for free, which can be a useful way to test something out, before deciding on whether to request the professional/commercial version. However, this is not always as straightforward as it sounds as university staff PCs are often so tightly locked down that users are unable to download any software at all without administration rights or the intervention of IT staff. Again, while such requests would usually be quickly accommodated, it still adds another obstacle, and can deter people from experimenting with different tools.

STRIVING FOR PERFECTION

While not a specific barrier to e-learning as such, the quest for perfection, particularly when recordings are involved (video, audio or screen capture) can significantly increase the time it takes to produce something. It is not unnatural to want the material you produce to be of a high quality, and there can be a tendency, especially when first experimenting with recording tools, to delete and start again if you get a word wrong, or are interrupted by a telephone ringing in the background. However, depending on the purpose for which you are creating the recording, absolute perfection is not always required. Obviously, if you intend to create a series of exemplary videos to be used as a showcase for your institution, then it makes sense to avoid extraneous sounds and mispronunciations. If on the other hand, you are creating a short database tutorial, designed to highlight how to perform a particular search, it may not be so crucial. Anecdotal evidence from a colleague at Nottingham Trent University backs this up. He decided to pilot individual audio feedback to his students for one assessed coursework, recorded via his webcam. Initially, whenever he stumbled over his words, or got interrupted, he would stop recording and start again from the beginning. He soon stopped this though, as it was taking too long, and instead just carried on talking regardless of slip-ups or interruptions. The response from the students was that they didn't care that the video quality wasn't great, or that a phone was ringing in the background; they just appreciated the individualized feedback, which they felt to be more personal, more helpful and more speedily available than traditional written feedback. Lunt and Curran (2010)[18] have written about a similar audio feedback pilot, which produced similar responses in their student cohort. Although not all academic law librarians will be involved in providing formal feedback on student feedback, for those that are, audio feedback might be worth exploring.

Compatibility – Proliferation of Browsers

As the number of different internet browsers increases, this can have an impact on how an online learning object is viewed by different users. The original object may have been created in Internet Explorer, but will it display in exactly the same way to a Firefox user, a Google Chrome user or a Safari user? Again, given the fact that the librarian's access to different browsers may be limited, for reasons discussed earlier, it may not always be possible to test the object in different browser environments. Some institutions have 'lab' environments specifically to test resources on a variety of interfaces and if you are lucky enough to have access to such a facility, then you should definitely take advantage of it.

Increasingly though, the browser is no longer the only variable. Students want to access information on their iPads or smartphones, so should institutions be looking at developing apps which can impart valuable information in an appealing way? In deciding whether or not to go down this route, there are a number of variables to take into account. Firstly, you need to consider which (and how many) platforms you are prepared to support. The iPhone, although probably most associated in the general public's mind with apps, could be out of the price range of many students, so is it cost-effective to spend time and money developing iPhone apps, which may only be accessed by a small minority of your users? Android apps for other commercial smartphones may be a better investment, as they may encompass a wider potential audience. Secondly, you need to consider the potential lifespan of the app, in relation to future advancements in mobile phone technology. Any app created could be redundant relatively quickly, unless you're prepared to update it when required. It is unlikely that most academic or library staff will have the technological or computer-programming skills required to create an app of any kind, so going down this route will require liaison with learning technologists, educational developers and IT staff.

Cornell University Library have developed an iPhone/iPod app for their library website, in support of their aim to make the library visible and useable outside standard library places, tools and services (Connolly, Cosgrave and Krkoska

2011).[19] In September 2010, Nottingham Trent University developed its first student smartphone app to support Welcome Week, its programme of events in Freshers' Week, but its originator questions the suitability of the app route to support wider e-learning, seeing the app as being more beneficial as a way of disseminating general 'housekeeping' information to students, such as library opening hours or pc availability (Foster 2011).[20]

All of the above barriers to involvement with e-learning could be said to have a common element running through them, which is described by Gray, Ryan and Coulon (2004):[21]

> *For e-learning to be successful, organisations often have to transform their attitude to e-learning and the way they adapt to it. Hence, the innovative element becomes not so much the technology, as cultural change within the organisation itself.*

E-learning permeates the very culture of an institution and may require a radical rethink of how that institution is organized and supported, to achieve staff and student engagement in the e-learning process.

Learning Repositories and OERs

Learning repositories are now a common way to locate learning objects which can be incorporated into one's online teaching. The term 'learning objects' comprises a variety of material types; examples could include a word document or pdf, a PowerPoint slideshow, a quiz, a video or an audio file. Wiley (2000)[22] defines a learning object as 'any digital resource that can be reused to support learning' – the reusability (or repurposing) aspect will be discussed later in this section.

Many universities will have their own internal learning repository, most likely closely linked with their VLE, into which staff will be encouraged to upload their own learning objects to share with colleagues. Objects held within the learning repository can then be extracted or linked from within the VLE. In many cases, the link to the original object can be made 'dynamically', which means that should the original object be updated or changed at a later date, the links from within the VLE will always point to the most recent version of that object.

The benefits of this approach should be plain for all to see. Where a subject is taught in different departments of the university, for example, sharing content via the internal learning repository makes a lot of sense. Law is an excellent example of a subject which spans many more schools or departments than just the Law School, as law modules often feature within business courses, forensic science courses and journalism courses to name but a few. In some instances, such modules may not be taught by academics from within the Law School, so the facility to include learning objects and materials created and updated by the acknowledged experts in the field can only enhance the student experience. Even within the Law School, the same subject may be taught by different teaching teams on different modes (for example, the same module will be delivered on the full-time programme and the distance learning programme by different staff). Using the same learning objects on each programme can make the teaching burden easier and also ensures consistent delivery between programmes.

Law librarians can use internal learning repositories to disseminate their own teaching materials to academics in a non-threatening way. The learning repository negates the need for the librarian to be given author rights to an academic's own learning spaces within the VLE, which has been a stumbling block previously encountered by librarians (Black 2008).[23] Instead, librarians can upload their training materials to the learning repository, and have them incorporated into the learning spaces associated with different modules, with minimal effort required on the part of the academic.

Librarians can also fulfil a vital role in relation to learning repositories, by developing a metadata schema for use when creating learning objects. Descriptors can be appended to learning objects, to aid searching within the learning repository, but without a structured classification scheme many valuable learning objects may languish unused in the learning repository, because no-one else has been able to find them. It doesn't have to mean implementing specialized schemes such as Dewey or Library of Congress, but a list of agreed headings to describe subject area, content type and originator will help to fully exploit the repository content, and will also reinforce the role of the librarian as the organizer of knowledge.

As well as internal learning repositories, there are also a number of external learning repositories on both national and international levels, which can be useful sources of material for reuse, as well as tools for benchmarking exercises, to see what other types of learning objects are being used at other places. Learning objects stored within external learning repositories are also known as open educational resources (OERs), indicating the 'open' manner in which they can be used by others. Atkins (2007)[24] defines OERs as 'teaching, learning, and research resources that reside in the public domain or have been released under an intellectual property licence that permits their free use or re-purposing by others'.

Most OERs will be licensed using a Creative Commons (CC) licence, which will indicate what you are entitled to do under the terms of the licence. There are six Creative Commons licences available, which vary from the most restrictive (where you are not permitted to do anything other than use the material as it is, with appropriate acknowledgements), to the least restrictive (where you are permitted to repurpose the material to your own requirements and may publish the repurposed object for commercial gain). Given that educational learning repositories exist to promote and share learning objects, most OERs are licensed under a CC BY-NC-SA (Creative Commons Attribution – Non-commercial – Share Alike) licence, to permit the repurposing of materials. If repurposing is permitted under the terms of the licence, then you may amend parts of the content to suit your own requirements.

Many institutions will have their own policy and guidance regarding ownership of copyright in educational resources, and the type of CC licence which may be applied. It is advisable to check for any such policies before uploading your OERs to an external repository.

As well as using external repositories to download useful OERs, law librarians can also upload their own resources, to be shared with the wider academic community. While many librarians are happy to upload resources to their own internal repositories, they are more reticent about making their material visible to the world at large. This may be because they feel their material relates too directly to their own institution, and won't be of interest to others – an unnecessary concern given the repurposing nature of OERs. Or it could simply be because it never occurred to them that their material might be of interest to others, in which case they are most decidedly wrong. Most law librarians sitting down to create or update their teaching materials long to see what others have done, and how they've approached a particular subject, so being able to do this via a learning repository is a definite benefit. On another level, there is the marketing aspect to be considered – by disseminating your materials to others you are promoting yourself, your library service and your institution, and you could gain valuable kudos for all three if your materials are acknowledged and used by others.

Jorum

Jorum is JISC's national learning and teaching repository service, focusing on open educational content available under Creative Commons licences. Teaching and support staff in UK Further and Higher Education Institutions can deposit their learning and teaching resources in Jorum and Jorum defines its target audience as teachers, lecturers, librarians, learning technologists and other support staff who wish to share and/or access learning and teaching resources. Jorum provides immediate statistics on the number of times a resource has been viewed and, on request, the number of times a resource has been downloaded – both of which could be useful from a marketing perspective.

Merlot

Merlot stands for Multimedia Educational Resources for Learning and Teaching Online, and is a free and open online community of resources designed primarily for faculty, staff and students of higher education from around the world to share their learning materials and pedagogy. Material is peer reviewed before being added to Merlot, but it does have a strong US bias in terms of content.

Using Google and Flickr to Locate OERs

Google's advanced search allows you to search for reusable learning objects according to their Creative Commons licence. Select the 'Advanced Search' option, then select the 'Date, usage rights, region and more' option to see the different licence restrictions available. If you are looking for images, you can apply the same licence restrictions within Google Image's advanced search options, or you could perform a similar 'Creative Commons Licence' search within the Flickr photo sharing website (http://www.flickr.com).

Lawbore and Learnmore

Academic law librarians will be familiar with the excellent Lawbore and Learnmore sites created by Emily Allbon at City University. Although not (currently) licensed under Creative Commons or accessible through Jorum, the sites can be linked to by other institutions. Some of the content is understandably tailored to City University students, but there are many useful sections which will apply to all students regardless of their place of study, including the mooting videos and the careers information.

Find out more:
- JORUM (www.jorum.ac.uk) – a JISC-funded Service in Development in UK Further and Higher Education, to collect and share learning and teaching materials, allowing their reuse and repurposing.
- MERLOT Multimedia Educational Resources for Learning and Teaching Online (www.merlot.org) – US based repository, but which also includes UK materials.
- OpenSpires (http://openspires.oucs.ox.ac.uk/) – collection of podcasts from the University of Oxford.
- Creative Commons (creativecommons.org) – an internationally recognized licensing system under which creators of a work offer some of their rights to others to reuse their work under certain specified conditions.
- Lawbore (http://lawbore.net/).
- Learnmore (http://learnmore.lawbore.net/).

As well as learning repositories, universities are also investigating other ways of disseminating their information and content online, in an environment likely to appeal to students. One such environment is iTunesU. iTunes is familiar to most students and many will already have an iTunes account for downloading music and video content. iTunesU (the U stands for university) gives educational institutions an area within iTunes where they can upload their own content. A large number of universities from across the world have a presence on iTunesU, with the majority of those being from the USA. British universities to have signed up and provide law content include Oxford, Cambridge, Plymouth, Coventry, Hertfordshire, Nottingham University and the Open University. Participation in iTunesU requires an institutional subscription, but the external hosting means less space required on internal servers, plus the opportunity to market your institution to the world. Although an iPhone (or other Apple device) is not essential to using iTunes as a media storage area, there is a strong correlation in the public mind between the two, so it may prove a challenge to engage non-Apple users with iTunesU content.

Another such environment is YouTubeEDU (http://www.youtube.com/education), which is a subsection of YouTube aimed at educational content. Again, an institutional subscription is required in order to upload content, and YouTube EDU accepts larger files than the standard YouTube, making it possible to broadcast lectures of over an hour long. Content is stored off-site by YouTube's servers, and requires a basic media player to view material.

Resource Discovery Software

Resource discovery tools and products have been in fairly common use in academic libraries for some years now, although their use is less common in the commercial sector for a variety of reasons. A resource discovery tool can allow 'cross-searching' or 'meta-searching' of a number of different databases at once, presenting the user with a single, combined list of results.

First Generation Discovery Tools

The first generation of resource discovery tools carried out federated searching, where the user's search is run across the selected databases in real time, and the results returned accordingly. Google could be said to be responsible for the development of federated search tools, as academic libraries recognized that their users were comfortable with using Google's simple search box, but became confused by the vast number of different databases and interfaces available to them through their institution. Federated search tools were seen as a potential way of engaging the 'Google generation' and encouraging greater use of subscription databases. Problems associated with the federated search approach include the limits on the number of different databases which can be searched together at once, accessing databases which don't permit federated searching and the speed at which results are returned in a federated search. In general, the speed at which the result set is returned is dependent on the slowest-responding resource. Where some resources are known to be particularly slow, a cut-off time can be pre-set, which means that the discovery tool will return all those results which it has been able to find, within the search time available to it. While this gets over the problem of user frustration at having to wait for ages for results to be returned, it introduces another problem, namely the fact that the results retrieved may be neither complete, nor necessarily the most appropriate, but simply the first results to be gathered. Users are given the option to fetch more results, which necessitates a second search being run against the selected databases, but just as they rarely progress beyond the first page of results of a Google search, so they rarely request additional search results in a federated search environment.

Accessing databases which don't allow federated searching has been a particular issue for academic law librarians, as the major UK law databases (Westlaw UK and LexisLibrary) do not fully interact with federated search tools. This has meant that law searches have had to be carried out in the relevant database's native interface, and the user cannot search Westlaw UK and/or LexisLibrary together or in conjunction with other resources. There are arguments both in favour of and against the promotion of federated search technologies, and the 'federated searching vs native interface' debate tends to polarize academic librarians accordingly.

The pro-federated search argument
Those in favour of federated searching technologies argue that students are familiar with the simple Google-style search box and expect to find everything in one place; they want to spend as little time searching as possible, and would be put off engaging in research if it meant interrogating a number of different databases individually and collating the results themselves. It is also argued that a federated search environment can significantly increase the use of databases (Hambling and Stubbings 2003),[25] but this does not necessarily mean that students are finding relevant resources on all of the databases that they have selected to search. On the contrary, it could mean that students are selecting the maximum number of databases which can be searched together at once, regardless of whether those databases are the most appropriate for their particular requirements. What is not clear from such studies is the selection process on the part of the user, and whether they are guided first and foremost by the appropriateness of the database itself, or by the fact of its metasearching capability.

The pro-native interface search argument
Those who favour the native interface search environment for a database argue that a federated search doesn't offer the advanced search functionality that can be accessed through the native interface. In a federated search, the user is more likely to use simple search terms, without specifying particular fields in which to search. Although relatively little time is spent constructing the search, the user may spend more time filtering the results to find the most relevant. A database's native interface offers more sophisticated search options, which may mean more time in the search construction stage, but considerably less time at the results stage, as the selection of appropriate keywords, use of Boolean operators and search fields delivers fewer, but more relevant, results.

Given the complexities of the leading legal databases in terms of structure, content and organization, it would require a significant contribution of time and effort on the part of the database providers to fully integrate their resources within federated search environments. And given the fact that the federated search environments used in the academic sector are rarely replicated in the commercial sector, is there any point in the database providers making that effort? If part of a university's role is to produce students with the necessary skills to succeed in the commercial world, then surely an academic law librarian should be teaching law students how to use the resources they are most likely to be relying on in the workplace.

Second Generation Discovery Tools

There are now a number of second generation discovery products (termed web-scale discovery tools) on the market, including:

- Primo Central, produced by Ex Libris
- Discovery Service, produced by EBSCO
- Summon, produced by Serials Solutions.

The distinguishing factor of web-scale discovery tools is that they pre-harvest content into one single index, allowing users to search across a greater amount of content more quickly and without the merging, deduplicating and ranking issues that are experienced with a federated search (Way 2010).[26] Although a distinct improvement on first generation tools, these technologies are still reliant on engagement from the database suppliers to ensure compatibility. The main law databases are still currently accessed separately from the web-scale tools, and the same arguments will no doubt rage on as to whether or not law content should be incorporated.

VIRTUAL LEARNING ENVIRONMENTS (VLES)

Virtual learning environments have become the norm in universities, and those institutions which don't have a VLE are now very much the exception to the rule. Use of VLEs in schools and sixth-form colleges has also increased in recent years, so university students are in general much more comfortable with the concept of a VLE and very often able to navigate their way around them with the minimum of training.

Many commercial VLE products are available, which can provide certain advantages – most of the development work has already been done, meaning only customization work and training is required before going live; and, for the more widely used packages, there will already be a community of users who can be called on for advice and support. Depending on the level of IT expertise and support, provided within an institution, a commercial product, and the technical back-up that comes as part of the contract, can be a more appealing option, in terms of staff time and costs. The disadvantages of a commercial product can include the limitations affecting what may/may not be customized and the lengthy and complicated process of suggesting enhancements and development for future updates. Often where a 'community of users' is involved, the community must be consulted and the majority voice prevails – great, if your proposed enhancement is welcomed by the majority, but less so if your suggestion is not seen to be of wider value.

Open source VLEs will give an institution the option to tailor-make a VLE to their own specific needs and requirements, providing that they are prepared to commit the staff time to developing the software initially, and to supporting it on an ongoing basis. The flexibility of an open source VLE means that changes can be enacted much more swiftly, with the possible result of greater interaction with the product by staff and students.

In reality, the purchase of a new VLE system would necessitate a tendering process, and involvement from a variety of departments; IT, library, academic representation, central data services (to ensure that the chosen system will integrate with existing data systems in order to populate registers, assessment lists and so on), disability support, purchasing and finance. Student input at the trial stage would also be incredibly useful, all the more so if it were possible to include the views of mature students, distance learning and part-time students, disabled students and international students.

The 2012 UCISA Survey on Technology Enhanced Learning (Walker, Voce and Ahmed 2012) found that Moodle (an open source VLE) was in use in 58 per cent of respondents' institutions, with Blackboard Learn in use by 38 per cent and Blackboard WebCT in use by 16 per cent. Although Moodle is the single product used most widely, Blackboard have the largest market share as they provide three products (Blackboard Learn, Blackboard WebCT and Blackboard Classic) which have a combined market share of 60 per cnet. Eighteen per cent of institutions surveyed were using a VLE or intranet-based product which had been developed in-house, and 6 per cent used Sharepoint. Other commercial products, used by between 1 per cent and 4 per cent of respondents included Sakai, FirstClass and Desire2Learn.

The principal components of a VLE, which are present in most products, whether commercial or home-grown, have been identified as:[27]

- Mapping of the curriculum into elements that can be assessed and recorded;
- Tracking of student activity and achievement against these elements;

- Support for online learning, including access to learning resource, assessment and guidance;
- Online tutor support;
- Peer group support;
- General communications, through a variety of media;
- Links to other systems, both in-house and externally.

The key elements are also identified by O'Leary[28] as:

- Delivery of learning resources and materials;
- Self-assessment and summative assessment, such as multiple choice questions with automated marking and immediate feedback;
- Management and tracking of students; for example, passwords to ensure only a specific group can access the course, analysis of assessments, monitoring of each student's use of the VLE;
- Navigation structure; most VLEs assume a linear sequence of materials;
- Communication between tutors and students, such as e-mail, discussion boards and virtual chat facilities;
- Shared work group areas;
- Support for students; for example, Frequently Asked Questions (FAQs);
- Student tools; for example dropboxes for handing in coursework, individual student web pages;
- Consistent and customizable look and feel.

A number of these key elements deserve more detailed consideration:

Self-assessment and summative assessment – summative assessments are easy to create using VLE assessment tools. Most support a variety of question types, including multiple choice (where only one answer is correct), multi-select (where a number of correct answers need to be identified), fill in the blanks and order ranking. Assessments can be randomized, so students will each get a different set of questions, and even the order of the possible answers can be randomized. These assessments work best when constructive feedback is provided for wrong answers. Self-assessments generally provide instant feedback, one question at a time, but an overall score is not usually recorded. These work well as a quick test of one's understanding after working through a topic. Summative assessments are more formal, and statistics are kept on scores and attempts. If desired, it is usually possible to set a time limit within which to complete the assessment, and also to limit the number of attempts each student may make.

Dropboxes for handing in coursework – dropboxes allow students to submit their assignments electronically, and allow tutors to manage submissions, give feedback and grade the assignments. In many cases it is possible to link a VLE's dropbox facility to Turnitin (www.submit.ac.uk), the UK's plagiarism detection tool, meaning submitted assignments can be automatically checked against the Turnitin content database.

Navigation structure – most VLEs assume a linear sequence of materials, but this is generally because VLE units relate to specific modules or subjects, and the structure replicates the order of lectures and tutorials. Content can be arranged in any order the content owner desires, and it is often possible to set release conditions on content items, which the student must comply with before being able to see the new content. So, for example, a bonus audio file giving more detailed information on a particularly difficult topic may only be viewed when a student has achieved a particular score on an assessment.

Copyright and VLE Content

The relative ease with which academics can create content within a VLE can lead, knowingly or unknowingly, to copyright infringement. In just a few clicks, an academic can download an article from a database and upload it to their learning space, or add a link to a paper, bypassing the copyright clearance procedures in place within their institution and potentially violating licence terms. Librarians can play an important role in ensuring academic staff are aware of the copyright licences held and what they need to do to comply with them. This could simply mean reminding staff that they must submit digitization requests for articles or chapters, so that the appropriate statistics are recorded for copyright reporting requirements, or advising staff not to deep-link within a website, as this means copyright statements on the home page can be missed.

VLE and Student Use

For more and more students, the VLE is their first port of call for academic information relating to their course, and they will be logging into it regularly, and at all hours of the day. This has huge implications for academic librarians, as it means that any information held outside the VLE (on the institutional or departmental website) is less likely to be accessed. There is a growing view that university websites, rather than being a source of information for current students, are becoming primarily marketing tools, aimed at attracting and providing information to prospective students. Although Maringe (2000)[29] found that students seem to be less influenced by press reviews and institutional website information in their choice of university, the radically different marketplace of 2013 means that marketing has taken on even greater prominence as an activity. Whatever the purpose of an institution's website, the need for academic librarians to 'be where the students are' (Daly 2010)[30] is becoming more and more crucial if our services are to be used. Law librarians need to have a presence in the VLE, to ensure students have access to the support they require, and to confirm our status as the experts in legal research.

CONCLUSION

Elearning and VLEs offer law librarians an excellent opportunity to develop their technical skills, capitalize on their unique knowledge and expertise, provide support to colleagues and promote their/the library's services to a wide audience, all of which should lead to an enhanced reputation. Let's grasp it with both hands, and show some of our academic colleagues how it can be done.

CASE STUDY

Using the VLE to deliver legal information skills at Nottingham Trent University:

Background

Prior to 2008, legal information skills had been delivered at NTU through a combination of lecture and workshops, but a significant increase in undergraduate student numbers in 2008/09 meant that this approach was unsustainable, and a new delivery method was needed. At this time, NTU was also introducing a new VLE, so it was decided to use this to create a legal information skills 'learning room' which would be the primary means of disseminating legal skills training to undergraduates.

The VLE Package

NTU's previous VLE had been an internally produced one, primarily managed and developed by academic staff. Library staff had minimal viewing rights only and were not encouraged to create content. The replacement VLE was a commercial product, supplied by Desire2Learn. The new VLE (known locally as NOW) was to be managed by the Educational Development Unit within the library. Liaison librarians were encouraged to get involved with it from the outset and were given as much training, if not more, than the academic staff.

Support for the Legal Information Skills Learning Room

Senior staff in the Law School saw the Legal Information Skills Learning Room as a way to raise the profile of legal skills among the undergraduates and GDL students, by giving it a programme-wide status, rather than by attaching it to one specific module. A principal lecturer acted as sponsor for the project, presenting the proposal at the various school committees and executive board meetings, where it was formally approved and accepted by the Law School.

Content

The content is divided into two main sections:

- Essential online training and compulsory self-assessment
- Additional online training

Within each of the two main sections, the content is further sub-divided:

ESSENTIAL ONLINE TRAINING:

○ Case law basics

- Case law and law reports
- Case citations
- Neutral citations
- Legal abbreviations
- Square brackets and round brackets
- Law reports hierarchy
- Court structure

○ Legislation basics

- Primary and secondary legislation
- Parliamentary bills
- Citing primary legislation
- Citing secondary legislation
- Historical versions of Acts
- Updated versions of Acts
- Regnal years

ADDITIONAL ONLINE TRAINING:

○ Case law advanced

- Old cases (pre-1865)
- Recent cases
- Unreported cases
- Checking the history of a case
- Direct history
- Indirect history
- Applied, distinguished, considered and so on

O Legal journals

O Halsbury's Laws

O Hansard

The content is supported by audio PowerPoint slideshows and a number of database tutorials, including ones created by the database providers themselves, and others created by the Liaison Librarian for Law. Different software packages were used to create the local tutorials, including Adobe Captivate (the commercial version, for which NTU has a licence) and the free versions of Jing and Go View. In addition, some of these tutorials have also subsequently been uploaded to YouTube.

A section of FAQs provides support for housekeeping matters, such as username and password queries, or problems with printing. The learning room also includes a glossary of legal terms and a live link to the Liaison Librarian for Law's Delicious bookmarks, suggesting further sources of information on a number of legal topics.

The Delivery of Information Skills

Full time 1st year undergraduates still attend a lecture, delivered by the Liaison Librarian for Law, which introduces the Legal Information Skills Learning Room and also includes demonstrations of the legal databases. This lecture is followed up with a small number of hands-on workshops, which must be booked in advance, although the take up rate for these sessions is very low. After the lecture and workshops have taken place, students will be directed to the learning room for any legal skills queries.

The Assessment

Law School staff were keen to ensure that students would engage with the room, and so a self-assessment exercise was included, which is compulsory for 1st year undergraduates. It was agreed that there would be no minimum pass mark and no limits to the number of attempts a student could make. In order to highlight the importance that the Law School placed on the skills being delivered via this room, the following convention was added to the Law School's assessment's policy:

> *Failure to complete the Self-Assessment exercise will be viewed as a failure to engage with the Programme as a whole, and will count against you at Exam Boards.*

The assessment consists of 20 questions, randomly selected from the central question bank, and includes multiple choice questions, fill in the blanks and matching order questions. Some of the answers can be gleaned from simply reading the content, but others require the student to look up an Act or case, in order to find the answer.

Feedback

The Learning Room went live at the beginning of the academic year 2009/10, so has now been in use for four full academic years. Feedback from students and from academic staff has been positive. Students have particularly commented on the value of the tutorials, and so these have been increased to cover more topics.

The numbers of 1st year students completing the self-assessment exercise have been significantly higher each year than the numbers previously attending the 'compulsory' workshops. In the year 2012/13, 87 per cent of 1st years completed the assessment, achieving an average score of 83 per cent. 1st year module leaders and 1st year personal tutors have all reminded students about the legal skills learning room, so this could explain the high completion rate.

The learning room was commended during the LLB programme revalidation process and held up as an excellent example of blended learning provision within the Law School.

Positive feedback has also been received from library colleagues and fewer basic legal enquiries are now referred to the Liaison Librarian for Law, as a result of colleagues being able to access the room and answer student queries from it.

Further Developments

At the start of the academic year 2011/12, the learning room was made visible to all students within the Law School, not just undergraduates and GDL students. Although some of the content may be considered too basic for LPC and BPTC students, it was thought that they could benefit from some of the advanced tutorials.

The Liaison Librarian for Law has subsequently created a similar learning room focussing on international law, to support the LLB International Law programme, which was launched in the academic year 2012/13.

NOTES

1   Hemming, A. (2008), 'E-learning, in a world with too much information', *Legal Information Management*, 8(1), 43–46.

2   Allan, B. (2002), *E-learning and Teaching in Library and Information Services*, London: Facet.

3   HEFCE (2009), Enhancing learning and teaching through the use of technology: a revised approach to HEFCE's strategy for e-learning. Available at: http://www.hefce. ac.uk/pubs/hefce/2009/09_12/ [Accessed 19 June 2013].

4   JISC (Joint Information Systems Committee), e-Learning. Available at: http://www. jisc.ac.uk/whatwedo/themes/elearning [Accessed 19 June 2013].

5   Garrison, D. and Vaughan, N. (2008), *Blended Learning in Higher Education: Framework, Principles and Guidelines*. San Francisco: Jossey-Bass.

6   Walker, R., Voce, J. and Ahmed, J. (2012), Survey of technology enhanced learning for higher education in the UK. Available at: http://www.ucisa.ac.uk/~/media/groups/ssg/ surveys/TEL_survey_2012_with%20Apps_final [Accessed 17 June 2013].

7   JISC (Joint Information Systems Committee) (2007), Student Expectations Study. Available at: http://www.jisc.ac.uk/media/documents/publications/studentexpectations. pdf [Accessed 19 June 2013].

8   Hartley, J. (1998), *Learning and Studying: A Research Perspective*. London: Routledge, p. 149.

9   Honey, P. and Mumford, A. (1986), *Manual of Learning Styles*, 2nd edn. London: P. Honey.

10   Pritchard, A. (2009), *Ways of Learning: Learning Theories and Learning Styles in the Classroom*, 2nd edn. New York: Routledge.

11   Higher Education Academy (n.d.), Deep and Surface Approaches to Learning [Online]. Available at: http://www.heacademy.ac.uk/resources/detail/subjects/engineering/Deep- and-Surface-Approaches-to-Learning [Accessed 21 June 2013].

12   Brown, G. (2004), *Effective Teaching in Higher Education*. London: Routledge Falmer. Supplement. Available at: http://www.routledgeeducation.com/resources/pdf/how_to_ learn.pdf [Accessed 19 June 2013].

13   Heaton-Shrestha, C., et al. (2007), 'Learning and e-learning in HE: the relationship between student learning and VLE use', *Research Papers in Education*, 22(4), 443– 464.

14   Januszewski, A. and Molenda, M. (eds) (2007), *Educational Technology: A Definition with Commentary*. New York: Lawrence Erlbaum Associates.

15   O'Neill, K., Singh, G. and O'Donoghue, J. (2004), 'Implementing eLearning programmes for higher education: a review of the literature', *Journal of Information Technology Education*, 3, 313–323.

16   Copeland, R. (2001), 'The usual rules apply online', *Times Higher Education Supplement*, May 18 2001.

17   Volery, T. and Lord, D. (2000), 'Critical success factors in online education', *International Journal of Educational Management*, 14(5), 213–223.

18   Lunt, T. and Curran, J. (2010), 'Are you listening please? The advantages of electronic audio feedback compared to written feedback', *Assessment & Evaluation in Higher Education*, 35(7), 759–769.

19   Connolly, M., Cosgrave, T. and Krkoska, B. (2011), 'Mobilizing the Library's Web Presence and Services: A Student-Library Collaboration to Create the Library's Mobile Site and iPhone Application', *The Reference Librarian*, 52(1–2), 27–35.

20   Foster, E. (2011), 'App-y Days! The pedagogic benefits and limitations of smartphone apps'. Available at: http://www.ntu.ac.uk/cadq/quality/events/ALTC/altc2011/109477. pdf#page=44 [Accessed 19 June 2013].

21   Gray, D., Ryan, M. and Coulon, R. (2004), 'The training of teachers and trainers: innovative practices, skills and competencies in the use of e-learning', *European Journal of Open, Distance and Elearning*, 2004 (2). Available at: http://www.eurodl. org/materials/contrib/2004/Gray_Ryan_Coulon.pdf [Accessed 20 June 2013].

22   Wiley, D.A. ed. (2000), The Instructional Use of Learning Objects. Available at: http:// reusability.org/read/chapters/wiley.doc [Accessed 20 June 2013].

23   Black, E.L. (2008), 'Toolkit approach to integrating library resources into the learning management system', *Journal of Academic Librarianship*, 34(6), 496–501.

24   Atkins, D.E., et al. (2007), A Review of the Open Educational Resources (OER) Movement: Achievements, Challenges, and New Opportunities [Online]. Menlo Park, CA: The William and Flora Hewlett Foundation. Available at: http://www.hewlett.org/ uploads/files/Hewlett_OER_report.pdf [Accessed 20 June 2013].

25   Hambling, Y. and Stubbings, R. (2003), The Implementation of MetaLib and SFX at Loughborough University Library: A Case Study. Available at: http://info.lut.ac.uk/ departments/ls/lisu/downloads/Metalibcasestudy.pdf [Accessed 20 June 2013].

26   Way, D. (2010), 'The impact of web-scale discovery on the use of a library collection', *Serials Review*, 36(4), 214–220.

27   Weller, M. (2007), *Virtual Learning Environments: Using, Choosing and Developing your VLE*. London: Routledge.

28   O'Leary, R. (n.d.), Virtual Learning Environments. Available at: http://www.alt.ac.uk/ sites/default/files/assets_editor_uploads/documents/eln002.pdf [Accessed 20 June 2013].

29   Maringe, F. (2006), 'University and course choice: implications for positioning, recruitment and marketing', *International Journal of Educational Management*, 20(6), 466–479.

30   Daly, E. (2010), 'Embedding library resources into learning management systems: a way to reach Duke undergrads at their points of need', *College & Research Libraries News*, 71(4), 208–212. Available at: http://crln.acrl.org/content/71/4/208.full.pdf+html [Accessed 20 June 2013].

CHAPTER 11

PLANNING A TRAINING SESSION

EMILY ALLBON

For those law librarians within academia, teaching or giving training in legal research skills forms a substantial part of our role; indeed it's probably one of the elements that we enjoy most. Within a commercial environment this may also be a key focus, especially at trainee changeover times. This chapter however will focus on training for law students, rather than trainee lawyers, but I hope to include ideas for all information professionals regardless of their place of work.

Teaching, in any discipline, is a pursuit that should be reviewed, adapted and tinkered with fairly regularly; but often when the subject matter doesn't change, it can be difficult to motivate yourself to look again at what you do each year. This chapter offers some practical ideas around planning a session as well as a little of the theory.

CHALLENGES

For many, just securing the opportunity to teach can be more challenging than the planning itself. We often have many restrictions on how and when our teaching must take place. In academia we strive towards being embedded within courses; teaching alongside lecturers, putting on hands-on workshops and being involved in assessments – not just being called up for a solitary en masse lecture in the induction period. In a law firm context you might have to spend time teaching an online source when you know a hard copy one would be more effective.

And what about our participants? They often want to be elsewhere because they believe they know perfectly well how to find material on the internet. At undergraduate level they are still in the 'just Google it' zone, at the Legal Practice Course (LPC)/Bar Professional Training Course (BPTC) stage they have a little expertise in legal sources and think they can work the rest out themselves and in practice … well they often don't have time for any refreshers, regardless of how much the sources have changed.

The first challenge is easier to tackle once you've made inroads into the second, when you can prove that your learners have gained skills as a result of the session (and maybe enjoyed themselves in the process). So what are the top trio of considerations when starting planning?

Learners | Learning objectives | Practicalities

WHO IS YOUR AUDIENCE?

This is really one of the key drivers of your planning process. Some teach every session the same, regardless of who it is aimed at, or the content involved. We should adapt our session style to match the audience. As an academic librarian, I would use a different teaching style for PhD students than I would for first year undergraduates, even if the content was inherently the same. That's not to say that the undergraduate session would be 'dumbed-down' but you would find different ways of both getting and (more importantly) maintaining their interest.

A quotation around education that I particularly like comes from London-born Sydney J. Harris. Harris grew up in Chicago and established a very successful career as a journalist, and his thoughts on the purpose of education are as follows: '*Turn mirrors into windows*'.[1] Any training session that you plan should be flexible enough to allow you the option to learn from those you are teaching and change it as you go along.

You need to find out as much as you can about the audience in advance, although this is not always possible. In an academic context you might consider what they are currently studying, as well as what coursework they may have on the horizon. Teaching them new skills that intertwine with work they already have on their 'to do' list is a great way to ensure they are interested in learning what you have to say, and equally to establish yourself as the person who can help. Similarly if you were doing a session for academic staff it would seem good sense to have an understanding of their research area as well as what sources they have used already.

Linking to very current events or using humour is a really good way to get your participants involved. Let's be honest, learning legal research skills is never going to be something that evokes air punches and whooping. Is it enough for you to give a professional session but one that isn't tailored in any way for the audience? Humour can be tricky too; not everyone will think a wacky scenario is very engaging. Thinking students are all the same will ensure you fall flat. Try to avoid the potential perils associated with getting 'down with the kids'.

LEARNING STYLES

Decades of educational research have established that each of us learns in a different way and whatever session we teach we're never going to please everyone. Different people experience the same teaching in different ways. There is also a lot of emerging research that has found the needs of younger people are changing and the stimulations that are all around us mean that their expectations of learning have altered. They expect to be entertained and their desire for a largely transmissive 'stand at the front and teach' style is on the wane. Marshall McLuhan's famous quote has never been more apt: 'Anyone who tries to make a distinction between education and entertainment doesn't know the first thing about either'.[2]

We all have our preference as to how we learn most effectively, and there are many different educational theories around learning styles as you've heard from Angela Donaldson in the previous chapter. Here is my take on a few:

Honey and Mumford are responsible for the learning style that you are most likely to have come across. There are lots of self-tests floating around the internet and despite being conceived in 1982 it is still heavily used. Their test focuses you into one of four classifications:

- Activist
- Reflector
- Theorist
- Pragmatist.

Honey and Mumford acknowledge though, that any preferred learning style is likely to be made up of two or more of these categories. Some people like to jump straight into a task and try things out without doing the prior reading, brain-storming madly and always thinking about what's next (activist), whereas others like to do all the research first, listen and observe cautiously rather than jumping in with conclusions (reflector). Theorists thrive on organizing, analysing and synthesizing – not happy until they can come up with a logical objective theory. Pragmatists are problem-solvers, flourishing when given practical tasks to test theories or techniques and easily frustrated by vague and open-ended discussion. Me? I'm a Reflector with weird Activist tendencies.

Kolb (1984) highlighted four learning styles as a result of his work around experiential learning: Converger, Diverger, Assimilator and Accommodator. Here's a summary (Fry, Ketteridge and Marshall, 2009)[3] of the strengths of these styles:

Learning style	Strength
Convergent	Practical application of ideas
Divergent	Imaginative ability and generation of ideas
Assimilation	Creating theoretical models and making sense of disparate observations
Accommodative	Carrying out plans and tasks that involve new experiences

More recent examples include Fleming's VARK model (2001), which asks with which sense does a person learn best? Learners may rely more heavily upon the visual, auditory or kinaesthetic/tactile. Quite simply we either like to learn by seeing – for example snazzy PowerPoint slides (visual), by listening – for example lectures, podcasts (auditory) or by doing activities like hands-on tasks, projects or experiments (kinaesthetic).

So where does all this leave us? Well just because it's impossible to plan a session that appeals to all possible learning styles, it doesn't mean we shouldn't try to weave different approaches into our sessions wherever appropriate.

You might consider some of the following ideas to appeal to those with different learning styles.

TOOLS

To give greater visual stimulus you might consider your PowerPoint slides: do they grab your attention? Are they overly wordy? Are they dominated by bullet points? Are they a direct copy of what you're actually saying? Remember slides should act as a prompt for you and a stimulant for the participants; the detailed information should come via your spoken words and any support materials you might provide (workbooks, VLE content).

Take the time to perfect these; ensuring that they are the ideal accompaniment to your words. Your slides should be full of impact but not dominate your part in the session. For good ideas on how slides can look use Slideshare[4] to get inspiration! Find your images on flickr.com by doing an advanced search for Creative Commons licensed material.

You might want to consider an alternative. If PowerPoint bores you Prezi[5] is a more recent yet very popular tool, which allows users to break out from the rigid linearity imposed by PowerPoint. It's a zooming presentation tool that allows you to compose your thoughts in any way you like, enabling you to draw your audience's eye to exactly where you want them. It's not the ideal tool for showing lots of screenshots or bulky text however.

Using images and video in any training is popular: especially as props to hammer a point home. There are lots of useful videos on YouTube[6] to illustrate concepts like information literacy, which we discuss below, or plagiarism. The ICLR[7] have some useful videos about case citation and research on their own YouTube Channel. Or maybe you might like to create your own resource? At City, I do sometimes use the videos or talking slideshows I've created for Learnmore[8] within my teaching.

You might want to consider creating an interactive book to support your sessions; Apple released the iBooks Author (free on app store), which allows you to put together a custom-made book with text and embedded content – you can add in your own videos and images.

What About Ways to Encourage Active Learning –
How Do You Get Participants to Interact?

This is certainly one of the toughest things to do in a session; some people simply just want to sit and listen – they don't actually want to do anything. I've certainly been guilty myself of this from time to time. Our biggest fear in a session is that line of blank, disinterested faces set in zombie-like expressions. How can we ensure that our attendees are interested and motivated? A session where participants are working together to feed back to the group as a whole can often hit home far more effectively than you churning out information at the front. Be careful though not to get too fixated on this; don't push collaborative activities for the sake of it. Active learning must only be included in order to aid the learning process. Here are a few ideas particularly useful for large groups:

Cephalonian method – first crystallized in Cardiff by Nigel Morgan,[9] this basically revolves around simple cards which you give the audience in order to get them to interact. The colour-coded cards display questions predetermined by the speaker, but the session seems on the surface to be driven by the participants. Excellent for breaking the ice and getting shy ones to get involved but can involve quite a lot of time to organize. Find more information on the method via the Cardiff University website: http://www.cardiff.ac.uk/insrv/ educationandtraining/infolit/cephalonianmethod/index.html.

Clickers – like in 'Who Wants to be a Millionaire', you can create questions within your PowerPoint presentation, which the audience can then answer using small handset clickers. This is really useful for icebreaking; getting them onside early on with a few silly questions to put them at ease. Excellent for checking knowledge too, allowing you to adapt your session midway if there are areas the audience still find a challenge. It is possible to use mobile phones in a similar way (Sellahewa 2012);[10] Poll Everywhere is gaining in popularity although you would need to pay to poll larger groups.

In smaller groups you can try all manner of 5–10 minute exercises using props. Here are a few examples:

- *Understanding the structure of a law report* – print one out and get them to label it up in pairs.

- *Understanding legal sources* – put a variety of sources onto individual cards and do the same with their descriptions. Ask the group to match them up.

- *Website authority* – give a website to each group and ask them to discuss if they trust its contents or not (and report back). Phil Bradley has some useful fake websites to use: http://www.philb.com/fakesites2.htm.

- *Keyword selection* – give a series of questions (examples below) out to small groups for them to think about what keywords they might select in a search, or give them a random object (for example fizzy pop can) to think about all the different words you would use as descriptors. Statsky's cartwheel method might be a useful tool to use to get groups talking about word associations and identifying potential search terms (McKie 1993).[11]

Example questions:

- *Do the courts have a wide range of offences open to them when tackling gang crime?*

- *Do the defences of insanity, provocation and diminished responsibility need reform?*

'Flipping the classroom' is a form of blended learning that many are finding useful in terms of increasing engagement in their teaching. The 'flipping' refers to the fact that the traditional teaching model is turned back-to-front; with the students being set work to do *before* the lecture, in order that they may use the time with their lecturer for hands-on activities, working through practical exercises in collaboration with their classmates and asking lots of questions of the lecturer. This pre-lecture work may include reading, watching a video or listening to a podcast and will mean that they arrive at the face-to-face element of their course fully equipped and raring to go – the responsibility for learning lies with them. Essentially the lecturer takes a step back and lets the students get on with the practical work set, only intervening when the students need help to work through a problem.

FRAMEWORKS

Everyone could do with a bit of inspiration when it comes to planning your training and there are several routes I have found useful for giving structure: information literacy models and learning outcomes.

INFORMATION LITERACY

Those readers within the academic sector may be far more familiar with the term than perhaps those within the commercial sphere, as its origins come from education. Information Literacy (IL) is a term created within the library and information field but there is still some work to be done in raising awareness in the wider sphere. Its principles have been reaching further afield notably in the Welsh Information Literacy Project, which seeks to promote the understanding and development of IL in education, the workplace and the wider community in Wales. The work done by this group has led to the publication of the Information Literacy Framework for Wales.

Library organizations across the world have written their own definitions along common lines, with the well-used CILIP (2004) definition as follows:

> *Information literacy is knowing when and why you need information, where to find it, and how to evaluate, use and communicate it in an ethical manner.* *(Armstrong, 2005)*[12]

The concept was embraced in the UK in 1999 with a SCONUL Working Group on Information Literacy publication 'Information skills in higher education: a SCONUL position paper'.[13] This included the well-known Seven Pillars of Information Skills model, which underwent substantial revision in 2011.[14]

The key aspiration of information literacy is to equip students (or other participants) with the skills they need to deal with information (selection, evaluation, application) in their studies and, crucially, in their working life. This is particularly pivotal in the training of our young lawyers, at a time when there is so much debate around legal education and training, as well as the sector itself.

Until recently the UK legal information community had no set of IL standards dealing with law specifically, and most librarians relied upon the SCONUL framework. BIALL's sister organization in the US, AALL, developed its own set of law-specific standards in 2011: the *Legal Research Competencies and Standards for Law Student Information Literacy*. The latest version of these standards was approved by the AALL Executive Board in July 2012.[15] Twenty twelve also heralded the creation of a BIALL Working Group on the creation of a UK specific set of standards, and the *BIALL Legal Information Literacy Statement*[16] was published in August 2012.

HOW CAN IL HELP ME IN PLANNING?

Having an agreed set of standards can give authenticity to your endeavours; the BIALL IL Statement is based upon learning outcomes from the SRA, BSB and ILEX. Tying your sessions into the standards will demonstrate value loud and clear, particularly as the Legal Education and Training Review (LETR) (2013)[17] endorsed use of the standards.

Using IL standards also gives you a useful starting point for what you are trying to achieve in your teaching. It serves as an excellent framework to ensure you are focussing the session around what they need to know, rather than just throwing everything you know at them.

SCONUL SEVEN PILLARS

See oposite for the Seven Pillars diagram; anyone familiar with the earlier model will see that the 2011 version is less linear: taking a circular form. The pillars represent core skills and competencies (ability) and attitudes and behaviours (understanding) with individuals mapping themselves at different levels, from novice to expert. When viewed from the side these pillars show as columns and illustrate that it is not assumed that an individual will always be on the upwards climb: with the information world changing rapidly and the shifting focus within anyone's learning life it is to be expected that sometimes we get left behind.

What Do the Pillars Actually Mean?

Identify – able to identify a personal need for information

Scope – can assess current knowledge and identify gaps

Figure 11.1   Information literacy model (2011)

Plan – can construct strategies for locating information and data

Gather – can locate and access the information and data they need

Evaluate – can review the research process and compare and evaluate information and data

Manage – can organize information professionally and ethically

Present – can apply the knowledge gained: presenting the results of their research, synthesizing new and old information and data to create new knowledge and disseminating it in a variety of ways.

BIALL LEGAL INFORMATION LITERACY STATEMENT ('IL STATEMENT')

Split into five research skills, the IL Statement offers a selection of learning outcomes for each of the five along with a breakdown of the knowledge, understanding and skills required, and some examples of how competency in these could be demonstrated.

Below I take a look at each of the five stages and offer ideas of how they might be incorporated into a session.

Research skill 1 – Demonstrate an understanding of the need for the thorough investigation of all relevant factual and legal issues involved in a research task:

1.1   Determine the scope and objectives of the research [Set a problem question, in groups get half the cohort to work out a suggested research strategy and the other half to do the potential research timeline]

1.2   Identify the legal context and pinpoint the legal issues [Give the whole group a legal problem, have a discussion in tutorial groups about the questions it raises and split into groups of 3–4 to research using a secondary source (journals, practitioner texts, legal encyclopedias, monographs and so on), before reporting findings back]

1.3   Determine whether non-law information is also required [Set a topic for discussion around something socio-legal, for example impact of stop and search procedure? Students would get to use government papers, statistics, criminology journals and newspapers].

Research skill 2 – The learner will demonstrate the ability to undertake systematic and comprehensive legal research.

2.1   Demonstrate the ability to create a research strategy appropriate to researching the problem at hand [In groups start with a problem – pull apart to key facts, select correct legal terminology from a selection of cards – extend to research strategy if time]

2.2   Determine which legal resources are most appropriate for the problem at hand. Reference to both print and online sources as necessary [Exercise involving selection of legal problems with students choosing which would be first point of call from a list of potential resources. Discuss as a group reasons why chosen (content, speed/ease of use/cost)]

2.3   Formulate lists of search terms [Short series of questions, individuals practice using different connectors in database, record the method to find answer and discuss in group levels of success, debating why]

2.4   Identify and find relevant case law [Worksheet: to practice using information within hard copy law reports. List of legal citations – students to find the case name reading abbreviations, find correct information within the text of case. In addition choose most authoritative citation from various groupings of four]

2.5 Identify and find relevant legislation [Answer a series of questions using the databases, exploring the status of both primary and secondary legislation].

Research skill 3 – The learner will demonstrate the ability to analyse initial findings effectively.

3.1 Demonstrate the ability to compare new knowledge with prior knowledge [Groups to look at a question with associated selection of student research findings. Groups to decide which is the most complete trail and fill in any gaps]

3.2 Demonstrate the ability to reflect upon initial strategies and findings and revise the use of information sources as necessary [Best done over a series of sessions; students attempting a piece of research into legal problem very early on, then drip-feeding more information about sources over future sessions, allowing students to make further attempts and refine their strategy as they gain expertise in different sources]

3.3 Demonstrate the ability to choose the right method of searching online and critically evaluate the information found [Take a look as a group at different strategies adopted by students in response to a question. Group to comment on the authority, currency and relevance of findings and sources used].

Research skill 4 – The learner will demonstrate the ability to present the results of research in an appropriate and effective manner.

4.1 Organize, structure and compile a written response for the problem researched and present the results of the investigation to the intended audience [Use the final attempt of 3.2 to gather findings into report with concise and accurate summary of relevant materials]

4.2 Provide clear advice, conclusions and identify courses of further action [As above but with addition of recommendations for further research]

4.3 Demonstrate awareness of ethics and legality of information use [Exercise with clickers (or pub quiz style), around scenarios of ethical use of information – both for study purposes and in the legal environment].

Research skill 5 – Continuing Professional Development – refreshing the legal research skills required of a modern lawyer.

5.1 Refresh and update legal research knowledge as part of career development [Set up a few RSS feeds from databases, blogs, publisher websites, find some influential legal people to follow on Twitter, key websites and write a short blog post with recommendations to help other law students]

SETTING LEARNING OUTCOMES

In order to evaluate sessions successfully, we need to have some objective standards to benchmark against. What are the most important things we want the participants in our session to achieve? In the past, we have used somewhat interchangeably the terms 'aims and objectives' and 'learning outcomes' to describe these short pithy statements around what you expect the participant to get out of your session. However the big distinction is really focussing around what the *learner achieves* rather than being so heavily weighted on what we, as teachers or trainers, intend. Here are a few definitions:

> *An (intended) learning outcome is an objective of the module or programme being studied. An objective is a succinct statement of intent. It signifies either a desired outcome to be achieved and/or a process that should be undertaken or experienced. Objectives can thus focus on outcomes/processes or a blend of each. An outcome usually comprises a verb and a context. (Stefani, 2009)[18]*

> *Learning outcomes are an explicit description of what a learner should know, understand and be able to do as a result of learning. (Bingham, 1999)[19]*

> *A learning outcome is a written statement of what the successful student/ learner is expected to be able to do at the end of the module/course, unit or qualification. (Adam, 2004)[20]*

Bloom's *Taxonomy of Educational Objectives* (1979) is the starting point for many when sketching out their objectives/outcomes – as it breaks down the levels of intellectual behaviour inherent from learning, into six classifications, arranged hierarchically:

Figure 11.2 Original Bloom's taxonomy

Source: Adapted from Benjamin S. Bloom, *The Taxonomy of Educational Objectives: Handbook 1* (1965)

The hierarchy demonstrates that learners need to build on each of the earlier levels in order to be capable of moving on to the higher levels, and thus onto the more brain-taxing synthesis and evaluation. The taxonomy relies heavily on the concept of learning as a process.

The taxonomy has been revised several times and many others have provided associated verbs that should be used in penning any learning outcome in each of the six classifications.

I've listed Bloom's taxonomy below; along with the categories from the revised version (in brackets) and some ideas about activities you could set your participants to help them achieve their learning outcomes. The verbs I've used come from the excellent *Writing and Using Learning Outcomes: A Practical Guide* (Kennedy, Hyland & Ryan),[21] and you'll find a more extensive listing in that publication.

Knowledge (Remembering): essentially this concerns retrieval – useful verbs include *arrange, collect, define, describe, identify, find, label, order, recall, tabulate*.

Examples of law learning outcomes would be:

- *Order* hierarchically a list of law reports;
- *Label* a case noting date of hearing, headnote, cases cited, name of counsel, judgment, formal order and so on;
- *Identify* the differences between Lexis and Westlaw when searching for international materials;
- *Collect* some useful links around legal aid reforms and organize within a social bookmarking service like diigo or delicious.

Comprehension (Understanding): this one is to benchmark understanding and interpretation of information given in the session. Useful verbs here include *classify, differentiate, discuss, paraphrase, explain, illustrate, review, solve*.

Examples of learning outcomes would be:

- *Explain* how to best reduce a large list of hits in Westlaw down to a smaller, more relevant one;
- *Paraphrase* text from a textbook and reference correctly;
- *Review* a collection of journal abstracts to identify the most useful ones;
- *Differentiate* between a blog and a wiki.

Application (Applying): this centres on putting material learned into practice – problem-solving with new knowledge. Verbs to utilize include *apply, assess, complete, construct, demonstrate, develop, employ, illustrate, modify, organize, predict, prepare, transfer*.

- *Develop* search strategies for your first piece of coursework;
- *Modify* existing Harvard citations into ones which follow the OSCOLA method of citation;
- *Construct* a checklist for using Halsbury's Statutes in hard copy;
- *Prepare* a blogpost on the importance of using authoritative sources within law.

Analysis (Analysing): this category focuses on the more complex business of breaking down information into component parts. Verbs of use here are *analyse (obviously)*, *arrange*, *calculate*, categorize, *classify*, *connect*, *contrast*, *debate*, *distinguish*, *divide*, *illustrate*, *outline*, *question*, *test*.

- *Analyse* the provision of legislation within available services;
- *Debate* the merits of Lexis over Westlaw and vice versa;
- *Calculate* the quantum of a broken collarbone;
- *Compare* the search functionality of Europa and Westlaw for finding EU case law.

Synthesis (Creating): this is the putting the pieces together, in contrast to the breaking down seen above in analysis: *argue*, *arrange*, *combine*, *compose*, *construct*, *design*, *develop*, ex*plain*, *generate*, *manage*, *plan*, *prepare*, *rewrite*, *summarize*.

- *Arrange* the courts in order of hierarchy;
- *Explain* the different types of EU secondary legislation;
- *Argue* for and against the creation of a UK Supreme Court;
- *Construct* a search strategy for recent articles on the viability of prosecution for sexually transmitted diseases.

Evaluation (Evaluating): the final category is around judging the value of material for a specific purpose. Verbs useful in this context would be *appraise*, *choose*, *compare*, *contrast*, *criticise*, *defend*, *discriminate*, *evaluate*, *justify*, *rate*, *recommend*.

- *Appraise* a selection of journal article abstracts and select the one with the 'best fit' for your essay;
- *Choose* five people to follow on Twitter to help with your commercial awareness;
- *Summarise* the main types of plagiarism;
- *Evaluate* the key methods of keeping up to date in law.

WRITING A LESSON PLAN

Lesson plans can vary enormously between individuals in terms of the detail included. When you are the only librarian teaching these sessions it is good practice to keep a record of what you are covering in each session, including structure and timings.

For a new session you're trying out, it's useful to have a structure to give yourself a bit of confidence, as well as something useful to annotate after the event, in order to improve things next time around. On the following pages is an example of a detailed lesson plan for one of my basic introductory sessions to first year undergraduates; covering using the internet generally and an introduction to Lexis. Note if this was a 'flipped classroom' session you would prepare materials for the students to watch or read before the session and then set them loose on a problem within the session. You would take a back seat, allowing them to experiment and collaborate, only stepping in when a group gets stuck and needs a hint to get started again.

Note: Chapter 4 of Peter Clinch's *Teaching Legal Research*[22] (2006) offers an excellent lesson plan template and a number of examples of how to structure different types of sessions (Demonstration, Discovery Technique, Lecture/ Workshop, Guided Searching).

BEYOND GOOGLE AND USING LEXISLIBRARY (115 minutes)

You can see the slides at: http://issuu.com/lawbore/docs/google_and_lexis_issu

Slide 1: Title slide

Slide 2: 1 minute
Run through of the learning outcomes.

Slide 3–4: Everything's on Google now isn't it? – 5 mins
Group discussion around how they used other sources during their A-levels, the kinds of things they'd used Google for, problems encountered.

Slide 5: Exercise – 15 mins
Exercise 1 Students given selection of websites to look at – they need to decide which are fake and what gives them away. Ask students to jot down on single pieces of post-its, key characteristics that should raise alarm. A3 sheets of paper round the room representing each site to stick post-its on. Work in pairs.

After lull, ask pairs to feed back one key point to class.

Slide 6: Summarise issues – 5 mins
Exercise 2 Ask for group feedback on what issues this raises for academic study and assessed work, as well as potential perils for lawyers. Show number of stories about lawyers and plagiarism.

Slide 7: Google Scholar – 5 mins
Is there another way of searching Google with more checks and balances? Overview of what makes Google Scholar different and types of materials found on it.

Quick demo of setting preferences and looking for 'super injunctions' – look at types of materials retrieved.

Slide 8: So why are databases so vital? – 5 mins

Summarize key reasons (searching by subject, huge amount of material, print/email options, value added info, authority, use in profession). Brief discussion of costs involved in subscribing to databases – get students to guess how much we pay (never fails to shock them) – link to why they need respect, time spent gaining expertise using them, difference between paid-for services and Google.

Slide 9: What do we have at City? – 5 mins

Overview of databases available to students – what they do and how they might be useful throughout 3 years studying academic law.

Slide 10: What is Lexis? – 2 mins

Summary of types of content included in Lexis.

Slide 11: How to access – 3 mins

Get students to login for first time – go around room to check all OK.

Slide 12: Why is Lexis an essential resource? – 3 mins

Brief summary of the sorts of thing that make it indispensible: all ER coverage, searching across fields, case history, practitioner texts and international content.

Slide 13: Looking for cases – 1 min

Explain that the session will now be very much hands-on with students following my lead and trying out examples, as this is the best way to get used to how the databases work. We'll be looking at the functionality of Lexis by types of content. So we'll start with cases!

Slide 14–15: Finding a case by name – 2 mins

Quick rundown of the front screen – *Quick Find* useful for 'quick and dirty' searching. Note the Bookshelf on right.
<u>Exercise 3</u> Look for *Airedale NHS Trust v Bland*.

Slide 16–21: Look at how a case displays – 5 mins

Formats, list, case history, annotations key, is it good law? Getting full text.

Slides 22–23: Exercise – 3 mins

<u>Exercise 4</u> Look for *Hamilton v Al Fayed* case and answer two set questions using the case history.

Q!

Slide 24: Keyword selection – 2 mins

Introduce difficulty students may find in selecting keywords and how important this is to the success of the search.

Slide 25: Exercise – 6 mins
Exercise 5 Ask students to look at selection of objects and brainstorm possible keywords for if you were searching in a database for them.

Slide 26–27: Statsky's Cartwheel – 5 mins
Look at Statsky's Wheel with whole group, talking through the different types of word association.

Slide 28: Exercise – 3 mins
Exercise 6 Ask students to think about the types of keywords they would use for locating this case. Just do as a whole group.

Slide 29–31: Introduction to and/or – 5 mins
Choosing the relevant tab within Lexis for type of material – *Quick Find* is sometimes too basic. Why is more detailed searching important? Introduce and/ or searching.
Exercise 7 Do the search 'defamation and internet'.

Talk about keyword hits and previous function, and scan through without looking at full text.

Slide 32–33: Or searching – 2 mins
Why useful – difficulties with legal vocab, synonyms, explain with 'medical negligence and baby or infant' example.

Slide 34: Summary – 1 min
General summing-up of Boolean operators.

Slide 35–37: Truncation – 5 mins
Why useful – how it works – Exercise 8 'unfair dismissal and pregnan!' Find *Queen Victoria Seaman's Rest Ltd v Ward* and answer two questions.

Slide 38–39: Wildcards – 5 mins
Why useful – how it works Exercise 9 g*psy and 'right to buy'. Spot occurrence of gipsy and gypsy.

Slide 40: Field searching – 5 mins
Overview of the Advanced Search screen – talk about why combining fields to search can often make your search more effective. Use the example of not knowing the name of a case, just a few details about it.
Exercise 10 – Find a case Lord Denning was involved in where he said something about a 'red hand'.

Slide 41–44: Legislation – 5 mins
Explain that this is brief as covered in more detail in a subsequent session. Reminder that this builds on previous work using hard copy of Halsbury's Statutes. Brief rundown of fields available under Legislation tab, and group discussion of what

types of materials would be found here. <u>Exercise 11</u> find Anti-Social Behaviour Act 2003 and find the date of Royal Assent.

Slide 45–46: Commentary – 5 mins
Introduce students to commentary – what it is used for, what it looks like. Talk through Halsbury's Laws and when it is useful. State that we'll be doing some searching with this title to illustrate another type of advanced searching called Proximity searching.

Slide 47: Proximity searching – 7 mins
Start with a very general search – one keyword 'asylum' and ask the class how we might reduce the number of hits. They hopefully (!) will suggest searching within results, so we add another word: 'detention'. Ask class why sometimes this might not be precise enough and what needs to happen to the keywords to make the search more specific (and get the list of hits reduced).

Slide 48: Commentary titles – 2 mins
Quick overview of what sorts of titles are included in LexisLibrary.

Slide 49–50: Journal introduction – 5 mins
Recap of a previous lecture on sources – prompt students for what kinds of people would write journal articles. Group discussion of why useful for essays. Note how journals are probably the most problematic content to find online as the rights are so split across providers. Note key journals in Lexis. Brief rundown of fields you can search under, and importance of picking out keywords (not typing details in full) and difference between journal article and journal title field.

Slide 51–52: Exercises – 10 mins
<u>Exercise 12</u> Three questions to find answers to within journals. Let students have a go at first one, wander round room checking methods, come back to group discussion of strategies used. Then let loose on others alone.

Slide 53–55: Silly exercises to finish – 10 mins
Prizes for the first to get it right, with each winner telling the rest of the class how they did it.

Slide 56: Summing up and final questions
How do you know if you've hit the spot?

Don't forget to find out what the lucky recipients of your session have thought about the experience. Often this will be pretty monosyllabic but most people are happy to tick a few boxes. Giving them a sliding scale of happiness is popular: for example quality of presentation 1–4 where 1 is very poor and 4 is excellent. Giving five options will mean many people sit on the fence in the middle.

You might like to ask questions around the following:

- Rating of personal knowledge before session
- How confident you are to work alone after the session
- Length of session
- How you liked certain elements within session (for example use of clickers, breakout discussions and so on)
- How you liked the teaching style.

You can ask open-ended questions of course, and the answers to these will often be illuminating, but human nature dictates that many of us skip over anything that requires more thought, especially at the end of a session. Be prepared for good or bad comments. I usually set up an online survey and ask students to complete it before they escape the room.

AND FINALLY … THE PLANNING CHECKLIST

Issue	Notes and Questions
Location	Go and visit the room you've been allocated – does it hold enough people? Is the layout right for the activities you had planned? If any collaborative work planned, is there adequate space to move around?
IT	Do all the PCs work? Do you have the right software and browsers available? Is the projector functioning?
Databases	Have you checked the e-resources you're using will work on the PCs in the room? Are there going to be any issues with pop-ups or authentication? Do you have screenshots if it absolutely goes belly-up?
Equipment	If you're planning to do some activities, do you have all the kit required (e.g. spare pens, post-its, board markers, big paper …)
Help	Do you have the telephone numbers of those who offer IT/AV assistance in case of meltdown?
Back-up	Do you have your teaching materials (PowerPoint slides, prezi.) saved on USB and in an email or a cloud-based file service like Dropbox?

NOTES

1   Sydney J. Harris quote reproduced in: http://www.goodreads.com/author/quotes/169034.Sydney_J_Harris [Accessed 18 July 2013].

2   McLuhan quote reproduced in: *International Journal of McLuhan Studies Blog* (17 April 2012) *Pattern Recognition, Probes and Ideas*. Available at: http://bit.ly/mcluhanquote [Accessed 18 July 2013].

3   Fry, H., Ketteridge, S. and Marshall, S. (2009), 'Understanding student learning', in *A Handbook for Teaching and Learning in Higher Education: Enhancing Academic Practice*. London: Routledge.

4   http://www.slideshare.net

5   http://prezi.com/

6   http://www.youtube.com/

7   ICLR on YouTube www.youtube.com/user/TheICLR. In particular: *A Tale of Two Citations*.

8   Learnmore: the legal skills wiki http://learnmore.lawbore.net

9   Morgan, N. and Davies, L. (2004), 'Innovative induction: introducing the Cephalonian Method', *SCONUL Focus*, 32, 4–8.

10   Sellahewa, H. (2011), 'Using an online student response systems in small group teaching: a pilot stud*y*', *Innovation in Teaching and Learning in Information and Computer Sciences*, 10(3), 38–43. Available at: http://journals.heacademy.ac.uk/doi/abs/10.11120/ital.2011.10030038 [Accessed 18 July 2013].

11   Statsky, W.P. (1978), *Domestic Relations*, West Publishing, reproduced in McKie, S. (1993), *Legal Research: How to Find and Understand the Law*, London: Routledge, pp. 42–43. Available at: http://books.google.co.uk/books?id=0xaKKGkkvI4C&lpg=PA42 &ots=lZ-GPt1IKX&dq=statsky%20cartwheel&pg=PA43#v=onepage&q=statsky%20 cartwheel&f=false

12   Armstrong, C., et al. (2005), 'CILIP Defines Information Literacy for the UK', *Library and Information Update*, 4(1), 22–25. Available at: http://www.cilip.org.uk/get-involved/advocacy/information-literacy/Pages/definition.aspx [Accessed 18 July 2013].

13   SCONUL (1999, updated 2003), Information skills in Higher Education: A SCONUL Position Paper. Available at: http://www.sconul.ac.uk/tags/7-pillars [Accessed 18 July 2013].

14   SCONUL (2011), The SCONUL Seven Pillars of Information Literacy, Core Model for Higher Education, 2011. Available at http://www.sconul.ac.uk/tags/7-pillars

15   AALL (2011), Legal Research Competencies and Standards for Law Student Information Literacy. Available at: http://www.aallnet.org/main-menu/Leadership-Governance/policies/PublicPolicies/policy-lawstu.html – see also article by Kim-Prieto, D. (2011), 'The road not yet taken: How law student information literacy standards address identified issues in legal research education and training', *Rutgers School of Law – Newark Research Paper*, no. 088 [Online] Available at: http://papers.ssrn.com/sol3/papers.cfm?abstract_id=1678146 [Accessed 18 July 2013].

16   BIALL Legal Information Literacy Statement August 2012.

17   Setting Standards: the Future of Legal Services Education and Training Regulation in England and Wales (2013). Available at: http://letr.org.uk/wp-content/uploads/LETR-Report.pdf [Accessed 18 July 2013].

18   Stefani, L. (2009), 'Curriculum design and development', in Fry, Ketteridge and Marshall, 'Understanding student learning', in *A Handbook for Teaching and Learning in Higher Education: Enhancing Academic Practice* (2009) London: Routledge.

19   Bingham, J. (1999), *Guide to Developing Learning Outcomes*. The Learning and Teaching Institute, Sheffield: Sheffield Hallam University.

20   Adam, S. (2004), 'Using Learning Outcomes: A consideration of the nature, role, application and implications for European education of employing learning outcome outcomes at the local, national and international levels' (conference report published as a pdf).

21   Kennedy, D. Hyland, A. and Ryan, N. (2006), Writing and Using Learning Outcomes: a practical guide [Online]. Available at: http://sss.dcu.ie/afi/docs/bologna/writing_and_using_learning_outcomes.pdf [Accessed 18 July 2013].

22   Clinch, P. (2006), *Teaching Legal Research*, 2nd edn. Warwick: UK Centre for Legal Education.

CHAPTER 12

MAKING THE MOST OF SOCIAL MEDIA TOOLS

JAMES MULLAN

INTRODUCTION

Organizations and individuals are actively exploring the use of social media tools and in particular social networking tools. This chapter outlines the social networking tools that are available to individuals working with the legal information community. This chapter encourages readers to think critically about some key issues when using online social networking tools and provides some suggestions for organizational and personal use of these tools.

WHAT IS SOCIAL NETWORKING?

For many professionals social networking has become an important feature of the way they do business. Traditionally most networking would have taken place in person but nowadays organizations and individuals are increasingly focusing their efforts on tools that allow their employees to network and maintain relationships online in new and interesting ways via social networking tools. Whilst often considered a recent discovery, resulting from participation on sites like Facebook, Wikipedia and YouTube, online social networking has its roots in the early days of the internet with bulletin boards and sites like Geocities and Classmates.

However it wasn't until the development of sites like Friendster, Friends Reunited and MySpace that online social networking really took off. For some people 'online social networking' implies trivia, gossip and non-work related activities. In reality, social networks span our professional and personal worlds and are more than just about having fun and meeting friends. Social networks include everything from project teams to sports teams, communities of practice to focus groups and many more. Within the legal information community, informal and formal networks have been playing a fundamental role in supplying us with the information and support we need to undertake our roles successfully – think LIS-LAW, the BIALL e-mail list and the BIALL wiki and you'll begin to understand why social networking has become so important.

Online social networking has also become widespread because of the rapid and visible rise of new types of software (such as blogs, wikis, instant messaging, microblogging and bookmarking tools). These tools are more adept at helping people organize themselves, interact, communicate and share knowledge and information. They are usually referred to as 'social media' tools and are developed with user friendliness in mind, so that individuals with limited or no technical expertise can upload, create and share content, form connections and communicate with other like-minded individuals on the same network.

Social media tools are usually defined as a group of online websites or tools which share some of the following characteristics:

- Participation – social media tools encourage contributions and feedback from everyone who is interested. They blur the line between media and audience.
- Openness – social media tools are open to feedback and participation. They encourage voting, comments and the sharing of information. There are rarely any barriers to accessing and making use of content.
- Conversation – whereas traditional media is about 'broadcasting' (content is published or distributed to an audience) social media is seen as a two-way conversation.
- Community – social media tools enable communities to form quickly and communicate effectively. Communities share common interests, such as a love of books, a football team or a favourite TV programme.
- Connectedness – social media tools thrive on their connectedness, making use of links to other sites, resources and people.

WHY USE A SOCIAL NETWORKING SITE?

The reality is that social networking sites allow us to have much richer, profounder and fuller conversations than many might have experienced in face-to-face conversations. Why? Well firstly we can draw on the entire population of the world to converse with, regardless of geography. Previously, conversation was limited to who was in the room or at the end of the phone. We can also easily find like-minded people to converse with and perhaps most importantly find high-quality discussions on literally any subject at any time.

It's true that you could use social networking sites for totally trivial purposes, but the opportunity to have real conversations with interesting people is now available to anyone in the world at any time in an unprecedented fashion and many people are taking advantage of it. Overall, conversation-wise, we are immeasurably better off.

WHAT ABOUT WEB 2.0?

Run a search for Web 2.0 on Google and you will return more than 1 billion results. Amongst those will be numerous results for definitions of Web 2.0 or thoughts on what Web 2.0 is and the following are some of the best attempts at defining the term:

- The development of applications where users are encouraged to collaborate and participate on and provide feedback about. This is broadly described as 'user generated content'.

- The web becoming more social with users sharing more information about themselves and about things they are looking at.

- The continual, automatic almost invisible updating of websites, making them more dynamic and user-friendly.

Key elements in the development of Web 2.0 sites were Really Simple Syndication (RSS),[1] Atom and Asynchronous JavaScript and XML (AJAX). Changes to how the internet works have also occurred because of increases in computing power, the increased coverage and availability of broadband connections and more and more users becoming confident in their use of the web and websites.

However the term Web 2.0 is actually somewhat of a misnomer and is being used less and less. It does not refer to a new and improved version of the internet, which has become ubiquitous over the last decade. There isn't a new physical version of the internet, merely a lot more interesting places to stop, relax and have a conversation. Social networking and Web 2.0 come together whenever a social networking tool's primary goal is to enable communities to form and interact with one another – in other words to have a conversation.

This chapter does not distinguish further between Web 2.0 and social networking because the terms are too closely related, however suffice to say that *social networking* is the more important of the two terms and the one that you are likely to hear used more often in conversations. This is especially true with the advent of Web 3.0 (the semantic web) and Web 4.0.

The rest of this chapter will look at some of the social networking tools that exist and that are being used by legal information professionals.

BLOGS AND WIKIS

When most individuals think about social networks they don't automatically think about blogs and wikis yet these tools can provide opportunities for individuals to make connections, understand what people are working on and perhaps most importantly engage in conversations with their colleagues. This part of the chapter will look at each of these tools in turn and the potential for their use.

Blogs

Blogs have been around for about 15 years with the word 'blog' being short for 'web log'. Blogs are effectively online diaries displaying entries in chronological order with the most recent first. On the web anyone can create a blog using any one of a number of free tools including Blogger,[2] WordPress[3] and LiveJournal.[4]

Many blogs provide commentary or news on a particular subject; others function as more personal online diaries. A typical blog will combine text, images and links to other blogs and web pages. One of the key features of a blog is the ability for readers to leave comments. Most blogs are text-based, although some focus on photographs (photoblog), videos (video blogging), music (MP3 blog) and audio (podcasting). Microblogging is another type of blogging, featuring very short posts, which will be discussed later in this chapter.

Many organizations within the legal information field have recognized the value associated with providing blogs to their users but it has only been in the last five years that blogs have become well used. Within law libraries, blogs tend to fall into two distinct camps: those that derive from within an organization or library, promoting the library service itself and providing a service for the library users, and those that are written by librarians, dealing with the issues involved in librarianship and the development of the profession. In addition to promoting their services, blogs within law libraries are being used to replace or improve many of the more traditional ways of delivering services or communicating with users.

One of the best examples of using a blog to replace an existing service is as a replacement for internal (hard-copy) newsletters or e-mails. Compared to hard-copy documents, blogs have the advantage of speed, lower cost and interactive features, which provide staff members with the opportunity to comment on items published and engage in a conversation without the confusion of e-mail trails.

Other ways blogs are being used in the legal information field include:

- Capturing knowledge around new purchases, websites, databases, research tips and news that the contributor feels is appropriate for the audience;

- Maximizing internal knowledge sharing by allowing people to post freely about content they might not have sent in an e-mail for fear of clogging inboxes;
- Encouraging individuals to network with colleagues and contacts by allowing people to record their observations and comments and to make connections to what other people are saying or reading;
- Providing a space for groups and projects to discuss ideas and initiatives. Used in this way blogs can be a much more effective and informal way to share knowledge.

For an individual a blog can be a great way to promote themselves or to discuss a particular subject with their peers. Bloggers might feel passionately about a topic whether that is on a personal or a professional level. Unlike traditional media there is no need to spend hours agonizing over an article or a letter – blogging is immediate and can be the perfect way to share an important issue. Blogging can also help build a sense of community as most writers tend to read and regularly comment on one another's blogs. This sense of community is fostered by the sharing of experiences on the social networking sites available to bloggers.

Blogs are also increasingly being used by individuals to record the details of informal and formal training they've received and to assist them with the CILIP Chartership or revalidation process. A good example of how blogs are being used in this way is as part of the 23 Things for Professional Development[5] course. This is a self-directed course (with a blog used for all course details) which aims to introduce individuals (usually librarians) to a range of tools that could help their personal and professional development. One of the first 'things' individuals are asked to do is to create their own blog and record all their 23 Things activities on it. Within the legal information field there are some good examples of blogs maintained by law librarians, from the BIALL Blog[6] to A dumpling in a hanky,[7] and each will offer something slightly different but appealing in terms of content.

Naturally it's important to consider some of the potential problems that can arise, especially if you're going to be blogging about work-related topics. If you're planning to blog at work and about the work you do, you'll definitely want to discuss this with your employers to ensure they're happy for you to do so. It should be obvious that you shouldn't reveal any confidential information; this might include the details of internal discussions, your organizational policies, or anything in relation to clients, customers and deals. You should certainly never use a blog to criticize your colleagues, and should respect the privacy and feelings of others at all times. You may also want to check whether your employer already has a blogging (social media) policy in place. This should make it clear what the organization considers appropriate. If you're going to be blogging primarily from your work PC then it's also advisable to check your organization's computer usage policy.

The different types of blogs available today provide a valuable, although different service – one serving the needs of the library users and the other the needs and interests of librarians. With their ease of use and immediacy, blogs are now regarded as legitimate sources of information for individuals both inside and outside an organization and will continue to be well used by legal information professionals.

Wikis

Of all the social networking tools available wikis have had by far the biggest impact in terms of knowledge sharing, capturing content and encouraging individuals to share knowledge.

Put simply a wiki is a website that allows for the creation and editing of any number of interlinked web pages via a web browser using a simplified mark-up language or a 'What you see is what you get' (WYSIWYG) editor. Wikis are typically powered by wiki software and are often used collaboratively by multiple users. Examples of how wikis are being used within organizations include corporate intranets, knowledge management systems and knowledge bases. Wikis are designed to be easy to use with low entry level and encourage collaboration by being 'open' with minimal restrictions in terms of editing and moderation. Wikis also promote meaningful topic associations between different pages therefore encouraging people to link to pages created by other people easily.

This combined with their ease of use means that wikis are becoming one of the most well-used knowledge sharing tools within organizations. Wikis are also being used outside organizations to publish content that would otherwise exist in a number of different content silos. The BIALL 'How do I wiki'[8] for example draws content from the LIS-LAW and BIALL mailing list into one place to provide a single knowledge base.

Other examples of how wikis could be used include the creation of knowledge bases, subject guides and frequently asked questions (FAQ). Wikis are great tools for law librarians to use because we maintain a lot of documentation which could be better managed online. This might include best-practice guides, information on how to use databases or documentation, information on contracts and contacts and documentation relation to IT applications and systems.

Although wikis are primarily used as knowledge sharing tools they also provide opportunities for individuals to interact with their colleagues, understand what they're working on and comment on content they've created; it's for this reason they're increasingly being used by project teams and groups to manage the projects they're working on. Wikis do this by adding a social element to the content creation process and user experience.

Confluence is a good example of how wikis have made creating and sharing content more social. For example when an individual first uses Confluence they will automatically be given their own 'Personal Space'. This space can be used by an individual to add content about themselves including links to their blog and Twitter account if they have them. The personal space can also be used to experiment with wiki functionality and content.

Confluence also lets individuals add 'status updates'. Similar to Facebook updates these will be seen by anyone who is following you and is therefore part of your network. If you follow someone in return, you'll be able to see the content and any status updates they're creating irrespective of whether you are part of their team or not.

Other wikis will provide similar functionality and most wikis will share some features, for example commenting, liking, notifications, watches, RSS feeds and activity streams. With this functionality in place, wikis allow insights and ideas to spread quickly and broadly and encourage everyone within an organization to work openly and to share conversations that might otherwise have remained hidden. Other popular wikis used within organizations include:

- ThoughtFarmer[9]
- TWiki[10]
- MediaWiki[11]
- PBWorks.[12]

Outside organizations, individuals and groups are looking at how they can use wikis to manage content and encourage other individuals to add content. The BIALL 'How do I' wiki is a good example of this. Two other examples of how this works in practice are the 'Library Routes Project'[13] and the 'UK Library Blogs/Bloggers' wiki. The Library Routes Project is open to anyone and is a place for individuals to document how they got into the library profession and what made them decide to do so. As well as being interesting reading for established professionals it also provides useful information for anyone thinking about a career in librarianship. The site is maintained by those individuals who have registered to add and edit content and uses the free wiki software Wikkii.[14]

The UK Library Blogs/Bloggers wiki[15] is a regularly updated list of blogs that can be identified as having been created and maintained by librarians. The wiki provides a list of blogs under six headings; Library Blogs, Individual Librarian Blogs, Chartership Blogs, Information Professionals, Industry Supplier Blogs and 23Things blogs. The wiki is maintained by a team of four but encourages individuals to add or remove a listing themselves. The wiki uses the free wiki software PBWorks.

Wikis are highly regarded within the legal information community and legal organizations. Their intuitiveness combined with their social features will ensure that they continue to be well used as tools to create, distribute and store knowledge and other content.

Microblogging

One of the most talked about developments in social networking in recent years has been the steady rise in the use of microblogging as a means to communicate and network with individuals. Microblogging is a form of blogging that allows individuals to post brief updates (usually no more than 140 characters) or other media such as photos, audio clips and websites to followers. Followers, who are individuals who have chosen to follow these updates, a bit like blog subscribers, then view them. These updates could be about anything, from what you had for lunch, to a new website you've seen, to something you have just blogged about or are thinking of talking about, your only limit is in most cases 140 characters.

Updates can be submitted by a number of means including text messaging, instant messaging and e-mail or directly from the web. There are also a number of tools which will help you manage both your updates and your followers.

In the next few pages we'll look at some of the most popular microblogging sites.

Twitter

Twitter[16] began life in 2006 as a research and development project and has now become the most popular microblogging site on the web. Twitter is part social networking site, part publishing platform, with the idea behind it that it offers a way for individuals to provide more detailed 'status' updates to their friends, family and other contacts.

Think text messages or Facebook status updates and you're pretty much there in terms of the concept, although with Twitter users can receive updates via the Twitter website, SMS, RSS, e-mail or through applications like Tweetie, TwitterFon, Twitterrific or even Facebook. A number of other services also exist which provide a similar service to Twitter or which combine microblogging functionality with other services, of these Jaiku, Plurk and Tumblr are the best known.

Yammer

Yammer[17] is an enterprise communication tool that was launched in 2008 which provides companies' employees with a site they can use to collaborate and discuss ideas in real time. Yammer is a corporate version of Twitter because it limits the reach of the network. It does this by only allowing individuals who have an authenticated company e-mail address to access the site.

This greatly limits the amount of unrelated background chatter you are generally exposed to on Twitter. Since only your colleagues are allowed to enter the network and participate in the conversation, information exchange is more focused on company-related issues, often breaking departmental walls, flattening the organization and increasing productivity and value.

Just like Twitter, Yammer allows individuals to send short messages to people who choose to follow them. Individuals can also choose to receive messages from employees whom they want to follow. The general question individuals are answering on Yammer is 'What are you working on?' But the exchange of messages following the initial post is what proves to be of greater benefit to those who use Yammer.

For those individuals already used to microblogging, Yammer provides a very similar interface to Twitter. Yammer also provides a number of other ways to post updates to the site including via Twitter and from an application which is available for the iPhone and Android phones. So what are some of the other benefits associated with using a microblogging tool internally?

One of the biggest issues facing many organizations is motivation and morale. Having an open culture where individuals can connect with other employees, direct issues to senior management and provide innovative ideas is one way to address motivation and morale. Microblogging can help by providing individuals with a channel through which they can post ideas and communicate informally with more senior colleagues. Microblogging also provides opportunities for individuals who might never have worked together before to chat informally and to share content without the need to send an e-mail.

Microblogging can also be a great way to introduce new employees to an organization. Traditionally, information new employees need to undertake their role has been available on an intranet or within document repositories. Increasingly microblogs are also being used as spaces both for providing content and as a forum where new employees can ask established employees questions about their role, other departments and the organization. Microblogging should of course not be used to replace face-to-face conversations or picking up the telephone, but rather to supplement those activities.

Even with a tool like Yammer which provides an intuitive interface and easy access the involvement of the senior management team is crucial to ensure that those more junior colleagues can see that the application is well supported. By gathering the support of senior management you're also gently introducing them to the concept of an internal social network and encouraging them to be more open both about their activities and the dialogues they have with other employees.

Tumblr

Tumblr[18] is a microblogging platform that allows users to post text, images, videos, links, quotes and audio to their 'tumblelog'. A tumblelog is a relatively new concept in the microblogging world and is essentially a variation of a blog, which favours short-form, mixed-media posts over the longer editorial posts frequently associated with blogging. Unlike blogs, tumblelogs are used to share the author's creations, discoveries, or experiences without providing a commentary. Users can follow other users, or choose to make their tumblelog private.

Tumblr does a great job at filling the gap between Twitter, where people tweet resources, images and thoughts, and traditional blogging platforms like WordPress or Blogger where each post is a proper article. Instead, Tumblr works with seven types of posts; text, photo, quote, link, chat, audio and video.

According to recent statistics, Tumblr has grown significantly over the past couple of years. Much of this is down to its vast number of social features, and its ease of use, which will appeal to individuals who don't have the time to blog and feel uncomfortable about using Twitter.

Why Use a Microblogging Site?

Despite many advances in technology, e-mail remains the most common online communication and collaboration tool used in organizations. The endless stream of e-mails leads to the almost inevitable information overload frustration for many employees. To address this problem some organizations are turning to microblogging tools.

The value of microblogging and Twitter in particular comes from the combination of exchanging information and links whilst engaging in informal conversations. In terms of immediacy Twitter and Yammer are both a step up from blogging and Facebook-style status updates. This immediacy has been highlighted by some of the events that have been reported on Twitter.

Despite Twitter and Yammer being sold as microblogging tools, they're predominantly referred to as social networking tools. Yammer in particular is often referred to as Facebook for the enterprise. Both microblogging tools can be a great way to expand your existing network. So you may consider yourself fairly well networked especially if you currently publish to a blog or speak at events, but what both Twitter and Yammer do in terms of your network is expose you to individuals or 'followers' from outside your normal network of contacts.

These followers are of course all potentially valuable. Twitter can also be a great way to keep in touch with existing contacts in the legal information field, friends and other colleagues.

Both Twitter and Yammer make it easy for users to keep up with what other users are doing and to share and collaborate on projects even if they are in different departments, buildings or even countries. Microblogging applications literally have no boundaries.

Twitter is also a great way to stay on top of the latest technologies, even if you can't see any applications on Twitter that will currently work for you or your organization. That doesn't mean they won't be reported on Twitter in the near future. You can also discover new content via profile pages on Twitter. These pages display a user's photos and are where the user can link to their blog or website.

An important part of many information professionals' roles is to read or scan news sources for information. Major news sites, like CNN, the BBC and other organizations will have Twitter feeds where breaking news will appear, often in advance of their main website or RSS feed. Spotting a breaking news story has now never been easier. Yammer can also be a great way to see what is happening internally and to identify a trend in what people are doing, what they're reading and what they might be working on.

Twitter has for a while now been used by individuals to post live updates from conferences so others can follow the conference virtually. Many conferences also now have Twitter feeds that let you keep up with registration deadlines, speakers and accommodation details without having to visit the conference site and of course most importantly connect with individuals before the conference has even started.

Twitter and Yammer are great examples of how you could use crowdsourcing and the power of your networks to ask questions. Twitter in particular, where you could have thousands of followers, is a fantastic resource that is built around individuals wanting to build relationships and share their knowledge and expertise. If you have a blog or a website you can automatically post these items to Twitter, which will ultimately drive more people to follow you. Some libraries, albeit predominantly in the US, have started using Twitter instead of traditional communication methods as a way to let users know about new services or to provide service updates (when photocopiers are broken, if a website is unavailable and so on). Users can follow these updates from wherever they are based.

Although the use and development of microblogging tools 'behind the firewall' is in its infancy, its impact in terms of collaboration and networking could be huge and we're just now beginning to see some of these efforts pay off. More and more organizations are reporting how they're using Yammer to encourage people to share content and communicate.

Concerns Around the Use of Microblogging Sites

Despite microblogging being well-established there remain a number of concerns around its usage. Of these, privacy is arguably the biggest issue with users potentially broadcasting sensitive personal information to anyone who views their public feed.

Security concerns have also been voiced within the business world, since there is a potential for sensitive work information to be publicized on microblogging sites such as Twitter. This might include information which may be subject to an injunction or potentially confidential information. As with other social media tools it's important to think carefully both about what content is being published and on what site and when: doing so will ensure you don't fall foul of any of the policies that your organization has in place in relation to social media tools.

SOCIAL NETWORKING SITES

After being much maligned for many years social networking sites are now considered serious tools for sharing and creating knowledge by many organizations. Within an organization social networking tools could be used in many different ways, for example to find someone who knows about a particular subject or to create groups around particular subjects or themes. These uses of social networking tools will be discussed later in this chapter. First we'll take a look at look at some of the more well-known personal and professional social networking sites.

Facebook

Facebook is one of the most well-known social networking sites in the world. Originally established in 2004 as a networking tool for college students, it has grown to become one of the most significant online social networks. Facebook lets users communicate and share information about themselves, in both a professional and personal context.

The main user interface aggregates individuals' activity to create 'mini-feeds' of information. This activity includes updates to a user profile or personal page, which can contain as much information as the individual wants. These feeds show when individuals have connected or communicated with each other, updated their profile, added new applications or tagged content. Content can also be pulled into an individual's 'mini-feed' from other sites, for example an individual's blog, Twitter Feed and Linkedin account. Combined, the mini-feeds provide a complete picture of an individual's activity on Facebook and other social networking sites.

Although at first glance it might appear that Facebook supports only frivolous interaction, there is also a lot of professional and work-related communication on the site.

Facebook groups are another way to engage in conversations with peers and colleagues. Any Facebook member can create a group, which can be public or private. However the existence of a Facebook group, especially where linked to an organization, does not mean that it has been officially 'sanctioned' by the organization. Anyone who has signed up to Facebook can join a Facebook group, although private groups require administrative approval or are by invitation only. In addition to a number of general law and law librarianship groups on Facebook (including BIALL), many organizations are using Facebook groups for recruitment, alumni and trainee networks, work-related social and professional networks and communities of practice.

Google+

Google+[19] was launched on the 28th June 2011 and is Google's latest foray into the world of social networking following the disastrous Google Buzz and Google Wave products. With a similar look and feel to Facebook Google+ is a collection of different social products including Stream (a newsfeed), Sparks (a recommendation engine), Hangouts (a video chat service), Huddle (a group texting service), Circles (a friend management service) and Photos.

Essentially the platform is built around 'circles' so understanding circles is essential to mastering Google+ as Google has opted not to let you simply 'friend' your friends, like you do on Facebook, or 'follow' different people as you would on Twitter. Instead, Google+ gives you more control over who sees your content using 'circles'. These circles are similar to groups on Facebook. However, what differentiates circles from groups is the ease with which users can manage their contacts, making Google+ very powerful and a potential game changer. But why? Well, let's take a look at how we might use Facebook.

If you use Facebook regularly, you probably wonder whether you should add professional contacts. I believe that you shouldn't mix business and pleasure on social networking sites but use Facebook for personal contacts, and LinkedIn for professional contacts. Well, Google+ changes this. There is no need for separate networks any more, as users now have the ability to seamlessly choose which circles (group of 'friends') sees what content, on a post-to-post level.

The reason why this is game changing is because a typical user on Facebook cannot be 100 per cent themselves, since they may have both colleagues, friends, family and so on in their network. They may not want to speak openly on Facebook about their personal life, hobbies and so on, since everyone can either see everything or are excluded from seeing new posts entirely. Users might not discuss their religious beliefs as this could be perceived as too personal to discuss with colleagues, and they won't use Facebook for professional matters, as this might be too boring for their friends and family.

Circles allows users to drag-and-drop their friends into different friend groups, which categorizes them. This allows users to put their mum into 'Family' circle, their line-manager in their 'Business' circle and their best friend from school in their 'Friends' circle. Users can create as many circles as they like, although making too many becomes cumbersome and diminishes their usefulness.

Once a user has created and populated their circles, they just have to write a post or a status update, choose which circle (or circles) they want to see it and post the message, knowing that only those they want to see the content will have the ability to do so. Ultimately this means that less effort needs to be spent on maintaining the different circles of trust. There are also many potential uses for Google+ beyond just using it to maintain your professional and personal contact, they include:

- As a potential authoring platform (create an empty circle named 'drafts' and write your content there prior to sending it out to the masses);
- As a blogging platform (no limits on amounts of characters);
- As a newsreader (create an empty circle named 'Read Later' and share interesting bits to this circle for later consumption);
- As a collaboration platform;
- As a conversation tool;
- A relationship management tool.

When Google+ was launched it was hailed as the next Facebook or Twitter. Whilst it hasn't quite lived up to those expectations Google+ is most definitely a social network. There are now more than 500 million Google+ users and the level of engagement on Google+ would appear to be increasing steadily. Whilst you don't necessarily need to be using Google+ any more than you need to use Facebook or Twitter, its impact is spreading and to be effective in our roles we need to understand its potential.

Linkedin

LinkedIn is an extremely well-known social networking site with over 100 million registered users from more than 200 countries. Likened to a giant online rolodex, with a virtualized interactive address book, LinkedIn not only contains the online resumes of individuals and organizations, it also allows users to demonstrate their experience and share the expertise of others.

The core feature of LinkedIn is to 'connect' users with people they know and trust in business, although there are options to 'connect' with friends. Many people think this is all there is to LinkedIn, but there is so much more.

LinkedIn was founded in 2003, with the site launching with 350 contacts on May 5th. By April 2004 LinkedIn had reached half a million members. In August 2005 LinkedIn launched its subscription services. By the end of 2005 LinkedIn had 4 million members and by the end of 2008 LinkedIn had 33 million members.

Now with more than 200 million users, LinkedIn is well ahead of its competitors like Viadeo (50 million). LinkedIn membership grows at approximately a new member every second. About half of the members are in the United States and 11 million are from the UK.

Using LinkedIn
Connecting with people you know is by far the most well-known feature of LinkedIn and for casual users is the main draw. Connecting with someone you know is as simple as searching for them using the LinkedIn search and then choosing to add them as a connection. As with most networking sites LinkedIn users can see how many 'degrees' away they are from people. In addition LinkedIn will show shared connections among people within your network. By showing these shared connections LinkedIn provides users with an opportunity to expand their network of professional contacts. Other ways you can use LinkedIn include:

- Get introduced – LinkedIn introductions are a great way for you to connect with people you don't know but your connections do. Say for example you know someone who works in a law firm and have seen that they are connected to someone you'd be interested in talking to or connecting with. With a LinkedIn introduction you can ask to be introduced to the connection you don't know.
- Broadcast what you're doing – LinkedIn is a great way to tell the world what you're doing by posting status updates. These status updates can include links to content you've seen, articles you're reading or projects you're working on.
- Publish other content – If you've created items like blog posts, PowerPoint presentations or Amazon reading lists, LinkedIn has multiple ways to 'post' this information to your profile. Your LinkedIn profile then becomes a quick way for a potential connection or employer to get a 'view' of what kind

of person you are. This publishing aspect of LinkedIn offers yet another avenue for you to demonstrate your expertise. However you should think carefully about whether you want to post content directly from Twitter as your Twitter account may not have such a professional focus.

- Recommend people or companies – LinkedIn also allows people to ask their connections for recommendations or to recommend connections. This is one way that connections on LinkedIn can help individuals raise their profile. And whilst you might consider it tacky or inappropriate to directly solicit recommendations, many people do use their LinkedIn profile to demonstrate their expertise, by posting recommendations received from their connections.

- Become part of groups that match your interests – as with other social networks, LinkedIn groups are designed to connect people with similar interests, industry or professional affiliation. Anyone can create a group, post questions amongst group members and share information. There are a huge number of groups to choose from, all of them include the details of members of a discussion board and a profile page which explains the aims of the group. There are even several groups specifically for BIALL members.

- Demonstrating and finding skills – LinkedIn has recently developed a new module as part of the site called LinkedIn skills. For example if you're interested in SharePoint when you navigate to the skill page for this application you'll see related skills, related companies, jobs, groups and individuals who have indicated that they have this skill. Individuals can also add skills to their profiles to enhance what they might have already written about specific roles.

- A relatively new addition to LinkedIn is endorsements. Endorsements enable LinkedIn users to 'endorse' skills that are listed on an individual's profile, which can then be seen by anyone who wants to connect with this user. So a connection can view another connection, visit their profile and 'endorse' any of the skills listed by hovering over the skill and clicking 'endorse' or by clicking on the plus icon to the right of the skill. Those users who have previously endorsed this skill are listed by means of a thumbnail image with a link to their profile.

LinkedIn will also display recommended endorsements at the top of an individual's profile. So when an individual visits a connection's profile page they may be presented with a list of skills they can endorse. If an individual chooses to skip this step they'll be presented with four of their connections and asked whether these connections have the skills or expertise listed. An individual can choose to display more of their connections and endorse these as they choose fit. Any endorsements an individual has received will appear within a user's activity and in their timeline. Any endorsements provided will also appear on the activity stream of the connection that has received it.

LinkedIn isn't just about adding connections though, the site has so much more to offer. What individuals choose to use and make the most of is entirely up to them but used effectively LinkedIn can be a great way to promote yourself, develop your connections and share knowledge.

NETWORKING WITHIN AN ORGANIZATION

The highly publicized rise of social networking sites like Facebook and Linkedin has meant that many organizations have questioned whether they should be offering Facebook like functionality behind the firewall. After all 'It's not what you know, it's who you know' is a phrase that is well used in business and establishing and maintaining connections across an organization means people are more likely to find who or what they want, whenever they need to.

In most organizations it's not uncommon for people working together to know very little about their colleagues aside from their role and work location. For organizations whose locations span geographical locations and time-zones this is even more acute. In the same way that profiles are a central feature of an external social networking tool like Facebook, Linkedin or Google+, employee profiles are crucial to providing information about an individual to other members of an organization. They should offer rich information about an individual including information about projects they've worked on, their experience, associations and interests. Although increased numbers of intranets include employee directories or know-who searches, sadly a large number of organizations don't provide employees with the opportunity to find out more about their immediate and more distant colleagues.

Social networks can also help flatten organizations, that is, by allowing communications outside silos and organizational boundaries.

Maintaining a social network inside an organization can also bring several other benefits including the following:

- Gaining better interaction within networks;
- Sharing hot topics with groups;
- Talking to and listen to groups;
- Collaborating and crowdsourcing ideas;
- Activating employees and encouraging better interaction;
- Making networks activities accessible outside the corporate network;
- Building trust and networking within groups;
- Encouraging ongoing interaction between groups.

Where internal social networking solutions have worked is where they've been within applications that combine a social networking element with collaborative content creation, for example within a blog, wiki or community space. Well-used networking platforms include the following:

- Microsoft Office SharePoint Server 2013 (MOSS)[20]
- ThoughtFarmer[21]
- Socialtext[22]
- Jive Social Business[23]
- IBM Lotus Connections.[24]

Unfortunately many organizations struggle to integrate social networks with some of their existing internal applications (intranets, portals and so on). There will also often be a lack of awareness that a social network exists because it exists separately from existing IT infrastructure. Until social networks are part of an individual's workflow they will continue to be the poor cousin to e-mail and other applications.

SOCIAL BOOKMARKING

Social bookmarking is one of the easiest social networking tools to use and legal information professionals have already discovered ways in which they can use these tools both to promote resources externally and to share resources internally.

Nowadays most individuals are comfortable with searching the web and spending a significant amount of time looking for information on the web. We're all familiar with saving websites we visit frequently into our favourites on Internet Explorer and organizing these via folders so that we can find them at a later date.

However this practice is inefficient for several reasons. Firstly if a website is relevant to several topic areas it has to be saved in multiple folders. Secondly if you use a PC at work and at home you may end up with favourites saved in two different places. Finally you might want to forward a favourite to an individual, but the time taken trying to find the favourite in amongst all your other favourites means you end up searching for it on Google again. With social bookmarking sites you can avoid all this.

Social bookmarking probably conjures up images of individuals swapping bookmarks they have collected, and although the concept of individuals sharing 'stuff' is a good way to think about social bookmarking, before we get into how it works lets think about what it really means. At its most basic level social bookmarking is a way for individuals to save, manage and search for bookmarks on the internet with the help of metadata, tags or categories.

On a social bookmarking site, users save links to web pages that they want to remember or share. These bookmarks are usually public although they can be saved privately, or shared only with specified people or groups, for example your colleagues, your friends or people you might work with on a committee. The individuals who have the rights to view these bookmarks can usually view them chronologically, by category or tags, or via the site's search engine.

To start tagging websites and other content you'll need to identify a suitable social bookmarking site. There are a number available including Delicious,[25] Digg[26] and StumbleUpon.[27] Once you've registered with a social bookmarking site you can start adding sites and perhaps more importantly start sharing them with your 'network'.

This is a simple process, which involves navigating to the social bookmarking site and entering the URL. Most social bookmarking sites also offer 'bookmarking tools', these are usually toolbars that sit within your browser ready for you to use whenever you find a site you want to save. Applying a tag to a piece of content is usually just a case of typing words into a text box, previously used tags will also be displayed on screen, which can then be chosen and applied to the item. Importantly you can change the title and description of the item when you save it and add notes or a description.

Once added, tags will appear as words near to the item. These are usually hypertext links which when clicked on will show all content that has been given that tag. Within a social bookmarking application saved items are usually organized by date, allowing users to view the last items saved as well as the tags that have been associated with the item and the number of other users that have saved this item.

This is a useful metric for anyone using the social bookmarking site.

Collections of tags are often presented as a tag cloud, which is an alphabetical list of tags where the most used tags are often a different colour or size. Using this method to organize tags quickly shows users which tags are used most often. The alternative to this is a purely alphabetical list of tags, which can be difficult to browse especially if you're trying to identify the most regularly used tags.

Tagging is also being used extensively in the world of blogs. Bloggers can select a tag when they are about to publish an item, then when anybody navigates to the blog they can display all posts that have been tagged using a tag cloud or a tag list. Tagging information resources and legal content with tags or categories has already changed the way we store and find information and will continue to do so. If you're using a social bookmarking site already it has become less important to remember where the information was found and more important to know how to retrieve it using your social bookmarking site.

Social Bookmarking Inside an Organization

While some social applications such as blogs and collaboration tools like wikis have been adopted behind the firewall in a lot of organizations, social bookmarking or tagging would not appear to have found as much favour. This seems odd as there are many possibilities for using social bookmarking tools behind the firewall which organizations could take advantage of.

Tagging or bookmarking could supplement information retrieval options in intranets and document management systems, allowing employees to use tags to enhance the findability of internal and external content without waiting for an information professional to categorize it. This might sound like a bad thing, but there is still a significant role for information professionals even where an organization is using a social bookmarking or tagging tool.

Internal social bookmarking tools could allow individuals to subscribe to what is called a 'tag stream' and monitor content being tagged. This is an excellent way to provide trend monitoring, news/blog aggregation and other external company-related information. Social tagging can also be used to help share documents, research and more, both within formal groups and informal groups. This increases not only collaboration, but also expertise location as viewing a tagger's staff profile can tell you a lot about their interests and expertise. Essentially, social tagging creates a richer set of options for users within an organization for locating content and colleagues.

Organizations are also looking at how social bookmarking tools could be used to create sets of bookmarks for their external clients. Traditionally libraries have always produced documents, websites or intranet pages that contain lists of links. Social bookmarking sites take this concept one step further by categorizing the links, showing users how many other people have saved the links and making them fully searchable.

Put into this context, social bookmarking/tagging within an organization sounds like a great idea. So why aren't more organizations using bookmarks or tags to help individuals find content and people? The major issue, and this will apply to all social media tools, is the difference between the personal web and the private web (an organization's internal websites).

The social web is a seemingly infinite collection with no clear edges, no authority and no structure. Allowing web users to organize content in this context makes sense as individuals are free to make up their own definitions and categories. From these categories and definitions and the sheer volume of tagging, a usable structure will emerge.

Corporate content is different: information is more defined and is meant to support specific tasks and users, entities are structured and there is authority to be respected. Finding information is critical in this context, so employees have a higher need for precise and reliable access to information.

People are also very different on the web vs. working in an organization. One of the big success factors with many Web 2.0 tools was the number of users. Within an organization, the level of participation tends to be around 10 per cent of users. People at work also have less time and motivation to participate in social networking tools: they are focused on deliverables and deadlines and do not often have the spare time or incentive to focus on sharing and tagging information. They also have more concerns about privacy and security, given that their tags and content they create may be made visible to other employees.

Another issue is the quality of tags being generated by individuals. Unfortunately, individuals are not especially good at tagging. They tag inconsistently over time and are usually more concerned about personal findability than the 'greater good'. This translates itself into tags of dubious quality: misspelled tags (for example Sharpoint), inconsistent tags (for example dog vs. dogs) and personal use tags (for example to read, general) and so on.

Given these issues it might seem that all projects involving social software are destined to fail, but you only have to do a quick search on the web to read about some highly successful implementations in many different organizations.

IMPLEMENTING SOCIAL NETWORKING TOOLS

The next few pages will look at some of the concerns around the adoption of social networking tools, how to work with your IT teams and some approaches to implementing social networking tools internally.

Concerns Around Adoption

A fundamental barrier to the adoption of social media tools within organizations is the required shift in culture, both from the perspective of an individual using these tools to someone in IT or management who might be thinking about how these tools could be used. For individuals the shift is seismic, from a culture of knowledge created and captured on paper and stored either on their own PC or within a know how management system, to a more collaborative way of working and sharing content.

One of the biggest concerns for any organization around the adoption of social networking tools especially where the content is being reused is the quality of the information that comes from them. Twitter could potentially be a great tool to monitor breaking news in a particular subject area or for a particular company but how reliable is the information that is returned from the searches? Is it just speculation, rumours and hearsay or can it be relied on as accurate? This concern can be applied to many of the free social networking tools available including Google Alerts and Google Blog Search, Wikipedia and many more. This concern will remain as long as the information is being created on a collaborative basis. To stop creating content in this manner would go against many of the principles behind the sites.

Another issue for many individuals is finding the time to use these tools – and then potentially spending too much time using them. A number of law librarians will work either as solo librarians or as part of a very small team. In practice this means that very often they will do everything from ordering new items for the library to loading know how to the intranet. As a result time – or lack of it – can be an issue. I would argue that these tools have the potential to actually make life easier and more productive by filtering and organizing content an individual receives.

Alongside a lack of time, information overload is another concern for both individuals and organizations. RSS feeds are great but not if you subscribe to a thousand. Twitter has the potential to be a useful tool for those within the legal information field but not if you're following too many people or don't manage it appropriately. Wikis are intuitive and easy to add content to, but you could quickly become overwhelmed by the number of updates. These tools all have the potential to add to what is already a very noisy world. Managed properly however these tools could make individuals' lives easier and provide value for both internal and external clients.

The language of social media tools can also be confusing. RSS for example has several different meanings from 'really simple syndication' to 'rich site summaries' to 'read some stories'. All of these descriptions are valid but none of them actually describe what RSS is and more importantly explains its potential. For individuals managing these tools the challenge is to ensure their users understand what the term means without using too much jargon or 'dumbing down' the application or process to the point where a user thinks it isn't relevant to the work they do.

Risk aversion in some organizations, while appropriate and desirable in certain contexts, is not so good if you're championing a project that looks at how staff can collaborate and share information. Many information systems will be designed with security as a major feature, for example document management systems which encourage users to apply security to the documents they create. Informing users that they have to forget about what they have done previously and start using tools that will expose the content they create for everyone to see may therefore not go down too well.

Another issue is the concerns that might be raised by IT about the use of social media tools and services. For an organization's IT department, social media tools present a number of challenges, some of these relate directly to the security of information, others around support and perhaps most importantly control.

Security, especially when sensitive information resides on a third party's computer system, can be a major issue. Its security then depends entirely on the soundness of the third party's security practices and integrity. This is especially a concern where the third party's servers are located in a different country and where security practices may not be as thorough. Although security is still a concern, the increased use of cloud services by organizations because of the benefits associated with that, means that IT Departments are more open to using these types of services.

Demand for new tools will usually come from management or from the top down. In contrast the demand for social networking tools will normally come from individual users who have either used these tools outside the organization or have seen their potential. The problem for an IT department is that an individual user might not appreciate the security implications. For example if someone requests a blog that leads to a security breach – will IT be the ones who are blamed?

Supporting social networking tools can also be an issue for IT departments especially as users may be using a whole range of freely available tools and services, many of which the IT department may not be familiar with.

The social media sector is a dynamic and rapidly moving environment. Many of the tools may continue to be developed and supported but what about the ones that aren't? It might appear risky for users to rely on services which may disappear at any time, where no support contract is available and there are no guarantees that issues or requests for changes will be dealt with.

The scalability of social networking tools is another issue. For an IT department, the ideal solution is something that can be rolled out organization-wide so that usage and the support provided is consistent. If other approaches are used it can become difficult to manage these. IT departments may just not 'get it' or they may not have realized or seen the potential of these tools.

So what approach should you take when looking at how you could use social networking tools internally? The most important thing you need to do is to have a clear strategy about why you want to deploy a particular tool and this and other success factors are discussed later in this chapter. In the first instance you need to have a 'grown-up conversation' with your IT department. Extolling the virtues of 'poking people' on Facebook or 'chucking sheep' isn't going to bring them onside. Neither is telling them about all the amazing songs you've saved to Blip FM.

The approach you take should make the use of the tools relevant to the organization in which you work. So if you know the marketing team are looking at different ways to talk to clients then extol the virtues of Twitter. If your marketing team is looking to monitor the web, demonstrate the benefits of using Google News, Twitter and RSS feeds.

Similarly if you know a team is looking at ways to share information outside e-mail then suggest to your IT department that they start looking at a blog or maybe even a wiki.

Identify 'friends' in your IT department, people who you know are going to be responsive to the idea of the organization rolling out a new tool. Once you've identified these 'friends' you might find that IT are quite keen to be part of something that they have read about and is seen as 'new'.

Identify someone or a group of individuals who could use a social media tool for a specific task or project. Once they're onside, your case for having access to a specific tool will be much stronger. If your IT department isn't aware of them, highlight the benefits of using social media tools. Not only are they easy to set up and maintain but social media tools also provide opportunities to innovate at relatively low cost, which at a time when there is huge pressure on resources can only be good.

If you have access to a social media tool and want to demonstrate the benefits of using it, why not just go ahead and use it? Being able to demonstrate how easy to use and useful the tools are that exist may well lead to your IT department thinking differently about their policies in relation to them.

While there will always be some information that organizations will want to keep in-house, to opt out of using externally hosted social media tools does not seem a sensible strategy. These technologies are already well embedded into many employees' lives. It's likely that many employees will belong to social networking sites and will join new organizations with the belief that they should be allowed to communicate using these technologies while at work.

Pretending that these tools don't exist or that they can be ignored will certainly make your IT department's lives easier but ultimately this approach will only backfire. If your IT department does choose to block social media sites then they need to be explicit about why and be prepared to back up the policy with well-documented guidelines on social media use.

Social media tools should be an opportunity for users and IT to work closely together, not create more barriers. Ultimately, organizations that are as externally focused as possible and which allow their employees room to innovate without compromising an organization's business activities will be the most successful.

So if you've got the go ahead and are ready to start looking at/deploying social media tools, what are some of the critical elements of any rollout/strategy?

Identify the Problem You're Trying to Solve

Whatever social networking tool you're looking to implement there has to be a very good reason for doing so within a business setting. It might be that an existing system isn't facilitating conversations with employees across different parts of the organization or employees would like to be able to generate ideas and solutions. Either way, identify the problem you're trying to solve before you even think about looking at a tool.

Match the Benefits of the Tool to the Organization's Goals

There has to be a point at which stakeholders buy into the use of any social networking tool. If this isn't addressed relatively early the project will ultimately fail. To sell a tool to a stakeholder you need to be able to demonstrate how using social networking tools can solve problems previously identified.

Integrate the Tools with Existing Systems

To ensure the potential of social networking tools is fully realized they should ideally be part of an individual's workflow. At the very least this means providing links to these tools via an intranet and if possible implementing single sign on so that individuals aren't asked to sign on to multiple tools multiple times during the day. Promoting the tools is another way to encourage their use, and this can be facilitated either through the internal communications channels available within your organization or by attendance at team or departmental meetings. Making content created with any social networking tool available within a search tool is another key integration issue. Having content created on a wiki or a blog returned in a search alongside intranet and other internally generated content will help promote the content and drive individuals to a site they may not otherwise have been aware of.

Find Champions!

In addition to your key stakeholders who will support the project but might not necessarily contribute, you need to have 'champions'. These are individuals who can encourage others to use the tools either through their own use of the tools or by talking to other individuals about the tools.

Provide Training and Guidance

Although most social networking tools are intuitive, providing training can be a key element in encouraging individuals to use a social networking tool. However you need to be clear about your objectives when it comes to delivering training and not try to 'force' people to use a particular tool as this may have the opposite effect to the one you're trying to achieve.

No matter what the social networking tool is, it is also important to have some guidance available. That might just be a broad set of principles governing what individuals can and can't do. Whatever you have in place it should be flexible enough to encourage individuals to create content within a social networking tool without thinking that they are doing something wrong.

Develop a Social Networking Policy

Crucial to the success of any social media rollout is the development and implementation of a policy relating to usage. However the policy should be developed not only to provide protection, but it should also work to encourage employees to participate in social networking and to educate them about doing so in a safe, appropriate way.

Written properly, a social media policy outlines what can't be done and states what should be done from a legal perspective to protect the company's assets. But it will also do the opposite, which is to promote and encourage and motivate employees to actually look at and start thinking about how they can use social media.

THE FUTURE OF SOCIAL NETWORKING

Social networks and social media tools are an integral and important part of our lives both at work and at home. They have become ubiquitous to the point that sometimes we might not even realize we're using a social networking tool. So what does the future hold for social networking and our use of the tools previously discussed in this chapter?

What I hope is clear is that social networking tools play a very significant role in facilitating communication, ultimately leading to better knowledge sharing and collaboration. They are for the most part an addition to other forms of communication tools, notably e-mail, but aren't currently replacing them. They have however had the positive effect of connecting individuals across organizations that may not have had the chance before, creating new opportunities to collaborate, share ideas and develop better working relationships. However for some organizations they may not be suited, for example within the legal community, where security and risk are important considerations, there may already be existing tools which are used in preference to tools like blogs and wikis.

The legal information community has also changed significantly over the last few years, including some significant developments around our use of technology. As technology has changed, so the way many legal information professionals work has had to change. Legal information professionals should remain abreast of changes and developments within the technology landscape and be prepared to advocate the use of any new tool that aids collaboration and knowledge sharing within the organization they work in.

Many individuals have also been affected by organizations outsourcing their support functions or some cases working 'offshore' or at a location away from the traditional law library. In these situations even greater emphasis is placed on how geographically displaced individuals communicate and collaborate with each other. Understanding how social networking tools could be used in these situations and helping developing these tools may well be a future requirement for law librarians.

As leaders in their field from a knowledge sharing point of view, law librarians are well placed to start using social media tools both professionally and personally. Within organizations, knowledge management and information services teams are ideally placed to oversee and manage the use of social media tools alongside their IT and marketing teams. The knowledge management or information services teams should be the first to start looking at developing these tools; even if that means starting small with a limited access blog or wiki that uses free software. Demonstrating the potential use of these tools within the organization should eventually lead to bigger and more inclusive projects for legal information professionals.

NOTES

1   http://www.bbc.co.uk/news/10628494 for more information RSS feeds
2   http://www.blogger.com
3   http://www.wordpress.com
4   http://www.livejournal.com/
5   http://cpd23.blogspot.com/
6   http://biall.blogspot.com
7   http://dumplinginahanky.blogspot.com/
8   http://biallpr.pbworks.com/w/page/5259189/How-do-I
9   http://www.thoughtfarmer.com/
10 http://twiki.org/
11 http://www.mediawiki.org/wiki/MediaWiki
12 http://pbworks.com/
13 http://libraryroutesproject.wikkii.com/wiki/Main_Page
14 http://wikkii.com/wiki/Free_Wiki_Hosting

15   http://uklibraryblogs.pbworks.com/w/page/7262285/FrontPage
16   http://www.twitter.com
17   http://www.yammer.com
18   http://www.tumblr.com/
19   https://plus.google.com/
20   http://sharepoint.microsoft.com/en-us/pages/default.aspx
21   http://www.thoughtfarmer.com/
22   http://www.socialtext.com/
23   http://www.jivesoftware.com/
24   http://www-01.ibm.com/software/lotus/products/connections/
25   http://delicious/
26   http://digg.com/
27   http://www.stumbleupon.com

CHAPTER 13

OUTSOURCING

KATE STANFIELD AND SOPHIE THOMPSON

INTRODUCTION

'Outsourcing' may not be a welcome concept to many, but it is a recognized method for increasing value. It is often driven by a strong financial expectation of value, that is, as a way of driving down costs, but there are other drivers which motivate organizations to outsource, such as the experience, breadth, specialism and buying power that an outsourcing supplier can provide.

Outsourcing is not a new concept. It is embedded in our market economy as a way of enabling us to focus on what we do best. It is a vehicle which moves us away from self-sufficiency and allows us to specialize. As households, we are perpetual outsourcers, relying on others to grow our food, build our houses, teach our children, make our clothes. These are services we are willing to pay for, as we are confident they are being done by specialists with a wealth of experience, contacts and knowledge and because they free us up to focus on our own ways of creating value.

In an organizational setting, outsourcing has long been used to enable the organization to concentrate on its core business, for example by using a catering company, a printer, a PR firm or a consultant. In its most formal expression, outsourcing is about contracting with another individual or organization to provide a service which it previously provided itself. Over the last 20 years, the outsourcing of IT and other 'back office' services (Business Process Outsourcing or BPO) has burgeoned.

In the legal world, even non-core legal work is now under scrutiny as law firms assess whether any of the more process-driven activities can actually be better and more cost-effectively undertaken by a specialist in the field, a Legal Process Outsourcing (LPO) provider.

In the last few years there has been more outsourcing of library services, and in particular several law firms in the UK have made the move to outsource their information services one way or another, so why is this happening now?

Legal Libraries and the Changing Legal Landscape

Within law firms, the Legal Services Act opened up the legal market to competition from the business world, with alternative business models and the influx of 'non-lawyer' senior managers. For many law firms this ability to look at how they structure some of their business services and their financial model differently becomes more attractive as other pressures develop within the legal landscape.

Clients are no longer resigned to the law firm chargeable hour, rates and services. Facing their own pressures, clients demand a lot more from their legal advisers.

Primarily these requirements are based around cost; fixed price deals, bulk discounts – some innovative pricing deals – but clients also require added value, often to augment their administrative services which might have been cut back in-house. Tie this pressure in to the need to accommodate globalization with many firms, demands for expertise in new jurisdictions and topics, together with capability and service centres in different geographic locations, and again, a less costly model would be attractive.

The financial crisis of recent years focuses these pressures and senior management look at the overall costs of running a law firm with a keen eye on support costs. A clue is in the terminology commonly used for law firm staff – the lawyers are 'fee earners' whereas the business services teams – Finance, IT, HR, Library – are 'support'.

Senior management in most law firms are looking at the bigger picture: the pressures facing their growth, profits and partner drawings, as illustrated in Figure 13.1 opposite.

Public and Academic Libraries

Public libraries have long faced many of the pressures that are now facing commercial legal libraries, cost, effective services, fluctuating demand for services and ever more innovative library provision.

For many years libraries have outsourced tasks to private companies as contracts, functions that are necessary to library operations, such as library cleaning, binding services, barcoding, RFID tagging, book cleaning, stock analysis, statistical reporting, reclassification, cataloguing and so on.

Public leisure services as a whole have been outsourced or run by external organizations for over 20 years now and the business is a mature market with plenty of systems and models. Many local authorities now appear to be looking

Figure 13.1   The changing legal landscape

at outsourcing as a way of meeting current library provision issues of cost saving while offering 'service improvement' and avoiding library closure.

Several authorities have announced they are considering outsourcing some part of their library services, although very few are currently running as fully outsourced contracts.

JARGON BUSTER – OUTSOURCING OPTIONS AND TERMS

As outsourcing has grown as an industry and continues to find new modes of existence, so the vocabulary around it has evolved. Before we look at the business drivers and what is involved, it might be helpful to define some key words or phrases which are used or have been coined during this evolution:

Outsource – outsourcing is where any task, operation, job or process that could be performed by employees within an organization is instead contracted to a third party for a significant period of time. Using temporary workers to cover a post is not a form of outsourcing.

The functions that are performed by the third party can be performed on-site or off-site, onshore, near-shore or offshore.

Backshore – using an existing, lower cost office of an organization to provide the majority of the back office services.

Captive – a wholly owned operation or subsidiary, not servicing other clients.

Near-shore or near-sourcing – the transfer of business to companies in a nearby country, often sharing a border with your own country.

Offshore – offshore outsourcing is where a company outsources services to a third party in a country other than the one in which the client company is based, primarily to take advantage of lower labour and location costs.

Onshore or domestic outsourcing – where the work is carried out by a third party but it is carried out within the same country as the organization outsourcing the work.

BPO – Business Process Outsourcing – is the outsourcing of a specific business process task, such as payroll. It's often divided into two categories: back office outsourcing, which includes internal business functions such as billing or purchasing, and front office outsourcing, which includes customer-related services such as marketing or technical support.

ITO – Information Technology Outsourcing is a subset of business process outsourcing.

KPO – Knowledge Process Outsourcing involves processes that demand advanced research and analytical, technical and decision-making skills. Less mature than the BPO industry, sample KPO work includes pharmaceutical research and development, data mining and patent research.

SLA – Service Level Agreement is a contract between a service provider and a customer that specifies, usually in measurable terms, what services will be supplied. Service levels are determined at the beginning of any outsourcing relationship and are used to measure and monitor a supplier's performance.

Critical SLA – this refers to certain SLAs that will normally determine how well (or badly) a service is being provided, and for which a financial penalty will be charged if those SLAs fall below a certain level in any given period.

Shared Service – is where an outsourcing provider is using the same facility/team to service a number of different clients. This is usually at a lower cost than a dedicated or a hybrid service.

Dedicated – the outsourced staff work only for one client. This is the most expensive form of outsourcing, as it cannot take full advantage of the economies of scale. Cost savings may be provided by low cost locations or improved processes.

Hybrid – in a hybrid model, unlike the full shared model, the 'hybrid' team are limited in what work they can carry out for other clients. This model will have some of the benefits of a shared team, and will be able to utilize a shared team for certain tasks, but will also have some of the benefits of a dedicated team, often in terms of compliance and confidentiality.

THE BUSINESS CASE

Key business drivers for outsourcing can include a variety of factors. It is important to understand what the key factors for your organization might be, as that will affect the set-up and structure of any outsourcing solution, as well as helping your understanding of why outsourcing may be considered.

Controlling Costs

One key business driver for outsourcing is to control costs. Outsourcing support services allows law firms, for example, to concentrate on their fee-earning practice, while delegating the running and cost reduction of their crucial support services to an expert organization.

All organizations will generally be faced with increasing overheads; the cost of people, the costs of maintaining office space in expensive locations, the need for improved systems, information technology, insurance, disaster planning and so on, meaning that to remain competitive, or in the case of public and academic libraries to fulfill their authorities' requirements, an organization needs to look at how they can achieve these goals while reducing their costs.

In recent years law firms have taken up various outsourcing models; some firms have utilized BPO specialists such as Integreon, Evalueserve, Accenture, other firms have centralized their non-core support functions in lower cost locations, such as Allen & Overy utilizing Northern Ireland, while Clifford Chance built a base in India. Each approach will have varying cost models, and benefits. Building a fully 'captive' centre may not be economic for anything but the larger firms, opening the market for 'shared services' offered by BPO and LPO companies.

A Legal Week Benchmarking survey in May 2011, found that only 14.6 per cent of private practices are currently using LPO as a way of cost cutting, even though a majority of those firms agreed that they were under pressure to reduce their costs. However 17.1 per cent of those private practices surveyed were utilizing BPO.

In-house lawyers were somewhat higher in their adoption of LPO at 16.9 per cent.[1]

A recent CILIP seminar reiterated that public libraries are facing the need to make savings of anything from 25 per cent to 50 per cent of current expenditure. The creative thinking to resolve this includes everything, from public libraries with geographical proximity working together to explore viable options for sharing services, including established services such as the national online reference service; 'Enquire' created in 1997 where authorities share the staffing requirements and for a small fee benefit from the shared full-time enquiry service; through to the tendering process being run at Slough Borough Council to find a strategic partner to work with the council to run their library service.

Whatever the solution there was a need to quantify and analyse services in much the same way as commercial law libraries have.

Maximizing Efficiency

The law firm model of legal services itself can be viewed as one of the oldest forms of outsourcing, going back hundreds of years; legal partnerships provide specialist legal advice for corporate and private clients. The business case here is to outsource specific processes to specialist providers, enabling firms to improve efficiency by gaining access to the experience and expertise of outsourcing partners – in the original law firm model, experienced lawyers who carry out legal transactions on behalf of a number of different clients.

With BPO, outsourcing services such as IT support allows organizations to gain flexibility and expertise according to the organization's own business requirements, everything from document creation, document management systems, data storage, system maintenance, e-mail support, archiving and the overall disaster recovery systems.

Within information services the same arguments apply, with organizations able to tap into expertise and capability as and when it is needed. Within a professional services provider there are bigger teams of professionally qualified and experienced staff, trained both internally and externally. A larger team exists to share and develop expertise to deal with difficult enquiries or handle peaks of demand.

The provider may have better enquiry logging systems, methodology or overall learning, and they will certainly be able to provide detailed metrics about the service, how it is used and how well it performs.

When looking at the cost and effectiveness of library services, metrics of usage, spend, performance and value are important measures to capture. Outsourced services will always have to provide such metrics and they are something worth capturing whatever your organization is thinking of doing, as they can be used in any discussion/analysis and help to quantify the value of your library.

The law firm or organization outsourcing their support service will also gain relative flexibility. As the organization grows and develops, the requirements for support in different geographic regions or specialist topic areas will change. Rather than having to fund the employment and location of additional staff in new offices, or the recruitment and training of new skill sets, the onus is on the outsourcing supplier to provide the additional expertise and geographic cover – for a price.

Economies of Scale

Large and small firms will derive some different benefits from outsourcing. When a smaller firm outsources support functions to a specialist outsourcing company, they can benefit from the economies of scale provided by that company. That can include available skill sets, training opportunities, cost sharing of systems and knowledge of processes.

Consolidation may be the benefit to the larger or global company, with the economy and skill set maximization that this will bring.

Innovation

As well as potentially gaining a more experienced and well-trained work force, companies increasingly use external knowledge service providers to supplement limited in-house capacity for product innovation. Learning and know how gathered from servicing a number of clients can spur innovation for other clients.

OUTSOURCING STRATEGY

To effectively develop an outsourcing strategy, there must be a business case that supports this strategy, including details of all of the financials that would be involved, costs as well as savings, and this strategy must align with the organization's objectives.

Outsourcing is part of the business toolkit and to be used effectively it is important to understand the business drivers as well as the practical details of the tasks and services concerned for that particular department, to successfully implement this tool.

To understand whether outsourcing is suitable for all or any part of a service, and in what form, it pays to give careful consideration to the many different tasks which currently make up that service.

ANALYSING THE SERVICE – PREPARING TO OUTSOURCE

This section looks at the practical steps you may wish to take in preparation for outsourcing a legal library (whether in part or in whole). It will be of course be of most relevance if there are existing plans to outsource, but even if outsourcing is just a concept occasionally mooted, you may find it helpful to review the steps below as a quick hygiene check for your library service or in preparation for discussion about the feasibility (or otherwise) of outsourcing.

Recognize Your Influence

It is at the beginning of any new project that you have the most amount of power to influence it, so it is now that you can exert the greatest influence over any outsourcing plans. Whether you are an information officer, or part of the management team, experienced information professionals are crucial to making these services successful.

There are many fears about the effectiveness of outsourced library services, such as confidentiality, flexibility and speed of response, quality of research, loss of competitive advantage and governance issues with regard to access to privileged information.

All of these things can be worked out in a well-planned service, and again this is why experienced information professionals are crucial to carefully plan the outsourced service. However confident you feel, reflect upon how you can positively influence and create the best service going forwards.

Identifying Your Services

So what do you do as a legal librarian? What services do you provide to your end-users? This next step is about listing out all the activities that you and your team are involved in. Once you have your list drawn up, you will be in a much better position to reflect on the value of the activities to your client and how they might be tweaked or radically changed to enhance their value. From this vantage point, you can also assess what activities could be outsourced, how they should be outsourced and who is best placed to do them.

It may feel pretty obvious to you what your service is all about. However, this is about expressing your value as a service to people who sit outside your specialist function. The modesty and professionalism of legal librarians often mean that they are the last people to shout about what they do. The irony of providing a seamless service, combined with a disinclination to draw attention to your work, is that your service may be undervalued by its end-users. So, this is your chance to rectify that.

As a starting point for your list, look at any existing materials that already document your services, for example on an intranet page, in a flyer or within induction packs. These probably list out the more tangible areas of your service, for example providing an enquiries service, setting up news alerts and training on the use of electronic resources. However, it is also vital to capture the activities which may go unseen by end-users, such as the administration involved when new joiners arrive, the tasks involved in arranging a purchase order and settling invoices, coding to budgets or the work involved in maintaining intranet pages for knowledge or service updates. If possible, ask everyone in your team to list out what they do, whether on a regular, ad hoc or annual basis, so you end up with a comprehensive list of activities. Include all those weird and wonderful historical activities that have somehow found a home with the library, but which you might not strictly categorize as a librarian's job.

Once you have your list, try and group the separate activities into discrete services. The following list of services and activities is provided as a prompt for your own list, but is certainly not exhaustive:

- Information enquiries service
- Legal information research
- Business information research
- Acquisition of new hard copy materials
- Provision of existing hard copy materials (for example lending, stock-taking, loose-leafing)
- Acquisition of new electronic resources
- Negotiation of contracts and subscriptions
- Maintenance of existing electronic resources
- Training of new joiners and trainees
- Regular training to legal teams
- Setting and managing the library budget
- Provision of current awareness or a press alert service
- Maintenance of knowledge systems or intranet pages
- General library service management, for example management reporting, participation in business services or legal team meetings and forums
- Services that you have inherited, which may not strictly be generic 'library' services, for example managing professional subscriptions, fielding non-directed calls from external clients, precedent updating.

Defining the Value of Your Services

Now that you have a list of all the services that you provide, you can begin to define exactly what value each of those services brings to your end-users. If you can appreciate and express the value you bring as a law librarian, it is more likely that your end-users will understand and value your services too.

As a helpful way of defining the value of your service, try to articulate its purpose: why do you provide this service, what is the point of it, how does it enable the end-user to do their job, how does it help the end-user create value? If you are unable to put your finger on the purpose of some activities, you may need to question why you are doing them.

It can also be helpful to grade these activities according to the key concerns that you face. This could be concerns of confidentiality, competitive advantage, quality or speed of service. Plotting tasks on a graph to capture where they fall with regard to these concerns can help decisions on whether the tasks are suitable for outsourcing.

Match Your Services to the Right Skills

If there are just a couple of librarians in your team, it is likely that you will share many of the activities you have listed out. However, if you are looking to outsource any or all of the law library services, it is worth being clear about exactly *who* should undertake these activities: what type of qualifications do they need, what level do they need to be qualified to, how deep does their understanding of the end-user need to be, what technical skills are prerequisites of the job? For example, you might end up identifying that 10 per cent of activities must be carried out by a senior law librarian, 30 per cent of activities must be carried out by a qualified law librarian, 25 per cent of activities require an administrator with some experience of working in a law library, 20 per cent of activities could be carried out by a graduate of any discipline and 15 per cent are suited to someone with strong IT or financial skills.

You can now use this analysis to ensure that any service or activities undertaken by an outsourcing provider are matched against the right level of knowledge and skills. Once an outsourcing arrangement is in place, it also gives both parties a clear historical point of reference should any of the activities increase or decrease in complexity (which might then necessitate a conversation about cost of service). It is also clear that if this provider has a much larger pool of professionals and experienced administrative assistants than your function can justify, the potential for you and the team to specialize on the core activities where you create maximum value becomes greater. The benefit of scale that an outsourcer can provide thereby improves development opportunities for individuals on both sides of the arrangement.

Assess the Implications and Opportunities of Geography

It may be that most of your services are provided from one location, with perhaps a few satellite libraries if your firm or organization has a wider geographic presence. This does not mean that every activity has to be continued from these locations.

Look back over the list of services and activities you have identified and consider whether it is imperative that any activities are undertaken in a specific location. Be clear about *why* it is important for these activities to be conducted in these locations.

If plans are already afoot to outsource some or all of the library services, find out which locations your outsourcing provider delivers from. You may find that by accident of geography (for example you have a satellite library in Leeds and the outsourcing provider also has an office in Leeds), you can benefit from the provider's wider reach.

With increasing use of electronic databases as central and dominant information resources, and with the permeation of IT generally as a means for delivering a law library service, there are many activities which could be undertaken remotely. Many outsourcing providers have an 'offshore' presence and it is worth thinking seriously about whether any of the activities could reasonably be undertaken in the offshore locations offered by the provider.

Of course there are various restrictions around the remote delivery of work. These should be reviewed, alongside all the considerations for outsourcing work generally. Some of the issues you may have to consider include:

- *Compliance with the SRA's Outcome 7.10*: the new SRA Handbook came into effect on the 6th October 2011. It applies to all types of firms regulated by the SRA, so that clients of all such firms receive the same level of protection. Typically this will require specific wording to be included within the contract.
- *Protection of client confidentiality*: for example careful planning of workflow within shared services, decisions on use of email domains and storage of data.
- *Compliance with the Data Protection Act*: use and storage of data.
- *Restrictions on your licences with suppliers*: if a third party is to use the organization's online licences on behalf of that organization, this will need to be negotiated with the database providers, and contractual amendments agreed.

Making Your Service More Efficient

One of the benefits of stepping back to review all the activities that your team is involved in is that you find it easier to spot wasteful activities: there may be some which are unnecessarily time-consuming, some which waste paper, others which waste people's time and talents, others which are just surplus to your end-user's needs. The work you have already done to identify the purpose of your services should help you focus on what you are aiming to achieve through the service.

You may now find yourself considering new and improved ways of delivering them. Or you might conclude that some services or activities are too far removed from the value that you bring and are better suited to other functions, for example marketing, finance or hospitality, and warrant a conversation with the heads of those departments.

Quantifying Your Services: The Baseline

This next step is about assessing the frequency and complexity of your services and how long it takes to provide them. This might sound excessively detailed and you may be tempted to leave this until things have settled down with any outsourcing arrangement. However, this kind of data gives you and the outsourcing provider a very clear understanding of what you are expecting them to deliver. Without knowing how many enquiries you receive each month, how can the provider ensure there are sufficient numbers of staff on board to manage your requirements? If the outsourcing provider tells you that the volume of press alerts they are providing to your organization has increased significantly, how do you know what they were before?

Questions of quantity you may encounter include: how many press alerts does your team deal with in one month, how long do you spend on looseleaf updating each quarter, how many bulletins do you produce and how long do they each take to produce, how much time is taken up each year with budgeting, how many hard copy acquisitions do you make each month, how much time is spent each month contributing to meetings with other functions, how many journals does the team catalogue and circulate each month? Also ask what level of experience is needed to do each of these tasks.

Clearly, there are some activities which are seasonal, such as training. In these cases, you can just extend your time frame, for example to a quarterly or half-yearly view. Some activities are easier to pin down than others. However, where any activities may come under the outsourcing spotlight, it is worth having a go at quantifying them. It will save you time and effort in the long run.

Sharing Your Knowledge: Documenting Processes

As a team, you probably regularly share knowledge about how to do various activities. It might be that you are a long-serving employee and hold a tremendous amount of vital, tacit knowledge in your head about the service. If someone new joins the team, there is usually another person on hand to provide initial training and then be available for any further coaching or questions. Outsourcing arrangements shake this up if the people doing some of the work are located in a separate location to you. With physical distance, the process necessarily becomes more formalized. This means you have to document how you do things.

You have already grouped activities into various services. Now identify those activities which are likely to be part of the outsourcing arrangement and create a 'how to' or process document. It is helpful to have a high-level view of the process involved, perhaps using a process flow chart. However, it is even more crucial that you document each individual step involved in delivering a particular service. Go into as much detail as you think appropriate – you may be surprised how complex your routine tasks are.

Be clear in the process document about who the end-user for each process is and what the 'end product' consists of, for example is it a newly acquired book reaching its requester, a legislation update reaching its reader, or library shelves being ordered and clean? Also document what resources you need to create the product and which other parties play a part in creating it, whether internal functions like IT and HR or external suppliers.

As you compile this 'handbook' to the service, it is also helpful to supplement it with best practice, tips and advice, for example setting out the search string you use for specific press alerts, advising for or against specific sources, highlighting shortcuts around a specific database, giving contact details of individuals for recharging.

If you regularly provide any research or current awareness bulletins, you will no doubt be using a template of some kind. Review these and consider whether any additional formatting guidance is required that you may need to share with an outsourcing provider.

You should now have most of the facts about your service at your fingertips and be in a good position to assess the optimum outsourcing model for your service.

CHOICE OF OUTSOURCING MODEL

There are various models to consider when outsourcing a legal library, and then within that model the suitability of location needs to be considered. The overall strategy in terms of whether the solution is a wholly owned captive or a partnership with an outsourcing provider may already have been taken by the organization. In the second section of the chapter we looked at some of the models and locations involved in typical outsourcing contracts.

For legal libraries, the main models are:

- *Shared Service* – where an outsourcing provider is using the same facility/team to service a number of different clients. This is usually at a lower cost than a dedicated or a hybrid service.

- *Dedicated* – the outsourced staff work only for one client. This is the most expensive form of outsourcing, as it cannot take full advantage of the economies of scale. All captive solutions are dedicated. Contracts to provide dedicated services can then be any combination of on-site, onshore, offshore and so on.
- *Hybrid* – a hybrid model is a mixture of shared and dedicated services. Unlike the full shared model, the 'hybrid' team are limited in what work they can carry out for other clients. This model will have some of the benefits of a shared team, and will be able to utilize a shared team for certain tasks, but will have some of the benefits of a dedicated team, often in terms of compliance and confidentiality.

A Shared Model

This model will normally provide the best cost benefit and most flexibility of service for the client.

The shared model utilizes a 'shared' service, consisting of a central team with professional expertise. A cost reduction is gained by sharing the cost of running an experienced team, and most of the team will be remotely based, with some onsite presence.

Typically there will be a clearly articulated workflow, with checks and measures to ensure confidentiality and competitive advantage are maintained for the clients. This will involve 'gatekeeper' vetting of enquiries received from clients, and strict controls on how work is allocated within the team to avoid conflict of interest for the clients concerned.

Storage of data should also be carefully analysed, including which domain information is stored on, the client's domain or that of the outsourced service provider.

Shared services must have clear policies, procedures, compliance and workflow.

A Dedicated Model

This model is the most expensive, but probably presents the least change to the way that the organization works.

Dedicated teams may be entirely on-site within the client, or may have any mixture of remote locations, onshore, offshore, near-shore, but they will only carry out work for the one client.

Although confidentiality may be easier to handle, strict policies, compliance, data protection and workflow must be carried out, as the employees still work for an outside company.

A Hybrid Model

The hybrid model, like the shared model, is reliant upon a 'gatekeeper' function, monitoring and allocating work across the team to safeguard confidentiality.

Unlike the full shared model, the 'hybrid' team are then limited in what work they can carry out for other clients. The end result being that access to the confidential know how for one client can only be utilized by the relevant hybrid team, and not by staff working on other client accounts.

Shared work that can be carried out by the wider shared team would be work without any sensitivity, and would include searching commercial databases for specific item requests (a copy of xyz cases, or specific legislation), much of the typical library 'information retrieval'.

Only the vetting procedure and then the work involving the utilization of client data and know how generation are at a dedicated level. The following flow chart (Figure 13.2) shows the basic steps.

Figure 13.2   A hybrid service

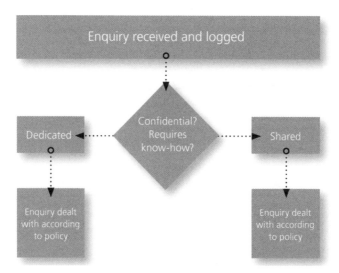

INFLUENCING OUTSOURCING AGREEMENTS

When putting together outsourcing agreements, some mechanism to ensure the best service is maintained at the best cost and speed is crucial. Such mechanisms will include Service Level Agreements (SLA), benefit sharing mechanisms such as gainshare, as well as incentives for innovation and service development.

Service Level Agreements should be both qualitative and quantitative, which can be quite difficult to achieve. They should cover the speed *and* quality of the work carried out, but the quality is very difficult to measure and can be very subjective.

For example, if a trainee asks for a case that covers a certain issue, and such a case does not exist, the client (the trainee) may give a low-quality mark for that piece of work, despite the work being done well and accurately. In some cases the response rates can be low as busy people do not always have time to respond to feedback requests or feel the need to do so. Surveys or quick 'voting buttons' to feedback on how a piece of work was done can be useful in these instances.

There is no replacement for face-to-face feedback, and it is important to continue presence at key organization meetings, for example at practice team meetings within law firms to gauge how well the service is performing.

Training and development for the outsourced library team is also essential, this can actually be easier within an outsourced service provider, with more opportunities to learn from peers, and perhaps more regular training within a larger team. Systems have to be developed and altered as each new client requirement comes along, making the work both interesting and challenging.

Typical SLAs will include the time taken to carry out an activity, which is why it can be important to measure how long such activities take before outsourcing was carried out, as a benchmark of reasonable performance.

It is important to identify some 'key' SLAs that would indicate how well the service is running. These SLAs can then be defined as 'critical' SLAs, which can incur penalty costs if they are not reached.

Relationships with suppliers are important throughout this process, and it is important to keep your suppliers informed of the change in service. If a third party is contracted to carry out enquiries for an organization, agreement must be reached with suppliers for that third party to utilize the organization's contracts on behalf of the client.

It is rare to have licences within the outsourcing organization, as information 'broker' licences are expensive and difficult to police.

Gainshare is a mechanism to incentivize third parties to continue to work on obtaining the best contracts, licences and purchase costs for their client. Typically the outsourcing agency will have agreed with the client a 'share' of any price reduction gained by the outsourcing agency on behalf of the client, sharing the benefit.

Contract

In a world where you and your end-user belong to the same organization, there is a good amount of assumed trust and common purpose. However, when any activities are moved outside the boundaries and remit of your organization, a carefully constructed contract should be used to embed controls into the agreement.

Time should always be spent on making sure that the contract accurately reflects the service required. Assumptions should always be qualified, and appendices can be lengthy in order to do this. Think of the future of the service required, how things may go wrong, how to protect your organization from risk and how to get the best out of any partnership with a supplier.

The best service is often gained when the relationship is a partnership with the outsourcing provider, rather than a 'vendor' or 'supplier' relationship, where time and quality can be compromised by unnecessary and often meaningless reporting and penalties.

Finally, the relationship with and choice of supplier is crucial, and should be managed carefully but all outsourced solutions should have an exit strategy.

Governance

It is important to have a clear understanding of governance for any outsourcing agreement. What are the reporting lines, who are the responsible parties within the client, what are the reporting requirements? Change processes will need to be in place for either party to put forward change requests for the way that the services are provided; resource levels, price changes, changing locations and any other eventuality.

Pricing

There are various ways to structure pricing within an outsourcing contract, including:

Unit or transactional pricing: the vendor determines a set rate for a particular level of service, and the client pays based on its usage of that service. This transactional pricing can provide a good incentive to the outsourcing provider to improve their services, making them more efficient, and also to innovate and provide a good quality service – encouraging more use of that service.

Fixed pricing: the customer pays a flat rate for services. Paying a fixed priced for outsourced services can look beneficial to customers at first because costs are predictable, however most fixed price contracts will have an 'uplift' clause, so that increases in work levels can be met by increases in the price of the contract. This is sensible for the outsourcing providers who will have to continue to meet service levels, whilst managing the increased work and therefore may need to obtain additional resources to do so. However, is there also a reduction in fixed price contract costs if work levels drop?

Finally, is there a good incentive for the outsourcing provider to become more efficient, to suggest innovations and to produce cost savings?

Variable pricing: this means that the customer pays a fixed price at the low end of a supplier's provided service, but allows for some variance in pricing based on providing higher levels of services.

Cost-plus: the contract is written so that the client pays the supplier for its actual costs, plus a predetermined percentage for profit. Such a pricing plan does not allow for flexibility as business objectives or technologies change, and it provides little incentive for a supplier to perform effectively.

Performance-based pricing: at the opposite end of the spectrum from cost-plus pricing, a buyer provides financial incentives that encourages the supplier to perform optimally. Conversely, this type of pricing plan requires suppliers to pay a penalty for unsatisfactory service levels. This can be difficult to implement effectively, but is becoming more popular among IT outsourcing customers who have been dissatisfied with performance in their previous forays into outsourcing.

Risk/reward sharing: with this kind of arrangement, the customer and vendor each have some benefit to improving service and innovating. The buyer and supplier each have an amount of money at risk, and each stands to gain a percentage of the profits if the supplier's performance is optimum and meets the buyer's objectives.

The buyer will select a supplier using a pricing model that best fits the business objectives the buyer is trying to accomplish by outsourcing. Whatever the pricing model, there is a need to consider the longer term implications of outsourcing. First year savings tend to be lower than projected because of implementation costs, TUPE and so on. An overview should include the longer term savings in year two or three and beyond.

CONCLUSION

Outsourcing as a business tool is being explored by a range of legal library organizations; it may not be suitable in every case and will always need to be carefully planned and organized.

The transfer of tasks to external third party organizations involves both risk and opportunity unique to that service, all of which have to be clearly understood and evaluated. When the right combination of process, service, pricing, location, provider, governance and quality is put in place as part of a planned change programme, outsourcing can provide many benefits. However if the main purpose of the service is compromised by lack of planning and judgment for the elements discussed here, then outsourcing may not work so well.

This was highlighted in the last ten years, when some high-profile call centres in the banking and finance sector were moved back onshore, because there had not been a full understanding of the service required by users. Public perception of outsourcing was adversely affected by such instances, and now 'outsourcing' is frequently associated with jobs being moved to India. A blended solution to outsourcing is far more effective, utilizing the best format, location and model for each individual service.

The key to successful outsourcing is to achieve a seamless interface between the client and the outsourcing provider. The users should experience as good a service or better than was previously provided, not encounter new barriers such as forms to fill in and restricted or non-intuitive access to the service. To achieve this, the expertise of information professionals at every level will be essential.

NOTE

1 'Send it out – senior private practice and in-house lawyers on outsourcing trends', *Legal Week Intelligence, Legal Briefing, Legal Week Benchmarker – Outsourcing*, May 2011.

CHAPTER 14

THE LEGAL SERVICES ACT

AMANDA McKENZIE

INTRODUCTION

The Legal Services Act 2007 (the Act) heralded one of the biggest shake-ups of the legal profession in its history. The Act was already beginning to impact on law firms, with the big law firms thinking ahead on how to become more competitive, but with the onset of the worst global recession since the Great Depression, the changes to legal aid and conditional fee arrangements, it meant that, for many lawyers, it was not just a matter of how to become more competitive and meet the challenges that could be presented by the Act, but of how to survive. Efficiency, fee flexibility, client service and regulation have jumped up the agenda for legal organizations and preparations have already been made to embrace or, as some may see it, withstand the impact of the Act. For some it has simply been a waiting game or a possible 'head in the sand' game but for many it has been a time to contemplate a very different future legal market.

THE LEGAL SERVICES ACT 2007 AND WHAT IT MEANS

The Legal Services Act 2007 received Royal Assent on 30 October 2007 following recommendations in Sir David Clementi's *Review of the Regulatory Framework for Legal Services in England and Wales*. It was introduced to reform the regulation of legal services in England and Wales, to liberalize the market, increase competition, protect consumers, increase access to justice and provide common standards across the profession. It was given the name 'Tesco Law' by the media to reflect the view that supermarkets could be offering legal services and that the provision of legal advice could potentially be no different to purchasing a tin of beans.

It only relates to the Scottish legal system in regard to legal aid and the setting up of the Scottish Legal Complaints Commission under the Legal Profession and Legal Aid (Scotland) Act 2007, but the Scottish Parliament passed their own legislation under the Legal Services (Scotland) Act 2010 which allows for similar, although not exactly the same, liberalization by the creation of alternative business structures (ABSs) which will allow external investors to take up to 49 per cent of ownership of the country's law firms. The Legal Services Bill (Scotland) was passed by the Scottish Parliament on 6 October 2010 requiring a majority share of 51 per cent to be owned by solicitors and other regulated professionals. It did not initially have the support of the Law Society of Scotland although there was a narrowly won referendum in favour of ABSs in April 2010. Members at the time also voted in favour of the Law Society of Scotland becoming an approved regulator if ABSs were introduced. The Scottish Government will be responsible for approving and licensing approved regulators who will in turn be responsible for licensing and regulating legal providers. The Legal Services (Scotland) Act 2010 also deals with regulatory objectives and professional principles, changes in the governance of the Law Society of Scotland, statutory codification of the regulation of the Faculty of Advocates, a regulatory framework for the Scottish Legal Complaints Commission and a new scheme for the regulation of non-lawyer will writers. At the beginning of 2011 the Scottish Government conducted a consultation on ownership and control of firms providing legal advice[1] and in May 2012 regulations were set before Parliament to permit the creation of ABSs which are also known as licensed legal services providers.

There also seems to be some appetite overseas for consideration of change in the structure of legal organizations.

In Ireland there was a review of the legal profession with the introduction of the Legal Services Regulation Bill 2011 which followed on from a study published by Anne Neary Consultants coming out of the International Monetary Fund's recommendations after the financial services bail out. The Bill will look at, amongst other areas, alternative business structures, the splitting of regulatory and representative bodies and the monopoly on legal training, but there does appear to be some strong opposition to some aspects of the Bill. A Ministry of Justice representative stated that: 'The Legal Services Bill 2011, in respect of which substantial work has been undertaken, is currently being developed and finalized in consultation with the Office of the Attorney General. It is a specific national commitment under the EU/IMF structural reform programme aimed at modernising the provision of legal services, reducing legal costs and supporting national competitiveness and economic recovery'.[2] The Bill has been heavily criticized by interested parties and has been slow to progress through the Oireachtas but in July 2013 the Bill was due to return to the Justice Committee to continue its Parliamentary journey.[3]

The American Bar Association (ABA) has considered the inclusion of non-lawyers in US law firms.[4] In April 2011 the ABA Commission on Ethics launched a consultation seeking feedback on three forms of ABSs for the US legal market which would include LDPs but would not include the ability to have external investment or be able to float. However in March 2012 the New York State Bar's committee on ethics announced that New York lawyers would be banned from running a New York office of a UK ABS with non-lawyer owners.

Back in 2004 an Australian law firm, Slater & Gordon, became the first to float on the Stock Exchange due to the changes to the profession brought about by the Legal Profession Act 2004, which governed legal practice for lawyers in the state of Victoria and allowed firms to become incorporated legal practices. Many states quickly followed suit allowing non-lawyers to become partners, directors or owners of a legal practice.

Meanwhile back in England and Wales, the Legal Services Act's main measures included the creation of the Legal Services Board (LSB)[5] which acts as a single supervisory body and oversees the eight bodies who are approved regulators named under the Act,[6] and the creation of the Office for Legal Complaints[7] (OLC) which acts as a single point for legal complaints, with the setting up of an ombudsman service to resolve disputes. The Act ensured that professional bodies separated their regulatory and representative functions, which meant that, for example, the Law Society is now the representative body of the solicitors' profession and the Solicitors Regulation Authority[8] (SRA) is the regulatory body. The Act allowed for the creation of alternative business structures (ABSs) which enables outside investment and non-lawyers to form partnerships with lawyers as legal disciplinary practices (LDPs). There is also set out in the Act statutory obligations and objectives for all regulatory bodies.

THE LEGAL SERVICES BOARD

The LSB is an independent body responsible for overseeing the regulation of lawyers in England and Wales. Its Chair and members are appointed by the Lord Chancellor and it became fully operational on 1 January 2010. It shares regulation with the approved regulators who have responsibility for the day-to-day regulation of the different professions. It has statutory powers and duties which include authorizing approved regulators and directing changes or sanctions if required. It also has the power to authorize ABSs and approve professional rule changes if necessary.

It has a role in commissioning, monitoring and investing in research into the legal services market, plus recommending to the Lord Chancellor which services should be reserved services and therefore compulsorily regulated, that is, activities which regulated lawyers need to be authorized to undertake.

These reserved activities are: the exercise of a right of audience; the conduct of litigation; reserved instrument activities; probate activities; notarial activities; and the activities of oaths. The Legal Services Institute (LSI) offered to consider the history of these reserved activities in order for the LSB to form an opinion on future reservation or reform.[9] The LSI found no coherent reasoning behind the reservation of these particular six areas although there seemed to be some history behind each individual area. Of course the significance of these reserved activities means that any reforms made by the LSB would have potentially far-reaching consequences. If an ABS provides a single reserved activity and that activity is subsequently removed the body will no longer need to be licensed as an ABS. The LSI argued that there should be a 'public interest rationale' for adding or removing reserved activities in the future. Obviously there is the argument that services such as will writing should be reserved based on protecting the consumer but it may also be argued that this goes against the liberalization of the profession and would prevent those wanting to write their own wills from buying a pack from a well-known high street retailer.

The LSB is also required to protect and promote the public interest and the interests of consumers, improve access to justice and promote and maintain adherence to professional principles.

OFFICE FOR LEGAL COMPLAINTS (OLC)

The OLC is accountable to Parliament and sponsored, via the Lord Chancellor, by the Ministry of Justice. It operates as a single gateway for complaints against all legal providers. It has a direct relationship with the LSB which will set out key performance targets, although disciplinary matters will remain with the regulatory bodies.

The OLC set up a Legal Ombudsman (LeO) service and has operated from offices based in Birmingham since October 2010. Its purpose is to ensure that consumers of legal services can access an independent and impartial ombudsman scheme to resolve disputes with lawyers of all kinds, including solicitors, barristers, licensed conveyancers and legal executives. The service is open and free to members of the public, very small businesses (less than 10 employees with a balance sheet of under £1.8m), charities, clubs and trusts. In other words the service does not really apply to the clients of large law firms despite the replaced Legal Complaints Service offering a service to all and it has been argued that this may cause confusion with some feeling obligated to tell clients about LeO despite the fact it is not really set up to assist them.[10]

The Chief Ombudsman will be able to order financial redress of up to £30,000 if lawyers are found to have provided an unsatisfactory service although there is no financial limit on interest on specified compensation for loss suffered, costs incurred by the complainant (if awarded), limiting fees to a specified amount or interest on fees to be refunded. Other actions it can take include asking for an apology, asking the party to put right any errors, omissions or deficiencies and limiting fees. If LeO considers there to have been professional misconduct then the matter can be referred to the relevant regulator.

LeO has taken two cases to court to enforce a decision against solicitors.[11] Birmingham County Court ordered the first firm to pay the ombudsman's costs of £1,215 and they paid compensation of £2,650 to the client. The second case in the same court was adjourned to allow the firm in question to comply with the ombudsman's decision to pay compensation for mismanaged real estate work. However when the firm failed to pay the compensation the ombudsman issued proceedings for the court's permission to enforce the decision as if it were a court judgment. The firm agreed to settle and pay costs after initially arguing that the decision was defective. This reiterates the point that once a determination has been accepted by a complainant then the decision of the ombudsman is binding on the parties and final, and the only recourse that would be open to the solicitor or other lawyer would be to have the process by which that decision was reached judicially reviewed. Given the cost of judicial review this is unlikely to be an option in many cases.

SOLICITORS REGULATION AUTHORITY (SRA)

The SRA is the independent regulatory body of the Law Society of England and Wales. Its role is to set standards, deal with rules and the Code of Conduct and support organizations in complying with those codes and standards. It also deals with investigations into misconduct and any subsequent enforcement. It is the Solicitors Disciplinary Tribunal, an independent statutory body, which will continue to hear cases, usually brought by the SRA. The SRA will also deal with continuing professional development, education and practising certificates. Additionally it will promote choice in legal services through various types of business structures including ABSs.

The SRA were approved as a licensing authority for ABSs by the LSB in June 2011, which was subject to Parliamentary approval. The legislative changes needed to allow the SRA to be a licensing authority involved allowing the SRA to examine spent convictions of potential ABS owners and inadequate time in the Parliamentary diary meant the 6 October 2011 target date could not be met. There was also some delay in getting agreement from the Ministry of Justice that the cost of appeals against SRA licensing decisions would not be borne by the profession. Eventually the SRA were approved and began accepting applications for ABSs in January 2012 and subsequently approved the first three applications in April 2012.

The SRA published its new Code of Conduct and Handbook in April 2011 which was formally approved, with some last minute changes, by the LSB on 17 June

2011. The new rules apply to traditional law firms, those converting to ABSs and new entrants to the market in the form of ABSs. The SRA Handbook and Code replaced the Solicitors Code of Conduct 2007, and all of its related rules and guidance which ceased to have effect after the new Handbook and Code came into force on 6 October 2011, except when the SRA reviews any conduct which took place prior to 6 October 2011.

The new Handbook is underpinned by 10 key and mandatory principles that legal professionals must adhere to:

1. uphold the rule of law and the proper administration of justice;
2. act with integrity;
3. not allow your independence to be compromised;
4. act in the best interests of each client;
5. provide a proper standard of service to your clients;
6. behave in a way that maintains the trust the public places in you and in the provision of legal services;
7. comply with your legal and regulatory obligations and deal with your regulators and ombudsmen in an open, timely and co-operative manner;
8. run your business or carry out your role in the business effectively and in accordance with proper governance and sound financial and risk management principles;
9. run your business or carry out your role in the business in a way that encourages equality of opportunity and respect for diversity;
10. protect client money and assets.[12]

This is a move away from a strict rules-based code to principles-based regulation and this is reflected in Principle 6 which states the 'provision of legal services' rather than the legal profession reflecting the introduction of ABSs which can include non-lawyers. Principles 7–10 are entirely new.

The new outcomes-focussed provisions in the Code of Conduct are supposed to show how 'the Principles apply in practice and provide clarity for consumers about the outcomes and protections they can expect'.[13] The difference between the outcomes-focussed regulation (OFR) to the previous rules-based regulation is, as the SRA states:

> *Responsibility for meeting the requirements in the Handbook, and for operating effective systems and processes, lies with you. In the SRA Code of Conduct (the Code) in particular, we have stripped out a lot of the detail of the previous Code to empower you to implement the right systems and controls for your clients and type of practice. You will have more flexibility in how you achieve the right outcomes for your clients, which will require greater judgement on your part.*

The changes are reflected not only in the new Handbook, but also in our approach to authorization, supervision and enforcement. This will be risk-based, proportionate and targeted and will involve a more open and constructive relationship between the SRA and those we regulate. Firms that are already well managed and providing a good service to their clients should have nothing to fear from this approach.[14]

The problem is potential grey areas and whether those principles are open to interpretation. A risk in one firm may not have the same outcome as in another firm. There does, it seems, need to be some cultural shift to be successful.

The Act requires ABSs to appoint a head of legal practice (HOLP) and a head of finance and administration (HOFA). The SRA stated that all practices regardless of whether they are ABSs would need to have someone assigned to these positions and have named the roles compliance officer for legal practice (COLP) and compliance officer for finance and administration (COFA). A COLP will need to be a lawyer of England and Wales (or a registered European lawyer or a European lawyer regulated by the Bar Standards Board) but a COFA need not be a lawyer but has to be an employee or manager of the organization and is of sufficient seniority and in a position of sufficient responsibility to fulfil the role. The same person could perform both roles. The compliance officers have a responsibility to ensure that the organization complies with its own compliance terms but also to record all failures and report such failures to the SRA.

A new 'suitability test' replaced the existing 'character and suitability test' and applies to all compliance officers. The main difference between the old test and the new is the widening of the types of offences that could bar an individual from working in the legal industry, with additional detail on requirements for rehabilitation. The new rules include being convicted for criminal offences involving dishonesty, fraud, perjury, bribery or racially aggravated crimes.

BAR STANDARDS BOARD (BSB)[15]

The Bar Standards Board is the independent regulatory body of the Bar Council. It sets education and training requirements for entry into the profession and deals with continuing professional development. Its role is to set standards of conduct and to promote high standards and quality of work. It investigates complaints and takes disciplinary or other appropriate action when required. The Bar Council retains overall responsibility as the approved regulator.

With the arrival of the Act the BSB made changes to the Code of Conduct, with the approval of the LSB, to allow barristers to work as managers or employees in legal disciplinary practices (LDPs) whilst retaining the ability to be self-employed and to offer services to consumers in a variety of ways, including sharing offices with others and to investigate and collate evidence and witness statements, attend police stations and produce correspondence. Barristers are allowed to be owners or managers in LDPs but need to put safeguards in place to manage conflicts of interest. In August 2011 the LSB approved proposals that were put forward by the BSB after consultation to make further changes to the Code of Conduct to allow barristers to be managers or employees or have owner interests in ABSs which are approved by other approved regulators.[16] Proposals have also been put forward to allow barristers to conduct litigation and for the BSB to regulate advocacy-focussed legal bodies, and barrister-led entities but not multi-disciplinary practices.[17] Owners of BSB regulated entities must also be managers, and there will be a 25 per cent limit on non-lawyer owners or managers of ABSs regulated by the BSB. A majority of the owner managers must be barristers or other advocates with higher rights of audience. In March 2012 the BSB launched a consultation on a new code of conduct, to be known as the BSB Handbook, which included proposals to regulate new business structures. The Handbook was launched in January 2014 following approval from the LSB with a view to the BSB being able to apply to regulate ABSs in late 2014.

LEGAL DISCIPLINARY PRACTICES (LDP)

An LDP is a recognized body, introduced by the Act from March 2009, to provide legal services. They consist of owners and managers who are not exclusively lawyers. They can include different legal professionals and up to 25 per cent non-lawyers. They are authorized by the SRA and the respective codes of conduct for solicitors and barristers were amended to reflect the changes.

Arguably the benefits of LDPs included the ability to raise equity from a variety of sources and have a breadth of service to offer the client, for example barristers, patent attorneys and so on, and to retain and reward high-performing non-lawyer employees.

A few of the top 50 UK law firms converted to LDP status, including Irwin Mitchell, Mills and Reeve and Berrymans Lace Mawer. Irwin Mitchell's finance director and costs manager both became members of the firm's equity structure[18] and Mills & Reeve added a barrister, Richard Sykes, to its partnership.[19] Berrymans Lace Mawer converted to a LDP and promoted non-lawyer Alistair Kinley to the equity partnership.[20] Interestingly, Bird & Bird decided not to convert after coming across problems in local jurisdictions when considering whether to allow lawyers in countries not recognized by the SRA into the partnership.[21] This highlights potential issues for international firms thinking of converting and trying to adhere to Bar rules in other jurisdictions. Kobre & Kim became the first US firm in London to convert to LDP status citing the fact that the firm was 'one of only a handful of international litigation firms that offers a conflict-free platform for litigation and advocacy through an integrated team of English solicitors, barristers and US qualified lawyers'.[22]

MULTI-DISCIPLINARY PRACTICES (MDPS)

The Act allows for the creation of ABSs operating as MDPs which are not subject to the same restrictions as LDPs in terms of minimum requirements relating to legally qualified persons and which permit outside ownership. There is, however, a requirement for a designated head of legal practice who is an authorized person and a head of finance and administration. In both cases there is a fit and proper person test.

ALTERNATIVE BUSINESS STRUCTURES

ABSs allow for external investment and ownership and enable different business structures for legal organizations. A law firm could accept investment from outside the partnership or could raise capital by floating on the stock market, or a non-legal organization, for example a retailer or a bank, could offer legal services to consumers.

ABSs will allow organizations to obtain external funding from a variety of sources other than the traditional bank loan, for example private equity, for greater investment in new projects such as IT, or expansion plans. It can also be argued that ABSs will open up legal services to a wider audience through channels other than law firms, for example retailers, and therefore will create greater competition and a better service for customers. This remains to be seen of course.

Those hoping that the UK's coalition Government, with Vince Cable's review of excessive regulation, would delay full implementation of the Act, including those protesting[23] against measures within the Act, were disappointed. The Ministry of Justice swiftly denied that there would be any delay and Justice Minister Jonathan Djanogly confirmed in a speech to The Law Society that the first ABSs would be up and running from October 2011.[24] Although the October date slipped, they came into existence in early 2012.

Firms could begin to consider external investment before the date of implementation but the SRA's guidance stated that they may only enter into non-binding agreements and may register company and domain names. It was found that Optima had breached this guidance by entering into an agreement with outsourcer Capita which gave Capita an option to obtain shares into the firm once ABSs came into force.[25]

The SRA has guidance available to assist those wanting to become ABSs and to understand what steps need to be taken to obtain a licence.[26]

WHAT DOES IT MEAN FOR LAWYERS AND HOW IS THE PROFESSION RESPONDING?

Barristers

The BSB proposals to be allowed to regulate advocacy-focussed legal entities and conduct litigation will arguably allow barristers to compete alongside solicitors for work in a rapidly changing landscape and offer an alternative to law firms for those who simply want a range of litigation services.

Changes were also made to Public Access which allowed greater direct access for consumers to barristers with a Public Access Directory being made available online.[27]

The BSB and Bar Council were proactive in creating model documents and guidance for barristers called ProcureCo which allows them to work together and with other professionals to obtain work by means of a procurement company.[28] The procurement company is not able to supply legal services, but can bid for work and then instruct its own panel of solicitors, rather than solicitors' instructing the Bar as at present. Although barristers have a tradition of independence, primarily because of conflicts and regulatory balances, the ProcureCo allows this model to work by going out and procuring a solution to the client's needs for legal services and then agreeing with a group of barristers that they will do the work. Barristers are then able to offer a wider range of services whilst retaining professional independence and avoiding conflicts. The ProcureCo model does provide additional mechanisms for barristers to respond to the needs of a competitive market place.

Barristers are also able to work within the traditional law firm and in February 2012 a fixed price legal services provider, Riverview Law, launched with a team of solicitors and barristers including 12 silks with a view to becoming an ABS.

Law Firms

After some enthusiasm for ABSs many law firms stepped back slightly and adopted a wait-and-see approach. Only a few of the top 100 law firms converted to LDP status and, although a survey of managing partners by Vantis found that most agreed that ABSs will be popular, not one said that they were considering it. A survey by Smith & Williamson questioning 121 law firms, including 60 of the top 100, found 20 per cent of those questioned would consider an IPO and 43 per cent would consider private equity as a means of external finance.[29]

There are many practical issues to consider for law firms, including the possibility that external investment may well mean a loss of independence, that private equity houses as external investors may want an exit strategy leaving firms vulnerable and there may be potential conflict and privilege issues. There is the additional problem for international firms of ABSs not being allowed in most jurisdictions other than Australia. The President of The Council of the Bars and Law Societies of Europe, Jose-Maria Davo Fernandez, stated that if a City law firm accepts external capital the matter will end up in the European Court of Justice.[30]

Despite the reservations of some solicitors, most are acutely aware that the legal services market has become more competitive. The response has been evident with some high-profile mergers including that of Clyde & Co with Barlow Lyde & Gilbert and Pinsent Masons with McGrigors, and in the number of firms deciding to outsource certain legal and operational functions and with the consideration and implementation of alternative billing structures.

There are those who have proactively considered the options available and personal injury specialist Plexus Law had early discussions with several private equity firms to see if such an investment could help the business. Parabis, Plexus' parent company, said that the main motivation for seeking to convert to an ABS would not be to take external capital but to allow it to form a structure that would permit non-lawyer executives to become LLP partners.[31] In August 2012 the SRA announced that Parabis was the first ABS to be backed by private equity.

Irwin Mitchell has been one of the more vocal advocates of ABSs and amended its management structure, splitting the business into a limited liability partnership and a separate holding company and appointed a new board to manage both parts of the firm in preparation for conversation. They became an ABS in August 2012 and were the first law firm to be granted multiple licences by the SRA.

Despite the 'Tesco law' tag being adopted for the Act, Tesco has shown little appetite to date and it does seem that most non-law organizations would initially only consider taking on high-volume legal work like personal injury or conveyancing. The Co-operative recently launched a high-profile campaign to promote its legal services to shoppers in its stores[32] and this may be a warning shot to high street law firms that they need to respond in order to compete. The Co-operative was the first announced ABS from the SRA.

There are some on the high street who have already responded and this includes an online residential conveyancing service called In-Deed, which involves a number of law firms doing conveyancing work, and which allows those buying a house to track the progress from instruction to completion,[33] and a grouping of 150 smaller law firms acting under the QualitySolicitors umbrella brand had agreed a deal with WH Smith to create legal access points in their stores.[34] This has recently come to an end and been replaced with an agreement with LegalZoom.[35] One law firm, Freeman Harris, which is part of the Quality Solicitors network has opened a 'shop' in Lewisham Shopping Centre in London.[36] They open during the week and on Saturdays and represent a huge shift towards lawyers being more accessible and marketing themselves in the wake of competition from the likes of the Co-operative.

Although it could be argued that the large commercial law firms will not feel the impact of ABSs in the same way as the smaller law firms or those doing more commoditized legal work, and many may not need the external investment, it would be remiss of them not to start thinking about the implications. If a large bank decides to deliver legal services, the cross-selling potential is huge, allowing it in turn to compete against the larger law firms with access to greater advertising and client development models. Many of the larger law firms are already failing to take advantage of marketing and networking opportunities through social media. The social media site Klout identified QualitySolicitors as having the most influential online presence.[37]

With the arrival of outcomes-focussed regulation, law firms will have had to start looking at their compliance departments. The SRA is putting the emphasis on the profession to proactively review their business models and risks and to choose models to minimize or manage risks. In such an environment the firm will have to plan ahead, assess risks, write policies identifying risks and develop policies on how to react and manage those risks. It is a risk model which aims to highlight issues before they become problems. One indicator of risk in regard to financial health is whether or not a firm has been put into the assigned risks pool (ARP) because it has failed to obtain professional indemnity insurance on the open market and this will be something the SRA will be focussing on and of course something law firms will need to be clear on. There are some reservations amongst lawyers on how this new model of outcomes-focussed regulation will work in practice. Results of a Legal Week Big Question Survey in March 2011 showed that 49 per cent of respondents at that time had mixed feelings about the change with 24 per cent saying they were 'not very' supportive and around 27 per cent supporting the change. Fifty per cent of respondents said they did not understand the move or the associated changes.[38] In a Legal Business Survey 68 per cent of respondents stated they felt the SRA's move to outcomes-focussed regulation created more confusion over risk management.[39] Since these surveys, more guidance has become available from the SRA but confusion or no confusion law firms have to show they are adhering to the new regime.

Legal Education and Training

A legal education and training review in England and Wales (LETR) was set up as a joint project between the SRA, the BSB and the Institute of Legal Executives.[40]

The aims of the review were to take into account future demands on legal services with the changing environment whilst ensuring the maintenance of ethical and competence standards. It looked at the educational requirements for those entering the profession and for continuing education and the requirements on those establishments delivering the education.

The review announced its proposals in June 2013, emphasizing that a good level of education and training was already in place. The recommendations included keeping traineeships and pupillages but giving more support to the development of less traditional routes such as non-graduate apprenticeships and licensed paralegal schemes.[41]

Following the report there was some suggestion that there is an oversupply of law students which may impact on the careers of those entering the legal profession.[42]

Even before the report, the recession and the Act was impacting on law students with many large law firms opting to cut trainee numbers or trial new trainee models which include those offered by Acculaw where trainees would be recruited by Acculaw from law schools and then seconded to firms on an ad hoc basis.[43]

There also seems already to be some enthusiasm within larger law firms to support legal apprenticeship schemes with Pinsents announcing in September 2011 that it had welcomed its first batch of apprentices.[44] The scheme works to allow those wanting to enter the profession to gain some valuable work experience. There are also similar paralegal schemes with DWF launching a Paralegal Academy.[45]

WHAT DOES IT MEAN FOR INFORMATION PROFESSIONALS?

There are opportunities for information professionals with the opening up of legal services including offering consultancy services to those entering the legal market for the first time and new positions becoming available with the creation of information and knowledge departments servicing the needs of lawyers within non-legal businesses. The legal information professional has knowledge of legal and business research, procurement and contract negotiation, budget management, information architecture, know how and knowledge management. These are skills that an organization would be dearly in need of when setting up a new legal department. Information professionals have to respond by marketing themselves in the same manner as lawyers will need to and they must market those skill sets that are required to meet the demands of the business.

Outsourcing can also create opportunities for freelancers and allow information professionals to join outsourcing companies where more expansive roles may exist. It is essential that information professionals are at the forefront of any changes and that they have considered how the Legal Services Act impacts on the business so they can prepare for any changes however difficult those changes are. The issue of outsourcing is unsettling as the face of the legal information profession changes and there is no doubt that positions have been lost due to outsourcing contracts. It is imperative that legal information professionals within any organization are involved in any outsourcing negotiations relating to information management and are aware of the consequences. There are many issues that need to be addressed when seeking to outsource information or knowledge departments which are not insurmountable but are nonetheless of huge importance and these include conflicts and confidentiality. The SRA have stated that under the new Code of Conduct Guidelines they expect firms to assess all existing outsourcing contracts to ensure they are compliant and that outsourcing companies have to meet with the SRA if requested.[46]

With the introduction of LDPs and ABSs an increased involvement at partnership or board level has become possible. With some law firms encouraging senior operational managers to enter the partnership, there is no reason why we cannot see a legal information professional becoming a partner or a manager within a law firm or within an organization offering legal services.

Despite the Act's efforts to streamline regulation there will be more for risk management and compliance professionals to deal with and there is scope for information professionals to become more involved in this area. Information professionals need to get involved in the implementation of change within their organizations.

The issue of training within the legal profession has now become prominent and this means information professionals working within the academic sector need to be aware of any changes and what this may mean for them. Hence it is equally essential that those entering the information profession be aware of the changes within the industry and where they may want to pitch their careers. BIALL and CSLIG run a joint annual Graduate Open Day which is aimed at student librarians, graduates trainees and those in their first jobs.

CONCLUSION

There is definite change afoot for the legal profession and for information professionals. It is more likely to be a slow burner than a big bang, but both those offering legal services and those working within the legal profession need to be aware and plan for the future. The legal services market is not likely to diminish and in fact it is likely to be heavily supported when it generates nearly 2 per cent of the UK's GDP and this is evident in the recent Legal Services Action Plan launched by Kenneth Clarke to promote London as the legal capital of the world.[47] However a wait-and-see approach may not be enough to allow survival for all and both legal and information professionals need to be prepared for change.

NOTES

1   http://www.scotland.gov.uk/Topics/Justice/legal/17822/10190/profession-reform-1/Bill/consultownershipcontrol

2   Harris, J. (12 September 2011), 'With wide-ranging legal reforms on the table, the Irish profession is set for a shake-up', *The Lawyer* (2011), 25(35), 30.

3   http://www.irishtimes.com/news/politics/cabinet-set-to-discuss-draft-laws-aimed-at-reducing-legal-costs-1.1456002

4   Peterson, S. (21 April 2011), 'US firms consider non-lawyer partnerships', *Legal Week*.

5   http://www.legalservicesboard.org.uk

6   The Approved Regulators are: The Law Society (through the SRA), The Bar Council, The Master of Faculties, The Institute of Legal Executives, The Council for Licensed Conveyancers, The Chartered Institute of Patent Attorneys, The Institute of Trade Marks Attorneys, The Association of Law Costs Draftsmen.

7   http://www.legalombudsman.org.uk/

8   http://www.sra.org.uk/solicitors/solicitors.page

9   Marley, O. (2011), 'Reserved legal activities: their history and future', *Legal Compliance Bulletin*, March 2011, 3–5.

10 Hill, C. (4 August 2011), 'Is anyone Listening?', *Legal Week*.

11 http://www.lawgazette.co.uk/news/leo-goes-court-enforce-decisions-against-law-firms

12 http://www.sra.org.uk/solicitors/handbook/principles/content.page

13 http://www.sra.org.uk/solicitors/freedom-in-practice/OFR/ofr-quick-guide.page?ref=search

14 http://www.sra.org.uk/solicitors/freedom-in-practice/OFR/ofr-quick-guide.page?ref=search

15 http://www.barstandardsboard.org.uk/

16 http://www.legalservicesboard.org.uk/what_we_do/regulation/pdf/20110824_barristers_in_abs_dn_final.pdf

17 http://www.barstandardsboard.org.uk/news/press/862.html

18 Ruckin, C. (27 May 2010), 'Irwin Mitchell converts to LDP status as non-lawyers join firm's equity', *Legal Week*.

19 Heine, F. (17 June 2010), 'Mills & Reeve adds barrister to partnership in LDP switch', *Legal Week*.

20 Dowell, K. (20 June 2011), 'BLM admits non-lawyer to equity in LDP conversion', *The Lawyer*.

21 Ruckin, C. (24 June 2010), 'Regulation difficulties force Bird & Bird to drop LDP plans', *Legal Week*.

22 Ruckin, C. (17 June 2010), 'US Kobre & Kim converts London arm to LDP status', *Legal Week*.

23   Croft, J., Peel, M. and Arnold, M. (22 September 2010), 'The legal sector's own Big Bang', *The Financial Times*.
24   Heine, F. (22 September 2010), 'Justice Minister Djanogly stresses commitment to ABS implementation schedule', *Legal Week*.
25   Dowell, K. (9 August 2010), 'Optima reprimanded by the SRA over Capita Investment', *The Lawyer*, 24(33), 4.
26   http://www.sra.org.uk/solicitors/freedom-in-practice/alternative-business-structures. page
27   http://www.barcouncil.org.uk/about/find-a-barrister/public-access-directory/
28   http://www.barcouncil.org.uk/assets/documents/ProcureCo%20260410.pdf
29   http://www.smith.williamson.co.uk/news/3183-1-in-5-law-firms-to-consider-an-ipo
30   Ames, J. (19 August 2010), 'Europe will block financing of law firms', *The Times*.
31   Lind, S. (14 April 2011), 'Plexus set to be one of the first major firms to convert to ABS', *Legal Week*.
32   Rothwell, R. (10 May 2010), 'Co-op launches new service for insurers', *Law Society Gazette*, http://www.lawgazette.co.uk/news/co-op-launches-new-service-insurers
33   Croft, J. (22 May 2011), 'Conveyancing site hopes to float on Aim', FT.COM, http://www.ft.com/cms/s/0/709e834a-84ad-11e0-afcb-00144feabdc0.html
34   Croft, J. (1 May 2011), 'Legal market gears up for Tesco Law', FT.COM, http://www.ft.com/cms/s/0/ed155b52-7430-11e0-b788-00144feabdc0.html#axzz1ZM4gvgW0
35   http://www.legalzoom.com
36   Croft, J. (27 March 2011), 'Lawyers "shop" is next to Poundland', FT.COM, http://cachef.ft.com/cms/s/0/77a46480-589c-11e0-9b8a-00144feab49a.html#axzz1ZMBXiwpK
37   Wozniak, V. (3 August 2011), 'Top firms losing out to upstarts in social media sphere', *The Lawyer*.
38   Lind, S. (31 March 2011), 'One in two partners lack understanding of workings of SRA's new regulatory regime', *Legal Week*.
39   McAteer, M. and Bennett-Warner, G. (2011), Moving targets, *Legal Business*, 212(March), 52–4, 56–7.
40   http://letr.org.uk/
41   http://www.sra.org.uk/sra/news/letr-report-published.page
42   http://www.thetimes.co.uk/tto/law/article3807265.ece
43   Begum, H. (19 September 2011), 'Trainees for hire: SRA backs revolutionary plan', *Legal Week*.
44   Manning, L. (27 September 2011), 'Pinsents join growing trend with launch of apprenticeship scheme', *The Lawyer*.
45   Manning, L. (23 August 2011), 'DWF launches legal apprenticeship scheme', *The Lawyer*.
46   Lind, S. (31 March 2011), 'Watchdog set to scrutinise legal outsourcing contracts', *Legal Week*.
47   http://www.justice.gov.uk/downloads/publications/corporate-reports/MoJ/legal-services-action-plan.pdf

CHAPTER 15

CASE STUDIES

CONTRIBUTORS:
DIANE RAPER
KAREN SCOTT
PENELOPE SCOTT
STEPHANIE CURRAN
KATHY TURNER
RACHEL ROBBINS
LOYITA WORLEY
NICOLA HERBERT
HEATHER SEMPLE

ACADEMIC LAW LIBRARIES

DIANE RAPER

Academic law libraries are normally part of a university library and will be very much influenced by the policies of the parent institution. The law librarian enjoys the benefit of having other professionally qualified colleagues. Only in the largest academic law libraries will there be more than one law librarian, but there will always be other professionally qualified colleagues.

The number of higher education institutions (HEI) offering qualifying law degrees giving exemption from the first stage of professional studies continued to grow in the early twenty-first century, and only with the recession in the UK have the Bar and the Law Society questioned the wisdom of allowing quite so many graduates to believe that they might enter the legal profession. Many undergraduate students will have decided to study law based on their parents' wishes and can often find the study of law at university not quite what they expected. This can provide challenges to the academic law librarian, who often shoulders the responsibility for teaching undergraduates to use legal materials. Although the Society of Legal Scholars continues to provide guidance on standards for academic law libraries (quite unique in the academic environment) encompassing both staffing and the collection itself, many HEI's have managed to ignore recommendations that an academic law collection should be staffed by at least .5 FTE librarian. Many librarians with responsibility for law will also be required to support other subject areas, often totally unrelated. Nevertheless, even though there is no career progression for most academic law librarians other than outside the legal area, many have remained as law librarians, very much thanks to the job satisfaction that can be gained from both the subject knowledge that they acquire and the imparting of research skills knowledge to generations of aspiring lawyers. Like all law librarians, their clientele have expectations that they have knowledge of a very wide area of legal resources. It should be noted that within academic libraries jobs are tied to salary scales, with none of the ability to increase remuneration that there can be in private practice. In the early twenty-first century in the UK, there is little possibility of moving beyond the five or six points of the salary scale advertised to applicants.

Academic law librarians have clearly defined job descriptions and may not need to become involved in the day-to-day running of the academic library other than to comment on policies for lending, acquisitions and cataloguing of stock. They are likely to be asked to develop the collections that they manage, advising on collection policy. Involvement of academics in selecting stock may be limited to the selections of specific course materials and the collection will often need to be expanded outside this rather narrow remit. This increasingly involves decisions as to whether the collection should run along parallel print and online resources. Many HEIs now have policies which put a preference on the sourcing of course materials in electronic format and this may still prove difficult when sourcing course books for undergraduates.

Academic law librarians will be required to design, and often deliver, training in the use of legal resource materials, often using the virtual learning environment provided by the HEI. Academic law librarians today are required to work with much larger cohorts of students than their predecessors and have to continually balance the demands of providing a level of training to all against the requirements of individual student needs.

Some HEIs offer courses for the professional stages of legal education and may set up separate (and expensive) law libraries for students on those courses. Both the Bar and the Law Society require use of both print and online sources at the professional stages of education.

Other HEIs will offer a wide variety of Master's courses to students who do not always have experience of either UK higher education or a qualifying law degree. Students on these courses require a special level of support and access to much more specialized materials than the undergraduate courses.

Providing support to any of these courses requires a clear collection development mandate. In an era when HEIs are uncertain where the funding for teaching will come from, this means that it can be challenging to provide the necessary resources within a budget that does not grow in line with the ambitions of publishers. Increasingly students and academics want to be able to access the material required for their studies from online resources and an important part of the role of the academic law librarian is to ensure that colleagues who maintain access to online resources are aware of the special needs and requirements of legal researchers. While students may long for the simplicity of a simple search facility, it is up to the academic law librarian to ensure that the requirements of accessing complex databases are provided for and that both academics and students have access to appropriate training services.

Academic law librarians often have greater involvement with academics, through involvement in the law school than many of their librarian colleagues with other subject responsibilities. Inevitably it is the course and module convenors who will have most influence over which legal resources are used and it is important for academic law librarians to ensure that training is offered to academic staff in an appropriate format as well as to students.

FREELANCE LEGAL INFORMATION PROFESSIONALS

KAREN SCOTT

INTRODUCTION

Freelance legal information specialists play an important role in supporting legal work in a wide range of organizations. This case study describes what is involved in being a freelancer, and how an effective freelancer will typically approach their role. It is based on the author's experience over 21 years, both in commercial law firms and the internal legal departments of other organizations

WHAT DO FIRMS WANT FROM A FREELANCER?

Firms use freelancers for a range of reasons. Usually the firm will have information resources which need managing, but cannot justify employing a full-time professional. However larger firms also use freelancers, for example to cover for maternity leave or while recruiting permanent staff. As the BIALL website has it[1]: 'Freelance law librarians … are a pretty disparate group …' The library might be anything from a collection of books and journals to a well-developed, comprehensive, high-profile support function. Firms will therefore expect a freelancer to have solid expertise in all aspects of setting up and running a library and information service. Freelancers also offer a breadth of experience across different organizations which can be very valuable.

A number of trends have affected the role of freelancers. As online resources have spread to fee earners' desktops, the demand for training and advice on these resources has increased. At the same time, publishers have sought to recoup their investment in these services by raising subscription rates substantially; freelancers often take the role of chief negotiator. As reliance on electronic resources grows, the paper library is often downsized dramatically. Lastly, the spread of remote working facilities can allow much information work to be done remotely. This can provide greater flexibility both to the client and the freelancer.

CONSIDERATIONS IN GOING FREELANCE

New freelancers nearly always have a number of years' prior experience of legal information work. Freelance life is attractive in many ways: it can provide more variety, the chance to develop a wider range of skills and greater potential flexibility.

However, freelancers are in business on their own account, and need to consider the same issues as any other small business. They have less security than employees and are not entitled to employee benefits such as sick pay. Many firms are unwilling to pay for training courses or professional seminars, or for professional memberships. Professional memberships are valuable to freelancers as a source of current awareness, contacts and future work, but cost money.

Before starting as a freelancer, it is important to understand the regulations and procedures for sole traders regarding income tax and national insurance. Sole traders also need to consider professional liability and other insurance. Tax advantages can often be gained by registering for VAT – the most successful may have to – or trading as a limited company. These options add further to the administration involved.

The following sources are useful when setting up as a freelancer:

- HMRC information on tax and national insurance: http://www.hmrc.gov. uk/startingup/
- Business Link guide to starting a business: http://www.businesslink.gov. uk/startingup/

FINDING WORK

The BIALL website has a list of legal library recruiters and online job boards.[2] However, many freelancers obtain much of their work through contacts and referrals. It is therefore essential to maintain existing contacts and make new ones.

The freelancer should ensure that ex-colleagues at other firms, both librarians and lawyers, know that they are potentially available for work. Freelancers can also get themselves onto the grapevine by attending meetings and events, for example:

- In London, the BIALL Solos group which organizes informal meetings;
- Other BIALL professional and social events. Events organized by the City Legal Information Group[3] and the CILIP Commercial, Legal and Scientific Information Group[4] can also be useful for certain areas of information work;
- Many established freelancers will also be invited to publishers' events;
- The BIALL conference, although funding and time can be an issue.

The world of online social media evolves quickly. Currently, many legal librarians participate in the LinkedIn business network. This has a number of relevant groups. The LIS-LAW mailing list[5] is also a useful source of advice and forum for discussion. Twitter does not appear to have had much impact so far. However those unfamiliar with the pitfalls of online networking should approach it with caution. It is easy to create a wrong impression through slightly misjudged wording.

There can be a temptation to accept work indiscriminately. The wise freelancer will avoid work where the client's expectations are unrealistic, or which does not play to the freelancer's strengths.

DEVELOPING THE INFORMATION SERVICE

For some time, information specialists have realized the importance of promoting the information service, and of highlighting opportunities for developing the service further. This is especially important for freelancers, who might otherwise be regarded as somehow less committed to the organization's success.

The first step is to develop a good understanding of the organization's needs and priorities. What are their strong areas? Which current developments concern them most? How good are the legal staff at research? Does anyone else provide information services, for example professional support lawyers or business development? Some of this can be understood informally – anyone who comes into the library or asks for support is worth talking to. However the freelancer should ask to attend events such as departmental meetings. These are good opportunities to introduce oneself more widely, understand the live issues and ask about perceived needs.

Even if not covered by the initial brief, an experienced freelancer would be able make a valuable contribution in many ways, including:

- Resource-specific training and individual coaching;
- Full coverage of information services during new joiners' induction;

- Tailored alerters and current awareness services;
- Root-and-branch stock reviews, possibly involving a move away from paper sources;
- Contributions to the organization's intranet;
- Increased support for business development – this can be a highly visible and valued role.

MAINTAINING SKILLS

Freelancers need to keep their skills current. The events and forums mentioned in the Finding Work sections will often include coverage of current issues. Formal courses are available through BIALL, TFPL and Ark among others. In any case, freelancers need to invest time and money to maintain their usefulness to their clients.

CONCLUSION

Being a freelancer is not an easy option. The professional role of the freelancer is as demanding as that of any other information professional, but often requiring even greater versatility, and with the added requirements of running a small business. However it is a career choice which can be extremely satisfying, and very valuable to organizations requiring legal information services.

GOVERNMENT DEPARTMENT LIBRARIES

PENELOPE SCOTT, STEPHANIE CURRAN, KATHY TURNER AND RACHEL ROBBINS

Some government departments have separate departmental and legal libraries, while others cover all subjects in one library.

MINISTRY OF JUSTICE

The Ministry of Justice (MoJ) is a large government department which was formed on 9 May 2007. It combined the Department for Constitutional Affairs with parts of the Home Office to create a department and associated bodies that oversee prisons, probation, courts and the judiciary, as well as various aspects of criminal and civil law. The Library and Information Services (jLIS) team comprises 14 professionally qualified librarians and 14 administrative staff. jLIS is divided into two teams: Customer Services (which includes the MoJ and Royal Courts of Justice (RCJ) libraries and the e-Services team), and the Publications Supply Team, which provides print publications to all courts, tribunals and judges across England and Wales.

MoJ LIBRARY

The MoJ Library is based in the headquarters building in London and serves ministers, civil servants, analysts, psychologists, lawyers and colleagues in sponsored organizations such as HM Inspectorate of Prisons and the Office of the Public Guardian. It covers a wide range of subjects including law; criminal justice; prisons and probation; offender management and mental disorders; parliament; and constitutional and electoral reform. MoJ's lawyers also have access to a range of legal databases and electronic journals through a portal which is primarily for the judiciary. The Library provides training on the databases and helps them with complex legal and parliamentary research, especially when they are drafting legislation. It also holds a collection of quasi-legislation concerning the management of prisons, which is often used by the Treasury Solicitor's lawyers in court cases and at inquests.

RCJ LIBRARY

The RCJ Library has two main libraries and several smaller collections around the RCJ complex. One Library is located in the main RCJ building on the Strand and the other is nearby in the new Rolls Building on Fetter Lane. The Libraries serve all the judiciary from the Court of Appeal downwards, RCJ lawyers, judicial assistants and other court staff. The collections are primarily legal and include a wide range of law reports, relevant textbooks and legislation. In addition to this the Library also holds a significant collection of old editions of key legal texts dating from the eighteenth century. The Library team is also responsible for the provision of personal publications to the judiciary and relevant procedural books to courtrooms.

LIBRARY SERVICES TO THE JUDICIARY AND COURTS

Every court in England and Wales has a legal library containing key legal textbooks, law reports, journals and legislation. The size of the library and the types of publications provided are determined by the jurisdiction and annual workload of each court. It is the responsibility of jLIS staff to supply publications for these libraries and to ensure that the libraries are being maintained to the expected standard. This is achieved with the co-operation of the local court manager, with the appointment of a local court library administrator, who, in addition to their regular administrative or usher duties, is responsible for the supervision and maintenance of the court's library collection. A court library administrator's duties include the booking in and distribution of new publications, and updating of looseleaf publications. jLIS staff support the work of the court library administrator through various training materials including CDs, a procedural handbook and guidance pamphlets. jLIS staff respond to their enquiries whenever these arise including chasing claims for missing looseleaf updates and law report parts. jLIS staff are also currently engaged in offering advice and assistance in helping courts that are closing with the disposal of surplus or old edition titles according to the correct procedure.

Members of the judiciary have access to comprehensive online legal information, accessed via a secure portal. jLIS staff negotiate the contracts, procure the databases and provide training and advice on accessing this online information.

A standing committee of judges meets with senior library staff every quarter to agree policy on the provision of legal publications to the courts and judiciary and is responsible for keeping their colleagues informed about revisions to this policy.

jLIS staff consult around full-time 1,250 judges and courts annually to gather information for ordering for the year ahead. This helps with budget forecasts and supply management.

This huge administrative process will soon be aided by the introduction of a new modern library management system with an acquisitions module, which will ease and simplify the process. Following the recent creation of Her Majesty's Courts and Tribunals Service, jLIS has taken on the supply of publications and online services to the tribunals and their judges.

LAW FIRM LIBRARIES AND INFORMATION SERVICES

LOYITA WORLEY

Law firms come in all different sizes – from smaller perhaps regional firms to large global law firms consisting of thousands of lawyers with offices all over the world. It follows therefore that law firm libraries too come in various guises. Each may provide a slightly differing service but all are key in supplying their lawyers with the information they need to keep at the top of their game and provide high-quality services to clients.

In most law firms the information service comes under the banner of 'support services' along with the other non-fee earning departments such as HR, Accounts, IT and so on. The Library overhead is made up of accommodation, staff and funding for resources, some of which can be quite expensive, so it is important that all are leveraged to demonstrate their worth to the business. This is a constant challenge to information workers who are always seeking ways to maintain a high profile, be economically astute and operate an efficient service. In some instances this may involve charging out librarian time.

SERVICES

The libraries are responsible for many information requirements throughout the firm, from the physical provision of printed materials such as law reports, text books and journals as well as managing the delivery of online materials to the fee earner desktops. Most operate enquiry and current awareness services and will be involved with training new joiners and trainee solicitors.

Whilst the need for current legal information is constant, there is an increasing requirement to provide business information as well. This is to help the lawyers remain up to date with what their clients are doing and to help them identify and target new clients or areas of business. Marketing and business development have taken on a new importance as a result of the tough commercial environment in which law firms now operate. Competition for legal business has never been keener and providing the necessary information to support this area of the business is common.

As a result of the recent recession, many libraries have seen their budgets and staffing reduced and have responded by becoming leaner and more efficient. It has been an opportunity for them to show their adaptability and demonstrate their ability to utilize their resources to the fullest extent. For some, this has also necessitated learning new skills and taking on additional responsibilities.

It is not uncommon to find law firm libraries involved in business development, anti-money laundering and conflict checking, knowledge management and registry services as well as more traditional areas such as copyright compliance for the firm.

STAFFING

Staff will deal with everyone from summer vacation students to partners – and in some cases may even deal directly with clients. Tasks may range from looseleafing and filing to high-level research, budgeting, contract negotiation and being involved with strategic planning. Staffing will range depending on the firm, from solo librarians to large teams. Most would fall somewhere in the middle and consist of qualified information staff with some administrative assistance. Some firms specialize in certain areas of law within a particular jurisdiction while others will cover many areas of law across a variety of jurisdictions. The information team will be expected to support all of these. In addition the positioning of the team may vary from firm to firm. Some law firms like their information team embedded within the practice groups which could mean that the information staff are spread out across the firm and located adjacent to the groups they work with.

WHAT THE JOB ENTAILS

The work involved will differ depending on the type of firm. A variety of skills may be required, ranging from understanding the legal system, knowing the various resources available, being a good researcher, having a general understanding of IT including the use of Excel for spreadsheets and so on, presentation skills for presenting at meetings and training and staff management as well as general awareness of issues affecting the profession. Most law firms will offer internal or external training on these competencies and encourage staff development. As with all types of information work, accuracy and thoroughness are critical as supplying incorrect information could have severe financial and reputational implications for the client and firm.

I have mentioned before that legal research is only one part of the service provided and that business information is equally important. Part of the law firm librarian's role is to keep all the lawyers up to date with their particular interests.

Librarians have provided current awareness services for many years although the content and delivery methods may have changed. Whilst some libraries still produce regular alerts, many of the online providers also do the same and so it is only worth the library doing so if they have something different to offer or are responding to specific requests from their users.

At the same time the lawyers' need for targeted knowledge on their clients and various industry sectors has grown, so many law firm libraries provide e-mail alerts tailored to a lawyer's specific requirements using RSS feeds and some other type of electronic delivery software. The online alerts that accompany topic-specific journals also provide useful information.

Firms have become increasingly cautious over their spending and whilst you may not be directly involved in the budgeting process, it is inevitable that you will be involved in assessing the various resources available and ensuring that the most cost-effective methods of research are applied.

As a consequence of the reduction in size of some law firm information teams, training end-users has become more important than ever. The trainee solicitors and junior associates constitute the heaviest information users and it is essential that they are taught to be independent and to be able to carry out research for themselves. Some global information teams offer 24/7 cover but most law firms need their lawyers to be independent outside office hours. The availability of online information is helpful in this context.

CHALLENGES

Lawyers work to tight deadlines which apply to the librarians too and law firm users can be very demanding. However, most are appreciative and the fact that the information that you provide makes a difference is very rewarding.

SOLO LIBRARIANS

NICOLA HERBERT

I am often met with surprise when I inform people I am a qualified information professional working in the legal department at Transport for London. While it does not appear to be unusual for in-house legal teams to include professional support lawyers, the employment of information professionals is still not commonplace. TfL Legal employs around 50 lawyers with 8 support staff. The role of Information Officer at TfL Legal is relatively new and I started in the post in 2006. I am the only information professional in the department and have responsibility for the management of all knowledge, information and resources.

Although there may be an assumption that working as a solo librarian can be isolating, I have found that the opposite is true: not being part of an information-specific team has allowed me to integrate fully into the wider legal department and I am able to engage with the colleagues I am supporting more directly.

It can be immensely rewarding and provides a wide variety of work. I am responsible for all aspects of information management at TfL, including knowledge, managing resources and subscriptions, liaising with publishers, finance and budget management, current awareness, strategic planning, development of the intranet and electronic resources, conducting legal research and general admin. This wide-ranging workload can be challenging and all levels of information tasks are completed by the librarian from basic admin tasks right up to strategic development. Such a variety of responsibilities means there is never the time or opportunity to get bored.

As my role was newly created, I have been able to develop knowledge processes and policy within TfL Legal. On joining TfL, I conducted an extensive information audit, asking each individual member of the department a series of predetermined questions about their existing workload, current awareness received, access to resources, intranet use, knowledge management procedures and training requirements. The results were then analysed to identify any recurring themes and resolve any individual issues. It offered the opportunity to learn more about the department's workload and has allowed me to develop information and current awareness services with their needs in mind.

TfL Legal does not have a dedicated library space and resources are situated locally with the relevant teams. Despite this, resource management is a core part of my role as the department has access to a number of books, journals and looseleafs. I am also responsible for online resource management and deal with subscription renewals. Liaison and negotiation with suppliers is becoming increasingly central to my role in order to drive down costs and ensure value for money is achieved.

Providing research and current awareness services are also vital to ensure access is available to all relevant information. As well as responding to information and research requests as they arise, I produce a weekly bulletin to raise awareness of news and current issues affecting TfL. This has proved to be an extremely useful resource and I regularly get positive feedback on how it has drawn attention to relevant materials that would have been otherwise overlooked.

The department has a knowledge management system, hosted on Visualfiles. This offers a centralized workspace to store essential business information and I have worked with the department to build up an extensive collection of documents. The information audit allowed me to identify several banks of knowledge to be stored on the system and I attended team meetings and consulted with individuals to identify further information. Promoting the knowledge bank is important to encourage people to utilize it to its full potential. As well as offering training to new users, I promote documents added through the current awareness bulletin. Regularly reviewing the system is also necessary so that it remains relevant and up to date.

Working independently means that the ability to be proactive is essential to identify ways to enhance the service. One of the issues that came up repeatedly in the information audit was confusion over how to access resources and where documents were stored. In order to resolve this, I set about initiating and developing a portal on SharePoint. This provides a single shared workspace from which everything can be accessed, including online subscriptions, links to useful websites, current awareness, details of resource holdings, information on forthcoming legal training and RSS feeds. I have also set up dedicated subsites for each individual team, allowing for more tailored information to be directed to specific areas of the business.

It has been absolutely imperative to the success of new services that they have been developed in close consultation with legal colleagues and the IT department. Discussing requirements with team leaders and encouraging feedback helped to ensure that SharePoint was developed with departmental need as a priority. I also worked closely with IT to ensure that the site had sufficient functionality to meet my vision and the needs of the department. Awareness is key and I regularly present new knowledge initiatives at departmental and team meetings to raise awareness of the full range of resources available and how they can be of benefit.

I have responsibility for wider TfL initiatives, including co-ordinating the Consultation Response Group, which facilitates TfL's responses to external consultations, and assisting the Legal Director in compiling the Legal Compliance Report. This has increased the scope of my role and has allowed me to become more involved in the organization from a wider perspective.

Working as a solo librarian can be both challenging and rewarding. Although I spend most of my time working independently, I am an integral part of the wider legal team. I am based in an open plan office with everyone else, which has helped greatly with visibility; rather than being isolated from colleagues in a separate library, I am able to engage with them directly to develop relevant and timely services. It also allows for a greater scope of experience as I am required to manage every aspect of departmental information and have had the opportunity to take responsibility for a wider range of projects outside the traditional library remit.

PROFESSIONAL SOCIETY LIBRARIES: THE NORTHERN IRELAND EXPERIENCE OF CHANGE AND REPOSITIONING

HEATHER SEMPLE

Eight years on from the first edition of the *Handbook of Legal Information Management*, this is an opportune time to comment on the changes of direction experienced by the Law Society Library which may, or may not, be reflected in other professional association library environments during this time.

The Law Society Library has the dual function of providing:

a) a library service to the Society professional and support staff as they discharge their statutory and non-statutory duties as a regulatory and representative entity; and

b) a library and information service to all members on the Society's roll.

Some significant change has occurred in the Law Society library in the last eight years, both as a result of change from within the Society and as a result of external market forces. We are fortunate that both these factors have enabled us to reposition and strengthen the library as legal information provider to solicitors in this jurisdiction.

Law Society House was demolished and rebuilt between 2007 and 2009, during which time we relocated to temporary, smaller premises. Nothing was taken for granted in the new building and it couldn't be assumed that a library would attract the same footfall and be given the same priority and prominence as in the old. During the relocation we shifted our emphasis to electronic subscriptions and dissemination methods. This initiated the debate probably familiar to all – do we need the same volume of hard copy material in the library? Do we need to duplicate hard and soft copy? Do we need a library?

This is where the professional society library may differ from commercial law firm libraries in terms of collection ethos. The Society took the view that the provision of a comprehensive library collection demonstrated a commitment to academic excellence for the profession, that a subsidized library service is an important component of the Society's member services and that it was essential to provide parity of resources with other branches of the legal profession. They also recognized the library's position as depository for historical legal records and documents.

A new library space allowed us the opportunity to develop more physical services, and we now house a Business Centre within the library. This has been used for training and development sessions for staff and members. It is also used by the membership as discreet office space if they have other business to attend to at the Courts. Both the Library and Business Centre have wifi access which is popular with users.

Apart from the physical changes to the library, economic factors have had a considerable impact on library services. As a professional society we have perhaps not felt the full rigours of the economic downturn facing many business entities. However, the Society's revenue is generated by practising certificate fees, and a reduction in the number of practising solicitors will have a cascading fiscal effect in all areas of Society business. If law firms were being forced to choose between losing a staff member or cancelling a subscription, then people are inevitably retained over paper. This has had several effects on the library.

Firstly, firms are using the library more often. They are expanding their traditional areas of work since they do not want to lose business. The library is heavily used by solicitors expanding their knowledge base.

Secondly, publisher relations have also been repositioned and developed. Publishers are aware that solicitors are using the Law Society library in preference to maintaining their own collections. Publishers also recognize that we are a route to market for them, and product endorsement using professional integrity is an important aspect of the library service. We have successfully negotiated a Resellers Agreement with a major online legal information vendor which acknowledges our positioning within the Northern Ireland legal information market. This enables us to e-distribute information as a mid-user within the terms of the Agreement, and both the Society and the vendor can move forward in a mutually beneficial way. We have adopted similar positions with statutory agencies such as the Copyright Licensing Agency whereby we provide advice and guidance as to the licensing requirements for our members and act as liaison for the CLA.

Our own library services have also been repositioned. The ethos of the Society in terms of corporate governance and fiscal responsibility has been changing from that of a club to that of a business, and the Library has been doing likewise. The Library is now run on a more commercial footing, and we are developing additional income streams and income generation, mindful of our core purpose as a subsidized resource for our members.

We concentrate on marketing and promotion with schemes such as a credit scheme for apprentices who successfully complete the Library Induction Programme. We have Service Level Agreements and Key Performance Indicators incorporated into the Library Business Plan, and our Annual Report contains analysis of performance across all these areas. We have been engaging with Solicitor Associations throughout Northern Ireland and I often go to their meetings and events to give talks on what the library can do for them. Online training sessions and CPD talks on the law-making process and sources of law are very popular with our members and provide a significant income stream for the library.

We have, however, noticed a decline in use of some library services where the charge for information received from the library cannot be attributed to a particular client file. One example is our general current awareness article service whereby solicitors ordered journal articles in line with the prescribed copyright fees. This has been replaced by Tailored Current Awareness services of local material which we offer free of charge to members who have an interest in a specialized area of law. We also produce focussed newsletters for Special Interest Groups and develop library services as appropriate for them.

Legislative changes have also led the library to reposition its services. A recent change to Northern Ireland primary legislation has granted solicitors rights of audience in higher courts. We have proactively developed our collections and services accordingly.

These have been significant years in the development of the Library Service. I have enjoyed the challenges. Whilst we have hopefully moved with the times, our mission statement remains steadfastly unchanged:

> *... to anticipate and satisfy the information requirements of existing and potential users through the provision of relevant, professional and specialised library and information services.*

NOTES

1 http://www.biall.org.uk/pages/where-do-legal-information-professionals-work.html [accessed 1 August 2013].
2 At http://www.biall.org.uk/pages/legal-library-recruiters.html [Accessed 1 August 2013].
3 www.clig.org [Accessed 1 August 2013].
4 www.cilip.org.uk/get-involved/special-interest-groups/clsig [Accessed 1 August 2013].
5 See https://www.jiscmail.ac.uk/lists/lis-law.html [Viewed 19 July 2013].

REFERENCES AND BIBLIOGRAPHY

CHAPTER 1

Abel, R.L. (1988), *The Legal Profession in England and Wales*. Oxford: Basil Blackwell.

Abel, R.L. (2003), *English Lawyers Between Market and State*. Oxford: Oxford University Press.

Adams, L. and Smith, R.L. (2006), 'The evolution of public law libraries'. *AALL Spectrum*, 10(5), 16–17 and 33, also available at http://www.aallnet.org/main-menu/Publications/spectrum/Archives/Vol-10/pub_sp0603/pub-sp0603-evolution.pdf.

Allbon, E. and Wakefield, N. (2008), 'Staying vital to the virtual learner – what role for future university law librarians?' *Legal Information Management*, 8(1), 18–23.

American Association of Law Libraries (AALL) (2000), *Leadership for the 21st Century: New Realities, New Roles*. Chicago: AALL.

American Association of Law Libraries (AALL) (2001), 'Competencies for law librarianship'. *AALL Spectrum*, 5(9), 14–15, also available at http://www.aallnet.org/main-menu/Publications/spectrum/Archives/Vol-5/pub_sp0106/pub-sp0106-comp.pdf.

American Association of Law Libraries (AALL), 'Special Committee on the Future of Law Libraries in the Digital Age (2002)', in *Beyond the Boundaries: Report of the Special Committee on the Future of Law Libraries in the Digital Age*. Chicago: AALL.

Aston, J. (2011), 'From Law Library Society to Law Library: the first 180 years, 1816–1996'. *Legal Information Management*, 11, 168–72.

Axtmann, M.M. (2006), 'Academic law libraries 2.0'. *AALL Spectrum*, 10(9), 14–15 and 17, also available at http://www.aallnet.org/main-menu/Publications/spectrum/Archives/Vol-10/pub_sp0607/pub-sp0607-academic.pdf.

Baker, J.H. (1990), *The Third University of England: the Inns of Court and the Common Law Tradition*. London: Selden Society, reprinted in *The Common Law Tradition: Lawyers, books and the law*, edited by J.H. Baker. London: Hambledon Press, 3–28.

Baker, J.H. (2002), *An Introduction to English Legal History*, 4th edn. London: Butterworths.

Baker, J.H. (2007), *Legal Education in London 1250–1850*. London: Selden Society.

Ballantyne, G.H. (1971), 'The Signet Library, Edinburgh'. *Law Librarian*, 2, 3–5, 15.

Ballantyne, G.H. (1979), *The Signet Library Edinburgh and its Librarians, 1722–1972*. Glasgow: Scottish Library Association.

Bar Standards Board (2011) *Bar Professional Training Course: Course Specification Requirements and Guidance*. London: BSB, also available at https://www.barstandardsboard.org.uk/media/28049/bptc_final_pdf.pdf

Best, K. (1983), 'The Supreme Court Library'. *Law Librarian*, 10, 13.

Bird, E. (2009), 'The Signet Library in the 21st century'. *Legal Information Management*, 9, 41–5.

Bird, R., Wills, D. and Winterton, J. (2009), 'Collaborating on collections: a structured approach'. *SCONUL Focus*, 46, 37–9.

Bird, R. (2011), 'Legal information literacy', in *IALL International Handbook of Legal Information Management*, edited by R. Danner and J. Winterton. Farnham and Burlington, VT: Ashgate, 115–33.

Birks, P. (ed.) (1994), *Reviewing Legal Education*. Oxford: Oxford University Press.

Birks, P. (ed.) (1996), *What Are Law Schools For?* (*Pressing Problems in the Law*, vol. 2). Oxford: Oxford University Press.

Black, G. (2009), 'The Scottish Law Librarians Group'. *Legal Information Management*, 9, 46.

Blake, M. (2000), *A History of the British and Irish Association of Law Librarians 1969–1999*. Warwick: BIALL.

Blom-Cooper, L., Dickson, B. and Drewry, G. (eds) (2009), *The Judicial House of Lords 1876–2009*. Oxford: Oxford University Press.

Boon, A. and Webb, J. (2008) 'Legal education and training in England and Wales: Back to the future?' *Journal of Legal Education*, 58(1), 79–121.

Breem, W. and Phillips, S. (eds) (1991), *Bibliography of Commonwealth Law Reports*. London: Mansell.

British and Irish Association of Law Librarians (BIALL), 'Committee on Cooperation (1971)', *Report of the Committee on Co-operation*. London: BIALL.

British and Irish Association of Law Librarians (BIALL), 'Sub-Committee on Standards (1981)', *Standards for Law Libraries*. London: BIALL. Appendices VI–XI (Recommended holdings for law libraries) were published as *Law Librarian*, special issue, January 1983.

British and Irish Association of Law Librarians (BIALL) (1985), 'National provision for legal information'. *Law Librarian*, 16, 70.

British and Irish Association of Law Librarians (BIALL) (2011), *Legal Research Training Packs*. [s.l.]: BIALL. Available in electronic form for customization.

British Library Working Party on Provision for Law [1985?], *Report*. London: British Library.

Brock, C.A. (1974), 'Law libraries and librarians: a revisionist history'. *Law Library Journal*, 67, 325–61.

Byrne, M. (2002), 'The Law Society Library', in *The Law Society of Ireland 1852–2002: Portrait of a Profession*, edited by E.G. Hall and D. Hogan. Dublin: Four Courts Press, 197–208.

Cadell, P. and Matheson, A. (eds) (1989), *For the Encouragement of Learning: Scotland's National Library 1689–1925*. Edinburgh: HMSO.

Campbell, L. (2011), 'Changes to legal education & training'. *SCOLAG Legal Journal*, September 2011, 201.

Cannan, J. (2007), 'Are public law librarians immune from suit? Muddying the already murky waters of law librarian liability'. *Law Library Journal*, 99(1), 7–32.

Cassidy, J. (2011), 'Chief State Solicitor's Office'. *Legal Information Management*, 11, 198.

Cheffins, R. (1999), 'National legal collections: the British Library'. *Law Librarian*, 30, 63–5.

Clavin, J. (2000), *Union List of Legal Periodicals and Related Stock in Irish Libraries*, 4th edn. Dublin: British and Irish Association of Law Librarians.

Clinch, P. (2001), 'FLAG Project: survey results'. *Legal Information Management*, 1, 45–58.

Clinch, P. (2002), 'FLAG: the new internet gateway to foreign law holdings in UK national and university libraries'. *Legal Information Management*, 2, 37–9, also available at http://www.llrx.com/features/flag.htm.

Clinch, P. (2009), 'SLS/BIALL academic law library survey 2007/2008'. *Legal Information Management*, 9, 205–20.

Clinch, P. (2010), 'SLS/BIALL academic law library survey 2008/2009'. *Legal Information Management*, 10, 291–305.

Committee on Legal Education (1971), *Report*. (Cmnd. 4595) London: HMSO (Ormrod Report).

Committee on the Future of the Legal Profession (1988), *A Time for Change*. London: General Council of the Bar and the Law Society (Marre Report).

Competition Authority [Ireland] (2006), *Competition in Professional Services: Solicitors and Barristers*. Dublin: The Authority, also available at http://www.tca.ie/images/uploaded/documents/Solicitors%20and%20barristers%20full%20report.pdf.

Constitutional Reform: A Supreme Court for the United Kingdom (2003). (Department for Constitutional Affairs consultation paper) London: HMSO.

Crawford, C. (2009a), 'Collection development and the history of standards for Australian law libraries … Part 1'. *Australian Law Librarian*, 17(1), 9–21.

Crawford, C. (2009b), 'Collection development and the history of standards for Australian law libraries … Part 2'. *Australian Law Librarian*, 17(2), 86–93.

Crommelin, M. and Hinchcliff, C. (2011), 'Global legal education and its implications for legal information management', in *IALL International Handbook of Legal Information Management*, edited by R. Danner and J. Winterton. Farnham and Burlington, VT: Ashgate, 65–75.

Cruikshank, E. (2003), 'Building a profession'. *Law Society's Gazette*, 100(25), 26 June 2003, 32–7.

Daintree, D. (1976), 'Law libraries and their users', in *Manual of Law Librarianship*, edited by E. Moys. London: André Deutsch, 31–58.

Daintree, D. (1983), 'Law libraries in the United Kingdom', in *Law Librarianship: A Handbook*, vol. 2, edited by H.P. Mueller and P.E. Kehoe. Littleton, CO: Rothman for AALL, 819–51.

Danner, R. (1998), 'Redefining a profession'. *Law Library Journal*, 90, 315–56.

Danner, R., Kauffman, B. and Palfrey, J. (2009), 'The twenty-first century law library'. *Law Library Journal*, 101(2), 143–56.

Danner, R. (2011), 'Defining international law librarianship in an age of multiplicity, knowledge, and open access to law', in *IALL International Handbook of Legal Information Management*, edited by R. Danner and J. Winterton. Farnham and Burlington, VT: Ashgate, 1–21.

Danner, R. and Winterton, J. (eds) (2011), *IALL International Handbook of Legal Information Management*. Farnham and Burlington, VT: Ashgate for the International Association of Law Libraries.

Dennison, M. (2011), 'Working for parliamentarians, contributing to Parliament'. *Legal Information Management*, 11, 176–81.

Dicey, A.V. (1883), *Can English Law be Taught at the Universities?* London: Macmillan.

Donnelly, J. (1996), 'The Judges' Library, Dublin'. *Law Librarian*, 27, 152–5.

Donnelly, J. (2011), 'The Judges' Library, Dublin'. *Legal Information Management*, 11, 202–3.

Furlong, J. (2011), 'The law firm sector in Ireland: an overview'. *Legal Information Management*, 11, 172–6.

Garavaglia, B. and the Board of the International Association of Law Libraries (2011), 'A research agenda for international law librarianship', in *IALL International Handbook of Legal Information Management*, edited by R. Danner and J. Winterton. Farnham and Burlington, VT: Ashgate, 342–58.

Gasaway, L.N. and Chiorazzi, M.G. (eds) (1996), *Law Librarianship; Historical Perspectives* (AALL Publication Series, no. 52) Littleton, CO: Rothman for the American Association of Law Libraries.

Gaynor, M. (2011), 'The Law Society of Ireland Library: serving the solicitors' profession in challenging times'. *Legal Information Management*, 11, 165–8.

Genn, H., Partington, M. and Wheeler, S. (2006), *Law in the Real World: Improving our Understanding of How Law Works. Nuffield Inquiry on Empirical Research: Final report and Recommendations*. London: Nuffield Foundation, also available at http://www.ucl.ac.uk/laws/socio-legal/empirical/docs/inquiry_report.pdf.

Gordon-Till, J. (2003), 'A code of ethics for BIALL'. *Legal Information Management*, 3, 38–43.

Gordon-Till, J. (2006), 'Ethics in law librarianship', in *BIALL Handbook of Legal Information Management*, edited by L. Worley. Aldershot and Burlington, VT: Ashgate, 273–81.

Goudy, H. (1909), *Introductory Address to the Society of Public Teachers of Law in England and Wales Delivered at the First Annual General Meeting*. London: SPTL.

Hall, E.G. and Hogan, D. (eds) (2002), *The Law Society of Ireland 1852–2002: Portrait of a Profession*. Dublin: Four Courts Press.

Harris, P. and Bellerby, S. (1993), *A Survey of Law Teaching 1993* (Association of Law Teachers Research Project on Legal Education) London: Sweet & Maxwell.

Havery, R.O. (ed.) (2011), *History of the Middle Temple*. Oxford and Portland, OR: Hart Publishing.

Hazelton, P. (2011), 'The education and training of law librarians', in *IALL International Handbook of Legal Information Management*, edited by R. Danner and J. Winterton. Farnham and Burlington, VT: Ashgate, 43–64.

Healey, P. (2002), 'Pro se users, reference liability, and the unauthorized practice of law: twenty-five selected readings'. *Law Library Journal*, 94(1), 133–9.

Heller, H. (2009), 'The twenty-first century law library: a law firm librarian's thoughts'. *Law Library Journal*, 101(4), 517–23.

Hewitt, A. (2010), *The Law Society of Northern Ireland: a History*. Belfast: Law Society of Northern Ireland.

Hogan, D. (1986), *The Legal Profession in Ireland 1789–1922*. Dublin: Incorporated Law Society of Ireland.

Holborn, G. (1999), *Sources of Biographical Information on Past Lawyers*. Warwick: BIALL.

Holborn, G. (2006), 'Lawyers and their libraries', in *Cambridge History of Libraries in Britain and Ireland vol. 3, 1850–2000*, edited by A. Black and P. Hoare. Cambridge: Cambridge University Press, 453–69.

Holborn, G. (2008), 'Inns of Court libraries in the 21st century'. *Legal Information Management*, 8(1), 46–50.

Holdsworth, A. (ed.) (2007), *A Portrait of Lincoln's Inn*. London: Third Millennium Publishing.

Institute of Advanced Legal Studies, 'Policy Review Sub-Committee (1986)', Report. London: IALS. Chairman: Sir Robert Megarry.

Jeffries, J. (1992), 'From cavalry to courts: impressions of law librarianship'. *Law Librarian*, 23(2), 91–3.

John, C. (1992), 'The Advocates' Library three hundred and ten years on'. *Law Librarian*, 23, 111–14.

Jones, D.L. (1998), 'The House of Lords Library'. *Law Librarian*, 29, 105–7.

Kehoe, P.E., Lyman, L. and McCann, G.L. (eds) (1995), *Law Librarianship: A Handbook for the Electronic Age*. (AALL Publication Series, no. 47) Littleton, CO: Rothman for the American Association of Law Libraries.

Kennedy, C. (2011), 'The Law Reform Commission's library & information services'. *Legal Information Management*, 11, 204–5.

Kenny, C. (1992), *King's Inns and the Kingdom of Ireland: The Irish 'Inn of Court' 1541–1800*. Blackrock: Irish Academic Press in association with the Irish Legal History Society.

Law Librarian, vols 1–30, 1970–2000. London: Sweet & Maxwell for the British and Irish Association of Law Librarians, superseded by *Legal Information Management*.

Law Library of Congress (1982), *Law Library 1832–1982: A Brief History of the First Hundred and Fifty Years*. Washington, DC: Law Library of Congress.

Legal Information Management, vol. 1–, 2001– onwards, Cambridge: Cambridge University Press for the British and Irish Association of Law Librarians (Sweet & Maxwell until Winter 2003), superseding *Law Librarian*.

Logan, R.G. (1987), 'Law libraries and their users', in *Manual of Law Librarianship*, 2nd edn, edited by E. Moys. London: Gower, 3–37.

Longson, A. (2009), 'The Advocates Library'. *Legal Information Management*, 9, 35–7.

Lord Chancellor's Advisory Committee on Legal Education and Conduct (1996), *First Report on Legal Education and Training*. London: Committee on Legal Education and Conduct.

Lorrimer, A. (2011), 'Legal information service provision within government in Northern Ireland'. *Legal Information Management*, 11, 205–9.

Lutyens, C.R., et al. (1973), *Community Law: A Selection of Publications on the Law of the European Economic Community and the Relevant Law of the Original Member States*. London: BIALL.

Mansfield, S. (1997), *Access to Legal Information in Public Libraries: a Case Study in East Kilbride, Glasgow, and Paisley* (Unpublished MSc dissertation) Department of Information Science, University of Strathclyde.

Mansfield, S. (1999), 'Role of legal information professionals in law firms', in *Now and Then*, edited by A.J. Kinahan. London: Sweet & Maxwell, 127–38.

Mansfield, S. (2009), 'The Scottish Parliament and its Information Service'. *Legal Information Management*, 9(1), 16–24.

Marsh, S.B. (1990), *A History of the Association of Law Teachers: The first twenty-five years (1965–1990)*. London: Sweet & Maxwell.

Martin, R. (2001), 'Local law societies: what's in a name?' *Legal Information Management*, 1, 26–8.

McCabe, C. (2011), 'The Library of the Office of the Director of Public Prosecutions'. *Legal Information Management*, 11, 199–200.

McKenzie, J. (2009), 'The Library of the Royal Faculty of Procurators in Glasgow'. *Legal Information Management*, 9, 38–40.

McTavish, S. (2012), *BIALL Salary Survey 2011/12*, compiled on behalf of BIALL by Dr Shona McTavish. [s.l.]: BIALL. Available to members on the BIALL website.

McTavish, S. and Duggan, F. (1999), 'Law firm libraries in Britain and Ireland'. *Law Librarian*, 30, 56–63.

McTavish, S. and Ray, K. (1999), *Law and Order: Trends in legal information provision*. London: Sweet & Maxwell for BIALL.

Meadows, J. (2006), 'The future for public law libraries'. *AALL Spectrum*, 10(9), 18–21, also available at http://www.aallnet.org/main-menu/Publications/spectrum/Archives/Vol-10/pub_sp0607/pub-sp0607-public.pdf.

Melling, Z. (2011), 'The Legal Aid Board and library and information services'. *Legal Information Management*, 11, 200–201.

Miskin, C. (1981), *Library and Information Services for the Legal Profession* (British Library Research and Development Reports, no. 5633) Boston Spa: British Library Lending Division.

Moys, E. (ed.) (1976), *Manual of Law Librarianship*. London: André Deutsch.

Moys, E. (ed.) (1987), *Manual of Law Librarianship*, 2nd edn. London: Gower.

Mueller, H.P. and Kehoe, P.E. (eds) (1983), *Law Librarianship: A Handbook*. 2 vols (AALL Publication Series, no. 19) Littleton, CO: Rothman for the American Association of Law Libraries.

Muir, A. and Oppenheim, C. (1995), 'The legal responsibilities of the health-care librarian'. *Health Libraries Review*, 12(2), 91–9.

Munro, K. (2009), 'The University of Glasgow Library and School of Law'. *Legal Information Management*, 9, 50–51.

National Legal Collections (1999), 'Historical co-operation' by David Wills; 'Funding co-operation among university libraries' by Jules Winterton; 'Future co-operation' by Barbara Tearle. *Law Librarian*, 30, 65–71.

Neylon, M.J. (1973), 'King's Inn Library, Dublin'. *Law Librarian*, 4, 3–4.

Noel-Tod, A. (1990), 'Wallace Wilfred Swinburne Breem 1926–1990'. *Law Librarian*, 21, 59–61.

O'Flaherty, R. (2011), 'The provision of library and research services in the Office of the Attorney General – a law office of state'. *Legal Information* Management, 11, 195–7.

Oakley, R.L. (2003), 'International public policy and libraries. Members' briefing on international policies'. *AALL Spectrum*, 8 (3), December, centre insert 1–4.

Paris, M.-L. and Donnelly, L. (2010), 'Legal education in Ireland: a paradigm shift to the practical'. *German Law Journal*, 11, 1067–92, also available at http://www.germanlawjournal.com/pdfs/Vol11-No9/PDF_Vol_11_No_09_1067-1092_Paris_Donnelly.pdf.

Pound, R. (1953), *The Lawyer from Antiquity to Modern Times*. St Paul, MN: West, 215–9.

Pue, W.W. (1989), 'Guild training vs. professional education: the Committee on Legal Education and the Law Department of Queen's College, Birmingham in the 1850s'. *American Journal of Legal History*, 33, 241–87.

Rider, C. and Horsler, V. (eds) (2007), *The Inner Temple: a Community of Communities*. London: Third Millennium Publishing.

Rowe, J. (2009), 'At the heart of Justice: the library at the new Supreme Court of the United Kingdom'. *Legal Information Management*, 9, 257–61.

Royal Commission on Legal Services (1979), *Report*. London: HMSO (Benson Report).

Rudge, S. and Andrews, C. (2000), 'The electronic saga: the changing role of the law librarian'. *Law Librarian*, 31, 239–42.

Ryan, G. (2009), 'University of Strathclyde Library'. *Legal Information Management*, 9, 52–3.

St Clair, J. and Craik, R. (1989), *The Advocates' Library: 300 Years of a National Institution 1689–1989*. Edinburgh: HMSO.

Seaton, J. (2000), 'SPICe – breaking new ground'. *Law Librarian*, 31, 104–7.

Shenton, C. (2011), 'The historic records of the judicial function of the UK Parliament'. *Legal Information Management*, 11, 35–41.

Sleator, J. (2011), 'The Public Prosecution Service'. L.I.M., 11(3), 209–10.

Small, W. (2009), 'Essential or 'nice to have'? The Impact of the financial downturn on KM in law firms'. *Legal Information Management*, 9, 287–9.

Society of Legal Scholars (2010), 'A library for the modern law school: a statement of standards for university law library provision in the UK – 2009 revision prepared by the Libraries Sub-Committee of the Society of Legal Scholars'. *Legal Studies*, 30(3), 442–3, also available at http://www.legalscholars.ac.uk/documents/SLS-Library-for-a-Modern-Law-School-Statement-2009.pdf.

Society of Public Teachers of Law (SPTL) (no date), *Handbook of the Legal Curricula Pursued at the Various Centres of Public Legal Education in England and Wales*. London: SPTL.

Society of Public Teachers of Law (SPTL) (1968), 'The Society's evidence to the National Libraries Committee'. *Journal of the Society of Public Teachers of Law*, X, 87–90.

Society of Public Teachers of Law (SPTL) (1995), 'A library for the modern law school: a statement of standards for university law library provision in England and Wales'. *Legal Studies* special issue (Includes an introduction by the then Convener of the SPTL Libraries Committee, Terence Daintith, the Statement of Standards, and the detailed research report compiled by Dr Peter Clinch. The 1995 version of the standards and the various later revisions are also available at http://www.legalscholars.ac.uk.).

Solicitors Regulation Authority (2012), *Information for Providers of Legal Practice Courses*. London: SRA, also available at http://www.sra.org.uk/lpc/.

Steer, S. (2008), 'Information managers in the 21st century'. *Legal Information Management*, 8(4), 263–6.

Stevens, R. (1983), *Law School: Legal Education in America from the 1850s to the 1980s*. Chapel Hill and London: University of North Carolina Press.

Susskind, R. (1998), *The Future of Law*, rev. ed. Oxford: Clarendon Press.

Susskind, R. (1999), 'The future of the law librarian: an interview with Richard Susskind'. *Law Librarian*, 30, 147–54.

Susskind, R. (2000), *Transforming the Law: Essays on Technology, Justice and the Legal Marketplace*. Oxford: Oxford University Press.

Susskind, R. (2008), *The End of Lawyers: Rethinking the Nature of Legal Services*. Oxford: OUP.

Susskind, R. (2011), 'Foreword', in *IALL International Handbook of Legal Information Management*, edited by R. Danner and J Winterton. Farnham and Burlington, VT; Ashgate, xix.

Symposium on Law Libraries (1964), 1: 'Law Libraries' by K. Howard Drake; 2: 'The new Bodleian Law Library at Oxford' by P.B. Carter; 3: 'The Squire Law Library at Cambridge' by W.A. Steiner. *Journal of the Society of Public Teachers of Law*, VIII, 71–88.

Tearle, B. (ed.) (1983), *Index to Legal Essays: English Language Legal Essays in Festschriften, Memorial Volumes, Conference Papers and Other Collections, 1975–1979*. London: Mansell.

Tearle, B. (2008), 'Law librarianship and legal information provision in the 21st century'. *Legal Information Management*, 8(1), 4–10.

Todd, K.M. (2006), 'Law firm libraries in the 21st century'. *AALL Spectrum*, 10(9), 12–13 and 16–17, also available at http://www.aallnet.org/main-menu/Publications/spectrum/Archives/Vol-10/pub_sp0607/pub-sp0607-firm.pdf.

Twining, W. (1994), *Blackstone's Tower: the English Law School*. London: Sweet & Maxwell (the 1994 Hamlyn Lectures).

Waldhelm, R. (2009), 'Legal information service provision within Government in Scotland'. *Legal Information Management*, 9(1), 25–9.

Whelan, D. (2001), 'Virtual law librarian: adding value in a virtual world'. *Chicago Association of Law Librarians Bulletin*, 180, Spring 2001, 16, also available at http://www.ofaolain.com/resources/articles/virtlawlib.

Whisner, M. (2008), *Update to Choosing Law Librarianship*, available at http://www.llrx.com/features/lawlibrarianship.htm.

Wilcox, C. (1995), *Directory of Law Libraries in Scotland*, 2nd edn. Edinburgh: Scottish Law Librarians Group.

Wilcox, C. (1997), *Union List of Periodical and Law Report Holdings*. Edinburgh: Scottish Law Librarians Group.

Wilson, J.F. (1966), *A Survey of Legal Education in the United Kingdom*. London: Butterworth, reprinted from (1966) *Journal of the Society of Public Teachers of Law*, New Series 9, 1–144.

Wilson, J.F. and Marsh, S.B. (1975), *A Second Survey of Legal Education in the United Kingdom*. London: Butterworth, reprinted from (1975) *Journal of the Society of Public Teachers of Law*, New Series 13, 239–331 and Supplement no. 1. London: Institute of Advanced Legal Studies in 1978 and Supplement no. 2. London: Institute of Advanced Legal Studies in 1981.

Wilson, J. (1993), 'A third survey of university legal education in the United Kingdom'. *Legal Studies*, 13, 143–82.

Winterton, S. (2008), 'Law firm libraries in the 21st century'. *Legal Information Management*, 8(1), 28–31.

Winterton, J. (2003), 'In celebration of Willi Steiner'. *Legal Information Management*, 3, 140–149.
Winterton, J. (2004), 'The way of ignorance. Members' briefing on international networks'. *AALL Spectrum*, 8 (6), April, centre insert 1–4.
Winterton, J. (2006), 'Law libraries and their users', in *BIALL Handbook of Legal Information Management*, edited by L. Worley. Aldershot and Burlington, VT: Ashgate, 1–42.
Winterton, J. (2011), 'Globalisation and legal information management', in *IALL International Handbook of Legal Information Management*, edited by R. Danner and J Winterton. Farnham and Burlington, VT; Ashgate, 23–41.
Worley, L. (ed.) (2006), *BIALL Handbook of Legal Information Management*, Aldershot and Burlington, VT: Ashgate.
Young, H. (2002), 'Law librarians' survey: are academic law librarians in decline?' *Legal Information Management*, 2, 50–55.

CHAPTER 4

Current Awareness Systems (*Dean Mason*)

Fahy, S. (2008), 'Outsourcing Know How in Law Firms – Strategies for Success'. *Legal Information Management*, 8, 104–9.
Fisher, R. and Ury, W. (1999), *Getting to Yes: Negotiating an agreement without giving in*, 2nd edn. London, Random House.
Fogden, F. (2010), 'Mashing Content: a Case Study'. *Legal Information Management*, 10, 222–8.
Fogden, F. (2011), *Mashing, Merging and Manipulating Content: Lessons in Harnessing Technology to Overcome Information Overload*. Paper to the BIALL Conference: Sharing Experience; Building Value in Legal Information, Newcastle, 18/06/11.
Fogden, F. (2011), 'Negotiation of contracts, planning for the unknown with boilerplate clauses', *Legal Information Management*, 11(1), 27–31.
Fourie, I. (1999), 'Empowering users- current awareness of the Internet'. *The Electronic Library*, 17(6), 379–88.
Google (2012), *Advanced options: Set the volume* [Online: Google], available at https://support.google.com/alerts/bin/answer.py?hl=en&answer=175929&topic=28417&ctx=topic [Accessed: 13/03/12].
Kemp, D.A. (1979), *Current Awareness Services*. London: Bingley.
McKenzie, A. (2008), 'Delivering a Current Awareness Service to Solicitors'. *Legal Information Management*, 8, 56–8.
Milford, H. (2004), *Charging for Information Services in Law Firm Libraries*. University of Sheffield: Department of Information Studies.
Mullan, J. (2009), *Could law libraries be more social?* KIM Legal [Online], 3(5), available at http://www.kmlegalmag.com/xq/asp/txtSearch.Culture/

exactphrase.1/sid.0/articleid.89887904-FA85-4AA1-8225-975F7357A88A/ qx/display.htm [Accessed: 13/03/12].

Nicholas, D. (2000), *Assessing Information Needs: Tools, Techniques and Concepts for the Internet Age*, 2nd edn. London: Aslib.

Nicholas, D. and Herman, Eti. (2009), *Assessing Information Needs in the Age of the Digital Consumer*, 3rd edn. London: Routledge.

Thomas, O. (2013), *Google Reader Is Closing – And People Are Absolutely Freaking Out [Online: Business Insider]*, available at http://www.businessinsider. com/google-is-closing-google-reader-2013-3#ixzz2Q4qm97gO   [Accessed: 10/04/13].

Platt, N. (2007), *Current Awareness* [Online: Strategic Librarian], available at   http://strategiclibrarian.com/2007/07/31/current-awareness/   [Accessed: 13/03/12].

PLC (2012), *About Practical Law Company* [Online: Practical Law Company], available at http://uk.practicallaw.com/uk/4-200-8304 [Accessed: 13/03/12].

Scott, P.D. (2011), *Twitter removes all search RSS links from its site, now users must resort to hacks to get feeds* [Online: The Sociable], available at: http:// sociable.co/social-media/twitter-removes-all-search-rss-links-from-its-site-now-users-must-resort-to-hacks-to-get-feeds/ [Accessed: 13/03/12].

Law Firm Intranets (Sally Roberts)

CMS Wire. *50 ways to a better intranet*, available at http://www.cmswire.com/.

Cody, K. (2011), *Intranet usability workbook*, available at www.smallworlders. com.

FUMSI. *Improving navigation with user research and testing*, available at http:// www.fumsi.com/.

Gallagher, M. *Top 10 mistakes in managing a corporate intranet*, available at http://www.gallagher.com.

Robertson, J. (2010), *Designing Intranets – Creating Sites that Work*. Sydney: Step Two Designs.

Spencer, D. (2009), *Card Sorting: a definitive guide*. New York: Rosenfeld Media.

Step Two Designs. *34 ideas for promoting your intranet*, available at http://www. steptwo.com.au/.

Step Two Designs. *Creating a strong intranet brand*, available at http://www. steptwo.com.au/.

Step Two Designs. *Improving your intranet task by task*, available at http://www. steptwo.com.au/.

Step Two Designs. *Naming the intranet*, available at http://www.steptwo. com.au/.

Step Two Designs. *Project Guide 9 – card sorting*, available at http://www.steptwo. com.au/.

Step Two Designs. *Sixteen steps to a renewed corporate intranet*, available at http://www.steptwo.com.au/.

View plc. *Defining and delivering a vision for your intranet*, available at http://www.viewplc.com.

Library Management Systems (LMS) (*Mandy Webster*)

Bailey, P. (2006), 'Be an innovator: invest less and gain more'. *Further Education Today*, October, 24.

Bailey, P. (2006), 'Get the best from your supplier'. *CILIP Library and Information Gazette*, 30 June–13 July, 7.

Bailey, P. (2007), 'Is your library software really user friendly?' *Further Education Today*, January, 20.

Bailey, P. (2006), 'Let someone else provide your online catalogue'. *CILIP Library and Information Update*, 5(10), 39–41.

Bailey, P. (2007), 'Procurement strategy: evaluating library software'. *CILIP Update*, 6(10), 35–7.

Bailey, P. (2009), 'You can find library books in your search engine'. *CILIP Library and Information Gazette*, 13 February–26 February, 7.

Beastall, G. (2010), 'Fast track to success'. *CILIP Library and Information Gazette*, 30 September–13 October, 6.

Beastall, G. (2010), 'Will your library survive or thrive?'. *CILIP Library and Information Gazette*, 11 February–24 February, 5–6.

Bissels, G. (2008), 'Implementation of an open source library management system'. *Program*, 42(3), 303–14.

Blyberg, J. (2009), 'Hey presto! New product claims to be the first true social library'. *Library and Information Update*, March, 7.

Buckley Owen, T. (2009), 'Is LibraryThing a good thing?' *CILIP Library and Information Gazette*, 13 February–26 February, 1.

Buckley Owen, T. (2011), 'Will all be revealed?' *CILIP Update*, June, 28–9.

Caldwell, T. (2009), 'LMS searches must go deeper'. *Information World Review*, 257, 4–6.

Calvert, P. and Read, M. (2006), 'RFPs: a necessary evil or indispensable tool?' *The Electronic Library*, 24(5), 649–61.

Chad, K. (2006), 'Free your data'. *CILIP Library and Information Gazette*, 16 June–29 June, 8.

Chad, K. and Leeves, J. (2010), 'Making it easier to specify systems'. *CILIP Library and Information Gazette*, 2 December, 5.

Creissen, S. (2008), 'Library management systems: find the one for you'. *Legal Information Management*, 8(2), 117–21.

Dimant, N. (2010), 'Open to new developments'. *CILIP Library and Information Gazette*, 11 February–24 February, 8.

Dimant, N. (2010), 'Open source branches out'. *CILIP Library and Information Gazette*, 11 February–24 February, 9.

Durrant, F. (2006), *Negotiating Licences for Digital Resources*. London: Facet Publishing.

Fortune, M. (2010) 'Can we work together on a dream system'. *CILIP Library and Information Gazette*, 30 September–13 October, 5.

Fortune, M. (2009) 'LMS and RIFID in co-operation or competitors?' *CILIP Library and Information Gazette*, 28 August–10 September, 1.

Harris, S. (2008), 'Library management systems embrace change'. *Research Information*, December–January, 20–24.

Hughes, M. (2011) 'Evergreen conference shows open source is flourishing'. *CILIP Update*, June, 18–19.

Hyams, E. (2011), 'Save costs and exploit the value of your LMS'. *CILIP Update*, January, 26–7.

James, Dean, et al. (2009), 'Discovering discovery tools'. *Library Hi Tech*, 27(2), 268–76.

Jannetta, V. (2008), 'Prove your worth: measuring the performance of library and information centres'. *Legal Information Management*, 8(2), 123–6.

Mitchell, G. (2009), 'Dealing with unusual practices'. *CILIP Library and Information Gazette*, 13 February–26 February, 10.

Raven, D. (2011a), 'Flexible systems for tough times'. *CILIP Update*, January, 28–9.

Raven, D. (2011b), 'We have to pitch in together'. *CILIP Update*, May, 29.

Richardson, J. (2005), 'Can't afford a big database application?' *Information Outlook*, 9(1), 35–7.

Ruddock, B. and Hartley, D. (2010), 'How UK academic libraries choose meta search systems'. *ASLIB Proceedings*, 62(1), 85–105.

Webster, M. (2003), 'System migration: the use of PenLib in a law firm library'. *Legal Information Management*, 3(1), 34–7.

Wolffsohn, P. (2010), 'Proving you're worth it: managing an information department in challenging times'. *Legal Information Management*, 10(1), 54–7.

Yang, X., Wei, Q. and Peng, X. (2009), 'System architecture of library 2.0'. *The Electronic Library*, 27(2), 283–91.

Zetterlund, B. (2010), 'Things are moving quickly'. *CILIP Library and Information Gazette*, 11 February–24 February, 7–9.

CHAPTER 5

Basker, J. (1997), 'Resourcing the Information Centre', in A. Scammell (ed.), *Handbook of Special Librarianship*, 7th edn. London: ASLIB.

Durrant, F. (2006), *Negotiating Licences for Digital Resources*. London: Facet Publishing.

Fisher, R. and Ury, W. (1999), *Getting to Yes: negotiating an agreement without giving in*, 2nd edn. London: Random House.

Fogden, F. (2011), 'Negotiation of contracts, planning for the unknown with boilerplate clauses', *Legal Information Management*, 11(1), 27–31.

'FT sues Blackstone over alleged login abuse', *The Times*, 2 February 2009.

McKay, D. (2003), *Effective Financial Planning for Library and Information Services*, 2nd edn. London: ASLIB.

Milford, H. (2004), *Charging for Information Services in Law Firm Libraries*. University of Sheffield: Department of Information Studies.

CHAPTER 6

Bennis, W.G. (1998), *On Becoming a Manager*, London: Arrow.

Berne, E. (1966), *Games People Play: The psychology of human relationships*. London: Andre Deutsch.

Grant, R.M. (1998), *Contemporary Strategy Analysis*. Oxford: Blackwell.

Lancaster, K., Spry, J. and Shoolbred, M. (2004), 'Knowledge harvesting reaping the rewards'. *Library and Information Update*, 3(2), February.

Lawes, A. (ed.) (1993), *Management Skills for the Information Manager*. Aldershot: Ashgate.

Maslow, A.H. (1970), *Motivation and Personality*. New York: Harper and Row.

Open University Business School (1998), *Foundations of Senior Management. People: Book 2, What's special about people?*. Milton Keynes: Open University.

Open University Business School (1998), *Foundations of Senior Management, People: Book 5, Core functions in managing people*. Milton Keynes: Open University.

Open University Business School (1998), *Foundations of Senior Management, People: Book 6, Managing people: a wider view*. Milton Keynes: Open University.

Open University Business School (1999), *Managing Human Resources: Unit 3, Managing for performance*. Milton Keynes: Open University.

Open University Business School (1999), *Managing Knowledge: Unit 2, Communication*. Milton Keynes: Open University.

Weightman, J. (1999), *Managing People*. Wiltshire: Cromwell Press.

CHAPTER 7

Copyright and Related Rights Regulations 2003 (SI 2003/2498).

Copyright and Rights in Databases Regulations 1997 (SI 1997/3032).

Copyright (Librarians and Archivists) (Copying of Copyright Material) Regulations (SI 1989/1212).

Copyright, Designs and Patents Act 1988.

Copyright in the Information Society Directive 2001/29/EC.

Copyright (Visually Impaired Persons) Act 2002.

Cornish, G. (2009), *Copyright: Interpreting the law for libraries, archives and information services*. London: Facet Publishing.

Data Protection Act 1998.

Digital Economy Act 2010.

Directive on the processing of personal data and the free movement of such data 95/46/EC.

IPO, 2011, 'Government Response to the Hargreaves Review of Intellectual Property and Growth, IPO', available at www.ipo.gov.uk/ipresponse-full.pdf.

Gowers, A. (2006), 'Gowers Review of Intellectual Property, HM Treasury', available at www.official-documents.gov.uk/document/other/0118404830/0118404830.pdf.

Hargreaves, I. (2011), 'Digital Opportunity: an independent review of IP and growth. IPO', available at www.ipo.gov.uk/ipreview-finalreport.pdf.

Directive on the legal protection of databases 96/9/EC.

Padfield, T. (2010), *Copyright for Archivists and Records Managers*. London: Facet Publishing.

Pedley, P. (2006), *Essential Law for Information Professionals*. London: Facet Publishing.

Pedley, P. (2008), *Copyright Compliance: Practical Steps to stay within the Law*. London: Facet Publishing.

Privacy and Electronic Communications (EC Directive) Regulations 2003 (SI 2003/2426).

CHAPTER 8

Burton, G. (2006–07), 'Unlocking Potential', in *Inside Knowledge* magazine, Volume 10 Issue 4, December 2006/January 2007.

Christian, C. 'Legal Technology Insider', available at http://www.legaltechnology. com/

Jarrett-Kerr, N. (2009), 'Strategies for Law Firms', blog at http://www.jarrett-kerr. com. See book, *Strategy for Law Firms: After the Legal Services Act 2007*. London: Law Society.

Lastres, S. (2011), 'Aligning Through Knowledge Management', *Information Outlook*, June 2011.

Parsons, M. (2004) *Effective Knowledge management for Law Firms*. Oxford, New York: OUP.

Rumizen, M.C. (2001), *Complete Idiot's Guide to Knowledge Management*. New York and Indianapolis: Alpha Books.

Susskind, R. (2010) *The End of Lawyers? Rethinking the Nature of Legal Services*, rev. edn. Oxford: OUP.

CHAPTER 9

Taxonomies and Indexing (*Christine Miskin*)

Aitchison, J., Gilchrist, A. and Bawden, D. (2000), *Thesaurus Construction and Use*, 4th edn. London: ASLIB.

Batley, S. (2007), *Information Architecture for Information Professionals*. Oxford: Chandos Publishing.

Bergman, M. (2010), 'Taxonomy management at Clifford Chance', available at http://www.iskouk.org/events/legal_knowledge_nov2010.htm Legal Know how: Organisation and Semantic Analysis ISKO UK Event – London, 10 November 2010 [Accessed 12 August 2011].

Booth, P.F. (2001), *Indexing: the Manual of Good Practice*. London: K.G. Saur.

Broughton, V. (2006), *Essential Thesaurus Construction*. London: Facet Publishing. Broughton, V. (2010), 'The use and construction of thesauri for legal documentation'. *Legal Information Management*, 10(1) Spring 35–42 (Bliss Thesaurus project).

Browne, G. (2010), 'Indexing of free web-based electronic sources'. *Legal Information Management*, 10(1) Spring 2010, 28–31.

Chowdhury, G. and Chowdhury, S. (2007), *Organising Information from the Shelf to the Web*. London: Facet Publishing.

Coburn, A. 2010. 'The real CIG – who are they?' *Legal Information Management*, 10(1) Spring, 45–7.

Dextre Clarke, S. (2007), 'e-GIF, e-GMS and IPSV: what's in it for us?' *Legal Information Management*, 7(4), 275–7.

Dextre Clarke, S. (2010), 'Thesaurus standards on a converging track'. *Legal Information Management*, 10(1), 43–5.

Duffield, C., Fallon, S. and Stopford, J. (2010), 'LIM meets LJI: an article on an abstract'. *Legal Information Management*, 10(3), 187–90.

Gilchrist, A. and Mahon, B. (eds) (2004), *Information Architecture: Designing Information Environments for Purpose*. London: Facet Publishing.

Hedden, H. (2010), *The Accidental Taxonomist*. Medford: Information Today.

Haynes, D. (2004), *Metadata for Information Management and Retrieval*. London: Facet Publishing.

Jacob, K. and Barker, L. (2010), 'Why lawyers need taxonomies – adventures in organising legal knowledge', available at http://www.iskouk.org/events/legal_knowledge_nov2010.htm Legal Know how: Organisation and Semantic Analysis ISKO UK Event – London, 10 November 2010 [Accessed 12 June 2013].

Jordan, P. and Lippell, H. (2010), 'The metadata model for Direct Gov'. *Legal Information Management*, 10(1), 7–9.

Lambe, P. (2007), *Organising Knowledge: Taxonomies, Knowledge and Organisational Effectiveness*. Oxford: Chandos Publishing.

McGlashan, M. (2010), 'Indexing the International Law Reports'. *Legal Information Management*, 10(3), 205–10.

Marley, E. (2010), 'Metadata at the UK Parliament: use of controlled vocabularies and indexing'. *Legal Information Management*, 10(1), 28–31.

Morville, P. and Rosenfeld, L. (2006), *Information Architecture for the World Wide Web: Designing Large-Scale Web Sites*, 3rd edn. Sebastopol, CA: O'Reilly Media.

Moys, E.M., et al. (1993), *Indexing Legal Materials*. Sheffield: The Society of Indexers.

Marty, J. (2008), Developing a global law firm taxonomy, inside-out (Case study of Baker & McKenzie's project), available at http://articles.technology.findlaw.com/2005/May/01/9903.html.

Park, J. (2012), *Metadata Application in Digital Repositories and Libraries: Tools, Systems, and Architecture.* Oxford: Chandos.

Scott, M. and Smith, N. (2010), 'Legal taxonomy from Sweet & Maxwell'. *Legal Information Management*, 10(3), 217–22.

Vyner, A. (2010), 'Textual information extraction and ontologies for legal case-based reasoning', available at http://www.iskouk.org/events/legal_knowledge_nov2010.htm Legal Know how: Organisation and Semantic Analysis ISKO UK Event – London, 10 November 2010 [Accessed 12 June 2013].

Whittle, S. (2010), 'Filling the frame: the role of practical metadata in online resources at the IALS'. *Legal Information Management*, 10(3), 191–204.

CHAPTER 10

Allan, B. (2002), *E-learning and Teaching in Library and Information Services*, London: Facet.

Atkins, D.E., et al. (2007), A Review of the Open Educational Resources (OER) Movement: Achievements, Challenges, and New Opportunities [Online]. Menlo Park, CA: The William and Flora Hewlett Foundation. Available at: http://www.hewlett.org/uploads/files/Hewlett_OER_report.pdf [Accessed 20 June 2013].

Black, E.L. (2008), 'Toolkit approach to integrating library resources into the learning management system', *Journal of Academic Librarianship*, 34(6), 496–501.

Brown, G. (2004), *Effective Teaching in Higher Education.* London: Routledge Falmer. Supplement. Available at: http://www.routledgeeducation.com/resources/pdf/how_to_learn.pdf [Accessed 19 June 2013].

Connolly, M., Cosgrave, T. and Krkoska, B. (2011), 'Mobilizing the Library's Web Presence and Services: A Student-Library Collaboration to Create the Library's Mobile Site and iPhone Application', *The Reference Librarian*, 52(1–2), 27–35.

Copeland, R. (2001), 'The usual rules apply online', *Times Higher Education Supplement*, May 18 2001.

Daly, E. (2010), 'Embedding library resources into learning management systems: a way to reach Duke undergrads at their points of need', *College & Research Libraries News*, 71(4), 208–212. Available at: http://crln.acrl.org/content/71/4/208.full.pdf+html [Accessed 20 June 2013].

Foster, E. (2011), 'App-y Days! The pedagogic benefits and limitations of smartphone apps'. Available at: http://www.ntu.ac.uk/cadq/quality/events/ALTC/altc2011/109477.pdf#page=44 [Accessed 19 June 2013].

Garrison, D. and Vaughan, N. (2008), *Blended Learning in Higher Education: Framework, Principles and Guidelines.* San Francisco: Jossey-Bass.

Gray, D., Ryan, M. and Coulon, R. (2004), 'The training of teachers and trainers: innovative practices, skills and competencies in the use of e-learning', *European Journal of Open, Distance and Elearning*, 2004 (2). Available at: http://www. eurodl.org/materials/contrib/2004/Gray_Ryan_Coulon.pdf [Accessed 20 June 2013].

Hambling, Y. and Stubbings, R. (2003), The Implementation of MetaLib and SFX at Loughborough University Library: A Case Study. Available at: http://info. lut.ac.uk/departments/ls/lisu/downloads/Metalibcasestudy.pdf [Accessed 20 June 2013].

Hartley, J. (1998), *Learning and Studying: A Research Perspective*. London: Routledge.

Heaton-Shrestha, C. et al. (2007), 'Learning and e-learning in HE: the relationship between student learning and VLE use', *Research Papers in Education*, 22(4), 443–464.

HEFCE (2009), Enhancing learning and teaching through the use of technology: a revised approach to HEFCE's strategy for e-learning. Available at: http://www. hefce.ac.uk/pubs/hefce/2009/09_12/ [Accessed 19 June 2013].

Hemming, A. (2008), 'E-learning, in a world with too much information', *Legal Information Management*, 8(1), 43–46.

Higher Education Academy (n.d.), Deep and Surface Approaches to Learning [Online]. Available at: http://www.heacademy.ac.uk/resources/detail/subjects/ engineering/Deep-and-Surface-Approaches-to-Learning [Accessed 21 June 2013].

Honey, P. and Mumford, A. (1986), *Manual of Learning Styles*, 2nd edn. London: P. Honey.

Januszewski, A. and Molenda, M. (eds) (2007), *Educational Technology: A Definition with Commentary*. New York: Lawrence Erlbaum Associates.

JISC (Joint Information Systems Committee), e-Learning. Available at: http:// www.jisc.ac.uk/whatwedo/themes/elearning [Accessed 19 June 2013].

JISC (Joint Information Systems Committee) (2007), Student Expectations Study. Available at: http://www.jisc.ac.uk/media/documents/publications/ studentexpectations.pdf [Accessed 19 June 2013].

Lunt, T. and Curran, J. (2010), 'Are you listening please? The advantages of electronic audio feedback compared to written feedback', *Assessment & Evaluation in Higher Education*, 35(7), 759–769.

Maringe, F. (2006), 'University and course choice: implications for positioning, recruitment and marketing', *International Journal of Educational Management*, 20(6), 466–479.

O'Leary, R. (n.d.), Virtual Learning Environments. Available at: http://www. alt.ac.uk/sites/default/files/assets_editor_uploads/documents/eln002.pdf [Accessed 20 June 2013].

O'Neill, K., Singh, G. and O'Donoghue, J. (2004), 'Implementing eLearning programmes for higher education: a review of the literature', *Journal of Information Technology Education*, 3, 313–323.

Pritchard, A. (2009), *Ways of Learning: Learning Theories and Learning Styles in the Classroom*, 2nd edn. New York: Routledge.

Volery, T. and Lord, D. (2000), 'Critical success factors in online education', *International Journal of Educational Management*, 14(5), 213–223.

Walker, R., Voce, J. and Ahmed, J. (2012), Survey of technology enhanced learning for higher education in the UK. Available at: http://www.ucisa.ac.uk/~/media/groups/ssg/surveys/TEL_survey_2012_with%20Apps_final [Accessed 17 June 2013].

Way, D. (2010), 'The impact of web-scale discovery on the use of a library collection', *Serials Review*, 36(4), 214–220.

Weller, M. (2007), *Virtual Learning Environments: Using, Choosing and Developing your VLE*. London: Routledge.

Wiley, D.A. (ed.) (2000), The Instructional Use of Learning Objects. Available at: http://reusability.org/read/chapters/wiley.doc [Accessed 20 June 2013].

CHAPTER 11

AALL (2011), Legal Research Competencies and Standards for Law Student Information Literacy. Available at: http://www.aallnet.org/main-menu/Leadership-Governance/policies/PublicPolicies/policy-lawstu.html

Adam, S. (2004), 'Using Learning Outcomes: A consideration of the nature, role, application and implications for European education of employing learning outcome outcomes at the local, national and international levels' (conference report published as a pdf).

Armstrong, C. et al. (2005), 'CILIP Defines Information Literacy for the UK', *Library and Information Update*, 4(1), 22–25. Available at: http://www.cilip.org.uk/get-involved/advocacy/information-literacy/Pages/definition.aspx [Accessed 18 July 2013].

BIALL Legal Information Literacy Statement August 2012.

Bingham, J. (1999), *Guide to Developing Learning Outcomes*. The Learning and Teaching Institute, Sheffield: Sheffield Hallam University.

Clinch, P. (2006), *Teaching Legal Research*, 2nd edn. Warwick: UK Centre for Legal Education.

Fry, H., Ketteridge, S. and Marshall, S. (2009), 'Understanding student learning', in *A Handbook for Teaching and Learning in Higher Education: Enhancing Academic Practice*. London: Routledge.

http://bit.ly/mcluhanquote [Accessed 18 July 2013].

http://learnmore.lawbore.net

http://prezi.com/

http://www.goodreads.com/author/quotes/169034.Sydney_J_Harris [Accessed 18 July 2013].

http://www.slideshare.net

http://www.youtube.com/user/TheICLR

Kennedy, D., Hyland, A. and Ryan, N. (2006), Writing and Using Learning Outcomes: a practical guide [Online]. Available at: http://sss.dcu.ie/afi/docs/bologna/writing_and_using_learning_outcomes.pdf [Accessed 18 July 2013].

Kim-Prieto, D. (2011) 'The road not yet taken: How law student information literacy standards address identified issues in legal research education and training', *Rutgers School of Law – Newark Research Paper*, no. 088 [Online] Available at: http://papers.ssrn.com/sol3/papers.cfm?abstract_id=1678146 [Accessed 18 July 2013].

Morgan, N. and Davies, L. (2004), 'Innovative induction: introducing the Cephalonian Method', *SCONUL Focus*, 32, 4–8.

SCONUL (1999, updated 2003), Information skills in Higher Education: A SCONUL Position Paper. Available at: http://www.sconul.ac.uk/tags/7-pillars [Accessed 18 July 2013].

SCONUL (2011), The SCONUL Seven Pillars of Information Literacy, Core Model for Higher Education, 2011. Available at http://www.sconul.ac.uk/tags/7-pillars

Sellahewa, H. (2011), 'Using an online student response system in small group teaching: a pilot study', *Innovation in Teaching and Learning in Information and Computer Sciences*, 10(3), 38–43. Available at: http://journals.heacademy.ac.uk/doi/abs/10.11120/ital.2011.10030038 [Accessed 18 July 2013].

Setting Standards: the Future of Legal Services Education and Training Regulation in England and Wales (2013). Available at: http://letr.org.uk/wp-content/uploads/LETR-Report.pdf [Accessed 18 July 2013].

Statsky, W.P. (1978), *Domestic Relations*, West Publishing, reproduced in McKie, S. (1993), *Legal Research: How to Find and Understand the Law*, London: Routledge, Available at: http://books.google.co.uk/books?id=0xaKKGkkvI4C&lpg=PA42&ots=lZ-GPt1IKX&dq=statsky%20cartwheel&pg=PA43#v=onepage&q=statsky%20cartwheel&f=false

Stefani, L. (2009), 'Curriculum design and development', in Fry, Ketteridge and Marshall, 'Understanding student learning', in *A Handbook for Teaching and Learning in Higher Education: Enhancing Academic Practice* (2009). London: Routledge.

CHAPTER 12

http://biall.blogspot.com
http://biallpr.pbworks.com/w/page/5259189/How-do-I
http://cpd23.blogspot.com/
http://delicious/
http://digg.com/
http://dumplinginahanky.blogspot.com/
http://libraryroutesproject.wikkii.com/wiki/Main_Page
http://pbworks.com/

http://sharepoint.microsoft.com/en-us/pages/default.aspx
http://twiki.org/
http://uklibraryblogs.pbworks.com/w/page/7262285/FrontPage
http://wikkii.com/wiki/Free_Wiki_Hosting
http://www-01.ibm.com/software/lotus/products/connections/
http://www.bbc.co.uk/news/10628494 for more information RSS feeds
http://www.blogger.com
http://www.jivesoftware.com/
http://www.livejournal.com/
http://www.mediawiki.org/wiki/MediaWiki
http://www.socialtext.com/
http://www.stumbleupon.com
http://www.thoughtfarmer.com/
http://www.tumblr.com/
http://www.twitter.com
http://www.wordpress.com
http://www.yammer.com
https://plus.google.com/

CHAPTER 13

Aldridge, A. (2011), 'Legal "near-sourcing" threatens to widen status gap between London and regions'. Thursday 16 June 2011, guardian.co.uk.

Bénaud, C. and Bordeianu, S. (1998), *Outsourcing Library Operations in Academic Libraries: An Overview of Issues and Outcomes*. Santa Barbara, California: Libraries Unlimited.

Goodman, J. (2007), *Legal Outsourcing 2007*. London: Ark/ Managing Partner.

Martin, R.S., PhD, et al. (June 2000), *The Impact of Outsourcing and Privatization on Library Services and Management A Study for the American Library Association*. Texas Woman's University School of Library and Information Studies: ALA.

'Send it out – senior private practice and in-house lawyers on outsourcing trends Legal Week Benchmarker – Outsourcing', May 2011, Legal Week.

SRA outcomes 7.10, SRA Code of Conduct 2011, Solicitors Regulation Authority.

Susskind, R. (2008), *The End of Lawyers? Rethinking the Nature of Legal Services 2008*. Oxford: OUP.

CHAPTER 14

Ames, J. (2010), 'Europe will block financing of law firms', *The Times*.

Begum, H. (2011), 'Trainees for hire: SRA backs revolutionary plan', *Legal Week*.

Croft, J. (2011), 'Conveyancing site hopes to float on Aim', FT.COM, http://www.ft.com/cms/s/0/709e834a-84ad-11e0-afcb-00144feabdc0.html

Croft, J. (2011), 'Lawyers "shop" is next to Poundland', FT.COM, http://cachef.ft.com/cms/s/0/77a46480-589c-11e0-9b8a-00144feab49a.html#axzz1ZMBXiwpK

Croft, J. (2011), 'Legal market gears up for Tesco Law', FT.COM, http://www.ft.com/cms/s/0/ed155b52-7430-11e0-b788-00144feabdc0.html#axzz1ZM4gvgW0

Croft, J., Peel, M. and Arnold, M. (2010), 'The legal sector's own Big Bang', *The Financial Times*.

Dowell, K. (2011), 'BLM admits non-lawyer to equity in LDP conversion', *The Lawyer*.

Dowell, K. (2010), 'Optima reprimanded by the SRA over Capita Investment', *The Lawyer*, 24(33), 4.

Harris, J. (2011), 'With wide-ranging legal reforms on the table, the Irish profession is set for a shake-up', *The Lawyer* (2011), 25(35), 30.

Heine, F. (2010), 'Justice Minister Djanogly stresses commitment to ABS implementation schedule', *Legal Week*.

Heine, F. (2010), 'Mills & Reeve adds barrister to partnership in LDP switch', *Legal Week*.

Hill, C. (2011), 'Is anyone Listening?', *Legal Week*.

http://letr.org.uk/

http://www.barcouncil.org.uk/about/find-a-barrister/public-access-directory/

http://www.barcouncil.org.uk/assets/documents/ProcureCo%20260410.pdf

http://www.barstandardsboard.org.uk/

http://www.barstandardsboard.org.uk/news/press/862.html

http://www.irishtimes.com/news/politics/cabinet-set-to-discuss-draft-laws-aimed-at-reducing-legal-costs-1.1456002

http://www.justice.gov.uk/downloads/publications/corporate-reports/MoJ/legal-services-action-plan.pdf

http://www.lawgazette.co.uk/news/leo-goes-court-enforce-decisions-against-law-firms

http://www.legalombudsman.org.uk/

http://www.legalservicesboard.org.uk

http://www.legalservicesboard.org.uk/what_we_do/regulation/pdf/20110824_barristers_in_abs_dn_final.pdf

http://www.legalzoom.com

http://www.scotland.gov.uk/Topics/Justice/legal/17822/10190/profession-reform-1/Bill/consultownershipcontrol

http://www.smith.williamson.co.uk/news/3183-1-in-5-law-firms-to-consider-an-ipo

http://www.sra.org.uk/solicitors/freedom-in-practice/alternative-business-structures.page

http://www.sra.org.uk/solicitors/freedom-in-practice/OFR/ofr-quick-guide.page?ref=search

http://www.sra.org.uk/solicitors/handbook/principles/content.page

http://www.sra.org.uk/solicitors/solicitors.page

http://www.sra.org.uk/sra/news/letr-report-published.page

http://www.thetimes.co.uk/tto/law/article3807265.ece

Lind, S. (2011), 'One in two partners lack understanding of workings of SRA's new regulatory regime', *Legal Week.*

Lind, S. (2011), 'Plexus set to be one of the first major firms to convert to ABS', *Legal Week.*

Lind, S. (2011), 'Watchdog set to scrutinise legal outsourcing contracts', *Legal Week.*

McAteer, M. and Bennett-Warner, G. (2011), Moving targets, *Legal Business*, 212(March), 52–4, 56–7.

Manning, L. (2011), 'Pinsents join growing trend with launch of apprenticeship scheme', *The Lawyer.*

Manning, L. (2011), 'DWF launches legal apprenticeship scheme', *The Lawyer.*

Marley, O. (2011), 'Reserved legal activities: their history and future', *Legal Compliance Bulletin*, March 2011, 3–5.

Peterson, S. (2011), 'US firms consider non-lawyer partnerships', *Legal Week.*

Rothwell, R. (2010), 'Co-op launches new service for insurers', *Law Society Gazette*, http://www.lawgazette.co.uk/news/co-op-launches-new-service-insurers

Ruckin, C. (2010), 'Irwin Mitchell converts to LDP status as non-lawyers join firm's equity', *Legal Week.*

Ruckin, C. (2010), 'Regulation difficulties force Bird & Bird to drop LDP plans', *Legal Week.*

Ruckin, C. (2010), 'US Kobre & Kim converts London arm to LDP status', *Legal Week.*

Wozniak, V. (2011), 'Top firms losing out to upstarts in social media sphere', *The Lawyer.*

CHAPTER 15

http://www.biall.org.uk/pages/where-do-legal-information-professionals-work.html [accessed 1 August 2013].

http://www.biall.org.uk/pages/legal-library-recruiters.html [Accessed 1 August 2013].

https://www.jiscmail.ac.uk/lists/lis-law.html [Viewed 19 July 2013].

www.cilip.org.uk/get-involved/special-interest-groups/clsig [Accessed 1 August 2013].

www.clig.org [Accessed 1 August 2013].

INDEX

Note: *Italic* page numbers indicate figures.